Individual Voices, Collective Visions

IN THE SERIES
**Women in the Political Economy,
edited by Ronnie J. Steinberg**

HM
22
.U5
I53
1995

Individual Voices, Collective Visions

Fifty Years of Women in Sociology

Edited by
Ann Goetting
and Sarah Fenstermaker

Temple University Press
Philadelphia

Temple University Press, Philadelphia 19122
Copyright © 1995 by Temple University. All rights reserved
Published 1995
Printed in the United States of America

The paper used in this publication meets the minimum
requirements of American National Standard for Information
Sciences—Permanence of Paper for Printed Library Materials
ANSI Z39.48–1984 ∞

Library of Congress Cataloging-in-Publication Data

Individual voices, collective visions: fifty years of women in
  sociology/edited by Ann Goetting and Sarah Fenstermaker.
    p. cm.—(Women in the political economy)
  Includes bibliographical references.
  ISBN 1-56639-250-0 (cloth: alk. paper).—ISBN 1-56639-
251-9 (pbk.: alk. paper)
    1. Women sociologists—United States—Biography. 2.
Sex discrimination in education—United States—Case
studies. I. Goetting, Ann. II. Fenstermaker, Sarah,
1949– . III. Series
HM22.U5I53   1995
301'.092'2—dc20   94-17296

Contents

Acknowledgments — viii

INTRODUCTION FICTIONS OF THE SELF
Ann Goetting — 3

PART I ECHOES OF THE BABY BOOM: MOTHERING AND CAREERS

One **Writing Papers and Stirring Soup: Career and Family in the Baby Boom Years**
Datha Clapper Brack — 23

Two **An Accidental Sociologist**
Beth B. Hess — 37

Three **Obstacles and Opportunities en Route to a Career in Sociology**
Hannah Schiller Wartenberg — 51

PART II UP THE DOWN ESCALATOR: TALES OF ACADEMIC MOBILITY

Four **Acquiring an Academic Room of One's Own**
Jane E. Prather — 69

Five **Reflections on a Serendipitous and Rocky Career: The First Twenty Years**
Janet Lever   87

Six **Paradigm Lost: The Journey from Normal Science to Permanent Marginality**
Judy Long   109

PART III   VARIETIES OF INTERNATIONAL SOCIOLOGY

Seven **Marginality, Migration, and Metamorphoses**
Britta Fischer   135

Eight **Bridging Worlds: A Sociologist's Memoir**
Suzanne Keller   151

Nine **Sociologist by Default: Reflections on Past Choices and Future Goals**
Martha E. Gimenez   169

Ten **The Life Course of a Sociologist**
Helena Znaniecka Lopata   185

PART IV   ISOLATION, MARGINALITY . . .

Eleven **Discovering Gender: My Paths to a Feminist Sociology**
Elaine J. Hall   203

Twelve **Isolation and the Woman Scholar**
Diane Rothbard Margolis   219

Thirteen **Slouching toward Sociology**
Helen Mayer Hacker 233

Fourteen **Working the Third Shift**
Lynda Lytle Holmstrom 251

PART V ... AND COMMUNITY

Fifteen **Seventeen White Men and Me**
Coramae Richey Mann 273

Sixteen **Marginality, Motherhood, and Method: Paths to a Social Science Career and Community**
Shulamit Reinharz 285

Seventeen **Kaddish and Renewal**
Gaye Tuchman 303

Eighteen **Becoming an Active Feminist Academic: Gender, Class, Race, and Intelligence**
Pamela Ann Roby 319

CONCLUSION "EDITING" WOMEN, MEMOIR, AND THE SOCIOLOGICAL "I"
Sarah Fenstermaker 343

About the Editors and Contributors 359

Acknowledgments

This book required the attention and skills of assistants in both Bowling Green and Santa Barbara. Special thanks go to Sheryl Reimers at the graduate division at the University of California, Santa Barbara, and to Julie Rafaelli, Deondra Wardelle and Shanon Willett at Western Kentucky University. In addition, Ann Goetting extends thanks to Judy Long and Pam Roby for their thoughtful and constructive comments on an earlier draft of the Introduction and to Carla B. Howery, deputy executive director of the American Sociological Association, for access to unpublished data used in the Introduction. Sarah Fenstermaker thanks Denise Segura and Candace West for their help with the Conclusion. And to our many authors, whether or not their stories finally appeared in the volume, our gratitude. All of our stories are worth the telling.

INTRODUCTION

Fictions of the Self

Ann Goetting

This collection of life stories of American women sociologists is the product of an idea long in incubation. As I recall, the idea germinated from a relationship that I have come to see as critical in my total development and the most defining force of my professional career. The relationship was kindled in the early 1960s in my sophomore year at Central Michigan University with Beth Dillingham, my anthropology professor. Beth was bigger than life back then and quickly became my first positive role model—someone I wanted to be like rather than not like. There, planted center-front-row before her week after week, I felt the cobwebs that had accumulated from a difficult childhood and adolescence magically lift from my brain. From Beth I learned of the American Kickapoo and the Kalahari San, and I learned that a pretty, smart, funny, and passionate young woman could do interesting things, be productive, and feel good. Beth freed me once and for all from the tyranny of a fundamentalist Catholic upbringing. She was relentless, or so it seemed at the time, in her pursuit of all that was morally right. She deferred to only that which earned her respect. In that sense she was outrageous. Beth introduced me to another world, one that I wanted for myself. She told me one day that she saw herself in me. Her mentorship healed and saved me.

As I came to know Beth during those undergraduate years, it became clear that life was more difficult for her than it should have been. I thought that she managed her personal and professional worlds miraculously; she was committed to mothering her four young children while maintaining steady progress on her dissertation. But obstacles persisted. The department head clearly hated her. It was always something. It was as though people wanted to stop her, wanted her to fail. Like many women whose stories are contained in this volume, I had no feminist framework then. It seemed that the almost daily assaults on Beth were unrelated. As a close observer of her life, I know now that those Michigan days were Beth's best. Later in the 1960s Beth and her husband relocated to the University of Cincinnati. But the "little murders" persisted. She told me, for example, that her typing was given lowest priority. As a woman, she was assumed to be capable of doing it herself. And there were rumors of illicit affairs. Over the following two decades, as Beth's talents, quick wit, and compassion continued nourishing me, they were failing her. Somewhere along the way she gave up. I was there with her and her family four years ago when, at sixty-one, Beth's diseased liver finally gave out and her body shut down. I was a full professor and she was an associate. With Eve, her three brothers, and their father, I sorted through Beth's belongings and in the process reconstructed her life—and my own.

Now that I am armed with a feminist perspective, the mosaic falls into place. Her journey from naive boundless optimism to debilitating fear and sadness could be explained after all. She just couldn't absorb it all forever, especially back then when there was no framework to make sense of it and little if any collective consciousness among academic women. Beth would have loved and benefited from the stories in this volume. They would have connected her, strengthened her, and liberated her.

Through most of my friendship with Beth, her tales seemed unique. That was until I entered graduate school and then later academic life. Deja vu! Somewhere in there I realized that there were patterns and that they were peculiar to women. About fifteen years ago, I noticed at professional conferences that women were talking. With the enthusiasm and wit of the young Beth, they were gathered in small clusters here and there comparing notes, planning strategy. By that time the stories were decidedly familiar. I signed up; after all, I too was in need of a few good tricks. I think that I knew by then that a book should be written. Clearly, women of the academy were different from their male counterparts. They had different "ways of knowing" (Belenky, Clinchy, Goldberger, and Tarule 1986); different styles of interaction, communication (Tannen 1990), and relationality (Cancian 1987); and they brought different things to their disciplines, universities, and students (Aisenberg and Harrington 1988). Often those differences were not well received.

Women sociologists are a diverse lot. They are not bound by the linear script for male success, or by any script for that matter (Rosenfeld and Stark 1987). Their lives, like those of women in general, move through fits and starts, through "fissures of female discontinuity" (Benstock 1988, 20), as they struggle to balance power with the men in their lives, to balance career and family, and to forge pathways through it all. The isolation and marginality of women in the academy require creative response and adaptation. Yes, this book was surely in process by then. It is not enough that I was poised to initiate such an enterprise. Two other factors were critical to its launching: timing was important in providing a receptive audience, and I needed a partner. A brief historical overview of sociology as it intersects with biography demonstrates the timeliness of this collection. Later, I address my partnership with Sarah.

Biography is a time-honored tradition within sociology that has vacillated in acceptance and popularity over the years. Pioneers such as Max Weber (1947), W. I. Thomas and Florian Znaniecki (1918–1920/1927), Clifford R. Shaw (1930, 1931, 1936), Robert Angell (1945), and C. Wright Mills (1959) have extolled the virtues of subjectivity in general or biography in particular as central to the understanding of social processes and social structures. To Weber (1947, 88), sociology "is a science which attempts the interpretive understanding of social action. . . . In 'action' is included all human behavior when and in so far as the acting individual attaches a subjective meaning to it." And Mills (1959, 5) argues eloquently that knowledge of social context leads people to understand their own experiences and to gauge their "own fates." This is the promise of the "sociological imagination." Biography reached its pinnacle in the discipline during the first half of the twentieth century when the highly influential Chicago School of Sociology emphasized personal documents in the study of modern urban life. At midcentury, when social surveys and statistical tools became fashionable and mainstream (Sjoberg and Kuhn 1989), it retreated to the background.

After a two- or three-decade hiatus, biography resurfaced and reclaimed favor in a new sociopolitical climate, but this time its use was limited to the study of deviant and marginalized populations. It was in the context of liberation consciousness in America arising from the political consensus developed by the civil rights and neofeminist movements that social constructionists borrowed from older sociological, literary, and ethnographic traditions to reactivate the subjective paradigm (Johnston 1993, 29). With an agenda to construct a social order free of hegemony in all of its forms, including patriarchy and colonialism, narrative was elicited from people of oppressed, silenced, and marginalized cultures in an effort to know their "experiences" (for example, the black experience, the female experience). Biography emerged as a central component of this new politicized "way of knowing." It became the focalizing literature for constructionist studies, including Native American studies, women's studies, and African American studies. Biography was viewed by these modern constructionists as the story of a distinct culture written in individual characters and, from within, a story that offered privileged access to their worlds (Olney 1980). Furthermore, it came to be valued as direct and raw access to the interaction process between individual experience and social structure, which shapes both. Lifewriting demonstrated the development of a culture and its institutions. Without the inclusion of individual biography, little sense could be made of the social order (Sjoberg and Kuhn 1989, 314).

Clearly biography is gaining ground as a method of choice among sociologists, especially those committed to social reform. This is evident with the recent international influx of autobiographical work and work about autobiography within the discipline (Bell-Scott 1994; Berger 1990; Bertaux 1981; "Biography and Autobiography" 1993; Brodzki and Schenck 1988; Coser 1993; Edwards 1980; Higgins and Johnson 1988; Long, forthcoming; McCall and Wittner 1990; Oppenheimer, Murray, and Levine 1991; Orlans and Wallace 1994; Riley 1988; Sarbin 1986; Sjoberg 1989; Stanfield 1993; Witherell and Noddings 1991).

Feminist criticism springs from and responds to the lives of women. From every location in the social order, women's biography is emerging to strengthen the feminist agenda. Recently, interest has extended to include women of the academy. Books (Aisenberg and Harrington 1988; Long, forthcoming; O'Connell and Russo 1988; Orlans and Wallace 1994), conferences, conference panels, and works-in-progress demonstrate the timeliness of a collection of life stories of American women sociologists in providing yet one more window on gendered process and structure and in inviting reconceptualization of the discipline—past, present, and future.

So I was ready and the time was right. Now I needed a partner. Until now I had worked alone. Although all around, colleagues were collaborating, it had always seemed just easier to do it myself. I knew that wouldn't work this time. Since the voices in the volume should come from everywhere in the organizational structure of the academy, there would need to be two editors very differently situated therein. I had heard that friendships were easily lost in collaboration, a risk that I was unwilling to bear. So I was off to find just the right stranger at an elite research institution.

I met Sarah in October 1991 at a not-so-high-powered social affair in Santa Barabara. Our mutual friend Harvey Molotch thought that we were a good match for the job, and Harvey was right this time. Sarah said yes, and we commenced immediately with a broadly circulated call for papers. We have not met since that very brief encounter in a crowd. This project was executed almost totally by e-mail, with a few phone conversations sprinkled in. Communication was daily and ran the full range of intensity. Both being amateur comedians, we often relied on humor, but sometimes it failed us.

Our differences that brought so much to this collection were sometimes hard on Sarah and me. Never was there occasion to lament a lack of diversity between us as did Kristine M. Baker and Katherine R. Allen (1992, viii) in the production of their feminist volume. But we agreed on virtually everything. Our vision of the product and of how submissions and their authors should be treated was mutual and clear from the beginning and that carried us through. We ran a tight ship. The project remained on schedule throughout.

Our method of coming to know one another has been unconventional, if not unique. The relationship has always been lively and is akin to that described herein by Janet Lever as her "most bizarre friendship." I have always felt Sarah tugging at the other end of the line. Just the other day while I was writing about Beth, the dictionary on my lap dropped open to the heading "Sarah." Seizing the opportunity to collect yet one more morsel of information on Sarah, I glanced below to learn that hers is a biblical name with the diminutive "Sally." So I did learn something. I learned the source of her nickname, "Sally." But then I don't know for sure. And so it goes with Sarah and me.

Biography and Women's Biography

As a form of social science research and as a method of intellectual, personal, and social enhancement for the reader, biography offers a unique set of strengths. Beyond those general strengths are still others specific to the biography of minorities, including women. Consider first the general qualities.

Sensitive Insight and Confirmed Connectedness

Biography recreates the experiential integrity of human existence. The life of the emotions, the life of the mind, the individual life, and the social life—all are contextually embedded to produce a comprehensible whole. The reader becomes immersed in the disarray of it all. From a single position in the universe at a single point in time, human "truths" are revealed through lived experience in social structure, process, and interaction. Stories are related in the context of passionate beliefs and partisan stands. Efforts are recounted to grapple with the world in all of its obscurity and with the normal lack of omniscience characteristic of the human condition. The many dimensions of the human experience unite and are expressed as one life story or as an assemblage of life stories. Truly, biography provides privileged access to the ways of humanity. One German sociologist touts autobiography as the highest and most instructive form in which the understanding (*Verstehen*) of life, both individual and collective, confronts us (Wilhelm Dilthey translated by Kohli 1981, 126).

While *Verstehen* of the human experience is valuable and rewarding in itself, biography provides the additional benefit of activating the readers to construct a benchmark in the interpretation of their own lives. It allows us to apply new meaning to our existence by furnishing yet another framework within which we can locate ourselves and make sense of our lives. We constantly test our own realities against such stories, asserting and modifying our perceptions in the light of theirs. In life stories, we find other persons who independently have discovered the same or similar forms of truth. (Of course, on the darker side, we also may encounter persons who have found opposing truths and perhaps still others who verify our weaknesses, losses, and deprivations.) The confirmations are comforting; without them one feels isolated or marginal. Consensus sustains us with shared consciousness and community. Biography is interactive. Two lives/subjects meet in that life-storytelling enterprise, that single narrative space shared by storyteller and listener/arranger/intermediary (Smith 1991, 124). Unlike the traditional hierarchical research model, where the researcher dominates both research subject and reader, the biographical relationship is symmetrical. The reader is empowered with the responsibility of interpretation. Jane Tompkins (1989) says:

> I love writers who write about their own experience. I feel I'm being nourished by them, and that I'm being allowed to enter into a personal relationship with them, that I can match my own experiences with theirs, feel cousin to them, and say, yes, that's how it is. (170)

Not only can biography bring delight and comfort, it can motivate informed life change. C. Wright Mills's promise of "the sociological imagination," cited earlier, reminds us that insights into social context can supply the resources necessary to not only understand one's own life but, as a result, to at least partially control its outcomes. Biography can provide readers with fertile ground for redirection of the life trajectory through its reconceptualization. In summary, in the context of two factors, finely nuanced understanding into the human experience and an engaging, interactive, intimate, empowering relationship, biography invites the reader to enjoy a sense of connection and to forge informed life changes.

For me this collection of stories delivered those promised connections. I could relate well to Pam Roby's account of her childhood relationship with her dog, Cherry. The image of her nestled safe from harm's way in that rose-colored stuffed chair with Cherry recalled in me my shiny black spaniel, Blackie, who followed me home from kindergarten in Circleville, Ohio. Blackie was no less important to me than Cherry was to her. We were called "Blackie and Whitey" (my hair color back then). When I first revisited that house on Main Street where Blackie and I were together, I retraced my steps to Blackie's burial site deep in the recesses of an overgrown garden at the foot of an extensive backyard. It had been such a very long journey that day as I followed in the shadow of my father as he carried a shovel and Blackie. The image is so clear. When I read Pam's story, I knew that she knew how I felt.

Another connection that I made with these stories is unsettling and relates to graduate education. I had always suspected, but now there is no doubt, that I was and am deprived. I read with envy and regret account after account of the joys of learning in "heady" times under the tutelage of inspiring professors. Reflections on my own graduate career recall, with one exception, departments plagued with hostile and debilitating climates, the likes from which Gaye Tuchman fled back to Brandeis. A solid graduate education was not available to me, and I have been attempting to compensate ever since. If I could choose from among the graduate programs described herein, I would take Brandeis. Gaye, Shula Reinharz, and Lynda Holmstrom beckon me there with their narrative.

Knowledge Gaps

In addition to providing fertile ground for sensitive insight and confirmed connectedness, biography can make important contributions to the more mainstream sociological enterprise. For one thing, biography fills knowledge gaps. It supplies privileged strategic information on human interaction and social structure. For example, critical to the study of formal organizations, biography accesses decision-making processes of powerful actors, documents organizational secrecy, and illuminates organizational deviance (Sjoberg and Kuhn 1989, 317–18). Additionally, biography provides a window on informal organizational structures that infiltrate the formal order. A striking example of informal organizational behavior derived from this collection lies in Hannah Wartenberg's account of her unconventional "graduate career" at Princeton during World War II, during which her "assistantship" funding source was highly irregular and, unbeknownst to her, she was not receiving official credit for her courses.

Informal power is an important dimension of informal organizational structure. The dynamics of all kinds of informal power relations and their consequences, including power inequities between women and men, can be charted through biography. Women's personal narratives are especially helpful in understanding the subtleties of sexism because of their capacity to chronicle not only the incidents in process but also response to those incidents. Biography of all subordinate groups in hierarchical contexts reveals informal rules of domination as it documents response ranging from mere annoyance to hostile rebellion (Personal Narratives Group 1989, 6–7). The voices of the women herein record a multitude of informal gender inequities and the responses to them. Datha Brack describes a small social gathering of couples where the men were talking and the women were listening. Her attempted contribution to the discussion was met with brief silence followed by resumption of the previous male-centered discourse—as though she had not said a word. She was rendered inaudable and invisible. Decades later, Datha remembers this incident, its impact on her, and her response to it. Beth Hess's and Janet Lever's stories of gender-integrated Harvard and Yale failing to install restrooms for women in their central facilities demonstrate another manifestation of informal social control. Datha's, Beth's, Janet's, and all other such accounts in this collection provide a basis for understanding informal gendered inequities in the larger social order and within the academy in particular.

The Intersection of Micro and Macro

A second way that biography in general can contribute to the mainstream sociological enterprise is as a tool for interpreting the intersection of the micro and macro levels of the social order. It is, perhaps, the central tool available to us (Sjoberg and Kuhn 1989, 314). If we acknowledge that these two dimensions interact and shape one another, we must recognize that clues to understanding their connection and its consequences to both are accessible primarily through lifetelling. One context in which micro/macro intersection and some of its consequences can be observed in this volume is that of the tenure process. Coramae Mann, Judy Long, Janet Lever, and Jane Prather tell stories of negative tenure decisions—stories of women's ways, women's styles, women's knowledge, and women's needs clashing violently with the patriarchal order of the university structure. Neither the individuals nor the organizations escaped those confrontations unscathed.

We each have a "favorite" story to tell of the horrifying encounters where institutional inequities are made plain in a single set of individual interactions—where micro and macro seem truly joined. Here is mine.

I have a friend who, as an assistant professor at a comprehensive public teaching institution, published moderately in a "pink-collar" area within the discipline. One day she was summoned to the suite of her white, Christian, able-bodied, heterosexual male colleagues; these two men were outspoken and pivotal figures at the informal level of a strongly androcentric, hegemonic department. Some referred to them as "gurus." Suspecting nothing of any consequence, this woman followed them into the coffee room. Suspicion was aroused in the woman when one of these colleagues, upon closing the door, positioned himself in front of it in a blocking gesture. But still she was not alarmed. Then the discourse began. These criminologists, my friend's story goes, had been alerted by the departmental secretary to the woman's having a manuscript typed that, while focusing within her designated "pink-collar" specialization, intruded somewhat on the criminology domain. She was trespassing on their territory, she was told, and she was to stop immediately. After all, her involvement in criminology would surely ruin the sterling reputation that they had built for themselves, the department, and the university—a "reputation," she notes, that was established and is maintained virtually without benefit of a refereed publication record. The woman was outwardly silenced by this confrontation. But inwardly she was mobilized by it. Her life changed forever that day, as did the lives of the two criminologists and that of the department, though such change was perhaps not immediately apparent. The threat inspired her not only to publish the paper in question but to pursue the topic further—and then to pursue other criminology topics. She was to become a "rate-buster" among these colleagues, operating now from a feminist perspective and as a criminologist. The life course of the department was altered in that it would now need to accommodate a feminist and nationally visible criminologist, strongly resented on both counts within the department. And the discipline lost a conventional researcher relegated to "pink-collar" concerns.

Strengths of Women's Biography

Women's biography can contribute to the correction of the "social production of obscurity" (Long, forthcoming). Here we are concerned specifically with women's obscurity within the academy and within the discipline of sociology. As is noted by many of the authors herein, women have been and remain woefully underrepresented in the academy and in the discipline. They are conspicuously absent in the classroom and in positions as mentors. In fall 1991, the majority of sociology students in U.S. graduate schools were women: 59 percent at the master's level and 55 percent at the doctoral level. Yet only one in four full-time tenured faculty members was a woman, and the mentors available in graduate departments remained overwhelmingly men (American Sociological Association 1993). This underrepresentation of women is self-perpetuating. Talented young women can be silenced and stopped when they see no women in influential positions and when they have none with whom to interact and identify—when they are presented no inheritance and no tradition (Long, forthcoming). Same-sex role models are critical to the recruitment of women into the professional ranks and to both their personal and professional development. For women to see the realization of their own aspirations in the lives of other women is a crucial source of support and inspiration, especially during difficult times. Women are energized by the combinations of wit, perseverence, determination, dedication, commitment, humor, and achievement in the lives of accomplished women. Consider, for example, my opening narrative about Beth Dillingham. In this volume, Beth Hess describes an equally committed long-term relationship with Matilda White Riley. Janet Lever expresses her strong captivation as a student with Helen Gouldner, as does Shula Reinharz with Mirra Komarovsky and Roberta Simmons. These professors provided compelling role models for these three women.

What is particularly relevant here is that the benefits of same-sex role models for women can also be achieved by reading about accomplished women (O'Connell and Russo 1988, 3). Diane Margolis verifies this with her opening statement, "As a young girl, I read Madame Curie's biography." Especially with the dearth of female professors, women's biography can provide a critical function to young women aspiring to enter the academy. At the same time, it can provide an equally critical function to the discipline by drawing in women to achieve some semblance of gender balance. Women's work, women's presence, and women's ways must be represented equitably to produce a body of scholarship, a teaching faculty, and an administrative organization reflective of and responsive to a changing social order.

A second value of women's biography in particular is that it is critical to understanding our gendered world. Unlike men, women are reminded, at every turn, of their subordinate place in a gendered hierarchy. From the point of view of the male autobiographical subject, the public world is not gendered. From the viewpoint of the female, gender is central to human life, thought, and identity. Woman's selfhood is inseparable from her sense of community with womankind (Friedman 1988, 28–40; Personal Narratives Group 1989, 4–5). Georg Simmel (1911, translated and quoted by Klein 1946) states:

> If we express the historic relation between the sexes crudely in terms of master and slave, it is part of the master's privileges not to have to think continuously of the fact that he is the master, while the position of the slave

carries with it the constant reminder of his being a slave. It cannot be overlooked that the woman forgets far less often the fact of being a woman than the man of being a man. (28)

Because of the ideological loading of gender and because of their subordinate seat in a gendered world, women, like people of color, develop a double consciousness. They "double think"; they are gifted with a "second sight"; they constantly see themselves not only as subjects but as objects from the perspective of the majority (Collins 1986, 11–13, 1990, 232–33; Friedman 1988, 38–40). It is because the salience of gender is so apparent to women and also because of their "second sight" that women's biography offers the most finely nuanced understanding of gender structure and dynamics. A woman's biography is one of women, one of gender.

Finally, women's biography forges change in the social order. As women write themselves into existence, class, race, gender, and other structures inevitably must respond. The notion of who has rights, whose voice can be heard, whose individuality is worthy comes under revision (Johnston 1993, 33). And it is not just that women are now heard, it is that what women say is different. As women enter the mainstream, their relationality permeates those political structures, altering them to conform to perhaps more humanely textured models of social organization. It follows that biography of academic women and sociologists in particular would promote similar change in the academy and in the discipline.

Autobiography: Truth, Fiction, or What?

It has been fashionable for a couple of decades now to speak knowingly of autobiography as fiction. Purporting to reflect upon or recreate the past through the processes of memory, autobiography must become storytelling. Memory is faulty. It leaves only a trace of an earlier experience that we adjust into story; and some critical life experiences escape memory altogether (for example, child sexual abuse and other forms of severe child abuse are often blocked from memory [Briere and Conte 1993; Schwartz 1993]). Furthermore, experience itself is mediated by the ways we describe and interpret it to others and to ourselves. Also, narrative is driven by its own fictive conventions about linearity: beginnings, middles, and ends. Perhaps most important, the language that we use to "capture" memory only approximates it, yielding its own residue of meaning or imposing its artificial closures (Smith 1990, 145). Succinctly stated, autobiography is not simply a "true" representation of an objective "reality";

instead, memory, interpretation, and conventions of storytelling and language combine to create a particular view of reality. In the words of Georges Gusdorf (1980):

> Autobiography is not simple repetition of the past as it was, for recollection brings us not the past itself but only the presence in spirit of a world forever gone.... It reveals no more than a ghostly image of that life, already far distant, and doubtless incomplete, distorted furthermore by the fact that the [person] who remembers his [or her] past has not been for a long time the same being ... who lived the past. (38)

The counterpoint to autobiography as fiction rather than truth is that storytelling is truth if concepts are properly defined. It is argued that in spite of inherent distortions, autobiography does reveal truths. These truths do not disclose the past "as it actually was" by some arbitrary standard of objectivity, but instead they are reconstructed truths. From this George Herbert Mead (1964) perspective, it is the reconstruction that we are interested in, not the event, because the reconstruction informs us of the way the author relates to the social. Our memories are in a continual state of reconstruction as we discover more satisfying meanings and frameworks for them. We continue to reinterpret old events from new positions (Crawford et al. 1992, 8; Mead 1964). The truths of autobiography do not spring from empirical research or the logic of mathematical deduction. Unlike the reassuring Truth of scientific Ideal, the truths of personal narrative are neither subject to proof nor self-evident. We come to understand them only through interpretation, paying careful attention to the contexts that shape their creation and to the worldviews that inform them (Personal Narratives Group 1989, 261). From this perspective, autobiography is a second or later reading of experience and is truer than those before it because it adds the element of seasoned consciousness to the original experience. Gusdorf (1980) states:

> In the immediate moment, the agitation of things ordinarily surrounds me too much for me to be able to see it in its entirety. Memory gives me a certain remove and allows me to take into consideration all the ins and outs of the matter, its context in time and space. As an aerial view sometimes reveals to an archaeologist the direction of a road or a fortification or a map of a city invisible to someone on the ground, so the reconstruction in spirit of my destiny bares the major lines that I have failed to notice, the demands of the deepest values I hold that, without my being clearly aware of it, have determined my most decisive choices. (38)

Our real concern with autobiography is not whether it is "truth" or "fiction" but what it can teach us about how humans participate in, respond to, and interpret their social world. The question of truth or fiction is not a productive line of inquiry. To pursue some objective truth in autobiography is to miss the point. There exist multiple truths in autobiography as in all other forms of research and scientific pursuit. What people tell us through some kind of consensus as determined by conventional social scientific method is one kind of truth. What one individual tells us, perhaps in opposition to that truth, is also true. There is something to be learned from it all. The truth of autobiography is in the interpretation of life processes. "Fictions of the self" (Michael Sprinkler cited in Olney 1980, 22) occupy a critical part of the sociological enterprise. Without them there can be no understanding of the human condition. Without them there can be no comprehensive sociology.

In Closing

A widespread call for papers elicited life stories from senior women sociologists. From the final selections emerged a way of loosely organizing the autobiographical accounts into five sections. Yet, we expect that readers will make their own connections among essays. Part I, "Echoes of the Baby Boom: Mothering and Careers," presents three accounts of women who delayed or interrupted their professional careers during the 1940s and 1950s to participate in full-time domesticity. Part II, "Up the Down Escalator: Tales of Academic Mobility," illuminates three variations of academic mobility that are more characteristic of women than of men. Part III, "Varieties of International Sociology," provides a window to German, Austrian, Polish, and Argentine experiences. In Parts IV and V, "Isolation, Marginality..." and "...And Community," eight authors express the often overwhelming experiences that come with the territory of inequality and social change. Finally, Sarah Fenstermaker concludes the volume with her observations about the collection.

This volume is a celebration of women's contributions to the academy and to the study of society. These stories do not constitute findings; rather, they are raw materials to be used to aid each of us in our own transformations of unique experience into sociological text. Biography should be respected in its integrity; it must not be dismembered and expropriated in the service of some good (or not-so-good) cause. There are no clear rules governing the interpretation of biography, but it is important to keep in mind that the agenda of the narrator and that of the interpreter are distinct and not always compatible (Personal Narratives Group 1989, 264).

In a world so preoccupied with youth and so judgmental of aging, especially among women, this collection of life stories of senior women sociologists provides insights for academic women at mid-life. There are even fewer same-sex role models for us in circulation than are available for the young. With aplomb and decisiveness, the voices of the older women herein assure us that there is still plenty to do and that there may well be enough time for it all. Their stories relax anxieties associated with anticipated aging and inspire us to grow into the now-established images of these compassionate, productive, and self-reliant mature women.

In this sense, this project is timely for me. One winter day in 1993, these women ushered me ever so gently into my second half-century. Britta Fischer refers to her fiftieth birthday as the commencement of her third quarter-century; I suppose that I am more optimistic than she about longevity. The voices of these women comforted—no, elated—me at what traditionally has been viewed a dreaded point of transition.

REFERENCES

Aisenberg, Nadya, and Mona Harrington. 1988. *Women of Academe.* Amherst: University of Massachusetts Press.

American Sociological Association. 1993. "Survey of Sociology Departments and Divisions, 1991–1992." Unpublished data.

Angell, Robert. 1945. "A Critical Review of the Development of the Personal Document Method in Sociology, 1920–1940." Pp. 177–232 in *The Use of Personal Documents in History, Anthropology, and Sociology,* edited by Louis Gottschalk, Clyde Kluckhohn, and Robert Angell. Bulletin 53. New York: Social Science Research Council.

Baker, Kristine M., and Katherine R. Allen. 1992. *Women and Families: Feminist Reconstruction.* New York: Guildford Press.

Belenky, Mary Field, Blythe McVicker Clinchy, Nancy Rule Goldberger, and Jill Mattucks Tarule. 1986. *Women's Ways of Knowing: The Development of Self, Voice, and Mind.* New York: Basic Books.

Bell-Scott, Patricia, ed. 1994. *Life Notes: Personal Writings by Contemporary Black Women.* New York: W. W. Norton.

Benstock, Shari. 1988. "Authorizing the Autobiographical." Pp. 10–33 in *The Private Self: Theory and Practice of Women's Autobiographical Writings*, edited by Shari Benstock. Chapel Hill: University of North Carolina Press.

Berger, Bennett, ed. 1990. *Authors of Their Own Lives*. Berkeley: University of California Press.

Bertaux, Daniel, ed. 1981. *Biography and Society: The Life History Approach in the Social Sciences*. Beverly Hills, Calif.: Sage.

"Biography and Autobiography in Sociology." 1993. Special issue of *Sociology: The Journal of the British Sociological Association* 27(1).

Briere, J., and J. Conte. 1993. "Self-Reported Amnesia for Abuse in Adults Molested as Children." *Journal of Traumatic Stress* 6(1):21–31.

Brodzki, Bella, and Celeste Schenck, eds. 1988. *Life-Lines: Theorizing Women's Autobiography*. Ithaca, N.Y.: Cornell University Press.

Cancian, Francesca M. 1987. *Love in America: Gender and Self-Development*. Cambridge: Cambridge University Press.

Collins, Patricia Hill. 1986. "The Sociological Significance of Black Feminist Thought." *Social Problems* 3(6): 14–32.

———. 1990. *Black Feminist Thought: Knowledge, Consciousness, and the Politics of Empowerment*. New York: Routledge.

Coser, Lewis A. 1993. "A Sociologist's Atypical Life." *Annual Review of Sociology* 19:1–15.

Crawford, June, Susan Kippax, Jenny Onyx, Una Gault, and Pam Benton. 1992. *Emotions and Gender*. Newbury Park, Calif.: Sage.

Edwards, Harry. 1980. *The Struggle That Must Be: An Autobiography*. New York: Macmillan.

Friedman, Susan S. 1988. "Women's Autobiographical Selves: Theory and Practice." Pp. 34–62 in *The Private Self: Theory and Practice of Women's Autobiographical Writings*, edited by Shari Benstock. Chapel Hill: University of North Carolina Press.

Gusdorf, Georges. 1980. "Conditions and Limits of Autobiography." Pp. 28–48 in *Autobiography: Essays Theoretical and Critical*, edited and translated by James Olney. Princeton, N.J.: Princeton University Press.

Higgins, Paul C., and John M. Johnson, eds. 1988. *Personal Sociology*. New York: Praeger.

Johnston, Jill. 1993. "Fictions of the Self in the Making." *New York Times Book Review*, April 25, 1.

Klein, Viola. 1946. *The Feminine Character: History of an Ideology*. London: K. Paul, Trench, Trubner.

Kohli, Martin. 1981. "Biography: Account, Text, Method." Pp. 61–75 in *Biography and Society: The Life History Approach in the Social Sciences*, edited by Daniel Bertaux. Beverly Hills, Calif.: Sage.

Long, Judy. Forthcoming. *Telling Women's Lives: Subject/Narrator/Reader/Text*.

McCall, Michal M., and Judith Wittner. 1990. "The Good News about Life History."

Pp. 46–89 in *Symbolic Interaction and Cultural Studies*, edited by Howard S. Becker. Chicago: University of Chicago Press.

Mead, George Herbert. 1964. "Time." Chap. 13 in *George Herbert Mead on Social Psychology*, edited by Anselm Strauss. Chicago: University of Chicago Press.

Mills, C. Wright. 1959. *The Sociological Imagination.* New York: Oxford University Press.

O'Connell, Agnes N., and Nancy F. Russo. 1988. *Models of Achievement: Reflections of Eminent Women in Psychology*, vol. 2. Hillsdale, N.J.: Lawrence Erlbaum Associates.

Olney, James. 1980. "Autobiography and the Cultural Movement: A Thematic, Historical, and Bibliographical Introduction." Pp. 3–27 in *Autobiography: Essays Theoretical and Critical*, edited by James Olney. Princeton, N.J.: Princeton University Press.

Oppenheimer, Martin, Martin J. Murray, and Rhonda F. Levine, eds. 1991. *Radical Sociologists and the Movement: Experiences, Lessons, and Legacies.* Philadelphia: Temple University Press.

Orlans, Kathryn Meadow, and Ruth A. Wallace, eds. 1994. *Gender and the Academic Experience: Berkeley Women Sociologists.* Lincoln: University of Nebraska Press.

Personal Narratives Group. 1989. *Interpreting Women's Lives: Feminist Theory and Personal Narratives.* Bloomington: Indiana University Press.

Riley, Matilda White, ed. 1988. *Sociological Lives.* Vol. 2 of *Social Change and the Life Course.* Newbury Park, Calif.: Sage.

Rosenfeld, Anne, and Elizabeth Stark. 1987. "The Prime of Our Lives." *Psychology Today,* May, 62–72.

Sarbin, Theodore R., ed. 1986. *Narrative Psychology: The Storied Nature of Human Conduct.* Westport, Conn.: Greenwood Press.

Schwartz, Mark F. 1993. "False Memory Blues." *Masters and Johnson Report* 2(1): 3.

Shaw, Clifford R. 1930. *The Jack-Roller: A Delinquent Boy's Own Story.* Chicago: University of Chicago Press.

———. 1931. *The Natural History of a Delinquent Career.* Chicago: University of Chicago Press.

———. 1936. *Brothers in Crime.* Chicago: University of Chicago Press.

Simmel, Georg. 1911. "Das Relative und das Absolute in Geschechterproblem." In *Philosophische Kultur.* Leipzig: W. Klenkhardt.

Sjoberg, Gideon, ed. 1989. *Journal of Applied Behavioral Science.* Special issue on autobiography, social research, and the organizational context. 25(4): 307–524.

Sjoberg, Gideon, and Kathryn Kuhn. 1989. "Autobiography and Organizations: Theoretical and Methodological Issues." *Journal of Applied Behavioral Science* 25(4): 309–26.

Smith, Sidonie. 1990. "Construing Truths in Lying Mouths: Truthtelling in Women's Autobiography." *Studies in Literary Imagination* 23(2): 145–63.

———. 1991. "The (Female) Subject in Critical Venues: Poetics, Politics, Autobiographical Practices." *a/b: Auto-Biography Studies* 6(1): 109–30.

Stanfield, John, ed. 1993. *History of Race Relations Research*. Newbury Park, Calif.: Sage.

Tannen, Deborah. 1990. *You Just Don't Understand: Women and Men in Conversation*. New York: William Morrow.

Thomas, W. I., and Florian W. Znaniecki. 1918–1920/1927. *The Polish Peasant in Europe and America*. New York: Alfred A. Knopf.

Tompkins, Jane. 1989. "Me and My Shadow." Pp. 169–78 in *Gender and Theory: Dialogues on Feminist Criticism,* edited by Linda Kauffman. Oxford: Basil Blackwell.

Weber, Max. 1947. *The Theory of Social and Economic Organization,* translated by A. M. Henderson and Talcott Parsons. Glencoe, Ill.: Free Press.

Witherell, C., and N. Noddings. 1991. *Stories Lives Tell: Narrative and Dialogue in Education*. New York: Teacher's College, Columbia University.

PART I

Echoes of the Baby Boom: Mothering and Careers

One

Writing Papers and Stirring Soup
Career and Family in the Baby Boom Years

Datha Clapper Brack

I began a professional career in 1967 when I was forty-five years old. I did not go far, if success is measured in terms of honors and publications; but the years I spent studying and teaching in the 1960s and 1970s were some of the most rewarding in my life, and the experiences I had along the way were some of the most enriching. And I cannot write about my work without writing about my family, because the two are intertwined, inseparable; the one influencing and being influenced by the other.

My first encounter with sociology was Willard Waller's introductory course at Barnard College in 1939. I say encounter because it shook up and rearranged the stable solid middle-class church-going world I grew up in. I remember a losing argument with Professor Waller about the function of religion in social life, an argument in which I was woefully outclassed. Then, in turn, I remember a losing argument with my mother, a faithful Presbyterian who believed that doubt itself is sinful and questioning the Church's authority a road to certain downfall. She had no patience with the idea that the saving of heathen by missionaries might have latent dysfunctions. I had no other sociology at that time because I was enrolled in the Barnard-Columbia Nursing program—two years at Barnard, three at Columbia-Presbyterian Medical Center—and was busy ticking off required courses. But I think I was hooked although I didn't know it then, since it was sociology I returned to nearly twenty years later when I was grasping for an escape from suburbia. By that time I had long since stopped confronting my mother about religion. The new bone of contention was why I had to go back to school and neglect my family.

I never completed the nursing program. I was still a probationary student in gray when Japanese planes bombed Pearl Harbor in 1941, and it was clear that the man I was engaged to would be drafted. We married secretly because it was against the rules for nurses in training to be married, and I kept my wedding ring pinned inside my uniform pocket. After twelve months as an enlisted man in the U.S. Navy, he was sent home for officer's training, and I asked for a leave of absence to be with him but was told that if I were to leave I must resign from the nursing program. So I resigned with ten months to go. Not long ago a young friend hearing this story asked why in the world we would want to marry if I had to give up nursing and he had a good chance of getting killed in the war. She was amused to hear that the possibility he might be killed was precisely why many of us married then. If you were a "nice girl" and wanted to grab one last chance to sleep with him, you got married.

Stirring the Soup

When the war was over in 1945 we settled into suburban life in northern New Jersey where housing developments and children and new schools grew like mushrooms and women worked hard at being perfect happy housewives. We had six children, one girl and five boys, all wonderful kids; that was three more than we planned. I suspect that the postwar baby boom had at least something to do with misplaced faith in the diaphragm, or more specifically with physicians' being poorly trained to fit them and monitor their use. We women were told that we "probably forgot to put them in." Nonsense. We all knew intelligent, responsible women, highly motivated to limit their families, who had unplanned pregnancies. We even had a rueful phrase for it: "diaphragm babies."

I liked raising children, and I did a lot of volunteer work, so it took me until 1957 to admit that something was wrong with my life, although I didn't know what. I was always tired and the house was never clean; it's the only time in my life I remember crawling back into bed after I'd gotten everyone off to school and work, fed the baby, etc., etc. I looked into completing nurse training at Presbyterian Hospital but ruled that out when I found I'd have to attend full time and move close to the hospital for "on call" duty. I looked into New Jersey colleges and was told I'd have to start from scratch for a degree, because the college credits I'd earned were "too old." This part of the story may not sound like professional development, but feeling trapped in the only life I knew, and hitting one barrier after another trying to get out, laid the groundwork for a solid commitment to feminism later on in my work. So did my observations of other women's lives. I knew women who were completely satisfied being housewife/

mothers, but I also knew women who started drinking as soon as their husbands left in the morning, and women who lived on tranquilizers. Two of my friends were in and out of mental institutions, one a very bright woman with five children and a master's degree in theology. A third committed suicide. None of the women I knew worked outside the home at anything other than volunteer activities.

Writing the Papers

In the end I returned to Columbia University, primarily because the Admissions Office counted many of my "old" Columbia credits. I enrolled in the School of General Studies, a program for older part-time students, with many courses offered in the evening. This meant a long drive into New York City for classes. At first I took one course at a time and worked a part-time job selling curtains at Bloomingdale's New Jersey department store (two nights a week and Saturdays) to pay the tuition. Our youngest child was one year old when I started doing this, the oldest fourteen. On the evenings I went to school or work I'd prepare supper, then leave as my husband came in the door from his job. It is no exaggeration to say that I never could have done this if my husband and children had not been wonderfully supportive. People asked how I found time, and my standard answer was that it comes out about even if you give up PTA, Cub Scout den mother duty, and collecting for the Red Cross. The truth is that I was twice as busy as before but had three times the energy.

Returning to school saved my life. It opened up a whole world outside suburbia I'd forgotten existed, an exciting world of books and ideas. But it set me out of step with the world I lived in. One incident in particular stays with me because I was taking a course in deviance at the time it occurred and recognized it as a dandy example of social control. My husband worked then as an administrator for the Reformed Church in America, and I accompanied him, as wives did, to the RCA annual meetings. One evening we sat with other couples, the men talking about the day's sessions and current issues, the wives listening, as wives did. The men were discussing prayer in the public schools, an issue then being challenged through the courts, and I jumped in with my new ideas. They listened politely then took up where they left off as if nothing had happened. I felt like a chastened child who'd interrupted an adult conversation.

It took me eight years to complete an undergraduate degree in sociology and two more for a master's degree—ten years of reading assignments while stirring the soup and typing up papers after the family was asleep at night.

Those years at Columbia gave me a solid foundation in sociological thought (long on functionalism), and an abiding respect for the Old Masters. I remember the sheer pleasure of working my way through reading lists, the happiness of sitting in lecture halls listening to the men who wrote the books—Robert Merton, William Goode, Thomas O'Dea. Sigmund Diamond's course in historical research gave me my first genuine appreciation of the rich lessons stored in old documents—floors and floors of them buried in the Butler Library stacks. I remember the delight of finding John Stuart Mill's *On the Subjection of Women* for myself, years before feminist scholars dusted it off and had it reprinted in a new paperback edition. I wrote a paper for Diamond's class with the ambitious title "The Nature of the Part Played by Industrialization in the Changing Position of Women in Society." That was 1965. It was years later that I found I wasn't alone in exploring women's issues then, before we knew that a new women's movement was brewing.

And I remember the fun of finding out you could actually do this stuff for yourself. Charles Kadushin's undergraduate research methods course was a turning point in my education. He was doing a study of music students at the Manhattan School of Music, and of course commandeered his methods students to code questionnaires, then turned them loose on the data once it was in the computer. Before that class I really had no idea what computers were about. For those of you who grew up on desktop terminals, the system then was to go to the key-punch room, punch in the tables you wanted on a stack of cards, present them at the room that held the big mainframe computer, wait three days to get them back, find out why they wouldn't run, and start over again. Once past the initial exasperation I was swept away. The computer, pumping out table after table, was irresistible, and I could not leave it alone. Without being aware it had happened, I was committed to sociology.

Beginning a Career

But my real education began after I left Columbia. In 1967 teaching jobs were plentiful, and with only a master's degree in hand, I was hired at Fairleigh Dickinson University (FDU) in Rutherford, New Jersey, to teach Sociology 101, Social Problems, The Family, Crime and Juvenile Delinquency, Minority Groups, and anything else left over, including Cultural and Physical Anthropology when the one anthropologist went on academic leave. I didn't know a thing about teaching and broke into a sweat every time I stood before a class. The only model I'd seen was the Great Man Authority presenting polished lectures to eager attentive note-takers, and I learned quickly that (1) I couldn't do it, and (2) it didn't work anyway for the average run of undergraduates. I spent the first few years going on trial and error and running to keep one chapter ahead of the students in the textbook. I believe I learned more from teaching—and from my students—than I ever learned "learning." Years later I attended a weekend teaching workshop sponsored by the American Sociological Association that should have been a prerequisite for letting people with degrees into classrooms.

Was there ever a time more exciting—more astonishing!—to begin teaching sociology than the 1960s and early 1970s? Every day the front page of the *New York Times* was more relevant than the supplementary reader: war protest, draft protest, marches to Washington; city riots, campus riots, prison riots; the assassinations of Malcolm X, Martin Luther King, and the Kennedys; the abortion debate, the rising divorce rate, the "sexual revolution," the counterculture; Black Liberation, Gay Liberation, Women's Liberation. One government commission after another, appointed to keep on top of things, published reports—the Kerner Report; reports on violence, on pornography, and so on—an abundance of information, all grist for the classroom mill.

Meanwhile my own family was a laboratory of social change. My husband's elderly parents and an aunt, no longer able to fend for themselves, had moved in with us early in the 1960s. My mother-in-law had classic symptoms of what is now called Altzheimer's disease, but we called it "senility" then, and I sometimes wonder if it was easier to cope with when we simply saw it as Mom's way of growing old. Certainly it was easier with a large family around us to share the constant watching, to help her with dressing, eating, finding lost articles—finding her when she lost herself. In 1966 one son was drafted for the Vietnam War and placed in the Marine Corps. He marched off dutifully as his grandfather and father had in previous wars, only to realize he could not in all conscience fight. By then he was unable to claim Conscientious Objector status but mercifully obtained an assignment to an intelligence unit posted in Japan and never had to aim a gun at another human being and pull the trigger. Late in the 1960s another son dropped out of college and another dropped out of high school. They grew beards and long hair, bought an old school bus, and with a group of their friends, tore out the seats, installed a wood stove, painted it purple, and set off across the country accompanied by their dogs and musical instruments. They picked up work where they could, were helped and harassed by authorities, befriended and exploited by a remarkable variety of people they met along the way. Before they left, in the months they were preparing for their journey, the basement of our rambling Victorian house became a hostel for their friends—friends who had left home, their parents begging them to come back, friends who had been turned out by parents and told *not* to come home until they cut their hair, took off patched jeans, or whatever. Many years later we learned that the whole group was dealing dope of one kind or another to finance their journey. I marvel now at our own naivete and that of parents like us in those beseiged suburban communities late in the 1960s. Alcohol, we knew. But when drugs hit the suburbs like a tidal wave from somewhere (New York City, we thought, of course), most of us, even those who were close to our children, had no frame of reference for understanding what was happening. Finally, early in the 1970s, my husband dropped out of corporate life and became the proprietor of a small general store in the Catskills. Unwittingly, I found myself a participant observer in a "commuting marriage."

Learning Feminism

During those years the primary influence on the direction of my work came not from members of the Social Science Department that employed me but from annual meetings of the American Sociological Association (ASA) and the Eastern Sociological Society (ESS). Compared with other campuses at that time, FDU at Rutherford was peaceful. The faculty was relatively conservative, and the majority of students came from conservative middle-class homes. But professional meetings in sociology, as well as those of other academic disciplines, were shaking with the same unrest that troubled the larger society. While most paper sessions continued to present sociology-as-usual, each year more of them dealt directly with the great upheavals in our country, and I wonder now to what extent I foraged among program offerings, not only for new teaching material, but also for information to help me make sense of what was going on in my family and my personal life. Young radicals were ubiquitous at those professional meetings, questioning establishment-oriented speakers and challenging them with power structure analyses. For the first time I caught on to how useful conflict theory could be. Even the business sessions grew heated—volatile—as members proposed and debated resolutions on the burning issues of the day. Out in the hallways, tables were spread with tracts and pamphlets from radical organizations, and bulletin boards bristled with notices for caucuses and action meetings that often drew larger crowds than scheduled program sessions. Can anyone who was there forget the first caucus on women's issues—was it during the 1969 or the 1970 ASA meetings? Those of us who were lucky filled the seats and crowded into standing room along the walls, while the overflow milled outside the door trying to find out what was going on inside. In those overwhelmingly male association meetings, I had never before seen a platform occupied entirely by women. I wish I could remember all who spoke so passionately about the growing feminist movement, and about women's position not only in society but in *sociology*. Alice Rossi and Jessie Bernard were among them, and, as I recall, it was Jessie Bernard who said how clever it was that young women had taken the concept of racism, used it to describe the condition of women, then coined a new term, "sexism," to mean that inequality for women was structured into the fabric of our social institutions. That was the first time I heard the term "sexism."

Sociologists for Women in Society (SWS) was formed soon after that women's caucus. I joined and attended every meeting I could get to. I learned that women sociologists were developing courses on the sociology of women, and I offered one in my department; students flocked to it. This was the spring of 1971, before there were texts for such courses. I pulled together a reading list from the classics: Mill's *The Subjection of Women*, Friedrich Engels's *The Origin of the Family, Private Property, and the State*, Simone de Beauvoir's *The Second Sex*, Betty Friedan's *The Feminine Mystique*, and material I'd picked up at conferences—*Notes from the Second Year* and pamphlets, essays, and manifestos by groups with revolutionary names like the Redstockings, Bread and Roses, New York Radical Women. Robin Morgan's *Sisterhood Is Powerful* had just been published, and I found Kate Millett's *Sexual Politics* before the semester was over. At first I determined to keep the course coolly and objectively academic; I was taking flak (not all of it good-natured) from members of my 80 percent male department and wanted to stay beyond criticism. So I started with a survey of women through history but soon found that students wanted to—*had* to—first find out for themselves what was happening then, why it was happening, and what it was doing to their lives. I scrapped the course outline, let them explore the resources in their own way, and learned some valuable lessons: that you can trust students to do their own learning, and that emotions don't preclude learning subject matter. I wish I could describe the emotional impact of that first "knowing" for those students—for all of us then—without sounding overly dramatic. Discovering women's issues for the first time was like waking from a sleep, like being in a room without windows or doors and suddenly having walls open out and the wind blow through, like being Peter Berger's puppet who looked up to see the hand manipulating the strings. Women told me the course had changed their lives—that they had changed their majors, had broken engagements to be married, had decided to study law, or engineering, or whatever. Often I heard them say that for the first time they understood their mothers' lives.

Again and again I was swept into this drama of raised awareness. Students from that class formed a consciousness-raising group and opened it to other women on the campus. I remember one meeting in particular to which one student came in obvious physical pain. When asked about it, she said she'd had an IUD inserted by her gynecologist, that she'd reported the pain to him and been told not to be a baby, that if she wanted an IUD she would have to put up with a "little discomfort." The room was electric with recognition, shock, and anger as each woman in turn recounted stories of mistreatment, paternalistic put-downs, and outright damage at the hands of male physicians. In spring 1970 I attended a conference organized by the newly formed Barnard-Columbia Women's Coalition. The young women in charge barred all men from the conference rooms, including maintenance personnel and even newspaper reporters, who staged an outraged, unsuccessful stand for their "rights." A cheer went up from hundreds of women who filled the auditorium. They cheered a rousing, hatted Bella Abzug; they listened, spellbound, as Florence Luscomb, a feisty suffragist in her eighties, recounted stories of marching, picketing, and being jailed for women's vote early in the century. Then they roared their approval when she left to catch a plane to speak at a rally for Angela Davis. I joined workshops on issues I hadn't then imagined were feminist concerns—sexuality, the power of money, the tyranny of the cosmetics industry. I came home and threw away all my makeup; it seems inconsequential now, but then it was the most militant thing I'd ever done.

Changing Gears

Fired up by these experiences, I plunged into a research project. By 1972 the elders my husband and I were responsible for had died, most of our children were off on their own, and at last I had a little disposable time. The project was on childbirth and infant feeding practices. I wanted to find out why breastfeeding rates in the United States were the lowest in the industrialized world. The question had bothered me since I first started teaching courses on the family and read in the texts that American women "preferred not" to breastfeed their infants, which certainly contradicted my experience. In the 1940s and 1950s I had known many women who *preferred* to breastfeed but had been disuaded by obstetricians, or had been treated so harshly in hospitals where personnel and policies were geared for bottle feeding that it hadn't worked out. Interestingly, I could find no studies in the sociological literature on either childbirth or infant feeding. It was as if these activities, which had used up a lot of time for a lot of women I knew, fell outside the realm of human social behavior.

I constructed a questionnaire, took it to meetings of suburban women's organizations, and saw those meetings spontaneously turn into consciousness-raising sessions. Many of the women said they'd never before been asked about their experiences when their babies were born, and they covered the questionnaires with long emotional stories, writing between the lines and in the margins and on the backs of the pages. They stayed after the meetings talking with one another, some of them angry and in tears. I'd found *Our Bodies, Ourselves* that same year; those women, sharing their stories, were like the women sharing stories in that book. Talking together raised awareness, as the book did, about who controls what happens to women's bodies. I'd thought of breastfeeding rates as a matter of women's opinions and choices; I began to see them as a consequence of the medical profession's power to define and control childbirth.

Our Bodies, Ourselves had a powerful impact. It redirected thinking for a lot of us then. Every feminist I know from my generation remembers finding her first copy. The first one I found was a skinny newsprint edition published by the New England Free Press that sold for thirty cents—ten cents for copies distributed free in abortion clinics or women's conferences. It had already gone through four printings in a little more than a year, the copies snapped up as soon as they were off the press and passed from hand to hand. I still have that tattered copy. The language sounds much more militant than the Simon and Schuster glossy paperback editions that followed. Listen to this: "The fact that there is no effective, safe, and esthetically pleasing birth control method serves to maintain the dependent-submissive relationship women have vis-à-vis men. . . . We women demand birth control, not so that we can be used by men in demeaning or inhumane relationships; a liberated woman does not mean a 'free fuck.' "

That research project became a catalyst that changed the direction of my professional life. First it led me back to graduate school for a background in medical sociology. In spring 1973 I began classes in the Ph.D. program at the City University of New York Graduate Center on 42nd Street, a flexible program geared to working students. But equally important, the project generated connections with other women working on women's health issues. I traveled to meetings of the La Leche League and the International

Childbirth Education Association for background material and discovered a network of women health professionals working to change obstetrical care. When programs on women's health began to appear on ASA roundtable discussions and SWS workshops, I met feminist sociologists whose work overlapped mine. In 1974, I presented a summary of what I was doing at an SWS session during the ESS meetings in Philadelphia. Norma Swenson and Judy Norsigian spoke on the same panel about their work with the Boston Women's Health Course Collective, the group that wrote *Our Bodies, Ourselves*. Through them I learned about women's health collectives and self-help health groups organizing across the country, and later about the National Women's Health Network. I joined the Network and worked for several years as its representative on the International Nestlé's Boycott Committee. The very bright, capable young women I met through these activities were dedicated not only to describing and analyzing women's health care but to changing the system, and they made a profound impression on me. What's more, they were fun to be with. If I wasn't a professed feminist when the project began, I certainly was by the time it was wrapped up.

Changing Jobs

But just as I was getting a good start on this work, things fell apart on my job. Early in the 1970s enrollments were down at small private colleges across the country, costs were up, and budgets were tight. FDU declared a "financial exigency" in 1973, and I was among several untenured faculty given "terminal" contracts. The reason I was given was "insufficient progress toward a doctorate, and lack of publication." It was a painful blow that caught me off guard, because I'd been recommended by my department for tenure and had seen others with fewer qualifications than mine tenured in previous years. And I knew I'd been running as fast as I could, given my family responsibilities. The fact that my unemployed husband was waging a fruitless job search at the time didn't help me gain perspective on the matter. Feeling a degree of panic, I took my case to the University Grievance Committee, and in the process learned something about workplace reality. I wrote an impassioned appeal drawing heavily on new feminist research about inequality for women in the workplace. I even quoted at length from a report by Jo Freeman, *Women in the University of Chicago,* in which she described the "invisible disadvantage" women suffered in university settings: "as long as the University does not concern itself with the variety of life styles prevalent among academic women and the many needs they have that differ from those of men, it will inevitably discriminate against otherwise qualified women. . . . The University is geared to serve the needs of [intelligent, highly educated men] and those [women] who most closely resemble these men, or who can organize their lives, however uncomfortably, into the environment created for intelligent, highly-educated men."

Ultimately I sent a considerably toned-down second draft to the committee after more experienced women faculty advised that a discrimination-against-women approach would alienate conservative committee members. (One friend suggested I compromise my "politics" and wear lipstick for the hearing.) I won one more year's contract—no tenure—from the Grievance Committee, but I could see the handwriting on the wall and looked for another job. When I received an offer from Bergen County Community College (BCCC), I felt fortunate and grabbed it.

At first, moving to a two-year community college seemed a step backward, but in the long run it was a good niche for me. Community colleges were expanding in the 1970s. BCCC enjoyed generous public funding, had a climate open to innovative ideas, and served a growing number of highly motivated mature women students returning for education. What's more, the pay was better. During my fourteen years at BCCC I worked with other women to develop the first women's studies program offered at a New Jersey community college. Four of us put together a team-taught course on the changing roles of American women; I developed a course on gender roles that I team-taught with an interested young male member of my department; and I developed a course on women's health, which was always my favorite. The enthusiasm was infectious in that cooperative venture, and we all shared a real sense of accomplishment. I believe those courses made a difference in students' lives. I also taught more sections of Introductory Sociology than I care to count; but the longer I taught that course the more I appreciated its potential to open students' minds and alter their perceptions of the world, as it had done for me some forty years before.

Reflecting

In 1979 I was awarded a Ph.D. from the City University of New York. By then I was a fifty-seven-year-old woman with five grandchildren, secure in my job, and close to retirement. No one, either at work or in my social life, cared a whole lot one way or the other whether I had a doctorate. There were times (such as during the months of reading for orals) when I'm sure my husband would have been glad to see me forget the whole thing. But it was a luxury to do it, not because I had to, but because I wanted to; it kept adding new resources to my teaching, and it was a great journey getting there. I took Cynthia Epstein's course on the role of women, in 1973, when women's studies were new and very exciting. I took Celia Heller's course on social stratification and spent several summer vacations on independent study projects for Patricia Kendall on the history of midwifery, obstetrics, the nursing profession, and women in medicine. In all the years I studied at Columbia, I'd never had a woman professor or been assigned a text written by a female scholar. There weren't many women role models then, and they were important to me. Two of the papers I wrote were published while I was in graduate school, one on infant feeding, the other on the displacement of midwives by male obstetricians. The midwifery study was reprinted in a collection of essays edited by Ruth Hubbard and her associates, *Biological Woman: The Convenient Myth*. I felt these publications gave me permission to call myself a sociologist rather than a sociology teacher.

Looking back, I realize how often women gave me a hand when I needed one—before I ever heard about mentoring or networking. When I wanted to enter graduate school at Columbia in 1964, and had no money for tuition, applications for fellowships and scholarships all stipulated that applicants be under forty or even thirty-five years old, and I could find none for part-time students. But the Women's College Club of Ridgewood gave me a no-interest loan from a fund they maintained for girls from the local high school. They'd never before had an application from an older woman, and they were very interested in what I was doing and extremely supportive. When I wanted to start a research project at Fairleigh Dickinson University, Dorothea Hubin from the Teaneck campus put together a group of colleagues to critique the research proposal and encouraged me to apply for a faculty research grant. Laura Liss, who was working on a study of women faculty in FDU in 1973 when I was fired, held my hand during my bout with the Grievance Committee. I met Barbara Katz Rothman through SWS during the lonely Ph.D. quest, and Judy Lorber, who became a member of my dissertation committee. The conversations I had with them helped me think straight and sustained me in times of doubt and terror. I suspect that Judy was the only member of my committee who read every word of my thesis. Carol Poll invited me to join her dissertation support group, women who met after their day's work was done, in various members' New York City apartments. I'm not sure whether I was more impressed by their sharp minds or by their fearlessness in negotiating New York subways and streets alone at night. Through all those years, SWS was more than resource; it was the most important reference group I had to validate what I was doing and who I was as a feminist teacher.

And my mother. How many years does it take to really appreciate a mother? She never quite understood why I had to go back to school, yet I always knew she took pride in what I was doing. As a young girl, early in the century, she left a small Ohio farm to become a nurse. Although she never worked for pay after my sister and I were born, I remember her stories about nursing, and I remember her tales about her own mother, who was the woman in that small farming community called to accompany the doctor when a baby was born. She gave me a lifelong interest in medicine and healing and health care. My father also left the farm to work his way through college, and I saw both of them struggle through the depression in the 1930s. They gave me basic training in true grit.

Learning Retirement

When I retired in 1987, my department chair and Mark Kassop, the "other" sociologist with whom I'd shared an office those fourteen years, set up a fund in my name to give a prize each graduation to the student submitting the best paper on women's issues. I don't have words to describe how wonderful that made me feel.

I enjoy retirement now, although it took me a while to get the hang of it. At first I missed the rhythm of going off in the morning to do something that has to be done, and the feeling at the end of the day when it's finished. I tried to keep a hand in by completing a research project on grandmothers, but my heart wasn't in it. One semester I taught a women's health course in Amy Kesselman's Women's Studies program at SUNY New Paltz. But being an adjunct wasn't the same as being a member of the faculty. From time to time Sue Davis sent me books on women's health for review for *New Directions for Women*, which kept me in touch with academic life until that publication closed its doors. These activities eased my way into this last phase of life, but now I see them as almost comical efforts to keep one foot on shore while my boat was already moving off on what turns out to be a pretty good journey now that I'm on board.

I volunteer now on a community crisis intervention hotline, which gives me a sense of satisfaction and belonging to my community. My husband and I enjoy a circle of interesting friends, and I've found a network of women I care about through my yoga class, my book group, and my writers' group.

But my most rewarding project is reconstructing a family history from diaries and letters written by my parents long ago, and written to our parents by my sister and me while our children were growing up. I send one or two chapters of this history off to our children each year. They enjoy seeing themselves and each other as little people, and their parents as young adults like themselves. They appreciate knowing that parents and grandparents also coped with failure and heartbreak as well as victories and good times. The history gives all of us a sense of continuity between generations.

And writing it has helped me put my own life aspirations into perspective. Sometimes I've wondered what I might have done if I'd started earlier on a career, if my life hadn't been so divided between family and work. Might I have written a book? It mattered very much to me once. But looking back shows me how full and satisfying my life was without it. I've been privileged to watch children and grandchildren grow into capable adults, finding out in their own way what they have to do with their lives. I was fortunate to have lived through a time of hope and remarkable change. It saddens me to realize that it was easier then than it is now to believe that things will, indeed, get better—for women, for disadvantaged groups, and for all our children the world around.

Datha C. Brack

Two

An Accidental Sociologist

Beth B. Hess

Observe due measure, for right timing is in all things the most important factor. —Hesiod, *Works and Days*

In pondering the task set by my editors, I was struck by the extent to which my story hinges on "timing," in C. Wright Mills's sense of the juncture of biography (social and life course locations) with history (the choices available to women at a given time). Yet, it is also the case that I am an "accidental sociologist," an unintended consequence of chance events, as is probably true of many others in this volume.

Early Years

I was born in 1928, the only child of college-educated, upper middle-class parents in Buffalo, New York. My parents enrolled me in private elementary and high schools, with the expectation that I would go to Vassar or Wellesley, meet the scion of a well-to-do Jewish family, and settle into a life of affluent domesticity bounded by country clubs and charitable volunteerism. These were more or less my own expectations, even as they coexisted uneasily with a disruptive intellectualism. As with many only children, I became an early and voracious reader and, lacking siblings with whom to share my experiences, I became somewhat of a loner, shy and introspective.

Although I was graduated by my elite high school with highest honors, I might have enjoyed it more if I did not also have an unruly streak, manifest in problems with authority. My most vivid school memories are of the principal's or head mistress's office, and the litany: "insolent, irreverent, and insubordinate." I was never a teacher's pet, with one exception. My high

37

school history teacher encouraged me to cultivate the intellect and aim for her alma mater, Radcliffe College. Because it was not Wellesley or Vassar and would, therefore, confound my parents while still being socially acceptable, I set my sights on Cambridge in 1946.

Here is where the accident of geography comes into the story. I must have been one of the very few applicants who was not a near-genius, but I was also one of the few not from Massachusetts or New York City; I could add regional representation to the entering class. It is unlikely that my fame as a field hockey player meant much in those days, although I did quite well on college entrance exams. In any event, I entered Radcliffe as one of about 240 women in the class of 1950, along with the several thousand Harvard men who were either entering that year or returning after varying terms of military service.

Cambridge Days

The late 1940s were a historically unique period for the university, not only because of the extremely large number of relatively mature male undergraduates, but also for the formalizing of coeducation in the sacred precincts of Harvard Yard—not unrelated phenomena. Before the war, a professor would deliver a lecture to the men in a Harvard hall, walk across the Square, and repeat the exercise for the "ladies" in Radcliffe Yard. But now, with the swollen student body, such a pattern became increasingly inefficient.

Women were not entirely welcomed in Harvard Yard; indeed, "tolerated" is about the strongest positive word I can use to describe our treatment. The undergraduate men, for the most part, were thoroughly preoccupied with completing a degree and getting on with a disrupted life. The teachers were something else: Many were deeply resentful of our mere presence; others delighted in taunting us; most simply ignored us; and the University completed construction of Lamont Library sans toilet facilities for women, effectively barring our access. We accepted these realities with nary a murmur.

It was not that we were politically apathetic. We marched at the gates of local industries in solidarity with workers seeking union recognition. We demonstrated at the State House in Boston each year when legalization of contraception was voted upon and voted down. We spent evenings in the common room, playing recordings of songs from the Spanish Civil War, tearfully joining in their mournful choruses. Joe Hill was as much in our minds as was James Conant. But we had no word, no concept, no frame of reference for sexism. To be sure, we realized that the behavior of some professors overstepped some boundary of propriety, but we attributed it to a personality flaw rather than any systemic factor.

My career at Radcliffe followed my earlier scholastic pattern. After a slightly rocky start—it was a shock to find out that there were at least two hundred "girls" very much smarter than I was—my grades picked up. But I also spent time in Dean Mildred Sherman's office being chastised for irreverence and for fomenting cynicism on campus. By my junior year, however, I decided to give up troublemaking for an all-out effort to see how well I could do academically.

For close to three semesters, I spent days and evenings in the bowels of Widener Library working on the undergraduate honors thesis to end all theses. It almost ended me. At that time I was a government major, as were all true idealists in the mid-1940s. We were going to establish the conditions for world peace. By 1950, our hopes were thoroughly dashed.

My specialty was political theory, and my thesis topic was the fascist Rexist movement in Beligum before and during World War II (mostly because Widener had a large holding of primary material and I could read French), which I thought would make for a pretty classy product. It did; the thesis won very high honors, and I graduated *magna cum laude*. But the effort had sapped my strength and health. Thus, even though I was assured of acceptance in the first class of Harvard Law School to admit women, I was so drained that, without strong encouragement, the game did not appear to be worth the candle, and I went home to Buffalo to recuperate.

Life after Harvard

If I have one regret in life, it is my failure to enter law school in 1950. My idea of the highest calling is to be a Sarah Weddington (the attorney who successfully argued *Roe v. Wade* before the Supreme Court in 1973). But in 1950 there were very few voices urging me to continue my studies. The messages of that era were heavily weighted toward marriage and motherhood. Indeed, by the time of our graduation in 1950, half of my Radcliffe classmates were married or would be by the end of the year. Yet forty years later, all but a very few had received graduate degrees or had entered the labor force on a long-term basis. Of course, the ways in which education and employment were combined with almost universal marriage and motherhood were extremely varied. A few never left school or the labor force; many reentered academe and the workplace after only a few years of exclusive homemaking; and almost all had done so by the early 1960s, well before the full impact of the new feminist movement. I, too, followed the culturally validated paths, although somewhat later and less fulsomely than most. I married at the relatively advanced age of twenty-four, and I raised only two children at a time when the norm was three or more.

Before marriage, lacking the skills required for well-paying employment, I worked in New York City as a file clerk in an advertising agency, where it took some time for my employers to realize that my spelling was somewhat problematic.

Marriage and Suburban Homemaking

By then, however, I had met Dick Hess, a graduate of the Massachusetts Institute of Technology and everything my parents could have wished, which no longer disqualified him immediately in my eyes. We spent the first two and a half years of married life in Paris, where Dick worked for a subsidiary of the International Telephone and Telegraph Company, before settling down in suburban New Jersey and becoming completely enveloped in the *zeitgeist* of the 1950s. Oh, how I tried to disappear into the validated roles!

Raising children was the best part; marketing was a chore; cooking an insurmountable challenge; socializing the most difficult. Finally, in the spring of 1962, when my younger child entered kindergarten, I wandered down to New Brunswick to explore the possibility of graduate school at Rutgers, the nearest university to my home. As the government department was not terribly encouraging, I walked over to sociology—it was nearby—and found that they would at least accept an application. It can't get more accidental that that.

Back to School

Yet timing was also absolutely crucial. The university was expanding its graduate program in anticipation of the influx of baby-boom undergraduates later in the decade. I like to joke that all they did was check my pulse; there were no entrance exams, not even a proper interview. I left a copy of my 1950 honors thesis and the completed application form. At this point, I had no formal training in sociology other than "Social Relations 101" fifteen years earlier, plus some auditing of Pitrim Sorokin and Talcott Parsons daring my Harvard days. Yet shortly after my visit, I was accepted into the graduate program contingent on my taking introductory courses in sociology and anthropology, which I completed that summer and passed with little difficulty.

That fall, the new graduate students were summoned to an orientation meeting with Jackson Toby. There were perhaps a half dozen women among the thirty or so candidates, all of us somewhat older than the men. Professor Toby looked at the women sternly, noted that most were enrolled part-time, and warned us that this was no place for "dilettantes." Of course, this was all that I needed to vow that not only would I never, ever drop out but I'd get the best grades he had to give. The other women must have been similarly motivated, for my recollection is that over the next several years, we stuck it out while most of the men peeled off.

It took me nine years to complete graduate school. I took two courses each semester, and I spent a year polishing my dissertation. The first several terms were relatively uneventful. I went down to New Brunswick once a week for whatever two courses were being given on that day, studied at home, and aced the exams. Contact with faculty was limited to the classroom; no one really advised me or checked up on me; and I blithely proceeded through graduate school. On the drive down, I would be wracked by fears of all the horrible things that might happen to the children and the house during my absence, but the moment I parked in the sociology department lot, I forgot that other life, only to resume my compulsive worrying on the ride back.

And so it went until I was summoned to the office of Professor Matilda W. Riley, who, according to the college catalog, had also attended Radcliffe. Fearful of being dropped from the graduate program for extreme dilettantism, I decided that the best defense was to call on the old school tie. But upon my entering her sanctum, before I could utter the very same words, the redoubtable Professor Riley rushed to welcome "another Radcliffe graduate." I learned then one of the most important lessons of my career—that Matilda Riley would always be at least one step ahead of me (and most others).

Working for Matilda

Matilda looked for graduate students who received good grades and yet were not claimed by other professors as teaching or research assistants, which left her a pool of achieving but unmentored women. I joined a long line of such assistants; my immediate cohort included Joan Waring, Anne Foner, and Marilyn Johnson. I served as a teaching assistant in her methods course and as a researcher on various projects over the next seven years. In return, Matilda offered us publication opportunities, encouraged participation in professional organizations, and introduced us to such luminaries as

Talcott Parsons and Robert Merton. Slowly but firmly, she transformed us into professional sociologists.

She also guided me through the administrative mazes of higher education. Although I had taken no entrance tests, the rules changed during the mid-1960s, so that doctoral candidates were now required to take the Graduate Record Examination. As Matilda knew that I would have great difficulty with questions about when trains traveling at different speeds would meet, she managed to get the requirement waived. By this time, Matilda's team was deeply engaged in a long-term research and publishing project in the field of aging. A grant from the Ford Foundation, funneled through the Russell Sage Foundation, kept us in business through three volumes of *Aging and Society*. The first volume was an inventory of research findings on aging as of 1965. As the most junior assistant, my task was locating and abstracting every study on aging published in the social sciences since the early 1940s. It took over a year, but for a brief moment, I was the only person in the world who knew everything on the topic. Matilda's genius was to take my hundreds of index cards and see how they should be arranged to produce a coherent overview of the condition of older people and the state of the art of research on aging.

The inventory became an essential resource for gerontologists for many years. But it was the third volume, *A Sociology of Age Stratification*, that stamped our imprint on aging studies and spurred the emergence of a sociology of age (as distinct from social gerontology). I contributed a chapter to this volume, "Friendship and Aging," that was based on my dissertation research. This essay remains one of the few systematic treatments of the structural determinants of friendship, although not many sociologists have discovered it, hidden as it is in the gerontological literature. To my eternal shame, however, the chapter and the entire volume, written in the late 1960s, refers throughout to the generic "he."

Back to the Big World

By 1970, I finally completed graduate school and left the groves of academe and the protection of Matilda Riley, to join the full-time faculty at a newly opened community college only a few minutes from home. This choice, as with the selection of a graduate school, was dictated primarily by geographic convenience and compatibility with child-rearing obligations. In the latter respect, I enjoyed the advantage of a highly supportive husband who was by then self-employed and whose place of business was also within minutes of home and the children's school. Full-time teaching at a community college typically involves fifteen class-hours a week plus three office hours, which may sound like an enormous load, but those eighteen hours are all that have to be spent on campus: no heavy administrative responsibilities, no graduate students to monitor, no grant applications to prepare, no articles destined for the *American Sociological Review*, and no major book contracts to negotiate. In addition, at least at the County College of Morris, pay and benefits are adequate, and working conditions are comparable to those at major institutions. One misses the collegiality of a large research-oriented department, but I understand that these also are often characterized by pettiness and professional jealousy.

The downside to community college employment is that it is the kiss of death. Few institutions with pretensions to academic grandeur will hire someone from the lower depths. On the few occasions when I have been approached to apply for a post, the process was abruptly terminated at the first level above the department. In other cases, I removed myself from competition out of reluctance to commute or because of the impossibility of relocating the family. But offers have not been all that frequent, and I am now in my twenty-fifth year of teaching five sections of introductory sociology, two semesters a year. Having been imbued with a strong professional identity by Matilda Riley, I could not simply fade away into my safe niche at County College. As I saw it, there were two available routes to academic visibility: writing textbooks and becoming active in professional organizations. Fortunately, both avenues were open to me.

Writing Textbooks

My entry into textbook writing was somewhat serendipitous. I favorably impressed an editor who asked me to evaluate an absolutely dreadful manuscript when I wrote back offering to pay Macmillan if they promised not to send the remaining chapters. When the editor asked if I would be interested in writing an introduction to gerontology, I said, in effect, "Why not?" I asked Liz Markson, then in the sociology department at Boston University, if she would like to coauthor, and she said, "Why not?" And so we did. The book bombed, and for reasons we should have realized. We wrote a book for sociologists, but most teachers of gerontology come from other disciplines, namely, psychology and social work, or hybrids such as adult development or family studies. But we wrote such lovely prose, and did it on time, that the editor asked us to try our hand at an introductory sociology text. For that mammoth task we asked Peter Stein to join us, and so began our decade-long partnership (actually, gemeinschaft is the more appropriate description.) Five editions later, we are still good friends.

My other writing has been strictly a cottage industry—literally. My home has always been the favored workplace, for everything but homemaking. My husband and children proved to be infinitely forbearing, although I often feel guilty at not having been a more imaginative cook. By 1980, both son and daughter had left home, and in 1986, quite unexpectedly and most devastatingly, my husband developed a fatal heart illness. Having always been something of a loner, I moved, in widowhood even farther into the haven of my home.

As anyone who has phoned me can testify, I work best when surrounded by Mozart operas or Schubert lieder. And I, who have never mastered elementary electronics (Dick Hess was the resident wizard), now live in a fully wired environment: a sound system that plays in every room; a study with computer, laser printer, FAX, and copier; and several large TV sets. I haven't the vaguest idea how any of them works, but I have learned how to read the illustrations in an operating manual, and I am quite astonished that so many other people find the text intelligible.

Aside from the friendship study, I have done little original research. The community college is not a fertile setting for high-tech research, nor is it especially encouraged. Thus, my subsequent publications have been largely synthetic in the sense that I rearrange the ideas and data of others. Thanks to all those years of private education, with their emphasis on great literature and grounding in Greek and Latin, I developed an ear for the language and a feeling for style that obscures my shortcomings with matters of substance—a gap filled by my various coauthors. In addition to the textbooks and readers in social gerontology, I also collaborated with Myra Marx Ferree on a study of the new feminist movement and an edited volume of gender analysis. These, plus book chapters and journal articles is not the prestige output that would earn promotion and tenure at a major university, but it takes up two shelves of a bookcase, and I look at it with some pride.

Professional Organizations

Far easier and more gratifying than the writing has been my involvement in professional associations. This also began with my work for Matilda Riley. In the late 1960s, I joined the Gerontological Society (later, Gerontological Society of America [GSA]), where the *Inventory of Research Findings* brought instant name recognition. As a raw recruit in the field, I was enormously lucky to fall in with an amazing and amusing group of well-established women from a number of disciplines: Millie Seltzer, Lillian Troll, Vivian Wood, Helena Lopata, Barbara Turner, Maggie Huyck, Corinne Nydegger, Carroll Estes, and various of their students came to form the "feminist mafia" of the GSA.

The GSA was in sore need of a feminist jolt. As late as the early 1970s, conceptual models based on the male experience still dominated academic gerontology, despite the fact that the great majority of older people in modern society are female. Furthermore, because gerontology was a new and relatively low-status field (having a home in no one academic department), it had been open to women scholars, many of whom held high positions in academe and the GSA. By the mid-1970s, the Society harbored a critical mass of members influenced by the new feminist movement. The occasion for mobilizing this mass was the GSA Council's decision to hold its 1978 annual meeting in New Orleans, Louisiana, a state that had pointedly failed to ratify the Equal Rights Amendment. Carroll Estes, Vivian Wood, and I hastily organized a petition campaign among friends and allies who threatened to boycott New Orleans, and without whom it would have been very difficult—not to say embarrassing—to hold an annual meeting. After an extremely acrimonious meeting of the GSA Council, where we were accused of subverting science with crass politics (among the milder charges), the meeting site was relocated to Dallas, Texas. The venu shift was costly to the GSA and although ill-will lingered for many years, the Society was never quite the same again. Nonetheless, my patience with GSA and its leadership, dominated by "real scientists" (medical people and biological researchers, primarily male) in contrast to the "soft types" (the primarily female cohort of practitioners and social scientists other than experimental psychologists), finally ran out in 1990. I had spent most of my time on GSA Council pushing vainly for a change in governance that would give the behavioral and social science section, with 40 percent of the membership, a proportionate share of decision-making power rather than a share equal to that of the medical sciences section, with its 5 percent of the membership (but they were M.D.'s rather than lowly Ph.D.'s). Having lost that battle and my appetite for the struggle, I declined to renew membership. Nonetheless, I owe much to the Gerontological Society, not only for visibility and honors early in my career, but for wonderful memories and dear friends.

During the following two decades, I was organizationally active in Sociologists for Women in Society (SWS), the Eastern Sociological Society (ESS), the Society for the Study of Social Problems (SSSP), the Association for Humanist Sociology (AHS), and, ultimately, the American Sociological Association (ASA). Each involvement emerged from a peculiar intersection of history and biography. My introduction to SWS came at the 1972 ASA annual meeting in Denver, where I was to make my debut as presenter in a session on aging organized by Matilda Riley. My family made the trip to Colorado and enjoyed a weekend at a dude ranch while I learned the routines of a professional meeting. As I wandered aimlessly through the hotel corridors, a long arm reached out to stop me in front of a table with an SWS sign. The arm was attached to Betty Kirschner who invited me to join the nascent organization. I needed little urging, and I have never looked back; indeed, anyone who wants to find me at the annual meeting need only poke her head in the SWS room. The company of feminist sociologists remains my most congenial environment, and SWS has given me much more than I can ever give back. My presidential term (1987–1989) covered the annual meeting in Atlanta, and I shall never forget the thrill of realizing that the hundreds of SWS members gathered for our annual banquet represented the most vital and creative force in contemporary sociology!

My career in SWS overlapped the years I was involved in the Eastern Sociological Society. When Matilda Riley became president of ESS in the late 1970s, she was sufficiently alarmed over the precarious financial situation of the organization that she engineered a change in the bylaws that made the executive officer an appointed rather than elected position. She then proceeded to ask me to step into the breach. Actually, Dick Hess was the key to straightening out and maintaining the financial records, and together we managed to run the organization for four relatively successful years. There was no money for a stipend, but we were amply rewarded in coming to know and working with the hundreds of presenters and committee members who formed the backbone of the organization. Nonetheless, it was with some relief that we turned the reins over to an executive officer and staff that could be suitably remunerated.

If I had to single out one moment as the high point of my accidental career in sociology, it would have to be the 1989 ESS annual meeting. Having decided to make a feminist statement, I immersed myself for an entire year in the literature on feminist theory in preparation for my presidential address. As this was not my field of expertise, the end product was more of a rhetorical exercise than intellectual contribution, but I had a hell of a good time delivering it. My euphoria, however, was touched with deepest regret that Dick Hess could not share the moment; he had always encouraged me to aim for the top, was a committed feminist, and had worked as hard as I had to preserve the fiscal integrity of ESS. I think he would have had a hell of a good time, too.

SSSP was also a very welcoming organization for those of us from the lower ranks. I often, half-jokingly, tell junior faculty that the quickest path to professional recognition is through attending the business meeting of a SSSP division and raising your hand when volunteers are asked to run for office or to edit the newsletter. Yours will be one of the very few hands on display. Editing a newsletter is especially salient because your name becomes the only one that many members ever associate with the organization.

I remember with great fondness the quality of intellectual debate on the SSSP board of directors in the early 1980s; we really fought about important things. At that time, SSSP was the intellectual home for those of us whose concerns as well as academic status placed us outside the charmed circle represented by the American Sociological Association. Here is where qualitative sociology was not only accepted but honored, and where topics rarely on the ASA agenda became central. Heady days, before Bill D'Antonio managed to democratize the older association and the dividing lines grew ever more blurred and permeable.

Even more marginal than SSSP to the sociological establishment is the Association for Humanist Sociology, which draws its members from a wide variety of schools, and which maintains a radical critique of the philosophy and practices of mainstream sociology. I enjoy AHS meetings for the range of unusual topics covered, for the primacy given to personal experience, and for the friendship of people who still believe in the ideals that motivated us in the 1960s. It refreshes and invigorates the soul.

Back in the mainstream, however, the ASA's move toward inclusiveness under the aegis of Bill D'Antonio, combined with our own growing numbers and confidence, made it possible for those of us who had honed our organizational skills in SWS and SSSP to work our way into the ASA committee structure, especially the committee on nominations and the committee on committees. Throughout the 1980s, we also moved into leadership positions in the various sections, so that by 1990 it was difficult to tell which organization was meeting: The same people, under different hats, were running the show and sitting in the audience at SWS, SSSP, and the ASA sections.

By the late 1980s, there were so many SWSers and SSSPers on the ASA committee on nominations, that feminists and relative outsiders could be nominated for council and other important offices. This is, ironically, where being located at a two-year college has conferred an advantage. In response to an implied mandate to make the ASA's governance as inclusive as its membership, I became a "token peasant." Earlier visibility in other organizations brought a modicum of name recognition when nominating committees groped for a candidate from a two-year college, or, as one past president of ASA put it, someone representing the "little people." I'd like to think that whatever influence I've been able to exert on ASA council and committees has opened the door even wider for us little folk, especially those who have also had irregular careers or who work in lesser-known venues.

All in all, it has been a very satisfying journey. The luck of the draw has worked both ways, as have the constraints of time and place. As the other essays in this volume attest, there may be no one preferred path for academic women, at least under current conditions. There are distinct advantages to completing graduate studies and establishing oneself professionally before concentrating on domestic roles; but there are also risks. Those of my generation who did it the other way around—family first, career later—sacrificed some professional goals but probably enjoyed more stable marriages and less stressful childrearing. It is unfair that women should have to chose the lesser among evils, but one can also marvel at the flexibility of our lives. Perhaps we cannot achieve perfection both at home and at work, but at least we have two sources of satisfaction, and we can move from one to the other as circumstances permit. I would like to believe that our lives are potentially richer, certainly far more varied, than those of our male counterparts who are so single-mindedly committed to a narrow vision of success.

Beth B. Hess

REFERENCES

Ferree, Myra Marx, and Beth B. Hess. 1985. *Controversy and Coalition: The New Feminist Movement*. Boston: Twayne.

———, eds. 1994. *Controversy and Coalition: The New Feminist Movement through Three Decades of Change*. Rev. ed. New York: Twayne.

Hess, Beth B. 1990. "Beyond Dichotomy: Drawing Distinctions and Embracing Differences." *Sociological Forum* 5:75–93.

Hess, Beth B., and Myra Marx Ferree, eds. 1987. *Analyzing Gender: A Handbook of Social Science Research*. Newbury Park, Calif.: Sage.

Hess, Beth B., and Elizabeth W. Markson. 1980. *Aging and Old Age: An Introduction to Social Gerontology*. New York: Macmilllan.

———. eds. 1976, 1980, 1985, 1991. *Growing Old in America*. New Brunswick, N.J.: Transaction.

Hess, Beth B., Elizabeth W. Markson, and Peter J. Stein. 1982, 1985, 1988, 1991. *Sociology*. New York: Macmillan.
Hess, Beth B., and Peter J. Stein. 1995. *Sociology*. 5th ed. Boston: Allyn and Bacon.
Riley, Matilda White, and Anne Foner. 1968. *Aging and Society*. Vol. 1, *An Inventory of Research Findings*. New York: Russell Sage Foundation.
Riley, Matilda White, Marilyn Johnson, and Anne Foner. 1972. *Aging and Society*. Vol. 3, *A Sociology of Age Stratification*. New York: Russell Sage Foundation.

Three

Obstacles and Opportunities en Route to a Career in Sociology

Hannah Schiller Wartenberg

I do not feel old at all, not as much a survivor as a person still on her way. I suppose real old age begins when one looks backward rather than forward, but I look forward with joy to the years ahead and especially to the surprises that any day may bring. —May Sarton, At Seventy: A Journal

Women born before World War II grew up in a different world from those born in the 1960s and after. Without denying that women still experience discrimination, I contend that not only were the obstacles we faced more pervasive but what distinguished us is that most of us accepted them at the time. A few women achieved academic careers by the direct route, frequently by sacrificing a personal life. More did so only after having had different working experiences before marriage, and then having been full-time housewives and mothers. Amanda Cross (a.k.a. Carolyn Heilbrun) speaks through her fictional heroine, Kate Fansler, who observes: "Many women's lives particularly were lived by another pattern beginning again just when it was supposed to end" (*Sweet Death, Kind Death* [1984]).

My life course illustrates such a case. While in part I conformed to "traditional" expectations, in other ways I was in the forefront of social change for women, becoming aware of it only with hindsight. Being determined and accustomed to getting my way, I simply followed my inclinations, unaware that I was part of a growing trend and perhaps a little ahead of it. I got my master's degree in sociology in 1963, the year Betty Friedan's *The Feminine Mystique* was published.

Early Years

Becoming a sociologist was certainly not my "childhood dream." I was born in Berlin in 1921. Since both my parents were physicians, it was always assumed that I would go on to higher education and prepare for a profession, but for years I resisted the suggestion of an academic career.

My parents' office was in our home. During my earliest years, my mother took care of me between patients. I was raised by a governess from the age of six. Most upper middle-class families had domestic help, so I did not consider that unusual. Instead, I was rather proud that my mother was a well-known doctor and did not spend her time playing bridge and going to afternoon teas like other women in her social class. Looking back, I consider it an advantage that I resented my governess rather than my mother for being the disciplinarian in everyday matters, though it did not entirely eliminate the mother-daughter conflict.

I had my first experience with discrimination against Jews upon returning to school from summer vacation in August 1935. My classmates suddenly stopped speaking to me. They made anti-Semitic remarks, and they treated me like a pariah. The major event of my youth occurred in December 1935, when at age fourteen-and-a-half I emigrated with my parents from Nazi Germany. We went first to Palestine (now Israel), where I stayed with relatives and attended school while my parents explored the country. They eventually decided not to stay, much to my regret. Having become a Zionist in Hitler Germany, I loved being part of the realization of the dream of a Jewish homeland, but I obediently returned to Europe with my parents. We stayed in Switzerland until we got our immigration visas.

We arrived in the United States in September 1936. I went to high school for two years in New Jersey, first in a public, then a girls' private day school, while my parents studied for the medical state boards. Since I did not know anything about American colleges, I followed the advice of my headmistress to apply to one of the Seven Sisters; I chose Wellesley.

I won a chemistry prize at high school graduation, so I began my college career at Wellesley as a chemistry major. My father wanted me to become a physician, but I had decided not to study medicine, in part because my mother told me that I would spend the best years of youth just studying and working, when I should be having a good time and dating. I found her argument somewhat persuasive, in part because I did not think I had her energy and stamina to combine career and family, but probably more because I wanted to have a career that would not tie me down to one place. I soon realized that as a woman chemistry major I would have little choice other than to test blood in a hospital (I did not like lab work) or teach high school chemistry. I was aware of the glass ceiling without having a term for it. In my first year at Wellesley, I became active in Forum, the student organization that invited speakers on political topics. I wanted to learn more about American politics and world events, so I switched my major to political science after my sophomore year.

Born in Germany to Jewish parents, I had emigrated to Palestine after exposure to the beginnings of virulent anti-Semitism, returned to Europe by way of Egypt on an Italian cruise ship, and then arrived in the United States. By age fifteen, I had set foot on four continents; through it all, I continued to attend school, in German, Hebrew, and then English. I was graduated from college in June 1942, six months after the bombing of Pearl Harbor. At age twenty-one, I was ready to leave the "ivory tower" and enter the "real world."

"Incognito" at Princeton

My first encounter with blatant sexism occurred right after college. I wanted to get a job where I could contribute to the winning of the war and the defeat of the Nazi regime. Many of my classmates became officers in the women's auxiliaries of the military services, while others had interesting jobs in government or the war industry. No such options existed for me because I was born in an enemy country. After December 7, 1941, the U.S. government virtually stopped giving citizenship to "enemy aliens." As such, my prospects of finding employment outside the secure walls of an academic institution were slim.

Dr. Louise Overacker, head of the department of political science at Wellesley, considered an academic career the right choice for me. One day, during my senior year, she showed me a letter from Professor William Seal Carpenter, head of the department of politics at Princeton University, specifically recruiting female graduate students. I was intrigued by the idea and made arrangements for an interview during spring break.

Professor Carpenter was a jovial, friendly man who explained to me that there was a dearth of eligible male candidates because graduate students were not exempt from the draft in World War II. The ranks of faculty members (all male, of course!) also were depleted by the draft, while others were on leave working for the government in Washington. The only ones left, as he put it, were "overage destroyers like myself," and they needed graduate students to grade tests and exams in the heavily enrolled introductory courses. He hit upon the idea of hiring two female graduate assistants, who would not be subject to the draft. They would receive a salary and free tuition for three graduate courses per semester. He was quite proud of this ingenious solution!

In all innocence, unaware of the implications of my decision and unprepared for the unusual academic experience that awaited me as a women in an all-male institution, I applied for the position and was accepted soon thereafter. I became a graduate assistant during the academic year 1942–1943, and I took graduate courses in political science and economics at Princeton University, an all-male bastion that had never admitted women graduate students.

After I had been accepted, I was informed that my colleague was to be Jane Ann Maier (now Laffey), who was graduating from Bryn Mawr. Dr. Carpenter suggested that we look for housing together. We followed his advice, which turned out to be a life saver; that mutual support saved both of us from almost total isolation. Our close friendship survives to this day. The term "sexism" was not part of the vernacular at that time, and we were not conscious that what we considered the department head's kind interest in our welfare was, in fact, evidence of his sexist attitude. He "took care" of us, in his traditional male role of the protector of helpless females, while "using" us to fulfill his and the department's personnel needs.

We arranged our course program under Dr. Carpenter's guidance. Having had no graduate school experience, neither of us was immediately aware of the irregularity of this procedure: We were merely allowed to "take" courses; we were not officially "enrolled" as graduate students. Only recently, I found out from Jane that we were not paid through the department but that we were on the payroll of the Princeton Surveys, of which Dr. Carpenter was the director and where he had his office on Nassau Street. We were not even token female members of the department; we were outside help.

Only after all my course work had been completed did I realize the full impact of not having been officially enrolled: When I did not receive a transcript, I called Dr. Carpenter to inquire about it. In response, I received a note signed by him listing the courses that I had completed and stating that "the same work has been exacted from her as is exacted from the men students."

My experience at Wellesley had not prepared me for this. Since it was a women's college, we learned that women can excel in all fields of knowledge. Our positions in college government proved that women can fulfill leadership roles as well. Nevertheless, I had been aware of the barriers faced by women in the "real" world. Like other female liberal arts graduates, I was frequently advised to go to secretarial school in hopes that that ultimately might lead to a career. I was determined to not go the indirect route.

The faculty at Wellesley had encouraged us to pursue careers, although everyone assumed that we would stop working once we became wives and certainly once we became mothers. However, having had a mother who had managed to combine a full-time uninterrupted career with marriage and family, I had a successful role model. The female professors also served as role models. At the time I did not fully realize that the almost 90 percent female faculty had been products of sex discrimination. Few women scholars and professors taught at coed schools, let alone at the prestigious men's colleges.

Indications of our strange status at Princeton accumulated. We had no contact with the undergraduate students, whose papers we were grading, and even our presence on campus was not known beyond the small circle of professors and administrators involved. During the second semester, we found out that the male graduate assistants in economics were, in addition to grading exams, teaching tutorials, the usual role for such a position. Being incognito, we naturally could not fulfill this role; we merely graded exams taken by students, who were, for us, "faceless." On a ski trip in Vermont during inter-session in January 1943, I mentioned to a group of young people at the lodge that I was a graduate student at Princeton. One young man responded reprovingly, "You flunked me." A professor had revealed our "secret" to him.

We were not included in university-related meetings or functions. However, the faculty wives invited us to innumerable baby showers for their daughters and to similar affairs appropriate to our status as women. Was this a way the male faculty tried to integrate us into the academic community of Princeton? Our classroom experiences with the professors were unique and could happen only in a traditionally single-sex setting into which two members of the other sex had suddenly intruded (Kanter 1977). After we had both earned A's, one of our professors admitted that he had initially tried to intimidate us so that we would drop the course. The most amusing incident occurred in an economics class. When the professor referred to the classical economists as "old women" (with whom at age twenty-two we did not identify), he became flustered and blurted out, "I am not used to having to watch my language."

Professor Harold Sprout was our only "ally." His wife had a Ph.D., but she had not been allowed to set foot in the university library when they arrived on campus in the early 1930s! In this respect, conditions had improved. Not only could we use the library and borrow books but we were even given a key to the "Seminar Rooms," special rooms in the library open only to seniors and graduate students. At the time, Dr. Sprout seemed to treat us no differently than his male students. He showed another side more than twenty years later when I visited Princeton with my husband and our college-bound son. He received us graciously and told me proudly that the department now had a number of women graduate students who were of better quality than the men because they were more carefully screened "to make sure that they don't get married before they finish their degree."

The news of Jane's and my presence leaked and created considerable consternation among the alumni. We were told that we were known "from here to California" and that Princeton alumni "would rather close the university than admit women." This prophesy did not come to pass. I found no reference to this female intrusion in the alumni publications for 1942–1943, which I inspected at the Princeton Club in New York City in 1987. Upon entering the club I saw, carved into the marble tiles on the floor at the entrance to the bar, the famous inscription that, though no longer enforced, still read: "Where women cease to trouble and the wicked stay at rest." Those tiles have since been removed.

In retrospect, we learned a lot in the courses, but above all we learned about discrimination against women. We had been used: We had spent a year in school without earning valid university credits, even at Princeton. We came to realize that sex barriers cannot be torn down by isolated individuals. It did not occur to us to protest, although we resented the treatment. And we could not sue or otherwise fight back. Who would have supported us? We could not claim a legal right. There was no social movement I could join to effect social and legal changes, so I explored new challenges.

Government Service During World War II

Whether as the result of that experience, or only because I still wanted to do my share, however small, for the war effort to defeat the Nazis, I did not apply to other graduate schools at the end of the academic year. Instead, I went to Washington for three days and, with the self-confidence of youth, knocked on office doors, offering my services.

In October 1943, four months after I applied, I was hired as junior propaganda analyst in the Central European Section of the Overseas Analysis Division of the Office of War Information (OWI). As a wartime agency, the OWI was allowed to employ noncitizens if they possessed special skills (for example, knowledge such as mine of German). The Analysis Division of the OWI was part of a combined office with the Analysis Division of the Foreign Broadcast Intelligence Service (FBIS) of the Federal Communications Commission (FCC), a permanent agency. The delay in hiring was due to routine security clearance; these procedures were extended in cases of foreign-born people, especially "enemy aliens."

My section was headed by Dr. Hans Speier, a sociologist on leave from his teaching position at the New School for Social Research. All senior people were professors on leave for wartime service. There was a young cohort of employees with bachelor's or master's degrees; it included some students from Antioch College on temporary assignment during their mandatory work semester.

Many of the younger employees were women, since young men were in the military services. The nonsexist atmosphere in this job stood in sharp contrast to my Princeton experience. Our civil service rating and pay was determined by our background and experience, regardless of gender. Speier expected us to work hard and do our best, and he worked at least as hard as the rest of us. His only criteria were competence and good work. We admired and respected him for his depth of knowledge and analytical skill and for his democratic way of administering the section.

We analyzed German radio and press reports that were monitored by the FCC; they were sent to us daily in written English translation. We developed and applied a method of combined qualitative and quantitative content analysis to ascertain conditions in Germany, for example, military and civilian morale, domestic economic conditions, evidence of shortages of food, and the effect of allied air raids. It was my first contact with sociological analysis. We wrote up the results in a weekly report that was distributed to other government agencies for use in pursuit of the war effort.

The atmosphere in the office was intellectually stimulating and congenial, and we cheerfully put in a lot of unpaid overtime. When, occasionally, we could take "compensatory overtime" by informal arrangement, I could never go away for the weekend because I was still classified as an "enemy alien," and I had to apply at least a week in advance for a permit from the FBI for any trip. When I told this to the director of the combined unit, a colonel in military intelligence, he wrote to the Immigration Service. Within two weeks, I was called for a hearing. I became an American citizen on February 14, 1944, Valentine's Day.

About that time, propaganda analysis was being phased out, and several people transferred to other government offices. When I heard of an opportunity to go to the London office of the OWI, I applied partly out of patriotic motives, but also, to be candid, because I was adventurous and liked to travel. I was immediately hired as a civilian radio news writer to write in German for broadcasts to the enemy.

I was transferred from Washington to the New York office of the OWI in

June 1944 for a two-week training course for civilians to be sent overseas. At the conclusion of the course, we were returned to New York City to await clearance from the British, only to find out that they did not grant visas to persons born in Axis countries. So, we were temporarily assigned for work in the German broadcast section of the OWI. Toward the end of August I was granted a British visa. The day before I was to leave, the program was cancelled, and I did not go to London. Rather than returning to the OWI in Washington, I applied for a position at CBS shortwave and I became a news and feature writer. CBS, under OWI guidelines and control, was beaming shortwave broadcasts in English to Europe and Latin America for the American government.

I worked at CBS from fall 1944 until fall 1945, shortly after the end of World War II. It was an exciting time; so much was happening as World War II was coming to an end. We had to write fast and put in a lot of overtime (we were paid time-and-a-half, because of a closed shop union contract). We all felt as though the news had not happened unless we wrote up the stories.

One of my most vivid memories is of a day in April 1945. I was just getting ready to leave after the day shift when the FLASH (highest priority in press wire lingo) came over all the news wires: PRESIDENT DEAD. The only other person in the office was writing the news for the Latin America broadcasts. We immediately informed the top directors, and then I went home. The European programs would not start until morning, and I had to return to work early for what would be a busy day assuring the Allies that America would pursue the war effort as before. I remember the strange feeling of being aware that, in that pretelevision age, I was the only person in the crowds hurrying home from work who knew that President Roosevelt had died. The special editions of the papers with banner headlines appeared only later that evening.

As CBS I again encountered gender discrimination. One incident alerted me to the relative ease with which men could get jobs. After I started working at CBS, I found out that the newest staff writer always had been expected to work the night shift. This rule had not been applied to me (in fact I was not even made aware of it) because the director of the news room would not permit a female to work the night shift. This naturally created some resentment on the part of those who were required to work this unpopular shift, and it was not likely to make them favor the hiring of women. In a conscious effort to be treated just like the men, I pleaded to be allowed to work the 11:00 P.M. to 7:00 A.M. shift. The director told me that he could not leave a woman alone in the office that late when the (grandfatherly) black elevator operator would be the only other person in the building!

In accordance with the law, a few months after the end of World War II, I was replaced by a returning veteran. Not long after, the operation ceased. It did not occur to me to look for another position in the media. Being a woman and nonveteran, I probably could not have found one at that time anyway.

Overseas Service and Marriage

After wavering for a while, I entered the graduate program in the political science department at Columbia University. In the spring semester of 1946, I took a course in foreign policy and one in sociology with Paul Lazarsfeld. My studies were interrupted again when my dream of going overseas was realized quite fortuitously. While I was in Washington for the christening of my friend Jane's son in April 1946, I had contacted Henry Kellerman, a friend from my days in the Washington office of the OWI. When he met me for lunch, he told me that a representative of the Office of Chief of Counsel for War Crimes in Nuremberg was in Washington recruiting personnel for various positions at the trials. I was hired as a translator to head a translation section. I would have preferred a research position, but this was the only position still available.

After some bureaucratic delays, I left for Germany in September 1946. I spent a year in Nuremberg. A few weeks after my arrival, wanting to get out of the translation job, I found out that tests for simultaneous interpreters were in progress. There were no training criteria for the new occupation; the only requirement was the ability to translate instantaneously. I was a "natural," and I became a court interpreter from German into English.

I set out originally to get some overseas experience because I wanted to earn a degree in foreign relations. Most of my classmates had married during or after the war, but I had decided to pursue a career instead. However, shortly after my arrival in Nuremburg, I met Captain (ret.) Rolf Wartenberg, who had just taken his discharge from the Army of the United States (AUS) and joined the reserves. He was working as a civilian interrogator at the war crimes trials. We got married in Nuremberg in March 1947, and we both continued to work there until the end of October of that year. In July 1947, I went to Geneva for a week to do some research on Radio Nations, the UN station. I made that trip at the request of Paul Lazarsfeld, who, in his inimical discerning fashion, had discovered that I had radio experience at CBS. That trip also reflected my desire to continue traveling and functioning professionally, even though I was a married woman.

My husband and I returned to the United States at the end of 1947. He started his own business in New York in 1948. Although I was totally unfamiliar with business, I assisted him, but I maintained my interest in sociological research by occasionally conducting interviews and doing coding for projects at the Bureau of Applied Social Research (BASR) of Columbia University.

From November 1949, when my first son was born, until 1959, I was a suburban housewife, mother, and community volunteer, conforming to the norms of the 1950s. I had never had much interest in little children but, always open to new experiences, I thoroughly enjoyed observing the development of my own.

Part-Time Graduate Work

By 1959, when the younger of my two sons started first grade, I had grown tired of doing volunteer work, and I decided to return to graduate study and master a field of knowledge. I reenrolled as a master's candidate at Columbia University, this time in the sociology department. Columbia allowed six credits toward my degree for the two courses I had taken earlier there, but the eighteen credit hours I had earned at Princeton were not accepted.

I chose sociology because of the interest sparked in me by Hans Speier and Paul Lazarsfeld and because I enjoyed the content analysis that I learned as a junior propaganda analyst in Washington. It was only later that I realized that I seem always to have had a penchant for sociological analysis. I had never taken a sociology course as an undergraduate but once, in a paper for an English class, I chose to analyze a nineteenth-century English novel as an illustration of Thorstein Veblen's *The Theory of the Leisure Class*. I had been introduced to Veblen's writings during a summer vacation in 1941. I participated in a work camp at Highlander Folk School in Tennessee that was sponsored by the International Student Service and supported by Eleanor Roosevelt. That experience profoundly influenced my thinking on social issues.

A pragmatic reason for my choice was that sociology offered more employment options and more opportunities for women than my undergraduate major of political science. I still resisted the idea of going into teaching, and I planned to pursue a career in market research. I went to Columbia to study with Paul Lazarsfeld, who was one of the pioneers in that field.

In 1959, it was still unusual for "older" women with children to return to college or graduate school. While there were no barriers to the admission of women to graduate school at Columbia, no special allowances were made for mature women. I commuted from our home in the suburbs. My part-time status made me marginal at a time when most graduate students went full time. I continued to fulfill my duties as a housewife and mother, albeit with the help of a housekeeper. In addition, I helped my husband with business entertainment, and I even interrupted my studies to go on a business trip with him. My graduate experience was hardly typical, and it was quite protracted. I must note that though I have a very supportive and helpful husband who is proud of my achievements, he typically regarded my career as secondary to his.

Two experiences from the Columbia days that were relevant to gender roles stand out in my memory. One concerns the subject of my master's thesis. It was entitled "Married Women's Return to Work: Sociological Determinants of Their Choice." It was based on interviews I conducted with a sample of mothers with children in junior high school. The U.S. Department of Labor noted at that time that the return to work of this cohort of women in mid-life constituted the largest increase in women's labor force participation. Thus, it should have been considered an important area for sociological research. At Columbia, however, my peers expressed the hope that now I would return to doing "real sociology." Hence, I did not attempt to pursue this line of research further, not realizing that I was "on the cutting edge" of research on women in the labor force. Only Paul Lazarsfeld was not opposed to such research. When he asked to see my thesis, and I replied deprecatingly, "Oh, it's just about women going back to work," he commented, smiling, "I like autobiographical theses."

In a seminar with William J. Goode, I continued to pursue my interest in women by writing a paper on changes in the status of women in India and Pakistan. It was based on original material I had obtained from the Indian and Pakistani missions in New York City, by writing to those countries for information, and by interviewing American women scholars who had lived in India and Pakistan. My family obligations prevented me from contemplating foreign travel to pursue the subject; and no one suggested that I might publish it.

My second recollection relates to my career choice. After receiving my master's degree in 1963, I was told that there were many full-time but no part-time jobs available doing advertising research in New York City. I was not ready to commute to the city from the suburbs for a full-time job, since I still had children at home. So, I remained at Columbia and, like other graduate students, worked on various projects at the Bureau of Applied

Social Research. I had been told that older women attending part time would not be accepted as Ph.D. candidates, but Professor Allen Barton, my M.A. advisor, persuaded me to apply. I was accepted. I continued to commute from the suburbs, and I took courses part-time and worked part-time at the BASR.

When I had completed my course work, Paul Lazarsfeld asked me if I would be interested in writing a dissertation on directors of academic research bureaus. I could use data that had been collected at BASR. I was not only flattered but pleased to have a dissertation advisor with an interest in my work. I have never regretted accepting his offer, for it was indeed a privilege, though not always easy, to work under the guidance of a "renaissance man," a real genius, an innovator and original thinker. My sessions with him were memorable. They gave me a chance to see his mind at work: analyzing data, pursuing leads, interrelating my findings, and opening up new ways of looking at them.

It was only after I had prepared for my comprehensive exams that I became interested in teaching. It occurred to me that it would be a challenge to present all this accumulated knowledge not only to my examiners, who, after all, knew what I was trying to say, but to students, to whom it was all new. In the 1960s, institutions of higher education expanded in response to the entry of the "baby boom" generation. There was an acute shortage of college professors. The colleges and universities in the New York area approached graduate departments, seeking students who could teach. While working on my dissertation, I taught part-time, first at Stony Brook and later at Hofstra. The atmosphere in the Stony Brook sociology department was very supportive. Kurt Lang was acting chair my first year, and I will always be grateful to him and to Gladys Lang, who introduced me to colleagues and included me at social events at the American Sociological Association (ASA) meetings.

I presented a paper at the Eastern Sociological Society meetings in April 1968. It was my first presentation, and it was based on my master's thesis. The subject evoked considerable interest. The eminent sociologist, Everett Hughes, asked me if I had ever reinterviewed the women to see if they carried out their intention to return to work. After I completed my doctorate in June 1973, I took his suggestion. I presented the results at a meeting in 1975. It was the first longitudinal study of working women. It has been cited, but I did not succeed in getting it published.

By that time I had been teaching at the State University of New York college at New Paltz for three years in a tenure-track position. After I obtained the position, my husband and I moved to Manhattan, where he had his office. It made commuting easier for both of us. Again, I seem to have been a precursor of things to come; I had a small "pad" in New Paltz and a commuter marriage.

The college, and particularly the sociology department, was very accepting of women and minorities. Our special scheduling needs were accommodated. There were a number of women on the faculty; the curriculum included a course on women; and, in 1973, a women's studies program was initiated. Of the various courses I taught, the most popular and my favorite was mass communication, which the catalog still listed as Public Opinion and Propaganda. I utilized my experience as propaganda analyst and in radio. I participated in discussions about the women's studies program and gave a lecture in the interdisciplinary core course, but I never taught the sociology of women course because the contingent of radical students and faculty did not consider me to be one of them. Although I developed a feminist consciousness, they were correct.

Developing a Network of Feminist Sociologists

While at New Paltz, I maintained a friendship with Natalie Allon, whom I had met at Hofstra. She invited me to attend one of the monthly evening meetings of the New York chapter of Sociologists for Women in Society (SWS). This had a profound influence on my career. It was here that I met other women sociologists; listened to works in-progress of interest to women; had my consciousness raised; and, as Natalie once said, became "a real professional" through interaction with a peer network. As a result, and at the suggestion of Judith Lorber, I became active in SWS. I served first as treasurer of the local chapter, then as membership chair of the national group, and as program chair when Judith was president of SWS. For the first time since Stony Brook, I again felt comfortable at ASA meetings, where I now had colleagues with whom I could engage in scholarly exchanges and interact socially.

In 1978, my husband's business made it necessary for one of the partners to move to Miami to take charge of the branch office there. Being the oldest, my husband volunteered. I agreed to go along with him and retired from New Paltz to move to Florida. If I had been of a younger age cohort, I probably would have stayed until I got tenure and tried a real "commuter marriage," but I was too traditional to chose that path.

Again it was my SWS network that helped me to continue pursuing my career. Beth Hess, a gerontologist and member of the New York chapter of SWS, suggested that I contact Aaron Lipman at the University of Miami, whom she knew from gerontology meetings. I wrote him a letter, in which I asked about the availability of research positions. In response, he offered me the opportunity to teach a course on sex roles that the department intended to offer for the first time in spring 1979. So began my association with the University of Miami sociology department as an adjunct assistant professor. The atmosphere in Miami and at the university was not receptive to women. Most of the women students were untouched by the women's movement, although the few who were feminists were a delight and among the brightest. There are more women on the faculty now; and even though a woman's studies program was started in 1989, they still are fighting an up-hill battle.

After I arrived in Miami, I enjoyed a certain prominence. As one of the few women in the area with a Ph.D., I was asked to participate on panels and in conferences and to give lectures to various groups. For a while I was "lionized" by the local media; I was interviewed by reporters and I appeared on talk shows. During my time in New York I collaborated with Natalie on a chapter on health spas for her book *Urban Life Styles* (1979). Health spas were a "hot" topic at the time, for they had started to proliferate. I rather enjoyed my fleeting "fame."

I taught at the University of Miami part-time, and one year I was a full-time visiting professor. I never got a tenure-track position, although at the beginning I was told that I had a chance, and I was promoted to adjunct associate professor. During my early years, I was treated as a member of the department. With each change of chair, my status deteriorated, and I became a convenient person to call on to teach a course or two, when needed, at low pay. Why did I stay? Lack of alternative opportunities in Miami, inertia, and eventually, my increasing age.

My experience in Miami raised my consciousness and transformed me into much more of a feminist. Again it was SWS that "saved" me. I got in touch with SWS-South at the first meeting of the Southern Sociological Society that I attended in 1979. Through my activities in the organization, I met outstanding southern women sociologists and feminists. From 1986 to 1987, I served as president of SWS-South.

My husband retired in 1982 and thought I would retire, too, but I could not quite let go. Like many other women of my generation, I had started late, and I was not yet tired of the daily grind, as my husband was. This typical pattern is documented by Lillian Rubin (1979). We now spend the summer months in our former weekend house on the eastern end of Long Island, but I continue to teach part time, mostly in the spring and to be active in SWS and SWS-South. I also take an active part in the national sociological associations and attend the annual meetings regularly.

In May 1991 I announced my retirement, but I continue to pursue my scholarly and professional activities. Through professional organizations, I maintain contact with my colleagues, many of whom have become friends. They don't think I'm as old as I am because I started late and because I was not a full professor. And I do not feel old, as demonstrated by my agreeing to be nominated for the first time for a committee of the ASA. I served a two-year term (1992–1993) in its sex and gender section.

Concluding Reflections

As I look back over my life, I realize that it was influenced by political upheavals, social changes, and the rise of the modern women's movement. My family background, exposure to anti-Semitism and sexism, my choice of a woman's college, as well as my marginality as an immigrant and as a female in a male-dominated society also affected my life, as did my affiliation with a feminist professional network in SWS.

My life history illustrates that potentially adverse events can become learning experiences and can even turn into assets. In my youth, the exposure to anti-Semitism reinforced my positive attitude to Judaism and made me feel relief, not pain, in having to leave the country of my birth during adolescence. My early exposure to different cultures, languages, and countries had the salutary effect of teaching me to understand diversity and oppose racial and religious prejudice and all kinds of discrimination.

My encounters at Princeton document the sexism that pervaded America and academia at that time and began to arouse my feminist consciousness. My fluency in German created unique job opportunities, but my wartime positions also illustrate the use of the "reserve labor force" of women that touched the lives of many American women of that era.

In the 1950s, I followed a typical American life-style, conforming to the prevailing norms of women's domestic role. But by the 1960s I had become part of a growing trend toward the pursuit of a delayed career. Obstacles due to sexism, my inability entirely to abandon the traditional values of my generation, and my late entry into the profession limited what has been nevertheless a gratifying career. While changes in the status of women have eliminated the blatant forms of sexism that I experienced, discrimination based on gender persists on a different and often more subtle level, and I shall continue to fight for equality for women through feminist activities.

Hannah Wartenberg

REFERENCES

Allon, Natalie. 1979. *Urban Life Styles*. Dubuque, Iowa: Wm. C. Brown.
Allon, Natalie, with Hannah Wartenberg. 1979. "Health Spas." Pp. 82–129 in *Urban Life Styles*, edited by Natalie Allon. Dubuque, Iowa: Wm. C. Brown.
Kanter, Rosabeth Moss. 1977. *Men and Women of the Corporation*. New York: Basic Books.
Rubin, Lillian Breslow. 1979. *Women of a Certain Age*. New York: Basic Books.

PART II

Up the Down Escalator:
Tales of Academic Mobility

Four

Acquiring an Academic Room of One's Own

Jane E. Prather

It is necessary to have five hundred a year and a room with a lock on the door if you are to write fiction or poetry. —Virginia Woolf, *A Room of One's Own*

Coming of Age in the South in the 1950s

My life has been a search for my own space. I've always felt marginal—not quite fitting into the worlds around me. As a child we lived in Little Rock on the western edge of the city where the paved road stopped two blocks from our home. Some houses did not have indoor plumbing, and most lacked telephone service until the late 1940s. I was a child of Yankee parents transplanted to the South after World War II. My parents were "old" by the standards of my playmates; my mother was thirty-nine and my father was forty-four years old when I was born. At school most of my classmates had very young parents; some of the mothers were as young as sixteen when they had their first child.

Few parents had had opportunities to acquire higher education. My parents, on the other hand, had struggled to obtain their educations: My father had a doctorate in physiology, and my mother was the only woman on our street with a college degree. My family's middle-class values contrasted in various ways with those of the working-class families. While my parents encouraged my sister and me to study classical music, the other kids were listening to country music. My father had grown up in extreme poverty in Kansas and knew how to hunt and fish for survival. He did not, like many Southern men, consider hunting and fishing as the ultimate in recreation. My mother did not identify with the other neighborhood women who strived to be Southern ladies. Although women in the South, especially in the 1950s, may appear polite and smiling, behind their smiles may lie a lot of pain and suffering.

In childhood, I knew my family was different. We talked Yankee style, although I later acquired a Southern accent, and my family did not have the same attitudes as someone with a traditional Southern heritage. For example, I remember an African-American household worker was shocked when my mother invited her to eat lunch at our table; she sat next to my father. As she exclaimed, "I've never eaten next to a white man before." In most homes, she would have eaten separately from the family—on the back porch, or in the kitchen, and even from different plates.

Religion was another area where I felt alienated from my peers. Most Southern children identified themselves as Christians, meaning Protestant, if not fundamentalist. My father was agonistic, and my mother had little interest in formal religion. In the South, it is taboo not to have a church affiliation. Even today, a new acquaintance will inquire about one's church membership. Obituaries in Arkansas newspapers mention the church affiliation of the deceased in the first sentence. The lack of a religious identity caused me a variety of problems. I dreaded Monday mornings in the second grade when my teacher called roll by reading names listed on a big blue chart. Students were to respond "Yes, Ma'am" or "No, Ma'am" according to whether they had attended church or Sunday school during the week. Since my family was not religious, I replied, "No, Ma'am." Every Monday I felt cold stares as I publicly admitted I had not gone to a religious service. On Easter, when I could reply in the affirmative, the entire class applauded. By the third grade, I succumbed to social pressure, saying, "Yes, Ma'am!" although I had not participated in any religious meeting. To this day, I assert that it was the Christian influence in my school that first rewarded me for lying!

I am opposed to prayer in public school because, in my experience, the religious views of the teachers, principals, or community are reflected in any attempt to be nondenominational. Christian fundamentalism dominated the public schools in Little Rock in the 1950s. Each class day began with Bible readings and prayer and occasionally teachers included a Bible lesson. Other academic topics could be subjected to religious interpretation. For example, my sixth grade teacher stopped a filmstrip showing Mount Vesuvius erupting with an exclamation, "If you ever had any doubts of what hell is like, here it is!"

Fundamentalist churches encourage their members, even children, to recruit "heathens." I was a prime candidate since I was not baptized or affiliated with a church. Once, I attended a Baptist service, where the preacher called for "sinners to come forward." My girlfriend begged me to go to the altar, almost pushing me down the aisle. I nervously walked to the altar with about twenty others, but most of the congregation remained in their pews singing a hymn. I couldn't understand why there were so few sinners.

I finally began to attend church regularly with my sister because she wanted a school letter for her sweater. Her junior high awarded these emblems to students who participated in community service, including attending religious events. This is another example of how school and church are intertwined in the South.

My high school reinforced male superiority. Boys' athletics and other masculine interests dominated the school. Men's service organizations sponsored boys' organizations such as the Key Club, an organization that socialized boys for involvement in community activities and Southern traditions. Their most successful fund-raising event, which was held in the school auditorium, was a minstrel where the members donned black faces and told racist stories.

Sports for girls meant cheerleading, drill-team, or tennis. Girls' service clubs socialized their members for "hostess" or junior homemaker roles. These girls smiled and served refreshments at school events. Southern mothers also reinforced social skills by encouraging their daughters to host formal teas. Girls sent invitations to their friends, who in turn responded with formal notes. At the teas we dressed up with our hats and gloves to sip punch and daintily eat little sandwiches. I recall not enjoying the teas; but, on the other hand, one did not want to be excluded.

Southern girls, especially in the 1950s, received many implicit messages about being ladies. The high school emphasized dating, partying, dancing, going steady. During a typical high school year, clubs sponsored as many as six formal dances, where the girls wore long formal gowns and boys bought corsages for the girls. There was an assumption that high school represented the best years of one's life. After graduation, a young woman would soon marry and settle down. Most women from my high school did marry by the time they were twenty-one years old.

My high school has a unique historical reputation because it was the first large public high school in the South to integrate racially. In 1957, nine black students integrated Little Rock Central High School, which had over twenty-five hundred white students. During this era, most white Southerners opposed school integration. They defined themselves as either "moderate" segregationists, who wanted to move slowly toward integration, or as "Citizens Council" segregationists, who vehemently opposed integration.

As I reflect on this experience, it is amazing that school administrators and faculty did not prepare students for integration. When the black students arrived at the high school for the first time, violence erupted as many parents and other adults—both black and white—crowded around the school entrance. Within the next week, Governor Faubus sent the Arkansas National Guard to block integration, and President Eisenhower ordered federal troops to uphold the laws prohibiting school segregation.

How did these events affect me? As coeditor of the student newspaper, I wrote an editorial, "Can You Meet the Challenge?" in which I advocated that students identify their primary goal as completing their education, not fighting integration. Reprinted in national newspapers, the editorial gave me some momentary fame. I had almost no contact with the black students until the end of my senior year when the vice-principal for girls informed four other girls and me that during Baccalaureate one of us would be marching into the stadium beside Ernest Green, the one black senior. If we did not want to walk directly with him, we could move in front of him. I had forgotten about the meeting with the vice-principal until I arrived home that evening to find my mother very upset. She had received hateful phone calls from white racists who saw any situation where a white girl might interact with a black male as a threat. The nasty phone calls continued throughout the weekend. My father had died the previous summer, adding to my mother's anxiety as she felt very much alone. I did walk with Ernest during the ceremony. The hate mail continued to arrive at our home throughout the summer. The incident had a profound effect on me. I was very angry at these racist and hateful people, and I became even more determined that I had to leave the South.

Although I was one of seven valedictorians, I do not recall any high school counselor seriously discussing college with me. The young women in my high school received mixed messages about college. We should attend a finishing school or THE university (meaning the University of Arkansas), or we should go to work. The end goal for us was marriage, which, of course, included children.

My family had higher expectations. Not only did my parents assume that my sister and I would graduate from college, but they also encouraged graduate school. Although I was awarded an academic scholarship to the University of Kansas, my accomplishment, like those of the other women in my class, was ignored at high school graduation. The young men, on the other hand, collected accolades for their scholastic or athletic achievements.

Few women from my 1958 high school class had opportunities for professional success. I am the only woman from my class who has an advanced degree. No women have become lawyers, doctors, or scientists. Even those few women who earned masters' degrees remain stuck in clerical positions. At high school reunions, the upper middle-class women proudly state they are "homemakers." Only when they are a distance from their spouses does one learn that they may have returned to school and that they do have major accomplishments outside the home.

Undergraduate Messages: "Major in anything you like. You know, you'll just get married and do volunteer work."

Money dignifies what is frivolous if unpaid for. —Virginia Woolf

From 1958 to 1964 I attended the University of Kansas. I majored in sociology and psychology for my bachelor's degree, I earned a master's degree in sociology. I again became aware of my marginal status in college. During this time, Southern whites experienced prejudice; we were perceived as "red necks, stupid, or bigoted." My Southern accent and Little Rock origins made me a prime target for ridicule. I deliberately tried to alter my Southern speech. (I'm not sure how successful I was. Today, my Pennsylvania roommate roars with laughter at my attempts to sound non-Southern.) Gender was a significant factor influencing my undergraduate experience. On the positive side, I was the first out-of-state woman to be awarded a prestigious General Motors scholarship. I met with the scholarship administrator every year, and each time I received the same advice: "Major in education (like my daughter) so that you can have a job and raise a family." This advice was omnipresent. My freshman academic advisor, a French professor, offered another version: "Major in anything you like. You know, you'll just get married and do volunteer work." Thank God, though, for my mother! She always told me I would want a career where I would get paid for my work. (She had been a victim of discrimination in the 1920s when women who married could no longer teach.)

In the late 1950s, the college environment was not conducive to women scholars. Many male professors and students believed women attended college only to meet men. In contrast, I never heard any woman say that was why she was in college. Women faced additional barriers in math and science classes. When I was one of two women in an advanced calculus class, I endured stares, glares, or flirtations from the thirty men.

Another problem college women encountered was the unofficial dress code. Sororities forbade members to wear jeans or pants on campus. Dormitory rules required women to wear skirts for evening meals; on Sundays, the dorm helpers would serve us only if we wore a dressy outfit including heels and hose! In freezing cold weather, and I do mean freezing, I walked a mile to class in skirts with knee-high socks. My legs turned bright red! Women also had to contend with dormitory closing hours—10:30 P.M. evenings, 1:00 A.M. weekends. Campus police or other official monitors literally locked women in campus housing.

Sexual norms! Where shall I begin? In the Midwest, women were expected to be virgins at marriage. For a single middle-class woman, becoming pregnant was probably the biggest taboo. Although sexual mores designated a woman as responsible for setting the limits on sexual behavior, the man's responsibility was to marry her if pregnancy occurred. Thus, marriage and early pregnancy impacted the college experiences of both men and women. A woman was expected to quit college and support her husband until he completed his education. Pregnancy was not uncommon because the only readily obtainable contraceptives were condoms. Available in drugstores, condoms were hidden behind a counter, requiring the customer to request them. In small towns like Lawrence, Kansas, there were no clinics where unmarried women could obtain birth control information or diaphragms. Some bold women pretended to be married and sought contraceptives in Kansas City. Contraceptive information was unavailable at college campuses at this time. For example, a popular lecture in my child development class consisted of a local obstetrician describing only one form of birth control—the rhythm method. He ended the presentation: "When you are engaged, come see me and we can discuss other methods!"

Peer pressure fell on both women and men to be engaged by their senior year and to marry after graduation. Fraternities and sororities had rituals to promote going steady (pinnings) and engagements. Popular notions about gender roles asserted that men and women could *not* be just friends. Dating was the only possible relationship. College women gained popularity by the quantity, not the quality, of their dates. In dorms, women elicited phone calls to validate their social status; fraternities and sororities gave "points" to members who dated members of the prestigious Greek houses. A caste system existed in which students ranked Greek associations. Senior women living in dorms, as I did, were often the most academic achievement–oriented students, yet we were considered to be at the bottom of the social heap. Fraternities reinforced the social popularity of women through their method of delivering invitations to "prized" women during dinner hours in the dorm or sorority. Music and skits accompanied the public announcements. Thus, everyone knew which young women had received invitations. In these ways, the university, by tacitly accepting the practices of the Greek associations and campus housing, reinforced a dating system that promoted the popularity of women as dating objects and, in turn, trivialized their presence in the university.

Female faculty were rare. If women instructors existed, they were graduate assistants or nontenured. I never had a female sociology professor in my eleven years of higher education. Subtle and blatant put-downs of women or feminine attributes flourished in the academic setting. I survived by being in a state of denial. I thought that I was different from other women and that, therefore, the derogatory comments did not apply to me. To illustrate, I had an economics professor who argued that women needed a different education than men. Consequently, he recommended that the women in the class write their term papers on domestic topics, such as the best home appliances to buy. Male students investigated the economic issues of their chosen careers. Indignant, I told him that, unlike the other women in the class, I was not interested in learning about home appliances. He remained unconvinced, but he did allow me to research a career in psychology.

Although I began my college education with an interest in psychology, I discovered sociology in my junior year. Courses in collective behavior and social movements excited me; I wrote term papers about my experiences with racial integration in high school. The sociology department at Kansas claims to be the first department of sociology in the United States under the rubric. (Evidently Yale had created a department earlier called social relations.) The department was exhilarating because of its close affiliation with the University of Chicago and the Midwest Institute. Howard Becker often strolled through the Department; he was completing his study of the Kansas medical school, *Boys in White,* (1961). I took a course in race relations that was team-taught by Everett C. Hughes and Helen Hughes (the latter a much more dynamic lecturer than the former). I was impressed by the newer generation of faculty: Ray Cuzzort, C. Dale Johnson, and Norman Jacobs.

I experienced challenging and dedicated faculty in the sociology department at Kansas. If it were not for my mentor and thesis advisor, Charles K. Warriner, I would not have had the confidence to continue graduate school. He encouraged me. He obtained financial support for my research on voluntary associations; and he coauthored with me a paper based on my thesis. In addition, during my last semester at Kansas, I received an assistantship that allowed me to teach my own introductory sociology class. What a thrill at age twenty-four!.

In spite of my insistence that I was not attending college to find a marital partner, I, too, married when I was a graduate student. I knew, however, that I needed a career to survive. My husband Kirk supported me ideologically. He promised my mother that marriage would not interfere with my academic goals; yet neither of us understood the implications of a dual-professional marriage.

Life at Berkeley in the 1960s from a Married Woman's Perspective

> *Women never have an half hour . . . that they can call their own.*
> —Virginia Woolf quoting Florence Nightingale

I did not contemplate leaving the Midwest to pursue my doctorate. Instead, I was considering schools such as Washington University in Saint Louis, Iowa, Michigan, and Minnesota. When the Vietnam conflict escalated, my husband sought engineering jobs in defense industries that would grant him a draft deferment. In an interview with General Electric, he mentioned my interest in pursuing my doctorate in sociology. In spring 1962, I received a phone call from General Electric headquarters asking me if I would like to attend the University of California, Berkeley, while my husband worked in nearby Oakland. It was surprising that recruiters had taken his request seriously and had investigated the location of outstanding doctorate programs in sociology.

Although past the deadline, I applied to the UC-Berkeley sociology department and was denied admission. Upon arriving in California, I made an appointment to discuss my rejection notice with Herbert Blumer, who was the chair of the Berkeley department. Nervous at being in the office of such a sociology giant, I was impressed with his kindness and concern. As he looked over my records, he remarked, "I don't see why you were not admitted." Immediately, and in my presence, he began telephoning the admissions committee, asking why I had been denied admission. I will never forget his comment: "Married? That's no reason!" And with that reaction, he signed my admission application and informed me that my record merited an out-of-state tuition waiver.

Fall 1964 was the infamous semester when the Free Speech Movement began. I was in the country's most celebrated sociology department at probably the most famous time in its history. The professors in both undergraduate lectures and graduate seminars gave the most outstanding intellectual presentations I had ever experienced. But classes, like student demonstrations, were often mass events where only a few people participated and many remained as observers. For example, the graduate theory "seminar" was held in a classroom filled to capacity with one hundred students. The semester was half over before I realized that I was one of approximately thirty enrolled students. The others were advanced students reviewing for their exams who engaged in dialogue (sometimes in French or German) with the professor, Leo Lowenthal. Probably, most of the enrolled students, like myself, felt intellectually outclassed. This experience was not uncommon. Celebrated professors attracted crowds of students, many of whom audited the class. Students had limited interaction and contact with professors. As a reaction to their worshiping hordes, most professors were not readily accessible to graduate students.

Sexism was so prevalent that I was not consciously aware of its presence. Classrooms appeared to be approximately one-third women, yet few women completed their doctorates. Rumors circulated that certain faculty feared that the increasing number of women enrolling in sociology would mean the lowering of academic standards. The women students, however, suspected that the qualifications for admission were higher for women than for men. There were no female tenured faculty. It was clearly male territory. Interest in any academic topic that might be considered a woman's field was taboo or considered beneath the investigation of such an academic elite. Male students dominated class discussions, aggressively arguing, debating, and reaffirming their status. Sexist jokes and put-downs were tolerated. (Male) faculty and female student sexual liaisons occurred. As a married female graduate student, I felt estranged from some student subgroups, which were usually organized by men with a few invited women. I formed friendships with several other women who also seemed to feel as I did, like outsiders in the men's playing field!

My goal was first and foremost to complete my doctorate. I knew no alternatives. From my perspective, the roles of women were so limited that if I did not receive my doctorate, I would be relegated forever to the role of housewife, teacher, nurse, or secretary, none of which appealed to me. It was this determination that kept me struggling to finish, even when I saw other women become discouraged or quit. My perseverance intensified with pregnancy. Societal expectations dictated that mothers should abandon any personal pursuits. For example, when I told my career objectives to my obstetrician, he reassured me that I would love being a housewife and mother and would soon forget graduate school. On the hospital admission forms, I listed my occupation as graduate student. The receptionist typed "housewife." It was 1967 when my daughter Juliana was born. Although several women graduate students had older children, no one had a baby. I felt estranged as I distinctively stood out from the other students as a pregnant graduate student. I received diverse reactions. The majority of faculty with whom I interacted were very supportive, most notable were Herbert Blumer and Neil Smelser. Even Erving Goffman, known for his blunt communication, asked my why I didn't just stay home after having the baby. Then he remarked that being a full-time mother was not necessary. "After all, British women had always hired nannies to rear their children!" After saying this, and perhaps convincing himself, Goffman was always supportive of me.

As "starving" graduate students (my husband was now also in a doctorate program), we could not afford a nanny. I did have wonderful baby-sitters who were usually mothers who wanted a child to play with their children. I experienced enormous guilt: I *should* either by studying or caring for my child. Fortunately, my husband and my mother were emotionally supportive, but neither was available to provide assistance with child care. Again, I felt marginal. I tried to make friends in our apartment building with other mothers with whom I could share baby chatter and occasionally baby-sitting. But most of them had no understanding of what graduate school involved or what a sociologist was. My fellow graduate students, regardless of gender, had no particular interest in my family concerns, since most of them were single. I felt alone and lonely, but I was too busy to become depressed.

I selected specialities in sociology that excited me such as: small groups and social interaction (Erving Goffman), socialization (John Clausen), and collective behavior (Neil Smelser). Berkeley was unique in that one had the opportunity to study diverse research methodologies. While most sociology departments then emphasized survey techniques, the Berkeley department was rich with experts in various methods. I took historical methods with Rheinhard Bendix, fieldwork methods with David Matza, and survey techniques with Richard Glock. Plus, being a student of Erving Goffman, I learned his distinctive approach to observational methods.

After completing my doctoral exams on April 1, 1968 (I always thought April Fool's day was appropriate for such exercises), I couldn't think or study. I wanted to do anything but open a book. As if my neglected selves were screening for diversion, I immediately bought a sewing machine and made matching mother-daughter dresses. I sewed continuously for a month. Finally, I emerged out of the sewing phase, but still I was unable to study. I sought help at the UC-Berkeley counseling center, thinking I needed some assistance with motivation. Fortunately, the therapist was an understanding older woman who diagnosed me as a pioneer coping with survival in academia. She persisted in asking me what I did during the day just for myself. I told her I felt too guilty to do anything just for myself: I *should* be studying or caring for my daughter. She reassured me that I would be better at both if I were to do something special for myself. I took up swimming. I swam regularly in the women's gym on campus in a pool built by Phoebe Hearst that was surrounded with beautiful marble statues of goddesses. I am indebted to this counselor who helped me overcome my studying block.

By fall, I was working on my doctoral dissertation on banking. Goffman insisted that if I wanted to understand banking interactions I had to take a job in the bank. I objected, but I finally followed his advice. Reluctantly, I had to admit my best data derived from the four months that I worked incognito as a bank teller. Some of my richest data involved the issues of women's employment, and it was this section of my dissertation that I published. Working full-time as a bank teller while writing and analyzing fieldnotes and caring for my young daughter was overwhelming. My interest in feminism intensified as I was leading the double life of a housewife/mother and an academic. At the American Sociological Association meetings in 1969, I participated in a panel of graduate students at the Women's Caucus. This event was a turning point as I nervously and angrily described the problems women encountered in the discipline and in society.

By summer 1969, the Berkeley scene erupted into radical disturbances and demonstrations. When an opportunity arose for my husband to work in Los Angeles, I was eager to go. Although I had not finished my dissertation, I decided to apply for teaching positions because I feared that if I overidentified with the housewife/mother role, I would not accomplish my dream of completing my doctorate. Just as Virginia Woolf argued that for women to write poetry they needed money and a room, I knew, subconsciously, that to write my dissertation I would need my own identity, my own money, and my own room.

To maintain my sociological identity and to get the money, I began seeking academic positions in southern California. Naively, I thought one merely sent out resumes and the best universities would be eagerly waiting to hear from an all-but-dissertation (ABD) student. My best offer was at San Fernando Valley State (now called California State University, Northridge), where I launched my career in fall 1969. I had very little understanding of how much energy and time would be required to teach full-time and remain an active member of the department. The department chair offered me a two-day teaching schedule and recommended I not volunteer for any committee service until my dissertation was completed. Years later I realized what a generous offer he had made!

For my own room, I converted the laundry/storage room behind the garage into my office. There was no heat or telephone, and the roof leaked. But it was my own space! I maintained a very disciplined schedule. For at least two days a week I became a hermit in my room and wrote my dissertation. The other days involved teaching, class preparation, and caring for my daughter and husband. During the summer of 1970, my daughter was in day care (a rare fine in those days) while I researched and wrote at the UCLA library. My second daughter, Kirsten, was born in July 1971. By August, I had completed my dissertation. I look back now and wonder how I did everything.

I will never forget the day I "filed for graduation." Waiting in line in the UC-Berkeley administration building, I grew apprehensive watching the file clerk actually measuring the margins on dissertations to verify if they were the "correct width." Although I had hired an experienced secretary to type my dissertation, she was familiar with UCLA's requirements that had margins one-eighth inch smaller than UC-Berkeley's. I had discovered my margins were smaller than the regulations pamphlet stated after the dissertation had been typed, but I had no idea that margin size would actually be verified. When I reached the window, I plopped my dissertation down while holding the hand of my wiggling four-year-old and with the baby sleeping in a backpack. I must have been a strange sight, because the clerk suddenly looked up and said, "How did you do it?" I was relieved when she quickly passed the ruler over a margin on one page, apparently ignoring the smaller margin. She scanned a few pages and said, "This is the most beautifully typed dissertation I've received all day." I could hardly smile; I just wanted to cry that my dissertation was out of my hands.

From there I went to the sociology department, where two graduate students—Susan Garfin and Diane Horowitz—broke open champagne to celebrate. Then I did cry. The epilogue to this story is that Susan finished her dissertation shortly afterward. Diane, suffering with the anguish of struggling with familial responsibilities and academic frustrations, ended her life several years later.

To this day, the academic women of this era describe the pain we suffered trying to flow against the tide. We remember our female colleagues who turned their frustration inward, becoming bitter and depressed. Women have not often publicly discussed the personal sacrifices they made in order to establish academic careers. In my case, my marriage did not survive the trauma of dual careers. While academic men are likely to have a spouse or companion who supports their goals, academic women rarely report this experience.

Seeking Tenure: What They Don't Teach You in Graduate School

Few women even now have been graded at the universities.
—Virginia Woolf

The sociology department at San Fernando Valley State was large—over forty faculty positions, and the faculty had a dual junior/senior caste system. Rank was not the distinguishing factor; job seniority and age were. Even some associate professors were treated as junior faculty. The men and women defined as "junior faculty" had similar profiles: politically active, interested teachers, and involved in research. In contrast, the senior faculty consisted mostly of disillusioned men who claimed to be very actively engaged in published research. For most of them this was mere talk. Opposing student evaluations of teaching, some senior faculty argued that good teaching did not encompass concern or empathy with students. The worst indictment against a junior faculty member was to assert that he or she was popular among students. Anyone who enjoyed teaching was suspect for fear research was not also a priority. I truly loved to teach and acquired a reputation for being student-oriented. Having designed, with a colleague from the department of psychology, the first women's studies course on campus, I became known as a "women's libber." Naively, I did not realize how these labels would impact a nontenured person.

The sociology department had only one tenured women when I joined the faculty. Although she had won the university's coveted Distinguished Teaching Award, she had had difficulty obtaining tenure. Another woman was ahead of me in seniority. Appearing to fit a traditional model of the academic woman, she did not encounter problems with tenure, but she had difficulty getting promoted to full professor. Personnel committees were dominated by a few powerful men who controlled the department. They did not want to promote or grant tenure to any one who would not support their regime.

The entire semester before my tenure decision, I was in a state of denial, discounting every sign of trouble. Since I had published more than most of my colleagues at my level and since I had good teaching evaluations, I was confident that I met the qualifications. In addition, the president of the university had just appointed me to the first affirmative action committee on campus, and a colleague and I were preparing a grant proposal to submit to the National Institute on Drug Abuse. Thus, when denied promotion because of insufficient "quality" publications, I still did not anticipate tenure problems. I knew I was an excellent teacher.

A bizarre problem arose during the fall 1972 semester. The department chair, a very authoritarian man, asked me to sort his mail because he did not trust his secretary. I refused, saying that I had not obtained a doctorate to be a secretary. Then, revealing his racism in addition to his sexism, he replied, "Then, you'll have to tutor minority students." I reported this incident to the dean, but he died before my tenure review.

Another strange event occurred the day preceding the tenure decision. The chair of the department personnel committee asked me to meet with the committee to discuss my research. I prepared as if to present a colloquium. The personnel committee and the department chair—six male sociologists—began interrogating me abut the political climate of the department. They raised such issues as: whom would I promote if I received tenure? Would I promote faculty popular with students or those engaged in research? (I tried to argue a middle position—someone excelling in both areas—although I knew what the committee wanted to hear.) Most of the questions were about colleagues, rather than about my research. Then as a final blow, one man told me that I was not liked by my colleagues. Since "collegiality" was an important criterion for tenure, the committee would not recommend tenure to anyone who did not get along with colleagues. At this point, I started crying. I couldn't believe people didn't like me.

In short, the department denied me tenure, even though the majority of the faculty never had an opportunity to voice their opinion. I appealed my case. I contacted both Blumer and Goffman, who wrote my department very supportive letters on my behalf. Students organized a letter-writing campaign and colleagues in other departments of the university added their voices of protest. After a thorough investigation, the dean was my rescuer, urging higher level committees to overturn the department's position. I won. I earned the dubious reputation of being the first person on my campus to receive tenure without a positive recommendation from my department. I later learned that my fate was determined by seven people in my department. Two men were vehemently opposed to me, three men voted against me for fear of personal retaliation by my enemies, and two were allies. The votes did not reflect evaluations of my qualifications, but political vendettas. The following year, the department personnel committee denied my request for promotion to associate professor because I had only one additional publication since the previous year. No one had been held to such a high standard for promotion to associate professor. I had a total of six publications; I was a coinvestigator for a grant from the National Institute on Drug Abuse; and I served as an assistant dean. The personnel committee, which was composed of members from the previous year's committee, apparently wanted to continue provoking me, perhaps hoping I would disappear. Again a dean (the third one) came to my rescue. He convinced the higher level committees to override the department's decision. My case and other controversial personnel decisions in my department resulted in a lawsuit and an investigation by the American Association of University Professors and the American Sociological Association.

The most important lesson I learned from my tenure/promotion struggles is that no one wins a battle alone. I had tremendous support from colleagues and students. I now perceive that my tenure situation exemplifies some typical problems that women encounter. As suggested by the Virginia Woolf quote, we do not know how to grade women in academia. Promotion/tenure committees are most often composed of faculty who may not value feminist scholarship or research about women's issues. Anyone who does not fit the mainstream pattern of an academic department—because of their research interests, their academic background, their ethnicity, gender, or age—has more difficulty gaining acceptance in an academic department. Most important, women like myself are naive about the political process. We are often not aware of how political decisions are made and what procedures are legitimate. I am also painfully aware of how a dominant few can sway the majority in a committee and how factors other than qualifications may enter into personnel decisions. After my experience, I vowed to help any junior colleague who might need assistance in comprehending how the system operates.

Finding My Space, and Flowering in the Minor Leagues

> *There is no mark on the wall to measure the precise height of women. There are no yard measures, neatly divided into the fractions of an inch, that one can lay against the qualities of a good mother or the devotion of a daughter, or the fidelity of a sister, or the capacity of a housekeeper.* —Virginia Woolf

Like other women with intellectual interests, I have spent a great part of my life searching for my niche, my own space. I perceive my life as a constant challenge to traditional socialization messages. First, I had to contend with the Southern traditions that helped transform girls into Southern ladies. Then, I struggled with the pressures in college to major in education or to become exclusively a homemaker. When I had young children I had to carve my definitions of "a good mother," even though I was a working mom. Finally, I had to reconcile my graduate socialization with my career choices.

In an elite program like UC-Berkeley, graduate students are socialized to follow in the footsteps of their mentors (that is, male senior faculty) and pursue careers at prestigious universities. Perhaps the mentor feels a sense of accomplishment as well as reinforcement of his values if the mentee selects a similar academic setting. Other career choices are viewed as failures. For example, I remember mentioning to Erving Goffman that I wanted to focus on teaching rather than research. Indignantly, he asked: "Then, why are you here?" I recall arguing that one still needed a Ph.D. for any college career. The implicit message was that teaching held low status and that institutions focusing on teaching were the "minor leagues" of higher education. Research holds the highest prestige and universities that produce the most research form the "major leagues." This socialization to seek the most prestigious academic settings resulted in frustration for female students like myself. We were not likely candidates to receive tenure-track positions in these elite institutions because discrimination against women was and has remained highest in the research-oriented universities. Yet most women students during the 1960s were very naive. We remained optimistic in spite of our training in male-dominated institutions with no female faculty. We thought the situation would be different for us. As participants in the women's liberation movement and as organizers of women's caucuses, we believed that barriers would decline. Furthermore, as participants in the 1960s social movements fighting for students' rights, we thought teaching would gain more recognition. Many women like myself found that our only opportunities for employment were in universities emphasizing teaching. Nonetheless, we had to reconcile our career choices of teaching in the minor leagues with our socialization for the majors.

What is exciting about the minor leagues? In a teaching-oriented university, a faculty member can have a significant impact on students. After twenty years of teaching at California State University, Northridge, I still receive letters and phone calls from former students who claim I was one of the faculty who helped them turn their dreams into realities. My university, like others in this category, recognizes good teaching. One of my greatest accomplishments was receiving the university's Distinguished Teaching Award.

In the minor leagues one can (after achieving tenure) engage in creative or nontraditional research that major universities might not recognize or would censure. Research is not evaluated by a single male-dominated standard. Feminist scholarship appears to flourish in the minor leagues much more frequently than at the elite institutions. In my case, I have investigated the pharmaceutical industry's marketing of psychotropic drugs (minor tranquilizers) for women. The major sociology journals rarely publish in this field, and the research remains controversial since it criticizes traditional medical practices and the pharmaceutical industry. My university, however, has been supportive—albeit minimally—of this research when federal funding has not been available.

In addition, the nonelite universities, like mine, have in the last decade recruited and retained cream-of-the-crop women faculty, many of whom had encountered discrimination in hiring or promotion in the major leagues. The result is a lively contingent of intellectual and creative women from many disciplines who support feminist scholarship. While the major leagues are still male-dominated, the minor league academies have provided more opportunities for women in administration. For example, I have held administrative positions both on my campus and in the California State University Chancellor's Office, the headquarters for all the California state universities. Yet, when I wanted to return to a full-time faculty position, I had that option. Other women in my university have held top administrative positions for several years and then returned to teaching. While the male faculty cannot comprehend relinquishing power, the female faculty have perceived this trend as another way to maintain a dynamic career. In short, women in the minor leagues are creating new definitions of academic careers.

Another positive feature of the minor leagues is the flexibility of time. In my experience, the teaching-oriented universities allow faculty some control over their work schedules. In the major leagues, research can become so demanding that the faculty member often engages in a self-imposed regime of long hours in laboratories or libraries. The elite private colleges require faculty to be omnipresent to students and to be available for many campus activities. The minor leagues demand heavy teaching loads but provide some time flexibility after teaching obligations are met. Having this flexibility has allowed me to strive for a balance between family and career. I could schedule classes when my children did not need me, and I could pursue my research interests on my own time schedule. My family responsibilities took on other dimensions when I remarried and participated in the care of two step-daughters, plus my own two daughters. In 1987, I helped my husband, Dick, start his own business—a coffee roasting store. On Saturdays, I am the tea specialist in the shop giving "tea lectures." My mother, now in her nineties, lives nearby, and I have the opportunity to visit her and learn from her wisdom.

My search for my space appears to be ending as I recognize that in my teaching-oriented university I can create an academic room of my own! Yet in the age-old feminine tradition of cleaning a room before beginning "real" work, I have just uncovered amongst the piles of clutter in my office a letter written by a student in 1973 denouncing my department's denial of my tenure. The student, who recently died, ends her laudatory comments with: "You are the hippest of cats and the most sensitive of all instructors. When you teach with your heart, how can you miss?" May I always live up to her evaluation.

Jane E. Prather

Five

Reflections on a Serendipitous and Rocky Career
The First Twenty Years

Janet Lever

Early Recollections

I consider myself a lucky person. The price is taking the bad luck along with the good. Sometimes I am in the right place at the right time; othertimes, there is no doubt I have been in the wrong place. It can take a while to know which is which.

I was definitely lucky to be born into my family in Saint Louis. My parents, Harry and Sophia, are good people who gave their four children lots of love and encouragement. Both are now eighty, going strong, vigorous, and spirited. They were high school sweethearts who married at age nineteen. On the surface, ours seemed to be an average family as I grew up in the 1950s: mom, a full-time homemaker, and dad, an accountant who supported the family. I had to educate myself about sex roles before I understood that my parents somewhat deviated from the norm. My dad is a highly principled, warm man with a "heart of gold" who is well loved by his many friends. My mom is the tougher of the two, pragmatic, and very focused on her family. We observed them sharing power and making decisions jointly. A photo that my brother took of me at age four shows that early on I rejected traditional sex roles, too: I'm dressed in my underwear with my dad's hat, tie, and gloves on, carrying his briefcase. I didn't understand where he went each day, but it already had more appeal than doing housework.

Both my parents were good athletes. My mother even continued to play team basketball through the early months of her first pregnancy. But sports were a lot bigger for girls in the 1930s than in the 1960s; early dating was discouraged, so the "Y" or "J" (Jewish Community Center) provided a place for teenage boys and girls to be together. Team sport was the organizing activity, and the socializing afterwards was akin to what 1990s teens do: hang out in groups instead of formal dating.

My brother senses that my dad was disappointed by his son's lack of athletic ability, but sport was nothing either parent pushed on their three daughters. When I was growing up, it wouldn't have dawned on my dad to take a little girl to see the Cardinals play as he had taken his boy. Just last week, when I was invited to speak to a large men's group, I sat next to a man my age who also grew up in Saint Louis, still in love with the Cards. You never forsake your boyhood team. I thought about the fun he must have had with his dad at those major league games, although I also appreciate that my lack of fandom has saved me an extraordinary amount of time over the years. It's odd that I fell into studying sociology of sport. All others I know in the field are ex-jocks or superfans, or both. I don't regret being neither player nor fan; I knew that my outsider's view gave me a special vantage point.

When it came to academics, both my parents expected their children to be special. I'll never forget my dad asking why I only got a "B" in physical education without first praising me for my seven straight "A's" in everything else, including high school chemistry and trigonometry. I reminded him that it was basketball season and that I'm just over five feet tall, but that didn't seem to be a satisfactory answer. I only knew how proud he was when I ran into a friend of his who congratulated me on my report card. High achievement was a given in my household; being ordinary was not okay. The notion that a girl could exceed some standard of excellence to her detriment was only apparent at the end of college, when I announced my intention to get a Ph.D. My mother expressed concern that a woman with that much education might scare off men. (I never did marry, but I had a lot of fun and several good opportunities for marriage along the way. And, at five feet tall, I rarely got the impression that I intimidated anyone.)

As an undergraduate at Washington University, I lived in my parents' house. I felt deprived being a "townie" while others enjoyed the liberation of living away from home. When my brother offered to arrange a clerical job for me at Macy's foreign shipping office in London in 1966, the summer after my sophomore year, I grabbed the chance to travel. I had no awareness that England was to host the World Cup soccer championship that summer. I quickly learned that soccer was the most popular sport, that the World Cup was the only truly global championship for professionals in a team sport, and that soccer fans were literally willing to die and figuratively willing to kill for their national teams.

Tourists poured into London from many countries to support their teams. One focus for the media was the Brazilian contingency, who came prepared to witness a tri-championship, as their national team had won the Cup in 1958 and again in 1962. But the Brazilians were disqualified in early elimination rounds. BBC-TV showed the Brazilian reaction to the embarrassing defeats: men and women in Rio de Janeiro openly wept; one ship-dwelling fan attempted suicide by throwing herself overboard; Brazilian flags were lowered to half-mast; and angry mobs burned players and coaches in effigy. Not only did I witness this reaction to loss but I also was lucky enough to witness the reaction to victory. England won its first World Cup in 1966, and the fans' celebration suspended British reserve for two days. I tucked away these vivid images when my summer ended.

The following summer, my Portuguese language studies prompted an invitation to join an exchange-student program in southern Brazil. In addition to completing coursework at the local university, I was required to write a term paper for Washington University. Fortuitously, on my first weekend, my host family took me to a soccer match. I was one of about ten women in the crowd of thousands. The BBC-TV images flooded back; I had my term paper topic. My sociology professors—Helen P. Gouldner, Joseph Kahl, and Dorothy Meier—were genuinely excited about my written report. They easily talked me into dropping out of school for a semester and using my tuition money to fund a return trip to expand the work for an honors thesis. What is far more amazing, in hindsight, was their willingness to come to my home to meet with my parents and convince them of this unconventional plan for my education. The same professors later prodded me to shorten that thesis for publication in the social science magazine *Trans-Action*. How lucky I was to have had professors who encouraged me to be serious about an undergraduate research project. I had excellent grades and respectable board scores, but I'm sure that having such a bold senior thesis helped me get special attention when I applied for graduate studies in sociology.

The Preprofessional Years

I was accepted into several graduate programs, but Yale, Northwestern, and UCLA expressed the strongest interest with personal phone calls. All three offers were very tempting. During my senior year at Washington University, Pepper Schwartz and I had struck up a friendship based on our mutual interest in sociology, and she was leaning heavily toward Yale. We decided that the Ivy League was less daunting if we faced it together, so off we went to what was a virtually all-male institution. Yale had been accepting women into its graduate programs since the 1890s, but when we arrived in the fall of 1968, there were still no ladies' rooms in the sociology building and no gynecologist on the student health staff. The one dorm for graduate women was hidden on the distant periphery of the campus.

At first we felt like kids let loose in a candy store, but soon we were overwhelmed by Yale's maleness. At best, we were treated like "visitors" being *allowed* into the social system. We had to fight to make people notice our minds as well as our gender. In case we missed any metaphorical reminders that females were unwelcome, the doors to Mory's, Yale's famous eating club, were closed to women, including the very few on Yale's administrative staff.

In our first year at Yale, we witnessed groups of student activists challenge Yale's 267-year tradition as a bastion of male learning. Coeducation became the hottest issue on campus as Vassar and Princeton announced intentions to admit students of the opposite sex. In response to rallies, editorials, and petitions, Yale president Kingman Brewster agreed to limited coeducation; 500 females—250 first-year and 250 transfer students—were to be admitted for the fall of 1969. Had the Old Blues seen the new light? Not really. Their own research indicated that many of the best young men who had rejected their offer of admission had chosen Harvard because it had a sister-school, Radcliffe. Now some would prefer Princeton for the same reason. Yale had to compete. Pepper and I came to think of this as the "Geisha Girl Theory of Coeducation."

In a year when women's liberation had become a national movement, Yale was to provide a dramatic stage for women's attempt to gain admittance to a male preserve. Our interest in gender issues irreversibly aroused, Pepper Schwartz and I, just finishing up our first year of graduate school, seized our opportunity to apply the sociological tools we were learning. We were there, where it was about to happen, and the event was already being intensified by the magnifying lens of mass media attention. By observing the trespass of traditional male territory, we hoped to delineate where the boundaries were drawn and how far people would go to protect them.

We ran around to see whether our elders planned to write about this natural experiment. Political scientist Ken Keniston had just written *The Young Radicals* (1968). There were sociologists of education on the faculty and others whom we expected to be professionally interested. But no one else saw it as worthy of serious study, so we got a contract for *Women at Yale* (1971) with Bobbs-Merrill and were on our way to writing a book before we ever took our comprehensive exams, a diversion not uniformly appreciated by all the faculty or other graduate students.

While I was at Yale, I had more opportunities to return to Latin America and continue my studies in sport sociology. No one warned me that it was not a respected subspeciality. In the Ivy League there's an arrogance that one can do whatever one wants as long as it's done well; I would have been well advised to consider the career implications of my choice. In 1969, I got a summer fellowship to return to Brazil just as the national team was competing to qualify for the 1970 World Cup. Because of my gender and the novelty of my study, I had already been introduced to Pele, then and still the world's most famous soccer player. That introduction led to an enduring friendship of which I'm very proud. I went to visit him and the other team members where they were sequestered for training; then I went on to visit northern Brazil where disaster hit me. I returned with an unidentifiable tropical fever that put me in Yale–New Haven Hospital for forty-five days. I vowed never to return to Latin America.

But the fates tempted me again. The following summer Ian Taylor, a British sociologist who writes about soccer "hooliganism," offered to share his two press passes to the World Cup Games in Mexico after he read my *Trans-Action* article. It was there and then that Brazil finally accomplished its tri-championship, and I was lucky to witness the celebration that was shared by the hosting Mexicans who identified a *Latino* victory as their own.

Two of my Yale professors, Anthony P. Maingot and Tony Obserschall, convinced me to apply for a Foreign Area Fellowship from the Social Science Research Council, and I proposed Brazil as the locus of a fan study for my doctoral dissertation. I feared another fever and honestly didn't want to go, but they were so supportive that I filled out the application and hoped to be rejected. No such luck—I got the fellowship and a flattering invitation to come to Harvard and meet with the renowned economist Albert O. Hirschman. He had reviewed the proposal and wanted to discuss my plan for the research. It seemed that I was on my way, but for another disastrous event. In 1971, I was in a head-on collision with a drunk driver on a local New Haven street. Bad luck to be there right then; incredibly good luck to have lived through it, given that I was driving a tiny Triumph while she was in a Buick. My left kneecap was crushed, among other injuries. Not sharing the jock mentality I studied, I took my time going through painful physical therapy and it took me over a year to walk again without crutches or cane. The cloud's silver lining, I thought, would be getting out of my commitment to return to Latin America. That didn't happen. Everyone, including

Professor Hirschman, felt so bad about my misfortune that they put the fellowship in a special account earmarked for me after my recovery.

Once I could manage to hobble around, I took advantage of my time between therapy sessions to explore my other academic interest, gender studies. The year before, while I was a teaching assistant for Lenore Weitzman in one of the first sex-roles classes in the country, I'd had an idea. It dawned on me that little girls could play with traditional girls' toys, like Barbie dolls, alone or with a friend whereas little boys often needed other boys to play with their toys. A catcher's mitt is not much fun unless someone tosses you a ball. The next day I went to Macy's toy department and simply listed whether a game or toy could be properly played with by one person or whether more were needed. The idea had merit: boys were put into social situations by the very nature of their innocent playthings.

That was the start of my interest in sex differences in children's play and games. With the help of my friend and teacher Louis W. Goodman, I began to expand the notion that boys' games were more complex than girls' games along dimensions other than mere size of group. I put together a committee and planned another dissertation project. I wasn't sure whether the study of American children's games or the one on Brazilian fans would be my dissertation, but it didn't really matter. Stanton Wheeler, R. Stephen Warner, and Lou Goodman all agreed to serve on my committee no matter which project became my thesis. Stan was an exacting chairperson and, ultimately, I was the beneficiary of his demand for precision. The fieldwork I began on crutches to help me get through my time in therapy eventually was the basis for my dissertation and two articles, "Sex Differences in the Games Children Play" (1976) and "Sex Differences in the Complexity of Children's Play and Games" (1978). I went to Brazil a year late and collected data for what would become my book *Soccer Madness* (1983). No one is lucky to be the victim in an auto accident, but I succeeded in turning that lemon into lemonade.

Reflecting on my undergraduate and graduate experiences, I happily cannot say that I lacked mentorship, a complaint made by many women and men in assessing their higher education. Helen Gouldner was my "idol at first sight." Sitting in a large lecture hall with four-hundred other students taking introductory sociology, I was in awe of her command of the audience and her obvious delight with her chosen discipline. I had a few other women professors, but none who taught in large lecture halls. Gouldner was different from the male lecturers who showed arrogant command over their materials and, when we were lucky, some good humor. She was not only compellingly interesting and very funny, but she also exuded warmth. Only a freshman, I quickly determined what I wanted to be when I grew up: a sociologist who could lecture like Helen Gouldner. After I got up my nerve, I want and met Helen, who kindly guided my studies for all four years of college.

When I got to Yale, there were no women on the sociology faculty. But I was the beneficiary of friendship and mentoring by several of the men there: Wendell Bell, Burton Clark, Tony Maingot, and—most of all—those already mentioned who labored through not one but, in effect, two dissertations with me. Jacqueline Wiseman was a visiting professor for one semester, and Pepper Schwartz, Kristin Luker, and I had a tutorial with her. It was a welcome women-only time-out in which we shared our perspectives on our Yale experience. I recall Jackie's indignation when she found out that the housekeepers in her residence hall were making the beds of male faculty but not hers because, they said, they'd assumed she wanted to make her own bed. Because there were no female role models for most of our time at Yale, the women in our cohort served as models for each other. Lifelong friendships with Pepper, Kristin, Michelle Patterson, and Maureen Mileski began as a survival plan at Yale.

It was time to fly out of the nest and get my first job as an assistant professor. The academic year 1973–1974 was a good time for women and minorities to enter the job market. Affirmative action—at least having a few "tokens"—was accepted as a necessity. I remember being shocked by the recruitment letter from a noted scholar at a major university saying his department already had a woman so they were seeking a "black Negro" (as opposed to someone light-skinned who might "pass"?). The letter served as a good indication of how self-conscious was the search for people to fill the emerging quotas. I knew I'd be a hot prospect. I had a conceptually interesting dissertation that was grist for lively presentation and audience response. While others in my cohort had to handle theoretical or methodological critiques, I got to hear sociologists indulge in recollections of the play and game scenes of their youth.

I interviewed at seven places and got six offers. The process was interesting: A flurry of frantic calls for visits came in late March. Rosemary Taylor from Berkeley was the "number one applicant" and she had been holding several good offers. When she announced her decision to go to Harvard, recruiters must have scrambled. I vividly remember a call from Barnard inviting me to lunch. Surprised, I replied that there must be a mistake; I hadn't applied to Barnard. They said they were interested in meeting me anyhow and considered me a candidate. (Today's deadlines and other guidelines assuring "equal opportunity" were not yet in place.) I received an offer to be an assistant professor at an appallingly low salary.

The incident taught me that the "old-boy network" was a reality and that names were being passed around informally. That, plus an offer to visit the University of Wisconsin, Madison (UW) (where I had applied and Rosemary had just refused), flattered me into thinking I must be the "number two girl" on the market. I regret turning down the faculty position offered by UW, then the top-ranked sociology department in the country. Serendipity intrudes in many of life's big decisions: The April blizzard that trapped me for days in Madison cooled my enthusiasm for what was otherwise a terrific career opportunity.

My First Professional Appointment Ends in Disaster

I am a "bright lights, big city" kind of person. The lure of Northwestern, just outside of Chicago, was too good to pass up. I had wanted to study under Howard S. Becker, but I had passed up Northwestern's acceptance to graduate school in part because I wanted to get out of the Midwest. Now was my chance to be a colleague of someone I so greatly respected. Members of the faculty were enthusiastic in their invitation for me to join them. Unlike Yale, where most assistant professors are not awarded tenure and accept their assignment as a "stepping stone," Northwestern was described as a place that rewarded scholarship and good citizenship with tenure. The course load was light, the students were quite bright, and I could easily commute from Chicago's vibrant Northside to Evanston, so I accepted. As it turned out, I often shared the commute with Howie Becker, who became my mentor and taught me the "do's and don'ts" for young faculty. He also read draft after draft of my papers and book chapters; he gave me support as well as excellent substantive and editorial advice. I count Howie as one of my closest friends, and my relationship with him stands as one of the few reasons I could never fully regret my decision to go to Northwestern.

While there, I was happy and, by all indications, I thrived in the environment. I published in the discipline's best journals, and I was making progress on my soccer manuscript. More important to my ego, I was turning into that ideal lecturer I had modeled after Helen Gouldner. Statistics calculated after my departure in 1982 showed that my classes accounted for 50 percent of the department's enrollment in nonrequired courses. I had developed a "sociology of sex roles" courses that grew from forty students when first offered in 1975 to over three hundred by the early 1980s. I was even prouder of the composition of the class, which changed from mostly female to 50 percent males. When asked, men said they signed up "because my girlfriend made me" and other reasons like "I didn't want to end up like my father." I also taught graduate seminars in sex roles and was very conscious of my responsibility to be a role model for our women graduate students.

Call me arrogant, or just out-of-touch with political realities, but I wasn't worried during my tenure review. I had delivered on all my promises. I was naive enough to think the process was fair, and I was taken by surprise when, late in the year, one of my colleagues let me know things were not going so well. I had a true unanimous first-ballot recommendation from my colleagues in the department and a unanimous recommendation from the three-person ad hoc committee based on outside reviews, which were summarized as strongly in my favor. However, the three men, all from other social sciences, produced a report in which reservations about the style and content of my work were expressed louder than praise.

In its letter of recommendation, the ad hoc committee also conceded that I was a "much better than average teacher; indeed, she is quite possibly outstanding. . . . As critic, counsellor and role model for students at all levels, Dr. Lever's conduct as a member of the faculty is clearly exemplary." The committee acknowledged service beyond the call of duty, quoting a dean's letter that said I had "benefitted the University in ways that cannot appear in the printed record," a reference to some delicate trouble-shooting shielding students and personnel from scandalous publicity.

What they questioned was the theoretical relevance of my work as well as its topicality and accessibility, both qualities of which I am proud: "Throughout her career she has carried out research on topics of wide public interest and has written about them in an understandable manner. This probably accounts for the high proportion of her works that have been reprinted in more popular sources. In this sense her writings on women in academia, on sex roles in general, on children's games, and on sports border on and even overlap with first-rate journalism."

In his Appendix to *The Sociological Imagination*, C. Wright Mills (1959) warned, "In many academic circles today anyone who tries to write in a widely intelligible way is liable to be condemned as a . . . 'mere journalist.' . . . The spurious inference: superficial because readable" (218). The chair of my department then was Arnold S. Feldman, himself a theorist, who rebutted the ad hoc report in a letter: "In Lever's case, her ability to write understandable prose deprives her of the superficial appearance of being 'theoretical.' Unfortunately, 'theoretical' has come to by synomous . . . with ill-defined concepts, garbled syntax, and long words. . . . Perhaps it is because her work is rich in empirical observation that the committee failed to see its equally rich theoretical contribution."

By Northwestern's tenure procedure, the department's and ad hoc committee's recommendations were then to be considered by the eighteen-member university promotions and tenure (P&T) committee. A two-thirds majority was needed for a positive recommendation to the dean who, in turn, was to make his own recommendation to the provost, who is described in the faculty handbook as the one having the final decision. The committee voted eleven "for" (64.7 percent) and six "against" recommending me for tenure; had the eighteenth member, my colleague, been allowed to vote, the recommendation would have met the tough two-thirds standard. The decision was now in the hands of Dean Rudolph Weingartener, who in the past had made positive recommendations for candidates who had received fewer affirmative votes from the P&T.

In my case, the dean recommended against tenure and informed me of his decision in a letter dated May 5, 1980. On May 9, Chair Feldman sent a strongly worded protest letter to the dean saying that the dean had acted improperly as an "additional and determining external referee" in overruling the judgment of departmental and outside experts in sociology. As news spread around the country, reviewers and others called the dean to add their protest to that of my colleagues. On May 14, the dean wrote to the chair saying that he would agree to reconsider his recommendation if I were to submit a completed manuscript on soccer in Brazil by November 1. I did, and he sent it out to two well-known sociologists at other universities for review. Neither had taken part in the first evaluation.

At Northwestern, faculty have six months from the time they receive notice of a negative tenure decision to request an appeal by a faculty panel. However, the date the dean proposed for his reconsideration was a few months after such a deadline would expire. Not willing to sacrifice a hearing by my peers and not sure whether the dean was sincere in his offer or whether he was just trying to cool us out, I went to Provost Raymond Mack, himself a sociologist. I knew him personally, and I felt I could be straightforward about my concerns. He stated that an appeal would be inappropriate at that time, but he gave me his word that I would be given ample time after the dean's second decision, should the outcome be negative.

The second decision was dated January 15, 1981, and it was negative. The provost accepted his recommendation. The provost was honorable in living up to his word and, over the dean's objections, I was granted an investigation by an appeals panel. P&T committee members were interviewed. According to the panel's report, "Several members of the P/T Committee expressed the feeling that Lever's opponents *were* biased against her kind of sociology, and that words like 'flashy,' 'trendy,' and 'opportunistic' reveal a suspicion of the whole field. . . . One felt that the feminist orientation of Lever's book *Women at Yale* might cause it to be polemical." Ending in a three-to-two split, the panel voted against a new tenure review given the limits of its jurisdiction, but the entire panel expressed an "uneasiness" "not only in the handling of Professor's Lever's case but in the system as a whole . . . a different group of faculty . . . might well have reached a more favorable conclusion."

Northwestern's Organization of Women Faculty wrote a letter of protest that accomplished nothing. My efforts to get that group to consider a class action suit (many terrific women scholars had been denied tenure in recent years) fell on deaf ears. The school paper had just published the 1979–1980 figures released by the AAUP showing that Northwestern ranked at the bottom of a list of major private universities for the number of women as a percentage of total faculty and at the bottom of the Big Ten for the number of women as a percentage of tenured faculty. Janet Abu-Lughod, a senior sociologist, gave the most support I got from a female colleague. Instead of words of protest, she used the tools of the trade to provide data to support my contention that the system was rigged in favor of men and against women. Abu-Lughod demonstrated that in the years since my entry, 65 percent of the male candidates but only 20 percent of the female candidates received tenure through NU's internal review process.

The Endless Lawsuit

I agonized over the decision to file a complaint of sex discrimination at the Equal Employment Opportunity Commission (EEOC). My men friends begged me not to file, saying "life isn't fair" and "you can't fight City Hall." Just pick up the pieces and move on, they urged. My women friends were unanimous in their position that I *had* to file. After teaching a few thousand students about issues of gender discrimination, how could *I* walk away without a fight? Research suggests that women often do not recognize when discrimination touches them personally. I had been successful in the male domains of Yale and Brazilian soccer, but I had been only a guest. Tenure was real—it was lifetime membership and voting power—and, in the moment of truth, I was as much a victim as other women. I knew that a man with my achievements would have been granted tenure. I did feel a sense of social responsibility to cry "foul play."

The one woman who cautioned me about taking steps toward legal remedy was Nancy Gertner, my first roommate at Yale, who by then was a distinguished attorney and law professor and now is a judge of the U.S. District Court in Massachusetts. She warned me about the plaintiff's onerous "burden of proof," the steep financial and emotional costs, as well as the difficulty of getting another job after bringing suit against a university. Nancy remembers that I was determined, and she gave me advice on finding a local lawyer to represent me. That was not easy. Several civil rights lawyers turned me down because of the low success rate in academic cases. Others claimed a conflict of interest because of staff and client ties to Northwestern. Finally, a dedicated civil rights lawyer came to my rescue. Len Cavise—then at Kent College of Law, now on the faculty at DePaul—agreed to represent me at sacrifice rates that I could afford.

In June 1981, within 180 days of the dean's decision on reconsideration—the event that started NU's own six-month time clock for a conventional appeal—I filed a complaint alleging sex discrimination with the EEOC, which investigated the case for over two years. Cavise and Gertner then filed a lawsuit in the U.S. District Court with three causes of action: sex discrimination in violation of Title VII of the 1964 Civil Rights Act, breach of contract, and wrongful discharge from employment. The last two charges had to be dropped, but we fought for over a decade to support the allegation of sex discrimination.[1] The battles over discovery, depositions, motions, and legal briefs were costly and wearing. NU's lawyer objected to everything, a typical strategy to get a plaintiff to drop a case. NU was represented by senior partners at the prestigious firm of Sidley and Austin. Their expenses were tax deductible; mine were not. *Lever v. Northwestern University* as in all cases, is a David versus Goliath story.

Years after the merits of the case had been developed, NU pleaded a statute of limitations defense. A charge must be filed with the EEOC within three-hundred days of the action complained of; otherwise, a plaintiff is barred from presenting evidence on the substance of the claim. Remarkably, the federal magistrate agreed with NU and ruled that the dean's original notice in May 1980 was final and unambiguous, notwithstanding the dean's agreement to consider new evidence to be evaluated by new reviewers. My case against NU was dismissed; my day in court, denied. Both the AAUP (American Association of University Professors 1991) and the EEOC filed friend-of-the-court briefs urging the U.S. Seventh Circuit Court of Appeals to reverse the lower court and rule that my EEOC charge was timely. In its news release, the AAUP stated, "As the *Lever* case illustrates, professors deserve clear and fair rules identifying the point in the tenure process which starts the clock on the deadline for filing an EEOC charge." Insofar as it is a matter of record that NU did not start its own clock in May 1980, but rather in January 1981, the university's eleventh-hour statute of limitations defense struck me as deeply immoral.

On November 9, 1992, the U.S. Court of Appeals concurred with the lower court ruling that my EEOC charge was untimely, while reprimanding NU for its lack of clarity about the tenure procedure. The opinion, written by Judge Easterbrook, has an arrogant tone: "Northwestern['s] . . . handbooks are vague and can be understood to describe steps inconsistent with the process that, according to both Dean and Provost, Northwestern actually follows. . . . However, anyone able to obtain a Ph.D. in sociology has read [or written] much worse" (see *Lever v. Northwestern University,* 1992). This is an ironic end to a case where clarity of writing was held against me. Easterbrook characterized Provost Mack's stopping of NU's internal clock as a show of "excessive kindness" and not an action that could intentionally or unintentionally confuse a layperson as to the start of any external clock. It is outrageous for Northwestern to benefit from the admitted ambiguity of its own process, and the policy implications of the ruling are horrendous. At a time when the courts are jammed, people should be encouraged—not punished—for exhausting internal remedies before calling in the lawyers.

As I was writing this essay, the clock was running out on my right to appeal the Seventh Circuit's ruling in the U.S. Supreme Court. My lawyers and I jointly decided not to pursue the case further. With just a few days left before the deadline, I received a call from the Lawyers' Committee for Civil Rights Under Law. This watchdog group tries to find major law firms to take cases where "bad law" has been set and fight them *pro bono* (free) in the Supreme Court for the social benefit and for the experience of junior partners. The New York firm of Davis, Polk, and Wardwell was interested in my case. I agreed to go the final round. On April 8, 1993, we entered a petition for a writ of certiorari. The lawyers who crafted our final document spelled out the implication of letting the Seventh Circuit's decision stand: "It provides an incentive for employers to follow Northwestern's example and cloud their employment decisions with doubt thereby insulating themselves from liability." On June 1, 1993, the Supreme Court denied our petition. Twelve years after I filed a complaint at EEOC, my ordeal was finally over.

Over the years, many women who were themselves denied tenure have called me to hear my reflections on the wisdom of pursuing legal remedy. In the early years, I believed it was important to fight discrimination in court; in the later years, even before I knew the disastrous outcome in my case, I had lost faith in the legal system. Of course, I know the high price I have paid; I also realize that I'll never know the price I would have paid for turning the other cheek. I was interviewing someone who counsels date rape victims to press charges even though prosecutors rarely take such cases to court. Although it seemed she was setting these young women up for frustration, she felt it was important to their self-esteem and healing that they stand up and cry "Rape." I had to fight back; yet now that it's over, like a rape victim, I feel doubly victimized, first by Northwestern and later by the courts.

All things considered, filing a lawsuit was the worst decision I ever made. No doubt my challenge made things better for the next generation of women scholars at NU, but the personal price was tremendous. The cost to my career has been even greater than the emotional and financial burdens. There is a subtle "blacklist" effect. Some of it is simple: "so-and-so wasn't good enough for Northwestern, so she or he must not be good enough for us." But other colleagues denied tenure all landed nice jobs, and relatively soon, whereas I have suffered countless rejections. The label "troublemaker" stigmatizes more than the label "failure." Several friends on recruitment committees confided that they were rejecting my candidacy because I was unlikely to get the support of their dean. As always, luck (this time bad) played a role here, too. The job market in the early 1980s was grim, but it was better for those doing mainstream sociology than for those working in the "fringe" subdisciplines. (It seems that "gender studies" moved from the fringe to the mainstream by the early 1990s; sociology of sport is still "fringe.")

While I was failing to get a secure job, I was also failing at conventional fund-raising. In the early 1980s I applied to over twenty feminist organizations for support, but the answer was always the same: we cannot fund private litigation. I felt betrayed by the women's movement, which had motivated me to file the lawsuit in the first place. There was plenty of money earmarked for the doomed ERA battle, but virtually none for the individual women who were trying to get the courts to enforce the existing antidiscrimination legislation. The Women's Equity Action League eventually adopted my case. I also received donations from the National Women's Studies Association and the Sociologists for Women in Society. In recent years, the American Association of University Women gave generous support. More important than the money received was the moral support that came with those endorsements. Fighting this protracted battle has been mostly lonely and very expensive . . . and that without a day in court.[2]

From Gypsy Travels to Creating a Home

I know now that I could have moved on with my life in Chicago, keeping my home, and staying with my dear friends. But at that time, I didn't have a clear vision of the many ways other than teaching to be a practicing sociologist. One of the great injustices we do to both our undergraduate and graduate students is our neglect of applied sociology. We have to equip people for options outside academe. As sociologists we know how to get answers to all kinds of questions about human behavior and, by providing students with new jargon, we can handily teach them to do the evaluation research that informs policy decisions large and small.

When Manny Schegloff called with an invitation to be visiting faculty for the winter 1983 quarter at UCLA, I jumped at the chance to be in a warm, faraway place. UCLA had been the second contender when I chose to go to Yale, and I always wanted to see what I had missed. Shortly thereafter Kristin Luker called to extend support by seeing if I were available for a visiting appointment at UC-San Diego. We agreed on spring of 1983, so off I went for a six-month stint in California.

My student supporters came up with the idea of "Rock for Janet," a farewell party and fund-raiser. We held it at Evanston's Orrington Hotel just off campus. Two bands played, one was chosen, for its apt name "Frontlines." Hundreds of students and many faculty came for what has been remembered by many as the only political event of their college career. The decision in my case made students aware of the administration's total disregard for their judgment about which professors were worth the high price of their tuition. The students launched a petition campaign to protest the outcome in my case, but no one in administration cared. I cared. Student support, more than anything, reaffirmed my sense of success in spite of being shown out the door.

There is another important detail to convey about my departure. My best friend in Chicago, Barbara Nellis, is a senior editor at *Playboy*. She and her colleagues designed a sex survey of their readership, 20 percent of whom are female, that was included in the January 1982 issue. I had recommended one of our graduate students to help them prepare the questionnaire. Another graduate student friend, Rosanna Hertz, suggested that I put together a team—including herself and a couple of the computer whizkids—and submit a bid to analyze the data. We were hired, and I became the senior analyst on the largest sex survey of men and women to date. We generated many hundreds of pages of printout that spring and summer, and that fall we began our work with the editorial staff to write up the first of several articles on the findings. Then it was time to leave.

I packed the printout along with some essential belongings and drove out west. I had gotten as far as my sister's house in Boulder when *Playboy* called and coaxed me to fly to the "21" club in New York City for a press conference to unveil our findings. I agreed to do some publicity on both coasts, including "The Dr. Ruth Show," and then continued on my solo car trip west.

I remember my first day teaching at UCLA. It was 93 degrees in January. The twist of fate didn't seem all bad. I greatly enjoyed that winter quarter. In addition to teaching a huge class in sex roles, I had a seminar in the sociology of sport. Among my students was a rookie from the Detroit Lions, and Jeanette Bolden, who, in spite of a life that began with two club feet and severe asthma, was a contender for the Olympic Gold medal in the 100-meter dash. The famed basketball coach John Wooden came out of semi-retirement to speak with us. Dr. Jerry Buss, owner of the L.A. Lakers, also accepted my invitation and arrived by limousine. L.A. seemed a friendlier place than reputed.

I reluctantly moved on to San Diego for the spring quarter, but a funny thing happened on the way. Hugh Hefner had liked the television publicity I had done for the magazine's sex survey, and I got called back to L.A. to discuss the possibility of being one of two hosts for a show to be named "Women on Sex" on the new Playboy Channel. The premise was to eavesdrop on women talking about sex when no men are around. There were to be two women hosts, only women guests, and only women in the audience. "And only women in the crew?" I asked naively. No, that was not their intention; they already had a great team of guys. "But the concept?" I countered. After tossing it around, Mr. Hefner, the executives at the channel, and the producers decided to go with a female crew because it was a "cute" publicity angle. They hired me, cohost Vicky McCarty (the only Phi Beta Kappa Playmate), and a female crew. So after a spring in San Diego, I returned to L.A. that summer to do a three-show pilot.

The tape date was a disaster. I got "pink eye" from a friend's dog and it erupted on the morning of the shows. Television is serious business in L.A. The producer arranged a 7:00 A.M. appointment with a doctor who applied medication with steroids to my eye. That evening most everyone flubbed her job. Only later did I realize that what had happened was a direct reflection of sexism in the television industry. We were all "moved up" to make an all-female production crew happen. The director previously had been an associate director, the first camerawoman (the one who must respond quickly to the director's fast-paced orders) had been a third cameraperson, and so forth. We were still there shooting at 2:00 A.M., with an executive producer practically apoplectic at the thought of paying everyone double-overtime.

Miraculously, the audience liked the shows, and we stayed on the channel from 1983 to 1987 (in reruns through 1989). We calmed down and replaced some key people, and the all-female crew was a beautiful sight and a special part of that whole experience. There is good reason to believe that ours is the only show in television history with an all-female cast and crew.

Michael Trikilis, the executive producer, put the show in the hands of our very competent producer, Melissa Hunt, and we cooked up some interesting themes. Several of my women friends from academe were supportive enough to accept invitations to be guests. A few shows were embarrassments (once I extended my hand to greet a dominatrix and she struck it with her riding crop; I feared then that Yale might try to revoke my Ph.D.), but most were both entertaining and informative, and several were downright "revolutionary" (as when erotic artist Betty Dodson did a "masturbation pantomine" with her Magic Wand vibrator, and when Margo St. James, organizer of the prostitutes' union COYOTE, told male viewers what she thought of men, declaring she'd "marched into the belly of the beast").

Over the years I have taken heat from feminists for lending my credentials to an enterprise that they say demeans women. One TV critic said our show was for the Playboy Channel what the interview is for the magazine. (By the way, Betty Friedan gave the interview in September 1992.) I was asked more than once "How do you look at yourself in the mirror?" "No problem," was always my answer because I felt good about the forum I was given to educate (roughly half of the channel's viewers never went to college to hear someone like me or my guests). Besides, I was using the extra money I was earning to pay my lawyer to keep my case going. I always felt that Northwestern's hidden sexism was far more insidious than Playboy's overt displays.

By the time the Playboy show can to an end in 1987, I was getting tired of my life as an itinerant teacher. After my spring 1983 visit, I was invited back to UCSD for another two years. Then I was rehired at UCLA as a full-time lecturer on two one-year contracts, the second one not renewable under a scheme to keep temporary faculty from becoming too entrenched. Meanwhile, people kept asking me where I was visiting from, which prompted a convoluted story. I was approaching forty, and I thought someone that age should have a short, snappy answer to the question, "Where do you live?" Los Angeles seemed as good a place as any, and by then I realized that I could make a good living outside academe if necessary. So I bought a home, even though I had no job.

At this point my good luck returned. As I was leaving UCLA, I heard about a mid-career fellowship at the RAND Corporation's Health Policy Research Center. I had already begun some AIDS-related research, and knew that the rich *Playboy* dataset with over eighty thousand cases tabulated could give interim answers to important questions about risk groups until better scientific data could be collected. Someone who had accepted the Pew-funded fellowship for the following academic year had just reneged for some other offer, and, after a series of interviews, I was invited to take his place. I was placed in stimulating courses with the three other mid-career fellows and the RAND graduate students, and I was excited to think that my tired career was taking new direction.

RAND is located across the street from the Santa Monica Pier on the Pacific Ocean. Its professional staff is filled with energetic, very smart researchers. The work setting is ideal. I began a colleagueship and friendship with David Kanouse, a cognitive psychologist who was doing mathematical modeling to predict the course of the AIDS epidemic. He realized the limitations of the model posed by the gaps in our knowledge about the size and activities of certain groups, including bisexual men and prostitutes. We got a small grant from the American Foundation for AIDS Research and a matching grant from RAND, and we began a reanalysis of the *Playboy* readers' sex survey to explore the correlates of risk behaviors (Lever et al. 1992). In 1989, I joined a team headed by David Kanouse and sociologist Sandy Berry to do a study of rates of HIV infection in a probability sample of one thousand female prostitutes in Los Angeles County. It takes the self-confidence of RAND to propose such a project, and we largely accomplished the goal with respect to those who solicit on the streets. Call-girls and escorts could not be systematically sampled, and it became my responsibility to learn as much as possible about the demographic composition and organization of this diverse, hidden subpopulation.

In 1990, I accepted a position as an assistant professor in the sociology department of California State University, Los Angeles (CSULA). The nine-course load (on the quarter system) was daunting and the rank was lower than I felt I deserved, but I would be on a tenure-track in a city I already called home. My departmental colleagues and the dean were supportive of my plan to keep my RAND affiliation. The reality is there is little time and energy left over for research when one is in a university with that teaching load, no graduate assistants, and with so many students ill-prepared for the rigors of college. The vast majority of our students got inferior educations in their impoverished communities. It is not only the one-quarter of the student body who are immigrants who have difficulty with reading and writing. Because our students work thirty to forty hours a week, most of us teach both evening and day classes; we are the working class of the academy. I had come full circle. At Yale I saw how the elite perpetuated its privileged position, and now I have a far deeper understanding of the forces that keep poor people down. We struggle with dwindling resources as our students struggle to pay rising tuition.

Cal State has provided a congenial base for me. When *Glamour* magazine approached me to write the monthly "Sex and Health" column in 1991, I hesitated to go to my chair and dean. I knew that people at elite schools view such a side enterprise as a diversion from serious scholarship, but I got a refreshing response at CSULA, where such an endeavor is consistent with its populist mission to serve community needs. I agreed to write "Sex and Health" with Pepper Schwartz on the twentieth anniversary of our collaboration on *Woman at Yale*. Pepper and I share the opinion that if more sociologists were to write for the general public, there would be a better understanding of the relevance of our discipline in people's everyday lives. Writing for *Glamour* is a lot of work, but it is worth it. The magazine's market research indicates that our monthly two-page column is very popular with its eight million readers. Besides, Pepper and I get to talk and laugh together more than we have in years.

Only a few days after the Supreme Court put to rest my past at Northwestern, I was granted "early" tenure at Cal State, effective on September 1, 1993. Nineteen years from the start date of my first appointment, I was to become an associate professor. I was at RAND when a friend called me with the bittersweet news. I know some readers might not believe this, but later that day—just ten minutes before I left to go home—a rotted coral tree in RAND's parking lot fell and smashed the hood and windshield of my car. Over 1,000 employees, and it got *my* car. I was shaken until I accepted it as a fitting punctuation mark to my long-delayed tenure. Now I wouldn't have to look over my shoulder to see what my karma would bring; the shoe had already dropped. And, as my father pointed out, it seemed my luck was improving: This time I wasn't in the car.

Conclusion

In his provocatively subtitled book *In the Company of Scholars: The Struggle for the Soul of Higher Education,* Julius Getman (1992), former president of the AAUP, describes my experience with Northwestern: "Denial of tenure was a personal tragedy for her, a loss to the students she might otherwise have taught, and a loss to the world of scholarship" (120). I admit there are days I see it that way, too. But on good days I prefer the vision of Mary Catherine Bateson (1990) in *Composing a Life:* "Young teachers who choose or are forced to leave often feel that their lives are ending.... For many of them this discontinuity has been a move from stagnation to new challenge and growth" (8). She describes the life of five artists, including herself, who worked by improvisation rather than pursuing goals set early in their lives. I'm proud of my adaptation to change. I've become a multimedia teacher.

Taking stock of the first half of my career, it's clear that I've never had a ten-year or twenty-year plan. I couldn't even guess where I will be or what I will be doing twenty years from today, at the end of my career. It was not so much improvisation as serendipity that I followed instead of staying focused on a straight or strategic career path. I used to live by the philosophy "say yes to everything unless you have a very good reason to say no." That kind of outlook can lead to excitement, but it opens the door for charges of social or intellectual dilettantism. Coupled with my distaste for institutional politics, my lack of conventionally defined success should have come as no surprise.

The serendipitous route is not only perilous, it requires luck. To paraphrase E. B. White, one must be *willing* to be lucky. And one must seize the opportunities that serendipity presents. Perhaps I would have come up with a master plan had I been less lucky. Maybe I would have been more career-focused if I hadn't found so much satisfaction in the friendships I made along my rocky paths. But I am a sociologist because I find people fascinating. At NU, I made time for punk rockers as well as the academic elite. I'm still wide open to interesting people: I have a new friendship with a high-class call girl whom I met through my last RAND project and a new friendship with my first *Glamour* editor that is bizarre because we have never met, although we talked about sex by phone nearly every workday for a year-and-a-half.

My life, with its concurrent jobs, is usually a hodgepodge. Every once in a while it comes together and makes beautiful sense. Recently, I enjoyed one of those moments. At the request of the Office of the Secretary of Defense, RAND's National Defense Research Institute accepted a short-term contract to analyze policy options for lifting the ban against gays and lesbians in the U.S. military. I was invited to be a senior researcher on a thirty-person team that included economists, psychologists, sociologists, anthropologists, historians, lawyers, physicians, and national security specialists. I was needed because of my early work on integrating Yale, my recent AIDS research that focused on male homosexuality, my consulting work on sexual harassment, and my knowledge of American sex patterns, which is up-to-date largely because of our *Glamour* column. At CSULA my chair and dean recognized this unique opportunity and agreed to a release-time contract with less than a week to go before the start of spring quarter.

This was a once-in-a-lifetime project. The stakes were high and the work was to have immediate impact on policy drawn at the highest level. Our findings could effect millions of people's lives for years to come.[3] We formed a high-caliber interdisciplinary team found only in dreams. The meetings were awesome. We worked together, often seven days a week, for over four months. The field trips I went on ranged from inspection of "close quarters" on submarines to separate focus groups with gay and straight fire fighters and police officers in four cities. If I were still at Northwestern, I would have missed this project where the products of my career's meanderings came together to serve my country. I never could have planned such a moment. I only can take credit for being willing to be lucky.

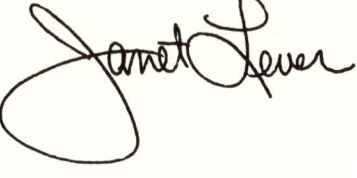

NOTES

1. Elsewhere it has been argued successfully that faculty handbooks serve in lieu of formal contracts that stipulate work agreements; however, in the Seventh Circuit, contract law has not been judged to be applicable where conventional contracts are absent; similarly, "wrongful discharge" is narrowly construed in the Seventh Circuit.

2. So many friends gave generous contributions that they all cannot be named here; however, special acknowledgment must be made to Kristin Luker, Jerome Rabow, Jonathon Goodson, Pepper Schwartz, Stanton Wheeler, Diane Vaughan, and my parents for their extreme efforts and generosity. I wish to take this special opportunity to let everyone know again how deeply appreciative I remain for their support.

3. On July 19, 1993, President Clinton announced a "compromise" decision—known colloquially as "don't ask, don't tell, don't pursue"—that ran counter to RAND's recommendations for a nondiscriminatory policy. RAND published our findings in a book titled *Sexual Orientation and U.S. Military Personnel Policy: Options and Assessment* (RAND 1993), which the defense department released to the public on August 26, 1993. The RAND study will very likely have an impact on the court challenges that have already been filed by civil rights activists.

References

American Association of University Professors. 1991. *Amicus Curiae*. U.S. Court of Appeals for the Seventh Circuit. No. 91-3571.

Bateson, Mary Catherine. 1990. *Composing a Life*. New York: Plume.

Getman, Julius. 1992. *In the Company of Scholars: The Struggle for the Soul of Higher Education*. Austin: University of Texas Press.

Lever, Janet. 1976. "Sex Differences in the Games Children Play." *Social Problems* 23:478–87.

———. 1978. "Sex Differences in the Complexity of Children's Play and Games." *American Sociological Review* 43:471–83.

———. 1983. *Soccer Madness*. Chicago: University of Chicago Press.

Lever, Janet, David E. Kanouse, William H. Rogers, Sally Carson, and Rosanna Hertz. 1992. "Behavior Patterns and Sexual Identity of Bisexual Males." *Journal of Sex Research* 29:141–67.

Lever v. Northwestern University 979 F. 2d 552 (7th Cir. 1992).

Mills, C. Wright. 1959. *The Sociological Imagination*. New York: Oxford University Press.

RAND National Defense Research Institute. 1993. *Sexual Orientation and U.S. Military Personnel Policy: Options and Assessment*. MR-323-OSD. Santa Monica, Calif.: RAND.

Six

Paradigm Lost
The Journey from Normal Science to Permanent Marginality

Judy Long

When my fiftieth birthday was approaching, I faced a kind of crisis. Intellectually I could distinguish between my work, which was exciting and challenging, and my career, which was disappointing. But that was only from the neck up. I still felt that I should take stock of my life and achievements at age fifty, and I wasn't eager to do so. I had planned that by this birthday I would either have achieved all I aimed for or, failing that, would have achieved serenity and resignation. As the birthday raced toward me, it was clear neither goal had been achieved; I panicked. I decided to hide behind a third alternative: I talked my husband into joining with me in a giant 110th birthday party. By summing our ages, I cleverly concealed the big 5–0, shifted the emphasis from achievement/failure to celebrating our lives, and brought other people into the act.

This worked pretty well in the short run. In the long run, I have become leery of any accounting that tries to sum up my whole life at a arbitrary moment. At any moment in living this life, I could produce a coherent chronological narrative that would make sense—but only that moment's sense. Writing my life in terms of socioeconomic mobility would be misleading: Professor-father to professor-daughter is no distance at all, but it has been quite a journey. So I am avoiding any chronological organization in this account. I have chosen another method of telling my life: I tell about a number of intertwined careers that have developed together, but not in parallel. This story is like a braid, with strands entering the stream at different moments and connected in different ways at different times. A cross section of the braid at any moment gives certain information, but the picture changes at the next cross section. Following any one strand of the braid provides a narrative of continuity, but it understates complexity by neglecting the other strands. The braid I have in mind is a French braid, with each strand continually increased and each strand continually bound to the whole by these new wisps.

My Roots

My roots define where the braid begins. They are contributions to who I am that I didn't make and didn't choose (except in the sense of claiming them now).

Being a professor's daughter was one of the most valuable accidents of my life. It was not that Daddy taught me how to play the game, or introduced me to powerful mentors, but that he provided a role model. During my childhood years in Burlington, Vermont, I got the idea that being a professor was a lot of fun. My father was a college marshal, and he led all the parades right by our house. He poked away at his typewriter with two fingers and allowed us kids to do the same. A dog that sat in on his classes was allowed to graduate (I'm told). And he had a radio show, and we eldest two girls got to be on "Let's Pretend" on a regular basis. These memories give a jazzy, show-business tone to academic life. As things worked out, I was good at schoolwork, won approval, and moved right along on a track that I didn't even know was there. This track would ultimately lead me into the academic profession. By the time I was of an age to think about a career, the option of being a professor was already winking away as a bright star in my motivational firmament (respectable, but jazzy).

There's a second influence on my career, which I would not have recognized during my long love affair with science in college and graduate school, that I think is significant now: I am a missionary's granddaughter. My sober, professional socialization was not able to suppress completely my desire to make my university and community a better place. I recognize now that I want to save the world; I think it is in the blood, like vampire genes.

Another influence on my life is more of a fantasy or archetype than a "formative early experience." It is an image of my Scots ancestry that I embrace: poor, proud, contentious, tough, hardworking, righteous—did I mention poor? A final factor was an elite education that gave me the habit of independent work, and gave me standards high enough so that I've never worried about meeting anyone else's.

None of my roots provides a source of deference or any other feminine virtue. My New England upbringing emphasized character, not conformity. I don't remember ever hearing that girls could or should do only certain things, or that girls should definitely not do what boys could or should do. This upbringing has stood me in good stead. Yet from somewhere I also got a good dose of "femininity." As a girl-child I was enamored of femininity. There was a period when I tried to rename myself Rosalie, Rosamund, Rose Marie, or at the very least Rose. I can still work up a convincing drool thinking about some of my favorite dresses when I was a child. I even remember a little pink patterned sunsuit with ruffles on the hips—the uniform of an eighteen-months femme. When I was in junior high school, I bought, with my own money, some of the most outrageous clothing: wooden mules with black woven straw uppers that twinkled with colored shells; a pink kerchief that had sewn-on gold hoop "earrings." My mother had ineffably glamorous grownup clothes: a velvet evening cloak with an ermine collar, and red satin shoes that had been, mysteriously, dyed after her wedding. For glorious years, Mother would lend me her clothes, and I got hand-me-downs that I treasured.

Family

Our family constituted a small society: parents, dog and cats, and "the four J's": Jean, Judy, Jill, and Jimmy. This was a good thing, because our family moved a lot: from New Haven to Burlington, as Daddy finished graduate school and became a professor at the University of Vermont; to Washington, D.C., when he left academia for government; to Paris; and then to Parkville, Missouri, when he returned to academia as a college president. Daddy's family had lived in China when he was a boy (his father was the missionary), and his brothers and sisters continued to live all over the world. I thought this was normal, and exciting.

Our family was tight-knit, with lots of family traditions and family jokes. But moving can be disruptive of schooling and social adjustment; it put us kids in a sink-or-swim situation. Repeatedly we had to start over in new schools, in new neighborhoods. Repeatedly we lost our old friends. In our case, for the most part, it toughened us and increased our independence.

I was the bad kid in my family. Later on, my brother competed successfully for this position and displaced me. At the same time, I was working hard to be a good kid, and the bad kid part of my identity became invisible, like the dark side of the moon. Yet I continued to carry the "bad kid" with me. That kid knew she was going to get in trouble and get punished, and she knew she was going to tough it out and not cry.

Community and Class

Many of my friends remember neighborhoods that were filled with kinfolks and that had boundaries beyond which dangerous "others" lived. Class, race, and ethnic difference define such boundaries. My childhood geography did not include much danger or difference. Residential segregation, never discussed, created a homogeneity of race and class; school segregation reinforced it. I was born into an "old" ethnic group, which placed our family in society to some degree. Ancestors of my grandparents had come to this continent early enough to fight in the revolutionary war. There are no family horror stories of mistreatment and ethnic labeling. This background, I think, made some things easy: The basic tenets of our family culture resonated with traditional American values.

I am amazed, however, when people assume that the privileges that came to earlier immigrant groups apply to both sexes equally. The professions have been within reach of the men in our family for generations. Maybe that provides an operational definition of class and race, if you define women's position as deriving from their male kin. Contrary to this model, however, the subordination of women is observed in every social group. If WASPs have the way paved for them, why wasn't my great-grandmother Long a doctor like my great-grandfather? Why was my grandfather Bain, and not my grandmother, a lawyer? Why is it only in my generation that the women have entered the traditionally "male" professions?

With experience, I have discovered some of the blind spots that come with my personal and familial history. The illusion of having no race is the delusion of pink-skinned people. My "discovery" of ethnicity came late where no sense of difference enforced it. I remember being told by a fellow graduate student, who had just discovered his own, that he was sorry for me because I had no ethnicity. But I did become aware of gender. It is only insurgent females who are known by their sex; dominant males are not, at least not among themselves.

My Student Career

I was one of those kids who loved school. I looked forward to being old enough to go to school, and I looked forward to the first day of school every fall. To tell the truth, it was easier to gain approval from teachers than from my mother, and I think by the second grade I realized this was going to be my salvation. Schooling brought is own form of "mobility": in those days schools didn't have tracking or "gifted" programs. If they thought you were smart, they "skipped" you. That meant being lifted, like Dorothy and Toto, from the now-familiar second grade to the third, missing the second half of second grade and the first half of third grade. I "skipped" again in the fourth grade. I know that everyone else got familiar with the map of Europe during those lost semesters, and I'll never know what else I missed.

Gender seemed to enter my parents' decisions about schooling, although I wasn't aware of it. My mother kept me out of school for a semester after I graduated from sixth grade at the age of ten. I think she thought I was too unworldly to go to junior high school and consort with "teenagers." (Later on I was "boy-crazy.") Instead, I spent a term with my grandparents in Florida, which was another whole culture. Mother protected us girls again when we moved to Paris in 1954, placing us in a convent school (I was the one who got thrown out). When we returned to the States, Jill and I went to the Barstow School (a girls' school) in Kansas City. When it came time for college, I considered a number of schools, and I picked Radcliffe. My parents bit their tongues while I was thinking things over, knowing if they indicated that they favored Radcliffe I would not choose it. Choosing Radcliffe turned out to be a happy surprise: a "girls' school" that was loaded with boys.

Radcliffe had both advantages and disadvantages. In retrospect, I have criticized Radcliffe's lack of a feminist spirit. But there's no question that I benefited from the educational opportunities at Harvard. The message I got was that the same set of rules applied to everybody, regardless of rank or sex: state your position and be prepared to defend it. I felt accepted in this bracing climate. I related unproblematically to concepts like "the fellowship of educated men." I felt included. As a student, I did not experience the hierarchy and anxiety that now seem ubiquitous in academia.

Many Harvard luminaries fired my professional ambitions. I particularly appreciate the respectful mentoring I received from David Riesman and Michael Maccoby. When I decided to go to graduate school, the professional fostering I received from Harvard professors and graduate students was significant. Still, I didn't realize that a Ph.D. means teaching. When Dr. Riesman said he'd like to nominate me for a Woodrow Wilson fellowship, I said, "Yuck. I don't want to teach," and declined. I thought I would do research all my life.

Research is what I loved. I was lucky enough to get a job at National Institute of Mental Health (NIMH) for the year following graduation. In the Laboratory of Socio-Environmental Studies, headed by Mel Kohn, I found an interdisciplinary team of social scientists who were welcoming, professional, and fun to be with. They helped me select a graduate school, and I left them with regret to move to Ann Arbor in fall 1962.

I flipped a coin between sociology and psychology and spent a year doing sociology for my master's degree. The next year, I moved on to the interdepartmental program in social psychology for my Ph.D. I felt that this was what I was born for. I had a wonderful time in graduate school. These were the golden years for the program. The atmosphere was full of energy and inspiration; the lunchroom buzzed with talk about research. In the vast Institute for Social Research, the research was theory-driven, with an activist dimension that descended from Kurt Lewin. Continuous achievements by senior staff kept the research funding flowing in and supported the small fry. If this was the end of my career as a student, it was a glorious end.

This period of my education was important for another reason. At Michigan in the 1960s there was the beginning of theoretical interest in the psychology of women: not *in* the curriculum, but alongside it. Judy Bardwick conducted a research seminar that pulled together everything that was then available in the research literature. From this period, and this professor, stemmed a whole generation of classic contributions to the psychology of women: the work of Matina Horner, Sandra Schwartz Tangri, Karen Paige, and others.

My Sexual Career

My sexual coming of age occurred at the point where the feminine mystique met The Pill. The contradictions between the two colored my sexual career. The 1950s, and a strict family, put a brake on sexual exploration when I was young, and my innocence no doubt protected me from many bad experiences. I was brought up to believe in virginity, love, and marriage as a package. Later, these pieces separated naturally. I never thought of marriage as a necessity, as a career, or as my ultimate destination. When I was young, doing well in school was my job, and that developed into a career. Besides, when I was twelve, I decided never to get married, after I figured out that although you were always supposed to be honest, in marriage you weren't. Grown-ups could not resolve this contradiction for me.

Somehow I knew, at a much earlier point than when I had to "make decisions" about it, that marriage could be an obstacle to my career. I don't know how I knew this; I don't remember any woman who had both a career and a marriage when I was growing up. There were teachers, but you didn't see their family life, if any; there were mothers, but they didn't have careers, or even jobs.

As adolescence went along, I enjoyed myself greatly. In college, particularly, I was captivated by the variety, abundance, and general cuteness of what I then thought of as "boys." At that time, I regarded "boys" as entertainment. I enjoyed valued friendships that weren't sexual. Some of these friends have come back into my life in recent years. I fell in love many times, but "ripeness is all." The one I fell in love with at the "right" time might have been "Mr. Right," but he was Jewish. His parents broke up our romance pretty expeditiously when they found out that he had proposed and I had accepted. Besides that little difficulty, I don't think he was prepared to be a partner to a career woman. He bravely anticipated that his parents would disown him when we married, and how would he go to law school? His proposal was that I should work as a secretary and "put him through." Remember this was 1961.

The breakup did disrupt my senior year to some extent, and my parents, at least, wondered whether I really had the motivation for graduate school (Ph.D. on the rebound?). I, in any case, wanted to work for a year between college and grad school, and I did.

But I did go to bed with this "boy." It's probably impossible for any reader in 1995 to understand how momentous that event was, and how thrilled I was. The sexual pressure and sexual suspense had built up enormously. It was romantic and fulfilling—just the way sex is supposed to be. It was also dangerous. In those days, finding a doctor who would provide contraception to an unmarried woman was something like trying to find an abortionist. It was against the law in Massachusetts. Word had it that in order to get fitted for a diaphragm (available only from a physician) you had to bring clippings from your hometown newspaper, to prove not only that you were engaged but that the wedding date was set. If you were not prepared with such documentation, you risked a hideous humiliation in addition to being denied contraception. Fortunately for me, the grapevine was correct about the doctor I consulted. He was professional and discreet, but I could tell he was concerned about me. I saw him watching as I walked down the path to the car where my intended was waiting. I didn't fully appreciate then what a risk he was taking to provide me with an essential freedom.

My heart was broken, but there was still plenty of variety available during my year in Washington, and then in graduate school. I was in charge of my own sex life, and there was no threat of AIDS. I was aware of sexually transmitted diseases only in the vaguest way. I enjoyed myself, and others. I stood off a number of marriage-minded men. But once again it all came together with a fellow student, another great love of my life. We swam along in tandem for years, until I could see the end of graduate school and the transition to "real life" coming up. I pointed out that if we wanted to marry, as we thought we did, we should start making some moves; he thought later would be time enough. I thought that when he got around to it, I would have made other plans, and that's how it worked out. That relationship provided me with a glimpse of what the options were for the "dual-career marriage" in 1967. This was before the great job market bust, and we both had many offers. My best offer was the University of Chicago. My *worst* offer was at the university where this man received his best offer, went, and stayed.

The professional atmosphere at the University of Chicago was exhilarating. I had to learn to teach from scratch, but I didn't think that would be hard. I wrote fragments of a journal that year (as David Riesman used to exhort everyone to do). I was embarrassed to find, reading it in later years, that it dealt exclusively with relationships with men. What about building my career?

I felt fine about my career, and after about a year I guess I felt established enough to be "ready" to get married. So, with a few fits and starts, I married the next man I fell in love with. I made an imaginative and unconventional choice: Ted was younger than I, he was not an academic, he was not going to dominate me, I was not going to be defined by him. Many academic women can have successful and satisfying partnerships with men who are in other occupations. Not this one, however. My ex told me in subsequent years that he "folded" in the first month. He was scared, and he figured out (again, later) that he'd be ready to marry at about age forty. Just my luck—he was twenty-four when I married him (I was twenty-nine).

I might have said, "I wish he had told me *before*," but of course he didn't know before. I didn't know what to do about our problems, but I wouldn't know much more now than then. We went for some counseling that didn't help us, and after about a year and a half we decided to separate. We were both miserable, and we spent a weekend coming to this decision, walking around the apartment holding hands and crying.

Since I had been fired from the University of Chicago, I was in the job market. Pretty soon I took a job at Cornell. Ted and I thought we'd get back together. But we didn't know how, any more than we knew how to be married. So after about another year and a half, we divorced. This was long before "no fault." He had to sue me for desertion in a courtroom in Chicago. He handled all the arrangements, and it was very painful for him.

Next I tried being single in Ithaca. In those days, there was still wife-swapping going on among the faculty, but this was a form of marital behavior that did not include me as a single woman. Within a few months, I realized that a single woman on the faculty in a conservative, upstate university would need a vice. So I took up smoking a pipe, which satisfied all sorts of antisocial motives. I also invented the Single Professors Cooking Collective, which is still in operation. I enjoyed dating in Ithaca (although I met some weird people, and I began to suspect that dating in my forties, fifties, and sixties might turn out to be a parade of weirdness). At one of the SPCC dinners I was placed next to a quiet, intriguing man with deep dimples and a gorgeous torso. Always frivolous when it came to love and sex, I figured that was a sufficient basis for infatuation. There ensued an embarrassing six months when my friends kept inviting him to parties where I tried to charm him. He couldn't stand me. After this we spent a chaste year getting to know each other and playing out the relationships we were already involved in. After this we fell in love, moved in together, and argued about most things. After about eight years we got married.

Getting married was strictly a pragmatic decision. I was involved with decisions about my grandmother's care when she was in her nineties, and, down the pike, I could see decisions that would need to be made about Dan's parents, who were older than my own. If we were going to participate in family decision-making as a couple, I thought, we'd do better married. Nothing to it.

But the personal was also political. The decision to get married was traumatic for me. When I figured out that we ought to get married, I had hysterics; I had to counsel for a year about my negative feelings toward marriage. We were doing fine as a nonmarried partnership organized along feminist principles, and we knew perfectly well that marriage is not a feminist institution.[1]

My women friends organized a big party to get my courage up the night before our wedding; it was the first shower I'd ever attended. Sure enough, Dan and I got married. I wore my red T-shirt that said "I do" on it and my Wedding Suit, which I wear to all weddings. We were married by a woman judge with no mishaps, then we took our small cheering section out to dinner. By 8:30 P.M. on my wedding night, I was perched in front of my own fireplace in a flannel nightgown, writing a thank-you note to my mother-in-law.

My Career as an Academic: Chicago and Cornell

My training was prologue. The "real world" began when I took up my first faculty appointment at the University of Chicago in 1967. As I prepared to leave the University of Michigan for my first job, one of the jolly older professors greeted me with the chivying remark, "Well, are you going to break the record and be the first woman to actually finish your degree?" I politely reminded him of several other women in my cohort and just before who had completed the doctorate, and went on my way. Years later, I met a new woman graduate of the social psych program at Michigan who told me that she had had the same interchange with the same professor. Only then did I realize that he wasn't misinformed or absent-minded: This was a shtick he performed in the great cause of sexism.

A job offer I didn't take was one where my then-intended was going as an assistant professor. This was my worst offer. Instead of offering me a faculty appointment, they offered me a postdoctoral fellowship for one year at half the salary Chicago was offering. I spoke to a professor on the phone about the offer. What would happen after that one-year postdoc? Well, of course, as the future Mrs. Male Name, they could not hire me in the same department. Marriage would effectively end my career. I pointed out to the man with hiring responsibility that his offer was not competitive, but *he didn't get it*.

At the University of Chicago I was the first-and-only woman in a faculty of one hundred in the graduate school of business. *I didn't get it*. In addition to the MBA program, the graduate school of business had an interdisciplinary doctoral program in behavioral science. The parent disciplines that provided faculty members had produced approximately 25 to 33 percent women doctorates for some decades. Why weren't any of these on the faculty?

One of the most significant events in my experience at Chicago was meeting Marlene Dixon, an assistant professor in the sociology department. She gets the credit for opening my eyes to feminism. I am embarrassed to remember exactly how dense I was. Marlene worked on me with some combination of the drop-of-water-on-the-rock technique and the loving-confrontation technique. When Marlene was denied reappointment as an assistant professor, the students protested and occupied a building or two on campus. The strike lasted all semester. The president went into hiding; campus mail sizzled with communications among faculty members. When the semester was over, Marlene was gone, and the students were expelled. The sanctions meted out to UC students were the most severe of any around the country that year, when student demonstrations were occurring on many campuses.

During this period, excellent women graduate students at the University of Chicago could not find faculty members who were willing to direct a dissertation that focused on women. Many women students tried and tried, and then dropped out. Jo Freeman and Nancy Hartsock were among the very few who made it through the system as it was then.

Women faculty members were not taken seriously. At the annual trustees dinner, women teachers in the lab school and women librarians were magically (and temporarily) redefined as faculty so there would be enough women to sprinkle among the tables at this black-tie affair. Since women faculty were so few, and we liked parties, several of us requested to be placed at the same table; our request was denied. Women were meant to be deployed as colorful and exotic decorations, one per table. During these years, I tried repeatedly to get my official mail addressed as other than "Mr." This also proved impossible. The university was programmed for Professor/Mr. In order to be addressed as Ms., I suppose I would have had to give up the professor part.

The history of women faculty at the University of Chicago is a ghostly one, haunted by the absence of women scholars who have been "disappeared."[2] At one time, I thought this was mainly because women had been so few. Now I know that there were outstanding women on the faculty who had been written out of history by the time I got there. The "invisibility" of women is deliberately engineered; women who are feminists and/or pioneers are particularly likely to be "disappeared." During my four years at the University of Chicago, my presence, my inspiration, and my confidence gradually faded, so that I left behind only the cheshire-cat grin that Marlene had left. I, too, converted one faculty woman before they came for me, and I am confident that she did the same. For all I know, feminism persists at the University of Chicago in the same distinctive form: each one teaches one and then expires.

It was at the University of Chicago that I began to concentrate on women. Coincidentally, when I began to do research on women, I was fired. I was shocked. But there was nothing I could do about it. The university had no due process, no appeals procedure, no female constituency to raise a protest. I went on with my work. My research was funded, in spite of institutional resistance. I moved it to the Institute for Juvenile Research with the sponsorship of some male colleagues, and I continued to collect data and look for a job. *I was beginning to get it.*

In 1971, I accepted a job at Cornell, with a joint appointment in sociology and psychology. I've been told that the faculty members of those departments thought they were rescuing me from the "philistines" at the graduate school of business when they voted unanimously to hire me. Why else would an outstanding person with an outstanding record be fired, as I had been? At Cornell I found out why.

I ran into some turbulence when I tried to make the graduate program in my department less oppressive for graduate students. I confronted racism, sexism and homophobia as best I could. I tried to get more women hired in the department. I tried to discuss the Vietnam War, somewhat at cross-purposes with men who were retelling their World War II stories. I was surprised to find that faculty members at Cornell had not been affected by the tide of antisexist awareness that was sweeping the country. My work in establishing the women's studies program was not appreciated by my colleagues. When I was up for tenure, I had a recurring dream of myself in the center of a ring of men in suits, all with their backs turned to me. I wanted to cry out for them to turn around, talk to me, pay attention to what I was doing, be colleagues—but I was too proud to. My waking life was pretty much like the dream. And, as a colleague to whom I told the dream said, it was the same for all of them, so why was I complaining?

During my years at Cornell, I witnessed some dirty tricks and updated my mental file on institutional sexism, but this was incidental learning. Most of my attention went to doing my work and building my career. I had high course enrollments and high teaching evaluations; I was writing and publishing; my graduate students were doing interesting things; I had a book in press (*Sexual Scripts: The Social Construction of Female Sexuality* [1977]) and one in manuscript form—and I was having fun. The typescript of *The Second X,* which was part of my tenure dossier, disappeared permanently during the tenure review. No explanation was ever made. Before the days of unlimited xeroxing (and computers with backup), this was my only up-to-date copy. This delayed the publication by at least a year; I suppose it could have delayed it permanently.

During the official conversation about my work and my future at my third-year review, the chair began to complain about feminist scholarship. "You're just like the Marxists," he said: "Johnny-one-notes!" I responded that Marxists trace their thought to a definable body of work, while feminist theories were many and proliferating. What body of theory did he have in mind? I asked. When he had no answer, I thought we had come to an understanding that this was a feeling, not a fact. This conversation was no doubt intended as a warning. But I didn't see any connection between the chair's prejudices and the criteria for evaluating faculty work. *I think that was the last time I didn't get it.*

I was denied tenure, and I was poleaxed by the negative vote. Looking back on that time, it seems I was sleepwalking while trying to discern what to do next. In truth, at that time there was no "next." Cornell had no procedure for appealing a negative tenure decision. The dean had a lot of discretion, but no obligation to investigate. The university ombudsman did not return my calls. The American Association of University Professors (AAUP) was not a player on the Cornell campus. Professional associations and women's caucuses had not yet developed a strategy for involving themselves in university personnel decisions. I did what I could do: I found a lawyer who was at least willing to *learn* about sex discrimination in higher education and went to see the dean of arts and sciences. I wrote long and painful memos to this dean challenging the decision. I carried on with my work in a deafening silence I hope never to experience again. "The word" got out with incredible speed (ironic, considering the official stance of "confidentiality"), and about 75 percent of the people I had worked with and partied with for six years stopped talking to me. Permanently.

The dean agreed that *no one* on the tenured faculty had expertise in the new field of sex roles, and on this basis he agreed to get three outside readers (whom he would select) to evaluate my dossier for tenure. In fact he got only two; both of them were males, and neither had done work in sex roles. Both were from departments more distinguished than Cornell's, and both recommended tenuring me, noting that in their departments I would merit tenure. This information was passed on to the sociology faculty, but they were not obligated to pay any attention to it. They denied me tenure a second time. This was the end of the line.[3]

I was devastated. The pain was indescribable. Understanding and nonunderstanding warred in my mind. The understanding said: This was intentional; my work didn't count in the decision; I was not being judged in comparison with *anyone* else. The nonunderstanding said: How could this happen? Has my whole life to this point been a mistake? How can I go on? Is there any future for me? Can I be a professor? If not, what can I do? I found a matchbook that said I could make big bucks driving a refrigerated semi coast to coast. I was thinking that I could support myself by doing this part-time, and hole up in an air-conditioned motel in some desert and write scholarly books. No one reached out to me; no one offered even a word of support. The only kindness I remember from this nightmare period involved the realtor who had sold me my house. She told me that she thought I could be a success as a realtor. This was the only indication I had for many months that anyone thought I might be good for anything.

Of course I went on with my work. I'm sure my civilized manners and stiff upper lip made things much easier for my erstwhile colleagues. But I was weighing suicide, for the usual reasons: unbearable pain and no prospect of a better future. The practicalities bothered me. To whom could I entrust my old bluepoint, Rasputin? I could take him with me, but that didn't seem fair: He wasn't suffering. I thought about it and thought about it. And in the meantime I taught, I advised graduate students, I worked on the book, just as if I had a future.

At last the year came to an end. Above the neck, I just wanted to finish the book. Below the neck, I just wanted the pain to stop. As usual, I went with above-the-neck. I hid out in my sister's little house in Fletcher, Vermont, with Rasputin; I took the job at Syracuse when it was offered; and I finished *The Second X.* In fall 1978 I joined the sociology department at Syracuse University, where I have been ever since.

My Academic Career: The Paper Trail

An academic career is summed up in a unique document that systematically foregrounds some of our work and obliterates the rest. I don't know about other academics, but I regard mine with ambivalence. My curriculum vitae is a curiosity, if not a disgrace. It is a ragtag compilation, with publications in offbeat places, and a notable lack of the initials *AJS* (*American Journal of Sociology*) and *ASR* (*American Sociological Review*). I preserve it as a unique and valuable historical document, rather like a tattered old flag from the time when there were only fourteen states. For every item on the vita, there are probably three or four unpublished papers. My vita reflects the micropolitics of sociological publishing in the dawn of feminist scholarship.

Many of my publications are books or invited contributions to books, forms that are more hospitable to ungainly, long, and theoretical pieces. I am grateful for these invitations. Nevertheless, I have had to defend my vita. The theoretical nature of many of my early contributions was out of step with the convention of brief empirical reports preferred by many sociological journals. In the late 1960s there was really no place to publish theoretical work—especially theoretical work on a nonexistent subject matter like women. Scholarly work on women was innovative, and it did not fit into mainstream sociological journals. There are studies on the rarity of female authors *or* women as subject-matter during the 1960s and 1970s that provide an estimate of the probability of getting *anything* published in the mainstream sociology journals.

The first crack in the wall appeared as a sort of intellectual tokenism, when journals published "special issues" with editors brought in for a single appearance. One of my most-cited articles, a review of the marital happiness literature, appeared in the very first of these, a special issue of *Journal of Marriage and Family* published in 1971 under the editorship of Pauline Bart. The journals devoted to feminist scholarship came into existence only after I had been writing and publishing on women for almost two decades.

Gender & Society, the first journal devoted to sociological work on women, did not begin publishing until 1987. Other journals, more interdisciplinary in emphasis, publish very little work by sociologists.

That's the bad news. The good news is that I was lucky enough to be in the right place at the right time to get in on the beginning of feminist scholarship. It has been exhilarating; I had a spacious scope in which to work. I didn't have to ask anyone's permission; there were no sacred ancestors (or mentors, either). Moreover, when I began, I had not yet been exposed to the put-downs and intimidations that cause many women to doubt their thinking. So I felt perfectly free to formulate what I thought were important issues and do the research I thought was most important. I was fearless. Some would say reckless. But since I've paid the price, I look back on the product with satisfaction. I have no doubt that if I had been "smarter" and concentrated on the rules rather than the questions, I would be more "successful" today. Maybe I would also be burned out, disillusioned, and even meaner than I am.

My Scholarly Career

I chose to become a professor because I loved research. It had a kind of glamour for me. I dreamed of making great discoveries. To tell the truth, I dreamed about winning a Nobel prize. My education at every level reinforced this motivation. The undergraduate honors program in social relations at Harvard provided opportunities to do research (including an honors thesis) and to learn different methodologies. Next, I did research while at NIMH that involved controlled experiments and some observational research with chronic schizophrenics. The University of Michigan was known for intensive methods training. During my first year there, I conducted a participant-observation study in a girls' correctional institution. Another year emphasized the design, execution, and analysis of experiments. Later, I spent even more time learning to design and conduct survey research, the methodology I used in my dissertation.

At the University of Chicago I began to focus on women's work. I looked at women's occupational aspiration and work motivation in the context of disincentives such as sex discrimination. I analyzed the specific means by which women were denied equal access and equal rewards in the workplace. Later, I extended my interest in women and work to include women in developing countries. When I was examining sex discrimination, it was a short step to begin to look at the way gender shapes the academic profession and its knowledge base. Much of my work over the years has been at the level of metamethodology and metatheory of social science, particularly focusing on the difference feminist scholarship makes.

My interests in role, identity, and subjectivity began with my dissertation research on self-actualization motivation, expanded to my work on women's sexual identity over the life span, and continues in my current work on women's personal narratives.

Originally, scholarship—an intense and respectful relationship with work that has been done before—and research—today's inquiry—were parts of the same whole. As time went on, a division appeared between what I thought of as scholarship and what counted as research. Increasingly, research came to mean studies that were funded by grants and the published reports they produced. Although I had several grants at the beginning of my career, I began to pursue questions that would not be supported by the traditional funding agencies. Pursuing research that was powered by feminist analysis separated me from the mainstream. Very little research funding supports feminist work, and the mainstream is fed by funded research that continues to ignore women. Much of my work didn't involve "research" at all. A good deal of it was developing theoretical frameworks that could be used to interrogate the research literature and its underlying assumptions. For me, scholarship, which is good for finding questions and more questions, seems to have beaten out research, which is good for finding answers, but only to some questions. The demands of scholarship continue to expand, for in order to pursue questions about women, I must read and understand what is being done across a number of disciplines. My scholarly career, like my academic career, has involved a lot of lateral movement.

My Career as an Activist

If I had written my autobiography at an earlier period, I would not have recognized my career as an activist. In the official version of my career (the vita) most of it remains invisible. But now, at mid-life, I am aware that my involvement in social movements is not a fluke and will hang on as long as I do. I still have an urgent feeling that this world must change: I can't live in it this way, and I can't leave it the way it is. At mid-life I can see a continuity between the deeply religious activism of my two grandfathers, my father's zest for public life, and my own desire to make a positive difference.

My activist career began in a very small way when I was a senior at

Radcliffe. I was spring 1961 (I was finally twenty-one), and freedom rides were happening in the faraway black South. In Harvard Square, people were picketing Woolworth's to desegregate the lunch counter. Walking by there scared me. When I gradually realized what was at stake there, it scared me more. I realized that I would have to get involved. I was terrified of going on the picket line. When I went to Washington, D.C., after college, I signed up with the Congress of Racial Equality (CORE). We received training in nonviolence, and groups of us went out every weekend to sit in at restaurants and diners all along the belt highway, trying to get them desegregated. The actual experience was a blur: I was always scared; it was like a punishment. I hoped that just being there made a difference, because I surely didn't engage anyone in life-changing, transformative discussions the way Gandhi would have.

I didn't dream of taking any leadership in those protests, nor did I feel any personal sense of closure or lack of closure when I left to go to graduate school. I simply stepped out of the picket line and someone stepped in to take my place. In Ann Arbor I became involved in the peace movement. This, too, involved my sense of justice, but I didn't have a personal place in the movement. Truly, a movement had to reach me where I *was* in order to change my life, rather than merely enlisting my body, my time, or my money. It had to be relevant to my life as an academic woman. The women's movement has been my movement. I have not felt that I was swimming upstream in this movement; I haven't felt controlled by it or invisible in it. I grow, it grows; it changes, I change. Today, I see the women's movement as an accomplished, tempered, determined, invincible woman with wrinkles and stretch marks: This is definitely my movement.

Some of my professional work counts as activism, too. Through my work on women in the work force, I became a consultant in the well-known A.T.&T. case. The precedent of this case was very influential in causing employers to discontinue the normal or reasonable-seeming procedures that impersonally and automatically reproduced job inequity for women—"institutional" sexism rather than personal sexism. I continued to analyze institutional sexism when I served as an expert witness in sex discrimination cases in academia. In 1978, I was consulting with General Motors, trying to help them identify women with management potential who were camouflaged by traditional female jobs. Another goal was getting women into previously all-male career pipelines. A third issue, which surfaced unexpectedly, was the sexual harassment targeting women who were entering nontraditional occupations.

My feminism led me to make these connections with the world outside the university. It also led me to activism within the profession. My consciousness-raising group in Chicago was part of the core of women who formed the Association for Women in Psychology at the APA convention in the early 1970s. Later, Division 35 (Psychology of Women) formed *within* APA. I also participated in a parallel development in sociology. I was one of the earliest members of Sociologists for Women in Society, which came together at the annual meetings in the 1970s, and led to the development of the section on sex roles (later sex and gender).

The accounting system used in universities—and the curriculum vitae that serves as a balance sheet—lack categories for innovation and for institution building. No record is made of this work. In our annual reports of our efforts, it is lumped under "service," a category even less respected and less rewarded than teaching. Nevertheless, program building has been an important part of my work life. I think it is intellectual work, yet I am reporting it as activism.

Women's studies has been an important part of my life and work. Women's studies flourishes today in a climate very different from the academic profession I entered in 1967. When I began, women were absent from the curriculum, absent from the politics of the university, and virtually absent from the faculty. But the idea of women's studies was in the air. I began to think about it, at first, only as a focus for research that would correct the lack of information about women. Like most people at this time, I thought women's studies would become obsolete when it became unnecessary. As time went on, I began to see that the study of women generated its own questions and its own paradigms. Today, I continue to be interested in the interplay between feminist scholarship and its host disciplines, but I no longer imagine that women's studies will ever become unnecessary.

When I moved to Cornell in 1971, I followed up on the work that a core of women—faculty, staff and students—had done to prepare the way for women's studies. I wrote and presented the proposal that established the women's studies program at Cornell, only the second in the nation. When I moved to Syracuse University in 1978, there was a women's studies program in place. Over time, an undergraduate minor was established, and then an undergraduate major. During my term as director of women's studies, from 1984 to 1987, I undertook building a graduate program as a major focus. During my term, a graduate certificate in women's studies was approved. Working to develop the intellectual community of feminist scholars, I organized a cross-disciplinary graduate seminar, led faculty retreats on feminist teaching and on research funding, and started the women's studies lecture series. Feminist scholarship in the rising generation is rewarded and legitimated by the graduate paper prize and the undergraduate paper prize that I initiated.

Institution building is required in revitalizing existing structures as well as in creating new programs. In the sociology department at Syracuse, I have developed the graduate field of sex and gender studies. Graduate students can qualify for a specialty in sex and gender through course work and a comprehensive examination in the area.

My Career as a Teacher

After twenty-five years as a university teacher, I have more to say about what I've *learned* than about what I *know*. Graduate school focused on training about the discipline but not training about teaching. My education about teaching began in my undergraduate classrooms. I found that young people reared on television rather than on books do not come to class ready to hear long pages of text and inscribe them in memory. My lecturing was taking too much for granted: It was based on a logic that had not been programmed into my listeners. I became aware that the traditional lecture format emphasized the expert role and maximized the information gap between student and professor. Learning by listening kept the student inactive, even passive. Recently, research has been published that shows lecturing is the least effective method of teaching.

So I used part of my 1987 leave to rethink teaching. I decided to abandon lecturing and develop a new format that concentrates on discussion and dialogue. I decided to teach specific intellectual skills, and I was determined to teach the students something about the tools of the trade as well. In my classroom, I discuss major traditions of sociological research, and I raise issues of value, bias, and rhetoric. The students learn how to read tables and how to access the primary literature. They learn how a multiple-choice exam item is constructed and how it can serve as a review of material. Written assignments start with cultural materials with which students are already familiar. As the semester advances, assignments demand an increasing level of skill and provide more choice. When I address students by name and mention their contributions to discussion, it seems to give them a stake in the course and creates a group history that increases the value the course has for them.

I have learned a lot through listening to students. That is how I learned that graduate students struggle with an almost universal sense of oppression.[4] Their learning experiences make them feel inadequate, unworthy, dumb, unprepared. When learning is paired with oppression it affects how they are as graduate students and, I have no doubt, how they are as professors. Like other "top dogs," professors underestimate the effects of the power differential between themselves and students; they do not perceive the oppression students feel. Some substantive areas, such as theory and quantitative methods, seem to be particularly powerful vehicles for oppression. I am experimenting with teaching feminist theory in a way that empowers students and invites them to claim theory as their work. I also deal with issues of "voice" and processes of intellectual production, so they keep in mind that theory is created by actual biographical people and is not handed down from on high. I think that sociological theory in general could also be taught in a way that is inviting, compelling, and empowering. Students remark that my graduate seminars form a community or family; that they feel an intellectual awakening has taken place; that open-mindedness and creativity rule; that discourse of this sort does not occur in other departments.

My teaching has certainly changed over the twenty-five years of my career. I've changed my perspective on the content, organization, and traditions of my field. The whole definition of what "counts" as knowledge has become problematic for me: The judgment of what "counts" and what does not is linked with social structures in which some folks have more of a stake than other folks. Knowledge-with-a-capital-K has legitimacy and becomes part of the society's mechanics of social control. Because I think this way, sociology seems much more subject to change (and to disputation) than I suspected. Thinking this way makes sociology more interesting to me and also more accessible to students who will not become sociologists. Thinking this way also separates me from some sociologists of my generation.

Conclusion

My life has been full of movement—much of it unexpected, some of it unwelcome. As a child and young adult I never minded moving. In fact, I connected mobility with success. Mobility was supposed to be upward, uninterrupted, and unambiguous (and, of course, unambivalent). I expected a fast climb to the top: full professor at Harvard by the time I was forty. That climb would have made a much shorter story than the life I've told here.

Unexpected events have shaped and reshaped my life. Preoccupation with success got displaced by concern with survival. My story (and my life) have had to deal with how I survived the denial of tenure. Tenure is referred to as an "up or out" decision; it is more like life or death. The unexpected brought trauma, but also serendipity. Teaching Harvard undergraduates (who would be like myself), I might have been able to take teaching for granted. Instead, I have had to listen and stretch in order to do my job as a teacher. I have learned, and, as a consequence, I am much enriched at this stage of my career. Staying at one university for fifteen years (by far the longest time I've lived anywhere), I have come to know colleagues intimately and appreciate them warmly. My long sojourn in upstate New York has also supported my personal relationship, for as much as I like to be on the move, Dan likes to stay put.

I will end this story the way I began, taking a cross section of the braid and date-stamping it. In terms of my multiple careers, today there is little mobility, but plenty of movement. The braid twists; there is an outer and an inner side. The outer part of my career is in stasis, but only in terms of rank and job. It is agreeable being a full professor. Then again, it is disagreeable being underpaid. In this account, I have neglected the inner side of the career braid for lack of time and space. But my work and thought are more powerful and more creative then ever.

I have told my academic career in terms of ranks and jobs, but also in terms of changing struggles with sexism. There is still plenty of motility there: institutional and intellectual sexism are part of the working conditions of every academic woman. I continue to be buffeted by the either/or thinking of male critics; I must try to teach them that the relationship of scholarship and activism is, not either/or, but both/and. In terms of my personal bent, I would surely be an ivory-tower theorist if only this were a just world. If that were the case, my intellectual work might be enough of a contribution. Or, if the university were as comfortable a place for me as it was for the white men who were my professors, I might be that serene, mellow character I was aiming for by my fiftieth birthday. But as a feminist employed in academia, I have necessarily raised issues and fought for change in our daily life—how we do what we do. My work, like the work of other feminist scholars, has been consistently politicized. Being a feminist theorist would mean being an activist even for someone who did not choose it. None of this is likely to change in my lifetime.

This account has given the impression that some careers came to an end, and that is misleading. I "finished" being a student when I became a faculty member, but, today, the opportunity to be a student is one of my greatest pleasures. My career as a learner is reviving. I don't mind being a beginner (even a dummy), and I appreciate teachers as I never did when I took learning for granted. I am beginning to learn how to use video in my work.

I recently learned self-defense; I don't need to become expert at it, only good enough. I am pursuing tap dancing, even after it has become apparent that I have no future in this field.

My career as a teacher is at a high point. Teaching undergraduates at Syracuse presented several challenges, and in meeting them I have developed skills I am proud of. I know we are making history in my graduate seminars.

My activism today focuses on civil rights of lesbians, gay men, and bisexuals; on women's reproductive freedom; and on ending sexual harassment in my university. It takes different forms today: I do less picketing and more advocacy, utilizing my expert knowledge when I can get people to listen.

My sexual career would seem to have come to an end with marriage. I remember from childhood that "happily ever after" was the end of the story. But with sex holding steady, I have noticed that love is creeping into other parts of my life. Children used to bore me; now they don't. I used to find undergraduates bland; now I find them fascinating. I have more time to talk with strangers. When I was was younger, I segregated my sex life and my work life pretty strictly, and that protected the independence of my career. But in recent years, relationships (including professional ones) are colored by love (or appreciation, awe, enthusiasm, whatever you want to call it). My world is expanding.

Judy Long

NOTES

1. I had been involved with reevaluation counseling for about ten years at this point. I thought of it as an invaluable aid to staying sane in insane places. I used it to work on my negative feelings about marriage, and I did not take them out on Dan.

2. Both Rosalind Rosenberg and Mary Jo Deegan have written about women faculty in the early days of the University of Chicago (Rosalind Rosenberg, *Beyond Separate Spheres: The Intellectual Roots of American Feminism* [New Haven: Yale University Press, 1983]; Mary Jo Deegan, *Jane Addams and the Men of the Chicago School* [New Brunswick, N.J.: Transaction Books, 1988]).

3. Almost. I joined in a class action suit led by five women challenging denial of tenure at Cornell. The name—The Cornell Eleven—is testimony to the fact that

although a number of women had grounds for legal action on the basis of sex discrimination, very few could afford the risk of direct confrontation. The Friends of the Cornell 11 met every Saturday for five years, strategizing, raising money, and serving as a life-support system for the plaintiffs who were still in Ithaca (and for our attorney). Living in Syracuse, it was difficult for me to attend the meetings; nearly three hours on the road meant that it took the entire day. I noticed that I would get nauseated when I entered the city limits of Ithaca. I was disappointed that my substantive expertise on sex discrimination was not utilized in the design of the case. Cornell settled the wage and compensation segment of the case. The agreement created some benefits for women currently employed at Cornell, and many people believe the situation for women faculty has improved as a result of the lawsuit.

4. I have been shocked to learn that many, if not most, academics have been shamed, humiliated, and mistreated somewhere in the course of their schooling. If this is true of the successes, what can have been the experience of those who don't persist to the Ph.D.?

PART III

Varieties of International Sociology

Seven

Marginality, Migration, and Metamorphoses

Britta Fischer

A Childhood in Germany

When I went to Germany in 1986 on the occasion of the twenty-fifth anniversary of my graduation from the Gymnasium,[1] I was going with the intention of studying my classmates as an anthropologist would study a distant tribe. After a weekend of intense recollections and rediscovery, I visited a half dozen of them in their homes in various parts of what was then West Germany. I kept copious notes, and I promised that I would follow up with a questionnaire to capture our collective experience. In the end, I did no such study. Only a skilled novelist, I felt, could have done justice to the life histories, the confidences, and the observations I made of upper-middle class domestic life. As a sociologist, I found myself shrinking from the idea of making my long-lost friends into objects of study.

We had been a small band of nineteen students who had shared the same room, the same teachers, the same courses for six years, until at the end of the thirteenth grade we passed the university entrance exams. Only three could not make it to the reunion, but we heard from them in writing. When we dispersed from our all-girls' Catholic school a quarter of a century earlier, we all went to a university or teacher's college. The seven who studied to be teachers were all from either working-class homes or had fathers who themselves were teachers. The daughters of business owners enrolled in business administration, the physician's daughter studied medicine, the organist's daughter took up music, and the local newspaper publisher's daughter went into journalism. That left the two who became engineers, a dentist, a pharmacist, a Sanscrit scholar, and myself, the sociologist. In 1986, all but two or three were working, at least part time, in their chosen field. All, except two, had gotten married and were raising an average of two children. Two were divorced.

We graduated in 1961, a time of profound change. Everyone remembers the infamous Berlin Wall, built in August of that year, and the "economic miracle" then beginning in West Germany that so attracted East Germans. At the same time, young women like us, whose mothers had been housewives, were now entering the professions in large numbers. It is rather striking how many followed in their fathers' footsteps. What, one might ask, was it that put me on a different course? To chose a nebulous subject like sociology with no known career path awaiting at the end, except possibly university teaching, was seen as foolhardy and daring as my oddball friend Helga's embarking on Sanscrit. Yet to me it seemed quite normal.

Except for two or three children of Eastern refugee families in my class, everybody else's ancestors had lived for centuries as farmers and tradesmen in the villages and towns on the fringe of the big industrial region of the Ruhr. In the years after World War II, they began to send their more gifted daughters to the Gymnasium to study with the nuns. In contrast, I came from an urban, cosmopolitan family, nominally Protestant but really agnostic, liberal Social Democrats in a sea of conservative Catholics. We had Jewish relatives and friends abroad, and the Nazi period was a frequent topic at the dinner table. In the 1930s, my father and his brothers had been caught pulling down Nazi election posters, an offense for which two of them spent time in jail. My grandmother's house in Düsseldorf had served as a temporary shelter for Jews being driven at night by her sons to safety in Holland. These stories, told and retold in our family, were part of the myths that nourished our sense of decency. We were different and proud of it.

I was born in 1942 in Berlin, and my conscious life began just after World War II. We lived in Bavaria then. My mother had contracted tuberculosis and was away in hospitals and sanatariums while my indefatigable grandmother ran the household that included, besides herself and me, my father, my younger brother, and my uncle. This uncle had lost his wife and one son in the war, and his other son had yet to be retrieved by the Red Cross from Poland. My grandmother's favorite child, by all accounts a brilliant lawyer, was missing or dead in Russia. Her daughter was safe with her Jewish husband in America.

I remember having only the barest of necessities because our household, like everyone else's, had been destroyed in bombing raids. My grandmother regretted only having lost her and her husband's library of several thousand volumes. Other material possessions were quickly forgotten, and I learned from this attitude an abiding sense of their unimportance. Books and ideas were all that mattered. My father strongly identified with the political and artistic tendencies of Weimar culture of the 1920s and he read us Bertolt Brecht's poems. Writers were heroes in my home, to the point where I am said to have stood on the kitchen table and announced that I planned to become famous like the Swedish Nobel Prize winner, Selma Lagerlöf.

By 1948, when I entered first grade, my mother came home an invalid from a grueling lung operation and my father had lost his job with the American military government, because fighting the cold war against the communists now preempted the previous policy of ferreting out former Nazis. My father moved to Hamburg in search of a job in the export business, since knowledge of four foreign languages was his greatest skill. My grandmother joined her daughter in Philadelphia, and my mother took in boarders to pay the rent. We moved to Hamburg, but my father's job did not pan out, and so he tried his luck as a traveling salesman. When my mother got sick once again, my brother and I were farmed out to different relatives in the countryside. Finally, my father secured permanent employment in a small town in Westfalia, where the somewhat wild little ten-year-old was to be domesticated by the nuns.

I was now in fifth grade, and I had lived in three different regions of the country and gone to four different schools. We finally settled down, yet it took me several more years to find full acceptance among my schoolmates. By the time it happened around age fifteen, in mid-adolescence, it was a great joy, but in the meantime, my parents' efforts to sustain our being different had taken root. I came to accept my marginality. I had learned to view society from the vantage point of the sometimes envious, sometimes detached, sometimes bemused observer. Over the years I had been teased because of my dialect; friendship groups had not accommodated me; the locals would let us know in countless ways that we did not belong. Yet some good came of all this, not just in later life, but right at the time. One benefit was that as an outsider you did not have to play as strictly by the rules as the locals. Thus, nonconformity reinforced my individuality. Another positive but also painful effect was that I learned to empathize with other outsiders in other times and places. When cramps augmented my emotional misery, I would think, much like the boy in the Swedish film "My Life as a Dog," of those who had suffered worse. I would try to imagine what Anne Frank must have felt when she rode in a freight car to the concentration camp. The images that I obtained from reading intensively about the Nazi period obsessed and haunted me. They also helped me put my own trials and tribulations in perspective.

When my mother divorced my father in 1956 and left without a word of explanation, I was not quite fourteen yet, but I had already built a little world of my own into which I could withdraw without being crushed. Considering how unable they both were to talk about emotional issues with each other and with us, it is remarkable how little lasting damage they really did. Perhaps it had to do with the fact that they had always defined for us other important issues.

Divorced parents were a rarity then, and children staying with their father (and the grandmother who was swiftly retrieved from America) were unheard of. Henceforth, I spent my vacations with my mother in Hamburg, where she, at age thirty-six, was an apprentice in a book business; later, she managed a bookstore. It took me many years to appreciate her act of courage and independence. At the time, neither she nor I could have imagined that twenty years later she would come to live with us in the United States. She has taken an active part in raising our children, thereby enabling me to work with peace of mind.

I dealt with adversity by escaping into books and films, yet I managed to appear to an outside observer as reasonably well-adjusted. Fantasy met reality when on one fine summer day in 1956 a pair of dashing young Harvard instructors, who happened to be my cousin and her husband, passed through our house on their way to a year's research in India. The cousin persuaded her parents in Philadelphia, my father's sister and her husband, that they had come upon a not altogether undeserving waif, dare I say a diamond in the rough, who might benefit from a year at an American high school.

American Adventure

In July 1958, at age sixteen and in the eleventh grade, I sailed for the United States aboard a passenger liner. Little did I know that I was headed for a new kind of marginality, this time entirely positive, for it was the marginality of near-stardom, of being the school's one foreign student, of becoming a goodwill embassador for a pariah nation. From the ten days on the ocean liner to the following summer when I found romance, the year in Philadelphia was one of wonder and learning beyond anything I could have imagined. I took on a heavy schedule at the selective Philadelphia High School for Girls so as not to fall behind my classmates in Germany. A history teacher, unwilling to concede that the talkative German girl might have trouble with concepts such as "lock out" and "Yellow Dog" contract, caused me fits of homesickness, but the enormously supportive environment created by my fellow students of many races and religions more than made up for it.

While some American contemporaries experienced the 1950s as a period of repression, hypocrisy, and misery (Breines 1992), I experienced a year of that decade as my personal liberation, a year of being appreciated and valued as an individual, as someone special. Would that every teenager could have such a lucky break! Of course this was possible only because as an outsider I was once again not held to the rules; this time, I was a sort of celebrity rather than an outcast.

By going to an all-girls academic high school, I missed out on the average American high school culture, something I don't particularly regret. The students at Girls' High were serious about their studies, about race relations, about personal integrity. Jewish students came to my rescue when someone wanted to hold me responsible for the Holocaust. It was an unwritten rule that the offices of class president and vice-president were typically held by one black and one white student; in my class it was an African American and a Chinese American student. The racial composition of the school reflected that of the city as a whole, which was at the time said to be 25 percent black. At Girls' High I saw the more liberal, democratic side of America.

Equally important was the care my family lavished on me. My aunt never tired of taking me to historic places and, even more astonishing, I never tired of being taken there. Valley Forge, Kitty Hawk, the National Archives, the Empire State Building: I saw them all. My cousins invited me up to the hallowed halls of Harvard University for Thanksgiving and expanded my horizons by driving with me the following July through the sweltering midwest to Chicago. I faithfully recorded all these miraculous happenings in my diary. There was no question that the upper middle-class life-style of American intellectuals greatly appealed to me. I had seen the future, and it looked good.

When I returned from America in 1959, I must have been one of a handful of German young people who had been exposed to the racial and cultural diversity, the glitzy cities, and the material wealth of the United States. Their effect was not lost on me. The following three years, when I finished high school and studied sociology for a year at the University of Münster, proved to be a mere interlude in the ineluctable attraction of the land beyond the Atlantic.

A German University

At the university, my professors were lecturing primarily about American sociologists: Thorstein Veblen, Talcott Parsons, David Riesman. That, combined with rumors in the student grapevine that many of these

German professors had been active Nazis, further fed my determination to leave. There were other reasons, as well, that influenced the momentous decision to emigrate from Germany. There was also the pull of something less readily definable, the presence of Jews in American daily life in general and in intellectual life in particular. In order to understand that pull, it is necessary to consider the "push" part that contributes to any decision to emigrate.

During my late teens, I had been immersed in trying to understand the systematic persecution and killing of Jews by the Nazis. Besides reading about concentration camps, I also came to study Berlin culture of the 1920s and turn-of-the-century Vienna. Who were the Jews? In Münster, I searched out contact with the Christian-Jewish Community, an organization of middle-aged non-Jewish and elderly Jewish Germans. A twenty-year-old was decidedly an oddity there. I considered working on a kibbutz, and I studied modern Hebrew with Mr. Schereschewsky, an old man with a yarmulke. My thirst for learning about Jewish life drove my friends crazy and could obviously not be quenched in Germany. I was rather embarrassed when one classmate at the reunion put it so directly, "Well, Britta, did you marry a Jew?" I did—some fourteen years after my arrival in the United States.

Another component of the push away from Germany was the thrust of my parents' upbringing and my political convictions. In 1962, Konrad Adenauer was chancellor. For all his efforts at European unity he was not a liberal statesman. Rather, he fed the fires of religious bigotry and dog-eat-dog competitiveness. True, war criminals were constantly put on trial, but others were found right in the government. Both facts merely increased the shame I felt at being a German. Neither at school nor at home were patriotic feelings, even healthy ones, fostered. I viewed myself as a citizen of the world, theoretically free to move where I pleased. In addition, the United States had just elected a glamorous, young president, who appealed to the idealism of the young and who was a cosmopolitan and a liberal. In 1962, the United States still had the magical appeal made in Hollywood, and this, too, tugged at me.

By the middle of my second semester at Münster I was deeply involved in researching to which colleges I should apply. My cousin had gone to Sarah Lawrence, so that was a logical choice. C. Wright Mills (the only American not praised by the German sociologists) was at Columbia, so I applied to Barnard. The third place was Smith. It seems rather interesting in retrospect that despite my being a student at a coed university and despite the fact that single-sex universities are unimaginable in Germany, I selected three women's colleges. I can only guess at the reasons. At Girls' High School the Seven Sisters colleges had been spoken of with great respect. Some of my American friends were attending Bryn Mawr and Radcliffe. I suspect so big a step as immigrating to the United States all by myself was cushioned by the prospect of pursuing my studies in a familiar, nonthreatening, supportive environment.

Barnard College Years

In April 1962, Barnard accepted me with a nearly full scholarship. I immediately took a leave of absence from the university to earn the $500 required for the passage. In early August, when Marilyn Monroe took her life, I was a young scholar full of hope on a freighter bound for New York carrying all my earthly possessions: a bicycle, a suitcase with clothes, and a trunk full of books and papers. I considered myself rich in spirit. From the material standpoint I was a fool. Just about everyone was beginning to be swept up by the German Economic Miracle. Certainly my classmates all ended up more prosperous than I did (all but the two who didn't marry, that is). But had I stayed, what would have been the likelihood of my making it into that small, select group of women who made up a mere 2 percent of German university professors then and only 4 percent today?

Things definitely looked brighter in New York. At Barnard there were women professors like the flamboyant and erudite Mirra Komarovsky (never seen without a hat), who impressed me with her willingness to look things up on the rare occasion when she did not have an answer to a question and who actually never referred to her research on women published as *Blue Collar Marriage* (1964). There was Renée Fox, vivacious and supportive. Most of the male professors were accessible and helpful, too, although Daniel Bell gave me the third degree when I wanted to attend a course at Columbia College on literature and revolution. Still, he actually spoke to me with sympathy about the woeful underrepresentation of women in German university faculties.

Beyond the classroom, there was Baker Library, in whose labyrithine corridors I expected to find skeletons of students who'd forgotten to eat or go home over their discovery of intellectual nourishment. Here I came upon Max Weber, Werner Sombart, Georg Simmel, Ferdinand Tönnies, and Karl Mannheim, and I read them in German. The revelation of the truly impressive German sociological tradition, of which I had never heard my professors in Münster speak, ironically came in America. Reading Weber's *Protestant Ethic and the Spirit of Capitalism* and the larger tome on *Ancient*

Judaism was like being admitted to the inner sanctum of the temple of knowledge. Here I was, an apprentice scholar, relishing the life of the mind. Karl Marx, presented by my teachers without passion, as one thinker among many, for the time being did not stir my imagination. It was not until the second half of the 1960s that political action sent us in search of his words.

Not only was I discovering intellectual history, to which Germans had contributed so much, but there were two books in particular about which I got truly excited. They said to me: Here are the cultural values, the religion, the geography, and the experience of your people. The two books were Max Weber's *Protestant Ethic* and Émile Durkheim's *Suicide*. They gave me a profound sense of discovery and identification, even a kind of pride, though a rather private one, since being German still carried a stigma. More than anyone in theory class, I could make sense of the maps and tables in *Suicide*, all those little principalities whose boundaries in mid–twentieth century still ran through entire German communities, if not physically, then through the mindsets of people, dividing them bitterly along religious lines. Diaspora. Everybody had heard of Jews in the diaspora, but here Durkheim was theorizing about my grandmother's experience in the 1890s. In her little Catholic town, Protestants and Jews alike were in the diaspora. On Good Friday, the highest Protestant holiday, the Catholics scrubbed their sidewalks, sloshing dirty water purposely into the churchgoers' shoes.

From Weber's essay, which has always given my Catholic students a fair amount of trouble, I learned that Martin Luther, our folk hero, who had brought us all out of the Dark Ages a mere five hundred years ago, who cut through superstition, intercession and corruption, was merely contributing to the general process of *Entzauberung*, or disenchantment of the world. The whole culture complex, called the Protestant ethic, was practiced religiously in my agnostic family. I relished the concepts of "calling" and "vocation." Hadn't I just found mine? When I reported about all this excitedly to my American family and mentioned that the translation had been done by Talcott Parsons, turning plain turgid German into excruciatingly turgid English, my uncle who had studied in Heidelberg in the 1920s, said, "Oh, Talcott Parsons, that little shrimp, he always carried an attaché case." This from a man who himself was no taller than 5 feet, 5 inches! Sociology was rapidly turning from a subject of reverence into sheer fun.

My forays into the city usually went no further than the bookstores around Columbia. There I eyed the classics and slowly filled the little shelf in my dorm room with 95¢ and $1.95 paperbacks, paid with money earned babysitting at 50¢ an hour. For graduation my ever-generous American aunt and uncle gave me Weber's *Wirtschaft und Gesellschaft* (Economy and society) and *Gesammelte Aufsätze zur Religionssoziologie* (The sociology of religion). They might as well have given me a Gutenberg Bible, I was so thrilled.

In the dormitories other issues prevailed. There were those who, I thought, agonized excessively over how to validate their existence through a steady stream of dates. It was painful to witness the desperation with which perfectly capable young women waited by the telephone. As the perpetual messenger who lived right next to the hallway phone, I was invariably greeted by, "Man or woman?" If I answered "woman," the eyes rolled upward and the pace of getting to the phone slowed markedly. With anthropological fascination (though, I am sorry to say, not with much empathy) I observed the Saturday night frenzy of getting ready for a date: hair-curling paraphernalia were traded across the corridor, shrieks of last-minute disasters could be heard, curly hair was straightened on the ironing board. Worst of all, however, was the near-nervous breakdown of one sophomore every time two weekends passed without her having received the longed-for phone call from a date, any date.

The same group waxed misty-eyed over the possibility of a native ritual called a "panty raid." I listened in disbelief to an explanation of this phenomenon: Boys (could one call them men?) from Columbia College would come into Barnard yard and yell en masse "Panties, panties!" When the event finally occurred it was not a very propitious night; dense fog hovered in the courtyard, yet underwear floated down from many windows. Mercifully, this custom was on the wane and happened only once in the two years I spent at Barnard. Another ritual that I have since seen dozens of times and that never ceases to amaze me is the excitement and the exaggerated oh's and ah's that fill the room when a woman sports an engagement ring for the first time. I recall when this happened in the seminar room of the sociology department. The student was a junior, and the diamond was apparently very impressive. Perhaps I was myself still too much of an adolescent, but the thought of marrying and keeping house right after graduation positively horrified me. There was so much that I still wanted to do, from travel to years of additional study, that I could not conceive of doing in tandem with someone else, no matter how much in love I might be.

I was a liberal and a pacifist, basically fairly apolitical, and this was the time of the civil rights movement. The irony of Barnard students going on freedom rides while our school carefully limited black students to four, or 1 percent, of each entering class of four hundred was not lost on me. I spent summers with my relatives in Washington, D.C. The summer of 1963 provided some excellent lessons of life in America. There was a recession.

My uncle had obtained a job in the Kennedy administration, passing out a billion dollars for emergency public-works programs ranging from building sewer systems in the South to campgrounds in the Virgin Islands.

For three weeks that summer I pounded the pavement, scaling down in the process my expectations of peddling my linguistic abilities to the local bookstores and settling for a job as a waitress in a German restaurant. My daily walk to work took me past the Library of Congress and the Supreme Court over Capitol Hill toward Union Station. In return for free rent at a settlement house, I did a visual survey of housing conditions in the southeast section of the city. I got somewhat of a feel for the poverty and unemployment among blacks in the area, but I also learned about family life and stability before drugs turned the capital into a war zone. I never felt threatened or unwelcome in the neighborhood. On August 23, my racist boss wanted to close the restaurant lest crowds of blacks would descend on it on the day of the March for Jobs. Greed got the better of him and he kept it open, only to find that protestors who come to Washington don't spend their time lingering in restaurants. He let us go early. Thus I joined the historic march, and I stood close to the front when Martin Luther King gave the speech now recited by millions of school children in January.

Another summer I visited every junior and senior high school in Washington; I interviewed many young women in the course of a study of teenage pregnancy. By the time I graduated from college in 1964, the ideal of life in the ivory tower was being supplemented by some real-life experiences.

In the early afternoon of November 22, 1963, I was sitting in my dorm room when the door flung open, and Elaine Cohen stood there, her turquoise plastic radio in hand, unplugged, tears streaming down her face, "The President has been shot." The next day I took the bus to Washington, spending that unforgettable Thanksgiving weekend glued to the television, joining the throngs of mourners at the funeral, and visiting the eternal flame at Arlington Cemetery, which was surrounded by fresh flowers. It was a gray and rainy day. I, who so yearned to understand the stream of history, was now consciously and irrevocably part of it.

Being a Sociologist

Upon a graduation from Barnard in 1964, I headed to Washington University in St. Louis. The now unfortunately extinct sociology department at Washington University was, in the mid-to-late 1960s, a place of intellectual ferment, where we learned as much from each other as we did from our teachers. Sometimes relations in the department resembled those of medieval knights in combat, complete with sometimes loyal, sometimes reluctant vassals. No wonder we graduate students withdrew into a culture of our own. Furthermore, the escalation of the Vietnam War and the Black Power movement caused us to look beyond the campus. Heated debates over the merits of racial integration versus separatism alternated with discussions of Fellini or Antonioni films. Our student life took on some of the flavor that I imagine my aunt and uncle had in the 1920s in Heidelberg or Berlin. Unlike students of earlier generations, however, our lives did not take place in cafés. Instead of rented rooms watched over by grudging landladies, we had spacious apartments at the fringe of the ghetto. There were lots of communal feasts and picnics, for some students of the 1960s also had cars. Over Mexican and Brazilian delicacies we became Marxists and activists who would demonstrate against Hubert Humphrey when he came to campus, and we would drive to Washington to protest the war. Undaunted by the Pentagon's failure to levitate at the sight of so many flower children, we marched again and again.

Not only were we part of a political revolution, the pill came into our lives just in time as part of the sexual revolution. Relationships became more relaxed, and we became more skilled at discussing emotional matters. Hours were spent in Freudian discourse analyzing personalities and problems. We never tired of each others' company. We popped in and out of each others' apartments, often in the same building; we babysat the communal baby, who is now an actress in Brazil; we commiserated with each other over unrequited love or being dragged into the conflicts between our teachers. Lifelong friendships, that have stood the test of time across continents, had their beginnings in these heady times. Just recently, twenty-five years later, several of us held a reunion in São Paulo, Brazil.

I left St. Louis in 1968, with all but my dissertation done, and I traded one university setting for another. I was a young instructor, first in Washington, D.C., and a year later in Boston at Emmanuel College, where I have taught ever since. By this time, my German classmates had completed their studies and were either working or beginning families or both. The student movement, which also swept Europe and which had such a profound influence on me, largely bypassed them. At our reunion I found out that I was the only Marxist—though by no means the only progressive, socially committed person—the only Ph.D., and the one with the youngest children.

During the first half of the 1970s, while teaching full-time, I was an activist in an organization called Science for the People. We took on the elitist science establishment, trying to demystify science and to forge ties between those working in the universities and high-tech firms around Boston and the inner-city community. Twenty-four years after we founded *Science for the People* magazine, it is still being published. I lived in a commune at the time, and both my parents visited me there on several occasions. My American family took a rather dim view of my radical rhetoric and concluded that I was perhaps living in a bomb factory.

My involvement in Science for the People had two important consequences, one personal and one professional. I met there a physicist, Herb Fox, with whom I have shared my life ever since. Also I found there the subject matter, but not the subjects, for my dissertation. Let me explain the latter. When Science for the People was founded in 1969, it had the cumbersome name Scientists and Engineers for Social and Political Action, yet there were never any engineers to speak of in the organization. When reports of relatively high rates of unemployment among engineers appeared in the newspapers, I went in search of engineers to interview. Some eight years and two babies later, in 1980, I received my doctorate for a theoretical dissertation on the class position of American engineers, having in the process also explored their history, ideology, conditions of work, and unemployment experience.

Writing a dissertation over such a long period of time and so far removed from Washington University had few advantages and many disadvantages. I was independent, so independent in fact that one European colleague who read the manuscript, which was dotted with Marxist terminology, exclaimed in astonishment, "Don't they make you write in slave language?" That, I suppose, was the good part. Over the years I lost two advisors, who were more involved with winning their own tenure battles than giving me timely comments on the chapters I sent them. The lessons of all the years of lack of mentoring have taught me to redouble my efforts with my own students. Perhaps an indirect measure of success in that area is the fact that, over the years, the small sociology department at Emmanuel College has generated a disproportionately large number of women who have gone on to obtain Ph.D.'s in sociology.

Having spent thirty-seven of my fifty-two years in women's institutions, I know that receiving support from women and giving support to other women makes for good practice. This is not the same as being a conscious feminist for that many years. For most of my life, issues of class, race, and ethnic discrimination, particularly anti-Semitism, have been paramount concerns. When the second wave of feminism arrived—and there was no ignoring it in Cambridge, Massachusetts—I was not swept up in it. Of course we had a women's study group, several in fact, within Science for the

People, but the very fact that we continued to work alongside men stigmatized us as insufficiently militant and single-minded about women's issues. As in many radical endeavors, the lines were quickly drawn and volleys of mutual condemnation were traded across them.

It may well be that, in addition to being at the time involved in building a stable relationship with a man and being a Marxist, there was what I now call the immigrant factor that made me, in Durkheim's word, "immune" to seeing myself as a victim of male supremacy. Petty bourgeois individualism, which I had studied extensively in my dissertation and from which I do not consider myself exempt, is particularly pronounced in middle-class immigrants who left their homeland of their own volition. After all, we are the ones who picked ourselves up and tried to seek our fortune elsewhere. A victim mentality does not readily grow in that soil. Moreover, for all my dwelling on my German past and my German reactions to the American scene in this essay, I have been an assimilationist. Like my German classmates who took up their fathers' occupations, I took my cues from the patriarchal culture and from my father, who wanted me to be a professional like his sister and his niece, Ph.D. and all.

And yet today I am a committed feminist. I teach feminist theory. I spent much of the 1980s creating courses bridging the gap between technology and women's lives and consciousness. The imptus finally came from feminist students and colleagues, radical and otherwise, who compelled me—not by derision but by dialogue—to catch up with the body of research and practice that has built up and transformed our lives over the past twenty years.

Looking back, I realize that I exercised a measure of control and initiative in my life that may have been unusual even for a woman of my generation. Nonetheless, I believe this account is accurate in its emphasis and is not the result of some nostalgic distortion. After all, there was pain and dislocation. But I also realize how fortunate I was in my early years to have enjoyed the support of relatives and teachers, most of them women who are still alive. Those who are now in their seventies and eighties serve as examples of how I might structure creatively and productively what I hope to become my fourth quarter-century. It is also cause for wonder and joy to be able look at the many continuing and sustaining friendships with women and men ranging from Germany in the early 1950s to Boston in the 1990s. As we were standing at the railing of a steamer on the Amazon earlier this year, a new friend, Tory, a woman from San Francisco, who, like me, had left husband and children behind for this adventure, turned to me and said, "Isn't it great to have been through so much and still be able to look ahead to decades of growth!"

At this point I am like the bougainvillea on the windowsill in my office from whom I am quite diligently trying to coax some subtropical blossoms: rooted in one place, yet branching out in many directions. I have been studying Portuguese and traveling to Brazil to do research on Chinese influences in its culture. At the same time, I have been immersed in studying feminist criticism and women's literature. I recently received an honorable mention in an international poetry and prose contest in honor of Elizabeth Bishop, Gabriela Mistral, and Carlos Drummond de Andrade.[2] My courses include one entitled Women in a Technological World (Contrucci and Fischer, 1990), which I initiated to be team-taught with three other women. It is designed to empower women to understand and act on the global technological and ecological issues of our time. Being the mother of a fourteen-year-old daughter and a seventeen-year-old son brings many creative challenges as well, requiring me effectively to invent the relationship that I did not have with my mother in adolescence. As I enter the third quarter-century of my life, I find myself drawn to more empathetic, expressive, nurturing, and interdisciplinary activities. Throughout the years my husband has given me generous support, and my mother, so different in temperament from me, has never blinked as I come up with yet another restless scheme, whether it be travel to China, to Norway, or to Brazil.

And my German classmates? Several of them have visited me with their families. Despite decades of separation, we have much in common: growing children, elderly parents, and our professional work, as well as living in countries whose history, persistent inequalities, and social unrest never permit a sense of complacency.

Britta Fischer

NOTES

1. A gymnasium is a selective school that one entered in my region by examination after fourth grade. The course of instruction at a gymnasium spanned nine years. In predominantly Catholic regions, gymnasiums were separated by gender. Boys' gymnasiums could be "humanistic," with a heavy emphasis on Greek and Latin; or "modern language," stressing English, French, and Latin; or "mathematical/scientific," with a corresponding downplaying of languages. There were only modern language gymnasiums for girls. Because Germany does not have a

formal separation of church and state, a gymnasium run by nuns, such as mine, could and did function as a public school.

2. Elizabeth Bishop (1911–1979), North American poet; Gabriela Mistral (1889–1957), Chilean poet, winner of the 1945 Nobel Prize for literature; Carlos Drummond de Andrade (1902–1987), Brazilian poet.

REFERENCES

Breines, Wini. 1992. *Young, White, and Miserable: Growing Up Female in the Fifties.* Boston: Beacon.

Contrucci, Joyce, and Britta Fischer. 1990. "Women in a Technological World: An Interdisciplinary Core Course at Emmanuel College in Boston." *Bulletin of Science, Technology, and Society* 10(4): 191–95.

Eight

Bridging Worlds
A Sociologist's Memoir

Suzanne Keller

My college years were drawing to a close. I had packed in a plethora of courses ranging from the classics and the Bible to history, literature, economics, and music. But when it had come to choosing a major, I opted for the natural sciences, physiology in particular, in preparation for a possible future career in medicine. And then, in my senior year, I had an encounter with a field I had never heard of but which was to change my life.

How can I, decades after this event, render the overwhelming impact of my first encounter with sociology? It was as if all the years of my life had been a prelude to this startling, exciting, original way of looking at the world. I read my way through the sociological classics with abandon, and my heart was filled with gratitude toward the teacher, a brilliant, provocative émigré from Berlin, for the gift he had brought into my life. Without a backward glance, I bid goodbye to the future physician and set forth on the intriguing, captivating quest into the mysteries of the sociological domain.

Needless to say, a shift so late in my college career caused major bureaucratic headaches, but I was determined to pursue my new path. What was it that so fascinated that nineteen-year-old? Why were the questions about social structure and personality, the power of the group, the inevitability of social hierarchy, and the lure of the sociological imagination so compelling?

Looking back some four decades later, I now feel that I was already a sociologist when I went into that classroom. The questions I encountered I had been asking implicitly for a long time; they were waiting within me, waiting for the magic key, the open sesame, to bring them to life.

Early Years

Two major biographical events had stimulated my sociological imagination. One had to do with a never fully understood family drama that had led to my being placed, for my health and well-being, into a peasant village about an hour from Vienna, Austria, for several years in early childhood in the 1930s. The other had to do with the triumph of Nazism, which for Austria meant conquest and submission (not without internal help) and for my family meant exile and flight. Both of these formidable experiences shaped my consciousness and character profoundly. They led me to be dissatisfied with the surface of things and to probe for deeper layers of meaning and to be attuned to the significance of collective forces for human destiny. I discuss both of these powerful experiences primarily for their impact on my professional development, especially in terms of the questions they posed for me for which there seemed to be no easy answers.

I learned two permanent lessons in the village: how to be a self-reliant individual yet also to be part of a hardworking community living precariously on the edge of collective survival. No one could evade the wrath of nature, the cycle of the seasons, the round-robin of birth and death. The pear tree bloomed magnificently for but a moment; the winter snows were followed by the explosion of spring. Mysterious ailments, for which peasant lore could find no cure, would periodically afflict infants and children, so that the bell tolled often and we knew early that it tolled for each and all. There was thus an elemental basis to life: one grew the food one ate; sewed the clothes; tended the living; buried the dead; celebrated holidays, especially Christmas, exuberantly; and prayed for guidance in the small village church in times of sorrow.

I do not recall when I first learned that I was a special child, a child who would one day leave the village and go to live in a grand city amid luxury and comfort. I never quite believed it until it came to pass. I was unprepared for it and the heartache that went with it.

I was special also in another sense: I was a Jewish child, indeed the only Jewish child, in a Roman Catholic village. Thus, although deeply, intimately, a part of that world, I was also, to draw on a distinction familiar to sociologists, early on both "insider" and "outsider." I went to mass with my peasant family as a matter of course, but everyone knew this was due to a special local dispensation. I knew the catechism by heart, but Austrian law decreed that each child had to receive religious instruction in its own faith, and so, when I was about five years old, they had to search for appropriate Jewish instruction for me in a place beyond the village. The search led to a larger town, an hour away by foot, where the railroad stopped and peasants bought and sold their goods. This is how one day I found myself before a large, heavyset man dressed in black, with a huge beard, pale glasses, and a wide black hat. He smelled powerfully of garlic, and he proceeded to teach me Hebrew. I no longer remember how many lessons I took. I remember only that I hated them as well as the weekly treks from the village and back. And the child with a ready facility for learning most everything proffered—reading, writing, arithmetic, piano—suddenly refused to learn.

Looking back it is easy to see what stopped me. It was not content but context. I did not want to be separate from those I loved. Religion, I concluded, was an arena of deep, intense feelings that united the faithful, but it was also a force for creating deep, intense divisions. Apart from this self-engineered failure, I thrived on school and its offerings. Our village teacher, a formidable woman, was strict and undemonstrative. She did not spare the rod for those who did not heed her rules, but she cherished those who shone in her classroom. I was one of the cherished. To keep order in a classroom that was home to four different grades, each in its own set of rows, required draconian measures, and one or another child was always being disciplined. It was, however, possible to skip from the first to later grades in the very same room and thus compress years into months. It was my first experience with symbolic boundaries, as a simple move from the window seats to the center designated a rise in status visible to only those privy to the code. Although the details are blurred now, I was dimly aware of an unacknowledged bond between that teacher and myself, and I remember her vividly. A love of learning would henceforth provide the thread that linked the world of the village to the many worlds I was to inhabit long afterward. Also, children in the village were given ample leeway to explore the world at will and were expected to learn from their own experience—bad and good. And we did. We learned to trust our senses, and we built up knowledge from firsthand encounters with the environment (snakes can bite; sun can burn; insects can sting). The rules to be heeded were aimed primarily at public conformity, and one was permitted a private, even a secret, life apart from the powerful village system of church, school, and household. This spawned an independence that sociologists have often missed in their studies of village life.

From Village to City

I had visited Vienna quite often to see and be fussed over by doting relatives, but one day, at age seven, I went to live there for good, with my "real" parents. My joy and excitement at the prospect was, however, overlaid by an immense sadness at the impending loss. The intensity of this loss would fade in time, as my new life amid a large extended family took hold, but even as the splendors of the metropolis came to absorb me, the loss was never fully erased. Deep within me, the village, my peasant parents, my peasant brother, and other members of that bustling household continue to live on, as do the themes of village life. One prominent theme was that of wholeness and interdependence, for regularities of the common life were plain to see, and everyone had a contribution to make. It was an intelligible world in which the dynamic interplay between individual and society was apparent to all. Human beings worked and prayed and schemed and plotted to protect their tiny places in the sun more or less in full view. Life could be hard because nature could be cruel, but there were moments of great beauty and bounty as well. The village provided one with a wide range of humanity, and this taught me that individual diversity need not be antithetical to community.

The contrast between this simple peasant village of a few hundred families with but one church, one school, one post office, and one restaurant and the fabled city on the Danube could not have been sharper. To speak of culture shock is to put it mildly. It was a profound transformation, a stripping away of one cultural skin to superimpose another. Almost immediately, I was plunged into the world of theater, ballet, opera, concerts, private schools, and all the comforts of an upper bourgeois life.

My father, a brilliant, erudite man trained in finance and the law, was a child of the enlightenment with a strong bohemian flair. He exuded worldliness and an ease of command that I attribute to his having been the eldest of seven sons and his mother's favorite. He was unconventional and challenging and a source of endless intellectual delight to me. My mother, sensual and seductive, intelligent but not intellectual, emotionally expressive and temperamental, presented quite a contrast. Their union of opposites reflected some of the stock gender stereotypes I would come to debate far into the future, but they were also vivid and compelling personalities, dazzling and vulnerable in different ways.

For a number of years, the clash of peasant and urban cultures—my early introduction to gemeinschaft and gesellschaft—was kept vivid by regular visits to the village, especially on major holidays, where the citified me tried, often unsuccessfully, to straddle both worlds. The one was solid, predictable, rule- and season-bound, its escapes well-disguised. The other was not only larger and more diversified but it was much harder to find a common denominator. By contrast with the closed world of the village, Vienna seemed a kaleidoscope of changing tastes, electrifying and filled with erotic innuendo.

The Viennese were a pleasure-loving people, who prized good food, music, flirtations, and *gemütlichkeit,* which roughly means a sense of ease and comfort. It was a charming backdrop for one's childhood. Of course, even in the best of times, childhood has its trials as one is poked and pruned into cultural shape. But these were nothing compared to the trials to come.

A World Goes Under

Those trials began one day in the spring of the year when sounds of Sieg Heils and marching boots invaded our world. All eyes seemed to be focused on one man who would come to symbolize war and devastation for untold millions. Seeing the agitation his appearance engendered—fanatic euphoria for some and despair for others—I found myself fascinated and terrified. How did such a man get his terrible power? I wondered. Who is responsible? Why can this happen, and what would become of us?

To see a society collapse is to see the raw and exposed nerve endings of a culture. It is a harrowing experience of anomie in action, for it turns everything on its head. From one day to the next, the flag was displaced, as were the currency, billboard messages, certain street names, and other staples of the society one had come to take totally for granted. The very air one breathed was permeated by fear and apprehension. People began to disappear or went into hiding; some committed suicide, others made haste to prepare their departure in secret. Prophesies and rumor circulated wildly. Children were warned to keep silent lest they inadvertently give away information that could harm their elders. The society that had once seemed impregnable and eternal was revealed as fragile and powerless.

The ins were now out and the outs were in, and, most importantly, they had taken control. Adults, once so sure of command and so knowing, now were neither. This then was the real truth: the old verities, namely, the flag, adults in control, a sense of order, were just provisional after all. It was obvious even to a child that these depended on invisible social forces to sustain—or destroy—them. A new order had taken over. For the unlucky, it would mean cremation or slaughter on the battlefield; for the more fortunate, it would mean permanent exile and the odyssey of flight. For us, the refugee experience with its Jobean bewilderment lay ahead. The sociology of immigration captures some of the uncertainties, the disruptions, the loss of roots, and the resolve to start over. If the transition is successful, it is probably conducive to the sociological capacity of *verstehen*, am empathic entering of other worlds.

The odyssey of exile is, above all, an extraordinary test of character. Fear and curiosity jostle one another, the anguish of departure and the excitement of arrival comprise a volatile mix of contradictory feelings. Adults may become highly agitated or strangely inarticulate as they endeavor to hide the full impact of the disaster from themselves and their children. But of course it cannot be hidden.

At the same time, this involuntary pilgrimage is crammed full of fantastic experiences. Along with the poignant internal dirge for the lost home, there is the adventure of new people and places—Berlin, Stockholm, Helsinki, Liverpool, London, New York—each a universe unto itself. And what extremes of human behavior to integrate: on one hand, the horror of the crematoria, on the other, the generosity of countless strangers. For me, school stopped for the duration. Any education now consisted of alighting briefly in some foreign port, unpacking suitcases that contained all our worldly goods, at times being put up with a local family who sought to make our lives a bit easier, and soon packing again before departing for the next harbor.

For half of this long journey, my mother and I were on our own; my father was stranded in Finland waiting for permits and visas that now controlled our fate. Always extremely close, my mother and I developed an almost symbiotic dependency on one another, an "us" against the world feeling that helped us survive.

We left England for the United States on a rickety, antiquated, overcrowded ship in which cabins for one were shared by four to six people. The journey seemed endless, and yet we did not really want it to end. People went out of their way to be helpful and solicitous; I had the run of the ship, and my mother, as usual, charmed everyone.

And then, at last, America, the golden land, came into view and with it freedom, safety, opportunity. At the dock, a troop of relatives waited, excited to meet us and take us home. And as I watched the garland of lights of the magnificent George Washington Bridge from the car speeding along the highway, I thought it a wonderful symbol of our new life.

A New World Looms

If luxury, high culture, and grand horizons were the key themes of our Viennese existence, deprivation and uncertainty marked the early days of life in America. Within five years, my family would have to be counted an American success story, but that was impossible to imagine then.

For one thing, with my father waiting for a visa in Finland, my mother became the sole support of the household. I did not then but do now marvel at her transformation from a pampered, fashionable lady of leisure to a hardworking, uncomplaining wage earner as a coat and suit model in Manhattan's garment district. Before her marriage, she had worked in the theater for some years, but with the wedding bells went any career aspirations she might have entertained. When my father finally joined us a year or so later, she had already established a base. Henceforth, I saw both of them struggle to expand it. As immigrant poverty made way for growing affluence, our residences changed from the most dilapidated rooming houses to more spacious and attractive apartments. And slowly, I saw them piece together a life in exile, by joining with other hardworking refugees to recreate some semblance of the lives they had left behind. Meeting at one another's houses or in a cafeteria they pretended was a café, they reminisced incessantly about the lost homeland. They were thereby able to share the fate of being permanent outsiders in a country for which they felt an immense gratitude but in which they would never feel completely at home. I noticed then, and hold it to be still true, that if one's childhood has not been spent in a society, one cannot fully belong to it. Still, my parents managed to learn the language fluently, make friends, socialize with relatives, and gradually cease the endless comparison of the new with the old.

Becoming a Native

By contrast, I rapidly became a "native." I learned to speak without an accent, absorbed the lore and legends of an American childhood, and moved through a succession of schools that ranged from inner-city public schools to the remarkable Hunter High School, accessible only to those who passed a difficult, citywide exam. In this way, it was like a private school for the academically gifted.

As is true for immigrants generally, the young gain a power base not available to the adult generation as they learn the new rules and ropes earlier and better and become emissaries to the new world. This also makes it possible to escape parental control, as the following story illustrates. My first U.S. school was an overcrowded inner-city public school composed of two groups, neither of whom I could relate to: one was largely working class with no interest in learning, and the other, likewise uninterested in learning, consisted of wealthy children bent on conspicuous consumption. Feeling isolated from both, barely understanding English, and bored with lessons that struck me as simplistic, I took matters into my own hands. Since I loved the movies, I decided to go to the movies instead of school. Daily, I took my small allowance (supplemented by tiny earnings for this or that errand) and walked some forty blocks each way to the heart of Manhattan to enter the magical world of a Paramount or a Roxy movie house. Often I got in without having to pay even the small sum of a ticket, and no one seemed to wonder what a ten-year-old was doing there at 9:00 A.M. on a weekday.

In addition to seeing the same film and the live intermission musical diversion three and even four times per day, I learned about the world (I thought), and above all I learned English. While school was boring and unrewarding, this was "real" life and excitement. The only problem was that my parents thought that I was in school. My response to their daily question, "How was school today, Dear?" was unvarying, "Fine. American schools are easy." Naturally this double life could not last. Judgment Day came in the form of a truant officer who exposed the deed one afternoon when I was carrying on my romance with Jimmy Cagney or Charles Boyer.

It is to my parents' everlasting credit that instead of punishing their wayward child, they sat down to learn what would prompt a child who had loved school and had flourished in it to so adamantly turn her back on it. I explained as best I could that I did not find schoolwork stimulating, that I felt out of place there, that I was embarrassed by my lack of English, and that I had not told them because I did not think they could do anything about it. Although both of my parents were visibly distressed, they were not at all angry. All they sought was to get me back into the fold. They succeeded by enlisting the assistance of the school and its remarkable principal. Upon hearing my story, this extraordinary woman offered to meet with me every morning, before her workday began, to teach anything I wanted to learn. Without hesitation I chose the Greek myths, and by way of this unusual detour and thanks to her generosity, I turned my attention permanently back to school. Soon thereafter, I became the top student of my class, the delight of the teachers, and, at last, at ease among my peers. Thus, from personal experience, I had come to understand how one could choose delinquency over learning and how little it really takes to get a child back on track—or off it.

Lessons Formal and Informal

As I reflect on my formal schooling up to that point I am struck by its high quality despite its disruptions and discontinuities. From the village school, with its high valuation of school performance despite the nonacademic destination of most of its pupils, to the Rudolf Steiner School in Vienna, with its holistic philosophical orientation, and finally to the intellectually competitive Hunter High School, with its superb teachers, I was exposed to a first-class education. Except for the high school and later, Hunter College, the schools I attended had students and teachers of both sexes. And in none of them did I receive a message that education was not for women. To the contrary, learning and the development of one's talents were viewed as desirable goals for everyone. The message that came through in diverse ways was that education mattered as an end in itself, not for a degree or a career, but for its intrinsic qualities. A mind was to be nurtured, and it was every child's responsibility to learn and to grow, a goal I took as my own.

Still, the message was not without its contradictions for a female child, considering the counter message from society and the fact that few of the mothers, aunts, and grandmothers one knew or observed were bent on developing their own talents. But, then, mixed messages are not unusual in childhood, and this permitted me to select the message I favored, namely, to follow the banner of self-development and intellectual growth.

My parents were surprised at the direction of my interests. They had envisioned my choosing writing or music, in which I had shown talent as a child, or perhaps the theater, my mother's arena. Instead, I was developing into an intellectual. Here, too, for the first time I noticed some ambivalence on the part of my mother, who had stopped school at age fifteen. My father, on the other hand, was ready to support the genesis of an intellectual peer in the family. What if he had not? Would I have persisted or would I have yielded to my mother's (and the society's) latent message not to aim for a career but for marriage and maternity? I suspect not. Both of my parents had a nondirective approach to childrearing. The major questions I remember hearing from them were "What do you think?" "What would you like?" "How do you feel?" They never dictated; they never usurped my feelings or views. There were some obvious rules, but beyond these they valued, both for themselves and for me, a spirit of independence. Hence, I expect that my choice for the life of the mind would have been as it was.

Choice is one thing, opportunity is another. It was my great and good fortune, given my limited economic resources, that there was a Hunter College for me to attend. Not only was it affordable but it had high scholastic standards; an excellent cadre of professors, many of them Europeans; and a first-rate reputation. In addition, there were all the resources of New York City, including that grand institution, the New York Public Library, where I spent many weekends devouring books.

The student body at Hunter, all-female at the time, comprised a wide range of talents and backgrounds. Nearly all had part-time, or even full-time, jobs, as did I. They were committed to obtaining an education, and they were grateful for the opportunity to do so. It was there, as I indicated earlier, that I found sociology, and it was from there that I embarked on graduate work at Columbia University.

Graduate School

Columbia's sociology department in the 1950s was a major center of intellectual enterprise with a roster of luminaries that included Robert McIver, Kingsley Davis, C. Wright Mills, Robert S. Lynd, and a young S. M. Lipset, among others. Its preeminent stars, however, were Paul F. Lazarsfeld and Robert K. Merton, whose collaboration constituted the centerpiece of our training. The passwords for students were theory and research, research and theory, which each luminary exemplified in quite distinctive ways. Lazarsfeld, an original and inventive mind, was a social psychologist with a bent for mathematics, who sought to discover empirical regularities of human behavior and operational measures for them. He was also a gifted entrepreneur successful at building far-flung professional networks and research institutes, the most famous of which was the Bureau of Applied Social Research. In that sense, the ex-Viennese was closer to the American temper as a problem solver and a builder. Merton, younger by a decade, was paradoxically more like the traditional European scholar, steeped in history and social theory. His fine analytic abilities, combined with a penchant for subtle conceptual distinctions, were linked to a magnetic lecturing style that attracted generations of students far and wide. They came year after year, some even after having launched their own professional careers, seeking in vain to capture his elusive magic.

Although trying hard to be a team, the two luminaries had quite different working styles and modes of relating to their students. Together they were an awesome force, somewhat like adored but unattainable parents for whose attention the student-siblings vied ceaselessly. Brilliant and inspiring models though they were, under the pressure of deadlines, expanding professional demands, and their own formidable ambitions, they could also be capricious, moody, and inaccessible. We all endowed them with enormous power over us, and for many years they were the measure of our professional worth.

First-year students rarely came to their attention, for they were concentrating on simply learning the ABCs, but a select few second- and third-year students might get assistantships, and the chosen ones carried a permanent aura of the elect. I set out and almost succeeded in taking every course offered and then sought, and obtained, apprenticeships with both the great and the lesser stars in my graduate career.

Social stratification was from the start my chief interest, as both my master's thesis ("Food Habits and Social Class") and my Ph.D dissertation ("The American Business Elite") would later reflect, and true to my earlier education, I explored this domain from multiple perspectives. I took courses with a number of teachers outside the department, among them Franz Neumann, Herbert Marcuse, and Alfred Kroeber. I also sought any and all research opportunities both to earn money and to add to my stock of skills. Here, Columbia students had the singular advantage of the Bureau of Applied Social Research, where apprentices could learn the craft on a variety of projects. I remember throwing myself into first one, then another, project with enthusiasm, often burning the midnight oil. When I was not busy learning to use fourfold tables, content analysis, questionnaire design, and data exploration, I devoured texts. Up to this point, my being a woman was not a drawback and may even have been something of an advantage, given the visibility of the minority of women among the male majority. In some respects, however, I did reflect a gender-linked naivete, I think. For one, I gave no thought to a career. I just assumed that I eventually would put my skills to good use. Nor did I have any inkling, as I was certainly to have later, that brainpower, and woman's brainpower in particular, could be exploited. So I worked on things without worrying about getting credit or letting others do so. I also had a somewhat cavalier attitude to my early work, imagining that I would always remember every word I had written since I knew it by heart at the time of submission. As a result, I did not build up a bibliography until much later, and so a number of items were actually lost. I marveled at my teachers and at the great works of sociology, carrying on many an internal dialogue with Durkheim, Weber, Mannheim, St. Simon, Montesquieu, the Encyclopedist, and Marx, among others.

My one and only ambition at the time was to master the essentials and then to pass the feared oral examination for the Ph.D. Two-and-one-half years after the start of graduate work, I presented myself before my committee, consisting of Theodore Abel, Paul F. Lazarsfeld, R. K. Merton, and, for my minor in social psychology, Otto Klineberg. I remember working feverishly through the night to absorb yet another crumb of knowledge before the appointed day. I entered the chamber that contained my destiny, nervous from lack of sleep and much more confident of my knowledge than of my ability to express it. It was a long and challenging two hours, at the end of which the test of fire had been met.

A number of job offers now came my way for which I was grateful, but which I refused. The time had come, I decided, to broaden my experience, and with the hubris of youth and no job prospects I embarked for Paris. I was twenty-three years old and, true to Thomas's four wishes, eager for new experience.

To Paris and Back

When I arrived in Paris after a six-day ocean voyage, I had very little money and even fewer acquaintances. Determined to make it on my own, I found myself again in what was to become a repeat pattern in my life: striking out on a new path without knowing where it would lead. My French was minimal, and except for a few swains I had met on the boat and a few names of friends of friends, I knew no one. The moments of anxiety were dispelled by the euphoria of being in the most beautiful city in the world. I followed any and all job leads, and, after a few months of scrimping and eating sparsely, I landed what would turn out to be the perfect job for me because it drew on my research and language skills, involved travel, and focused on an interesting topic: French, Dutch, German, and Benelux receptivity to the Common Market (a precursor of today's European Community). The project culminated in a lengthy, widely circulated report, my first published article ("Reference Groups in France" [1953]) and to subsequent jobs in other parts of Europe, all of which broadened my perspective on *la comedie humaine*.

Around this time, pressure began to be exerted independently by two important figures in my life, my father and Paul F. Lazarsfeld, to the effect that life experience was all to the good but not at the price of a Ph.D. In truth, I had more or less decided to abandon the doctorate, for in my view, I had gotten what I wanted from my graduate work. In other words, I still had no notion of a career, as indicated by a conversation between myself and Kingsley Davis, my professor in demography prior to his departure for Berkeley. When he asked me about my future plans, I told him I really did not have any, and I just wanted to become a very good sociologist. "Well," he said, "that's because you're a woman. Men always make definite career plans early on." That observation has stayed with me through the years. I think he was right, certainly for me. An interesting life, doing sociology, exploring human behavior, advancing causes I believed in—these were my goals at the time. Of course I expected to earn a living, but I wasn't very particular about how or where, provided it was interesting work and used my skills. Of one thing I was sure in my mid-twenties: I did not want to teach. For the rest, I sought to keep my options open.

I probably would have continued my open-ended journey following this or that bend in the road, grasping opportunities as they arose and improvising along the way, but the alarm signals from father and professor grew louder. The message varied according to its sender, but the point was clear: "Don't become an international floater being exploited as a permanent female assistant by a male boss, director, or supervisor. As a woman you need that union card. Come back and get your Ph.D." And so with several years of self-support in Europe behind me, I was persuaded by their arguments, and returned to Columbia to go the last mile—the Ph.D dissertation.

One of Paul F. Lazarsfeld's many virtues was his availability to students and the support he generously extended to those who worked with him. Since he had pressed hard for my return, he now put me in touch with people who could be helpful to me. Among them was a historian, William Miller, who was looking for someone with my training and interests in stratification to work with him on a massive study of the American business elite. After several lengthy discussions, I agreed to interview, code, and analyze over one thousand dossiers of the nation's top corporate executives over the century and to put these fascinating data into written form. Supported by a grant and several part-time jobs, I spent twelve-to-fourteen-hour days in my charming one-room apartment in an old brownstone house to complete the analysis and first draft some eight months later. Up to that point, my thesis advisor, R. K. Merton, had hardly been involved in the process, but with a first draft in hand he went into high gear and worked with me step by step, giving generously of his precious time to help me shape the final product. My chief deficiency at the time was not in extracting meaning from a vast amount of data but in rendering it in readable prose without violating its complexity. To have the benefit of such a brilliant mind at close range was extraordinary. His exceptional ability to express sociological findings in felicitous language was a lasting source of inspiration.

Naturally, given Merton's perfectionism, I had to rework long sections, add yet another historic reference, rethink yet again a particular conclusion, and rewrite until the master approved. Somewhere between his perfectionism and my impatience, the thesis was completed and successfully defended. My career was launched in spite of myself. A Columbia degree was in those days a passport to professional opportunities, and for a decade thereafter I worked in a great variety of settings. Among them was the Center of International Studies at MIT, the department of psychiatry at New York Medical College; a first teaching position at Brandeis, followed by one at Vassar. Those years saw the publication of many articles and book reviews and of *Beyond the Ruling Class* (1963), my first book.

Greece

And then one day, in the 1960s while on a brief vacation in the Greek Islands, I promptly lost my heart to Greece. Armed with a Fulbright grant, I packed up my worldly goods and set forth once again for an unknown land whose language I did not know and whose alphabet I could not even read. I was assigned to a Greek-based international planning firm whose director was a visionary architect-planner by the name of C. A. Doxiadis. His goal was nothing less than to transform the design of human settlements and to put planning on a scientific basis. To this end, he created a school and a research institute to which flocked architects, planners, and apprentices from all over the world. He also instituted a yearly international symposium, the Delos Symposium, where notables in architecture and planning as well as in business, academe, government, the arts, and film met to exchange ideas—on a yacht that sailed the Greek Islands—and to create new visions of human habitats.

My role in this complex undertaking was to supply the sociological perspective to the discourse as well as to educate future architects and planners. To do this properly, I followed a program in architecture and design, which added a whole new dimension to my work. The entire experience was unique in manifold ways and enriched all who participated in it, not least because of the complexity of Doxiadis himself—thinker, planner, impresario, evangelist, and builder rolled into one.

Princeton, Women, and Men

Five years after I had created a very rewarding life in Greece, Princeton University beckoned and, eager to touch home base, I accepted a visiting appointment for one semester. This one semester turned into a lifetime. Although Princeton was still an all-male institution at the time, the department nonetheless sought a permanent appointment for me. And thanks to the skillful strategies of the then chairman, C. F. Westoff, precedent was shattered in 1968, when I was appointed to tenure several years before the advent of coeducation.

In retrospect, the pandemonium that greeted my appointment must have reflected an implicit agreement with Dr. Samuel Johnson's infamous comment about women preachers. He likened a woman preacher to a dog walking on its hind legs, the issue being not how well she does it but that she does it at all. The publicity generated by Princeton's decision to break through the gender barrier was stupefying. I was hounded by photographers and by the ringing of the telephone at all hours for interviews. I learned to appreciate the desperation celebrities must feel when there is no place to hide. A woman at Princeton!!!, accompanied by a barrage of mental exclamation points, followed me for months. What better proof that Dr. Johnson's smug sally still had bite. What better proof of a secret ranking of gender capacity and the androcentric yardstick used to sustain it. In that light, the sociology department's unanimous invitation to me was pace-setting indeed.

To return to a point made earlier, in a curious way, being the token woman in a man's world could be a plus if that token woman managed to combine a conventional "feminine" style with unconventional feminine performance. This combination could elicit admiration for the individual woman and thereby mask the deflation of the gender. Thus, it is generally not the first or the only woman invader of the masculine terrain who sets off the panic buttons but the tenth, twentieth, and hundredth woman. The first is seen as an anomaly, unusual or peculiar, but the nth is perceived as a threat.

As a novice professional and a woman in the 1950s, I knew instinctively that to succeed in the "men's house" I had to act the woman at some points and the man at others. Also, as I look back on my peers, I believe that the women were held to a higher standard.

Of course some men were threatened and resented us for perceived favoritism, superior performance, or our just being there. And of course there was some sexual harassment at parties where alcohol dissolved the civilized male veneer. I should also emphasize that in both graduate school and later on the job, it was generally the less gifted and less successful men who had the greatest difficulty accepting women as equals, and it was most often they who were overtly patronizing or resentful of their presence. But basically, and contrary to the retrospective assessments of then and now, I experienced male teachers, supervisors, colleagues, and fellow students as supportive more often than hostile. The academic and professional subculture that valued intellectual achievement and merit helped women who excelled just as it hurt men who did not.

If a woman (writ small) felt confident, able to withstand the stereotypical discounting of Woman (writ large), could cope with the unwanted (as distinct from the wanted) sexual overtures, and was determined to succeed, she had a reasonable chance to do so. But keep in mind the special social conditions that made this the case: The women were a tiny minority who excelled in but did not challenge the system and who sought to prove their worth by living up to its demands in excess of expectations. Still, rarely, if ever, would the luster of achievement eclipse the hidden yardstick of gender.

Gender Identity and Role Models

By way of conclusion, I would like to say a word about gender identity and role models. For most children, their parents are their primary role models, both negative and positive, in the early years of childhood. In my case, I had two sets of parents, and so I not only had a more complex set of identities to absorb but quite different gender models at an early age. In that contrast, too, there was a measure of freedom. My peasant mother was the original earth mother who kept everyone and everything going. My peasant father was a shoemaker on whose knees I would perch to watch him transform multicolored skins into sturdy shoes for the villagers. He was gentle and retiring, while she was forceful and enterprising. Although there were no obvious manifestations of rank, she was to my child's eyes clearly the dominant one. Their union was peaceful, and household arrangements seemed to fit their talents and temperaments.

What a contrast to my parents in Vienna! Here the man was the dominant partner. He held direct power and controlled the purse strings; she proceeded by indirection and manipulation. Her main task was to oversee the domestic enterprise (not to do housework) and to create an agreeable, attractive atmosphere, which she did graciously and with considerable flair. But most important in my recall is that before the exile, she sought power and validation via her beauty and glamour and the male admiration it aroused. Here, then, the image before me was quite sharply gender-divided. I cannot tell what impact this would have had had this been my only model, but having an alternative permitted me to extend the symbolic boundaries of gender and incorporate its attributes selectively. I do recall being aware quite early that men held power formally and that the public facade stressed a definite gender hierarchy. At the same time, women often took actual charge and simulated a dependency and obeisance they did not really feel.

All in all, I did not see either sex to have an absolute advantage over the other. Both men and women seemed bound to role obligations, and although the cultural favoritism gave men a visible edge, to me they always seemed much less powerful or secure than their roles decreed.

I should also mention that in important respects, the man-woman question took on a sharper edge in the United States than in the European countries with which I was familiar. There, there was a kind of tongue-in-cheek attitude, among women especially, that softened the categorical divide and a secret woman's world from which men were excluded. In the United States, by contrast, the gender divide seemed more rigid, unyielding, and literal, and both sexes seemed more poised for the conflict that would be unleashed by the stunning impact of the women's liberation movement. As was true for millions of women worldwide, this movement expanded my own horizons, and I worked assiduously at the university, in the profession, and in the local community to introduce change. I like to think of the women's liberation movement as my generation's gift to the generations to follow.

In my own case, my peripatetic existence could not have occurred had I embarked on the traditional path of marriage and a family. And since every choice involves trade-offs, mine was not to have children. At the time I saw no way of fulfilling two such demanding commitments. Had I not been well-launched in a career in my twenties, I might have made a different choice; or perhaps if I had been born a generation later, I might have been able to combine them. But lacking a support group (and not even knowing I lacked it), I could not even imagine two such antithetical paths converging peaceably. I assumed I had to choose between them.

Indeed, as is still true for women with strong professional commitments, I found it difficult to integrate romance and vocation. My typical pattern was an either-or format, either immersion in romance or in work, but rarely the two simultaneously. When romance took center stage, work was put on the back burner. When work, usually a major piece of writing, was the focus, romance receded. Freud supposedly saw the ability to love and to work as critical for human existence. It is not clear whether he meant pursuing these simultaneously or alternatively. For me they came in zig-zag.

In part, this reflected an assumption, widely shared at the time, that, for women, a serious vocation meant the sacrifice of alternative goals. Fortunately, the sacrifice was not complete or permanent. In time, I would have stepchildren and now, grandchildren, to cherish. And for two decades I have been very happily and harmoniously joined with a remarkable man who has helped me combine love and work in a way I once thought impossible.

Conclusion

In offering this bird's-eye view of my "journey to Ithaca," I have become aware of a number of themes, heretofore implicit, about my stance toward life as a drama in motion—open-ended, unpredictable, ever poised for surprise. The drama contained tragedy and sorrow, of course, but also joy. And being a woman at this historic juncture had a special momentum of its own. On the one hand, one had to become skilled at deflecting the often outrageous arrows of male chauvinism, especially if, as in my case, one chose an unconventional or nontraditional way of life. On the other hand, however, being something of a maverick has meant that I was freer to improvise and experiment than would a man in my place. (Men tend to get roped into definite tracks early and firmly.)

Sociology was a splendid professional choice for me. Socrates' commandment "know thyself," an exemplary goal for individuals, is relevant for sociology, too, for at its best it is a means to collective self-knowledge. This is perhaps more the case in Europe than in the United States, a less reflective culture and one impatient with abstract ideas. But with the accelerated pace of contemporary technical and moral change, the sociological imagination is likely to be ever more in demand in the coming years.

Sociology is also generous in its inclusiveness, which has permitted someone like myself, more fox then hedgehog, to follow a serendipitous rather than a single-minded course. Thus, I have worked and published in some five different subfields, and I have reached very diversified and seemingly unconnected audiences. But a connection is there, at least in my mind. And one of my central questions, formed when I saw illiterate proles overthrow a civilization that claimed some affinity with the Enlightenment, has focused on the nature of social hierarchy and its origins, persistence, and impact, with special emphasis on the top rungs where the essence of the social system is distilled. The sociological house has many mansions and, at this still early phase of systematic probing for the secretes of the sociological universe, no single key as yet unlocks those secrets. We must, I believe, cast our net wide and deep.

Sociology has also made it possible for me to combine theory and praxis in a fruitful way, to bring the ivory tower of intellectual discourse in contact with arenas of action. In this regard, Robert Lynd's "Knowledge for What?" which made a deep impression when I first read it many years ago, continues to be a persistent refrain. Thus, by all these highways and byways, the depths and the heights of this mortal coil, the peasant and the cosmopolite have been joined, and the art and the life become one.

Suzanne Keller

◧◧ Nine ◧

Sociologist by Default
Reflections on Past Choices
and Future Goals

Martha E. Gimenez

Existence is the process whereby the hitherto meaningless takes on meaning. —Maurice Merleau-Ponty, *Sense and Non-Sense*

I credit my love of learning and the written word to my grandmother, who taught me to recite poems and to read when I was four, and my love for argumentation and politics to my father, who shared with me his political frustrations and dreams from the time I was old enough to listen. To my mother I credit my ability to love, to endure, to survive.

I was born in Argentina, where I grew up, went to high school during the 1950s, and, later studied law. At the time I entered law school, sociology as a profession did not exist at the University of Cordoba. One of my first courses was "The Sociology of Law,"[1] but it gave me few clues to what sociology was all about. This essay is about how I, brought up in a middle-class, Catholic, politically conservative family, ended up becoming a feminist sociologist specializing in Marxist theory and working in the United States. Of my career, my professional specialization, my political views, and my current place of residence, none is the product of a direct conscious choice. They comprise the cumulative results of many other choices that, at the time, seemed wholly unrelated. Hence the quotation from Merleau-Ponty, which I came across in a seminar on ethnomethodology (taught by Harold Garfinkel at UCLA) and found enormously appealing. It is like a revelation of sorts that time and again has made me aware of the dialectics of patterns and randomness. I believe individual lives are defined by those dialectics.

In the sections that follow, I discuss some aspects of my education in Argentina, the circumstances of my coming to the United States in 1960 to study political science, and my discovery of sociology after my return to Argentina in 1962. I end by examining some of the connections between my background and experiences, and my intellectual and personal development.

From Argentina to Missoula, Montana; From Law Student to Sorority Girl

I grew up in a medium-sized city. Cordoba was founded in the 1500s; it has a university that dates from 1613, several interesting churches, and a lovely cathedral. I entered law school when I was nineteen, in 1957. Like all my friends (male and female), I took higher education for granted. Studying law was, to me, as unremarkable as having finished high school, and I do not remember having any special feelings about becoming a university student. My main interest was international law. Argentina's chronic border conflicts with its neighbors have always been decided by foreign arbitrators whose decisions have often been perceived as contrary to Argentina's interests. I wanted, therefore, to become the kind of expert who could defend Argentina's interests in international disputes.

Entering law school was not an unusual choice for women in Argentina at that time. It was and still is very common for women to be lawyers. One of my mother's sisters was a lawyer; the other was a professor of mathematics. Several of my friends studied law. Others studied engineering, dentistry, architecture, medicine, biochemistry, and pharmacy. Only two studied psychology and literature, fields of study that are more associated with women in the United States. I grew up in an environment where professional women were not considered exceptional.

It is true that primarily upper- and middle-class women attended the university, but, since state universities were free, working-class men and women could, with sacrifices, become professionals. In fact, many did. Many years later, as I reflected about this with a mind informed by sociological and feminist insights, I realized that women's intellectual space did not by any means entail full equality. Limited as it was and is, that space is real. At the time I was growing up, those limitations were not visible to me, and my sense of freedom knew no limits. Furthermore, the fact that I never had the chance to work in Argentina deprived me of experiences that might have led me to develop a less positive perception of what growing up female in Argentina was like. My family and my friends' families always encouraged learning, but they did it without defining it as something out of the ordinary. Our career goals were treated as natural expressions of who we were. I cannot give substantive reasons why education was equally valued for sons and daughters in the setting in which I grew up. Nora Scott Kinzer (1973) suggests that Argentine women's educational aspirations might be the effect of massive European immigration and immigrants' desire to see their children succeed. While I was in high school, the issue was not whether I would have a university education, but what kind it would be. Father, in fact, was a bit disappointed when I chose law because it was such a common career choice. He cheered up when I told him about my interest in international law, and he even dreamed of my pursuing a career in diplomacy.

Besides the supporting immediate environment, the fact that I grew up during the first presidency of Juan Peron (1945–1955) may have been an important contributing factor in shaping my outlook and self-image as a woman. Searching for information about what was actually happening in those years, I found out that women's attendance at the university, if compared to the 1931–1940 decade, increased substantially during the 1940s and 1950s. For political reasons far removed from modern feminist concerns, the Peronist government sanctioned the 1947 law that granted the vote to women; introduced women's rights in the reformed Constitution of 1949; and made considerable efforts to incorporate women, especially working-class women, into politics. Argentine governments had always maintained a very conservative attitude toward women regardless of their growing presence in the labor force, where they occupied a secondary position in traditional women's jobs (for example, elementary and high school teachers, typists, clerks, secretaries). Peron, who in 1943 was the secretary of the Department of Labor and Welfare, understood the political significance of women's labor-force participation, and he capitalized on it. In 1944, he created the first Women's Division of Labor and Assistance, stating that, as "more than 900,000 Argentine women are part of the paid work force in all kinds of jobs and professions . . . it is our duty to morally and materially dignify their efforts" (Hollander 1973, 150–51). Among the goals Peron outlined at the time were "improvements and implementation in protective legislation and a law establishing women's right to equal pay for equal work" (Hollander, 1973, 151). The Peronist party had a women's branch, and women were elected to serve in provincial legislatures and in Congress. Eva Peron was highly visible and indefatigable. Through the foundation named after her, she did a great deal to help the working class, particularly needy women and their children.

I was fourteen years old when she died in 1952, at the age of thirty-three.

As a child and as an adolescent I was fascinated by her beauty and her activities. She traveled widely and I have vague memories of newsreels that showed her visiting the Pope or European heads of state. While the environment that surrounded me encouraged me to believe that I could do anything I wanted to do, I think this belief was strengthened by Eva Peron's powerful personality, by her passionate involvement in politics, and by her public-speaking skills. She addressed crowds without faltering and I, always shy in front of strangers, admired that more than anything else. It was only as I grew older that I learned about her flaws and her ruthlessness toward her enemies. Looking back now as a sociologist, I think it would not be far-fetched to assume that, regardless of her politics, she must have had a substantial impact on most Argentine women of my generation, thus strengthening the effect of other structural and ideological supports for women's aspirations. She was a charismatic woman, living proof that women could be powerful, assertive, and active in public life. Although she attained power through her relationship to General Peron and only later developed a power base of her own, such facts were inaccessible to me as a very young person. What impressed me, as it must have impressed countless other women who were children or teenagers during the time of her brief appearance in Argentina's political life, was her presence. Whatever her personal flaws, she was an extraordinary role model, even though, in my youth, I simply took her for granted.

I have since learned that gender inequality is indeed present in Argentina; it creates problems for all women regardless of educational levels. But that knowledge came much later. Throughout my adolescence and early adulthood I was unaware of women's unequal status. While I had self-doubts and hesitations like everyone else these were, in my mind, unrelated to the fact that I was a woman. Therefore, I never thought of my gender as an impediment to anything that I might want to learn, do, or become. When I was twelve, I read a biography of Marie Curie and, for a while, I toyed with the idea of studying science and making an important discovery myself. Being a woman was, of course, an important part of my identity, but it was not the most salient one; social class and nationality were more prominent and, to some extent, they still are.

Today in the United States, where class politics have been supplanted by the politics of identity, the salience of gender as a core identity that supplants others is taken for granted by scholars and lay persons alike. In my view, such an identity necessitates specific historical conditions to emerge and become dominant, conditions that social scientists have yet to identify in all their complexity. Before the women's movement, I never thought of myself primarily as a woman (that is, in abstraction from other dimensions of life) except in the context of my personal relationships with men. In the university, I thought of myself first as a student and later as a professor and as a sociologist. I did not think of myself as a "woman student" who was bound to find life more difficult because of her gender.

While I was in law school, I also attended classes at the Institute of Cultural Exchange between Argentina and the United States. I was encouraged to apply for an Institute of International Education fellowship. I applied to study political science because that seemed the closest field to law. My application was successful. The one-year fellowship included airfare, tuition at Montana State University in Missoula, Montana, and room and board in Sigma Kappa Sorority.

It was quite a change to go from a large city and a large university (more than forty-five thousand students) to a tiny university (about five thousand students) in a tiny town. The year was 1960. I was twenty-two years old, older than my sorority sisters who were eager to meet me and whom I found rather intimidating and confusing at the beginning. There is nothing in Argentina comparable to the sorority/fraternity system, and I was totally unprepared for it. I thought we were going to be robbed during the first panty raid. I was told never to confide in anyone that I had studied law in Argentina because nobody would believe me and I might not get any dates if the dreadful truth were to be known. My sorority sisters seemed more interested in the fact that I was old enough to buy beer than in most other things about myself. Thanks to the housemother's lessons, I learned, among other things, how to pick up matches or anything else from the floor "like a lady." Looking back, I can laugh. But my early days were not easy, especially because I had difficulty in understanding spoken English. In Argentina, my teachers had taught me reading rather than speaking skills, and I was unprepared for the variety of accents I encountered.

Student life was indeed different! In Cordoba, I met with friends after classes (which were, for the most part, in the evening) to discuss, besides our lessons and related matters, politics and poetry. We drank espresso in smoke-filled cafes. We read Neruda, Garcia Lorca, Eluard, Rimbaud, Baudelaire, and Apollinaire, with passion. We read Sartre and Simone de Beauvoir and Heidegger, and we diagnosed ourselves afflicted with metaphysical angst. We eagerly followed national and international events. In Missoula, women students worried about fashion, dates, and little else, while boys focused on girls, sports, and drink. At home, while interest in the opposite sex and, among the women, fashion were taken for granted, we gave primacy in our conversations to films, novels, poetry and, above all, politics. I was therefore struck by the generally apolitical stance of my American classmates, males and females. I found foreign students more congenial for they, no matter where they were from, shared with me this overriding concern with politics. Of course, had I been in a more cosmopolitan university setting, my experiences would have been very different.

Besides political science, I studied history. I read some C. Wright Mills for one of my social history of the United States courses, something that would later influence my education. I was given additional aid by the university, and I stayed for a second year. The school gave me enough credits based on my law studies in Argentina to enable me to graduate in spring 1962 with a B.A. in political science and history. I returned to Argentina soon after graduation.

From Law to Sociology

It was not easy to fit into Argentine society again. I missed the personal freedom I experienced in the United States. Women of my generation and social class growing up in Argentina had less personal freedom than comparable American women; we were more closely supervised by our families and the community. But we had greater intellectual freedom, for we were psychologically free to make educational and career choices that seemed unthinkable to the women I had met in the United States as an undergraduate.

I tried to continue with my law studies, but I found them increasingly boring and difficult. To the consternation of my family, I drifted about for several months until I learned about the creation, at the University of Cordoba, of a master's-level program in sociology that was open to graduates of any discipline. I had no clear idea about what sociology was, through I had some inklings based on my readings of C. Wright Mills. I applied, was accepted, and so started my studies in sociology out of the need to do something with myself, without really knowing where I was going.

The sociology education I received in Cordoba was provided by several Argentine professors with Ph.D.s from Europe or the United States (Berkeley, Columbia, Indiana) and a few American professors with Fulbright fellowships or other sources of funding. Some names come to mind: Rose Coser, Alex Inkeles, David Nasatir, Aaron Ciccourel, Melvin De Fleur, Delbert Miller, but there were others. The program was experimental, and it had fewer than twenty students. Men and women studied together without self-consciousness.

I remember those days with both pleasure and pain. I was visiting my parents during the fatal winter of 1976. The struggle between the new military junta and urban guerrillas was intense; there were numerous violent encounters, and the number of the dead, the kidnapped, and the "disappeared" began to mount. I read in a newspaper that one of my former fellow students was among those detained for having "subversive literature" at home and using it to teach. The books listed in the paper were harmless sociology texts, such as Ralph Dahrendorf's and Max Weber's works. As far as I know, he was never seen again. We used to meet to study at his home, where his wife would give us coffee and we would play with and fuss over their lovely baby.

The sociology we learned was standard American sociology enriched with large doses of Weber. We never studied Marx; the program director characterized Marxism as a monocausal economic determinism. There were, among the students, some economists who had read Marx and who questioned the cursory dismissal of his work. Those students constantly argued that sociology could not adequately explain social change, class struggles, imperialism, and the distortion of our economies.

For us, imperialism, social class, class struggles, class interests, oligarchic power, and exploitation were not just "analytical categories" with varying degrees of academic legitimacy. They were ordinary terms that were encountered in everyday political discourse and a commonsense understanding of Argentine and Latin American reality. I lived in a country where coup d'états and rumors of military uprising were ordinary events; where class issues and conflicts of interest were out in the open; where strikes, including general strikes, were commonplace; and where students' political activism and organization mirrored, to some extent, the class cleavages of the society as a whole. I began to realize, as time went on, that the sociology to which I was so committed had a limited scope. There was a gap between our methodological (for example, public opinion, survey research, focalized interviews) and theoretical (for example, Parsons, Merton, modernization theory) studies and the macro-level economic and political issues that mattered to us.

Back to the United States: Learning Sociology in the Late 1960s

I completed my studies, and I earned a certificate equivalent to a master's degree. The Institute's director advised me to get a Ph.D. to improve my chances in the academic market. He indicated that I would be welcome to work at the Institute in the future. I decided to return to the United States. I had visited California during the summer of 1961, and I wished to return to familiar territory. I chose to attend UCLA. Since education in the United States is expensive, I came as an immigrant so that I could work to support myself while going to school. I began graduate school in the fall of 1967. It never occurred to me that graduate work and a Ph.D. were something out of the ordinary for a woman, either in Argentina or in the United States. The presence of many women in my cohort at UCLA reinforced my sense of the commonplace nature of my career choice.

Today many of us look back to "the sixties" with nostalgia, surrounding them with a romantic aura and yearning for a return to heady days of demonstrations, "happenings," political activism, and an exhilarating sense of being alive. As a foreigner, it took me some time to learn about the controversial nature of the Vietnam War and arrive at an understanding of the reasons why it was so bitterly opposed by so many. In the meantime, I observed and sometimes participated in what was going on without thinking that those were exceptional years. Like most everyone I knew, I took in the spirit of youthful California, dressed outlandishly, and had great fun. Because of what my experiences growing up in Argentina had taught me, I perceived the mobilization and political organization of American students during the late 1960s and early 1970s as a sign that they were finally learning their politics, something that Latin American students of my generation took for granted. I figured the time had come for the young to be radical and politically aware in the United States. Consequently, unlike my American friends, I do not perceive the events and experiences of those years as watersheds in my political development, at least not in the profound way in which they remember their politicization. This does not mean that my views remained unchanged; on the contrary, they changed in ways I never anticipated. It happened at UCLA, when I took a course on classical sociological theory, taught by John Horton, and discovered Marx and Marxism.

My interest in Marx was awakened by the power of his prose, the complexity of his thought, and the relevance of his work for understanding how present institutions function. Reading Marx and classical and contemporary Marxist scholarship, I found these writings the antithesis of the "economic determinist" caricature of Marx and Marxism that I had learned in Argentina. Unfortunately, this view is still prevalent in academic circles in the United States. Marxist and neo-Marxist theory and research, I found out, were very useful for making sense of both U.S. and Latin American societies. Thus, without having made a conscious decision, I became increasingly conversant with Marxist theory.

At about this time, I began to hear some women graduate students talk about "women as a minority group." The idea seemed strange to me at first. There were many female graduate students and very few female professors at UCLA at that time, but I had not found the situation remarkable. Looking back upon my graduate student years, I cannot identify instances of blatant sexist behavior toward me. If they happened, I was not aware. I remember asking a friend, at a time in which I was still not sure about what sexism meant, How do we know that someone's behavior is sexist instead of just plain rude? It was in the early 1970s that I began to learn and understand what the women's movement was all about. Although I found most of its claims reasonable, I did not champion the slogan "Sisterhood is powerful," because I could not overlook the fact that women and men did not form homogeneous groups but were divided by social class.

Another important learning experience occurred through the reaction of a Mexican American student to the possibility that I might participate in a research project about Mexican Americans that required Spanish-speaking interviewers. He objected because I was a foreigner. At first, his attitude was incomprehensible to me, for I naively had assumed that there were no substantial differences among Spanish-speaking people, whatever their national origin might be. I was, as it is now obvious to me, terribly ignorant about the realities of race and ethnic relations in this country. I talked with other graduate students about this, and I began to learn about the oppression of Mexican-Americans and Chicanos and about the social, economic, and political implications of minority status. I then understood why the student had reacted that way, and I became aware of the qualitative differences between foreigners like myself and people who had, for generations, been excluded from full participation in this society. I had no idea at the time of the importance of what that incident had taught me and how its lesson would become clear to me later on and would help me develop a theoretical and political understanding of the labels currently used to classify the U.S. population.

Theory and Praxis

I have always been aware of the relationship between my life experiences, my theoretical choices, and my written work. The fact that I became a Marxist sociologist and that my work on feminist theory is outside the mainstream of U.S. feminist thought are, to a large extent, results of the experiences and knowledge acquired growing up as a middle-class Latin American, which led me to identify some of the limitations inherent in universalizing sociological and feminist theoretical perspectives.

Marxist social scientists have to contend with the misperceptions of colleagues and students. In that sense, I am no exception. Many identify Marxism with Stalinism. One of the worst experiences of my life was when I was accused of being a Stalinist by a drunken professor from another department during a faculty party. Many have asked me, upon learning about my theoretical work, whether I "came out" after I was hired. It is very difficult to counter the stereotypes people have formed, within and outside the universities, about what Marxist scholars do. Non-Marxist sociologists and lay people share many assumptions about the way society is put together and how it works (I believe that, with good reason, Pitirim Sorokin [1956] once defined American sociology as "the tortuous elaboration of the painfully obvious" or words to that effect). That is not the case with Marxism; the dominant modes of thought are not dialectical but analytical, and they support a psychologistic and constructivistic view of social reality. Consequently, it is almost impossible to counteract effectively the typical accusations of "class reductionism" and "economic determinism" and convey the complexity and subtlety of Marxist thought in a few "sound bytes."

Again, given the lack of common theoretical assumptions, my relationship with feminism and feminists has never been easy. Marxism makes one very much aware of the historicity of the categories of analysis one uses and skeptical about the value of ahistorical categories and abstract theories of origins. And, as a sociologist, I could not accept theories that seemed to exempt men from social determinations. I could not avoid noticing, therefore, as soon as feminist literature became available, the problems inherent in the use of "women" and "men" as categories of analysis, in the stress on the power of "sisterhood," and in the development of ahistorical theories of "patriarchy." Early feminist works examined the oppression of women without taking fully into account the historical specificity of feminism itself (that is, the conditions under which people would self-identify primarily in terms of gender rather than class) as well as some of the grievances that fueled the movement (for example, women's responsibility for domestic labor). Having grown up in a society where class divisions and identities prevail and where domestic servants were taken for granted in most middle-class households, I could not help being critical of theories about women in general. In my work, I argued that women might share some interests because of their vulnerability to sexual and reproductive controls; but, given their class and socioeconomic status differences, women differ in their vulnerability to economic forces and the extent to which they are responsible both ideologically and in practice for the care and management of their households. The "liberation" of some women requires the oppression of other women as part-time or full-time "housekeepers." Of course, upper-class and wealthy women have always been "liberated" from domestic labor. Furthermore, most men, under capitalism, are socially and economically as powerless as women, although their wages and salaries are higher. To think of them as "patriarchs" seemed to me a barrier to understanding gender as a principle of social organization, something which by its very nature is irreducible to microfoundations. I was also very much aware of the importance in this country of perceived racial and ethnic differences. These differences, I thought, should also be taken into account in the analysis of the oppression of women. Today it is commonplace to utter "class, gender, and race" as a sort of mantra, but I still remember the criticisms I received in the early and mid-1970s when I brought up those points in my consciousness-raising groups, in discussions with other feminists at the university, and in my first published article, "Marxism and Feminism" (1975).

Another area where my work became quite different from the mainstream is the area of race/ethnic studies. The topic of race was not one I studied in graduate school, although I did support the civil rights struggles of people classified as racial and ethnic minorities. Naive as the proverbial sociologist who needed a substantial grant to find a whorehouse in Chicago, I was not aware that I had been classified as a minority by the university where I currently teach. I think it was in 1985, when a colleague asked me to participate in a search committee as a minority representative, that I realized what was happening. He told me he had called the affirmative action office and had been told that I "counted" as one. In disbelief (I am a foreigner and still have Argentine citizenship), I called the office and was told I "counted" as a "Hispanic." Later on, I received a letter informing me who I was in the eyes of the law. That was, in my view, objectively a racist practice for it deprived me and people like myself (other Latin American immigrants) of our historical and political identities, while imposing a contrived "Hispanicity" that one could find amusing were it not for its objective or latent ideological and political functions. Equally important were the implications of the label for U.S minorities of Mexican and Puerto Rican descent. The label misrepresented the reasons why they have consistently been subject to racial discrimination and economic exploitation. It is not because they spoke Spanish or had Spanish-influenced culture but because a large proportion were descendants of the union between Native Americans or Blacks and Spaniards.

The university, of course, was doing nothing illegal. In fact, because foreigners "count" as minorities, one way universities and other employers can increase their minority recruitment is to advertise their job openings in Africa, Asia, and Latin America. I tried to extricate myself from what I considered to be an impossible situation, tantamount to crossing a picket line, but I was given the run-around for several years. Finally, the department chair succeeded in getting my classification changed. This experience was an object lesson on the relationship between social practice and knowledge. I would have never attained the theoretical insights I have attained in this respect had I not challenged what for those in positions of authority was a nonproblematic situation. And, I would have never developed the political sensitivity to understand the unintended effects of the minoritization of foreigners had I not had that encounter with a Mexican-American student.

Looking Forward, Looking Backward

In 1970, while I was still a graduate student, I began to teach full time at Pitzer College in Claremont, California. In the spring of 1981, I taught at Dartmouth College, and during the academic year 1983–1984 I had the pleasure of teaching at the University of Kent, in Canterbury, United Kingdom. My contract at Pitzer College was not renewed in 1972, but early in 1973, the year I received my Ph.D., I was offered a job at the University of Colorado at Boulder, and I have been there ever since. As I look back on these years as a professional sociologist, I realize I have been privileged. Unlike other women in the profession, I do not have experiences of harassment and loss of employment except briefly. My professional life, however, has not been free of upsets and disappointments.

My theoretical commitments have kept me outside the mainstream, both as a sociologist and a feminist. I work mainly in isolation, sharing my work with a few friends in the United States and abroad. I must say that, while women rightly complain about the old-boy network, old-girl networks fulfill similar functions of gatekeeping and paradigm construction, setting the basis for acceptable scholarship. Someday someone will write the "sociology of feminist sociology." It will be, as it is said these days, a "good read." But, having reflected on my personal and professional development, despite the intellectual isolation that I have experienced I can truthfully say that I regret nothing.

Professionally, I chose particular intellectual paths because in each instance they seemed to be the best. I worked "against the current" without having deliberately set out to do so. In fact, I have longed for the sense of integration and belonging that I thought would be provided by membership in an intellectual community. I was unable to join, however, because of the problems that I identified in dominant paradigms. I cannot adjudicate how much of this perception of insufficiency is due to my commitment to Marxism and how much can be attributed to the knowledge and insights that my personal background has given me. Both contributed to my choosing a style of work that brought me problems and great pleasure at the same time. They also contributed to my developing an identity that ran against the stereotypes within which people wished to constrain me. Well-grounded in the complexities of Marx's work, I did not play the heavy-handed orthodox Marxist role; and, as a middle-class Argentine woman, supportive of U.S. minority rights, I did not play the exotic (that is, "ethnic") Latin American role or the "Hispanic" minority role. The middle-class experience is the same everywhere; I belong to a privileged professional/scientific stratum that feels at home anywhere in the world. It is my location in this stratum that has protected me from the ravages of racism and sexism to which I would have otherwise been exposed in this country.

Personally, I marvel at the decisions I made, beginning with that application for a fellowship to study abroad. I have often pondered about why my life might had been like had I not left home to study in the United States. Would I have become the kind of lawyer I once wanted to be? What would it have been like to live in the same place one grew up, close to one's best high school and university friends? Given my political and theoretical views, would I have survived the years of dictatorship had I returned after graduating from UCLA? Also, I often wonder about my relationship with my parents and how it might have developed had I not left them to live apart for so many years. Sometimes I think that we get along so well because I am not there most of the time, so that we meet in a unique terrain, under different rules. They are always with me in my thoughts, and I visit them almost every year, staying anywhere from a few weeks to a couple of months, depending on time constraints. This has helped me maintain my identification with Argentina, my language, and my awareness of the gap between what Argentina and Latin America are all about and the stereotypes prevalent in this country. I live in two worlds. I feel at home in both, but I do not belong fully in either one; I am always an observer. Sometimes I like this for it is like having an escape door, as those travelers from the past or the future one reads about in novels, who depend on their time machines to save their lives. Other times I long for that which I knew all too briefly: the experience of being fully part of one's surroundings. Sociologically and existentially, however, I know this kind of social integration never lasts, even for those who never leave. To young women today facing the question of whether to go abroad to study, I would advise they go. Why? Because the contemporary processes that undermine state boundaries and loyalties are irreversible. It is only by becoming "world citizens" that we can appreciate more keenly what we leave behind, experiencing it in freedom, not constraint.

It is now time to reexamine the overall tenor of this paper and use it as data for sociological reflection. It is a text framed by the quote from Merleau-Ponty, which stresses the meaningless nature of the separate and discrete incidents that constitute personal experience and our active role in giving meaning to our lives. In that sense, this version of my story is what it is because of the audience it intends to reach. Depending on who elicits the tale, I could come up with several overlapping but different accounts, introducing other details while keeping silent about some stated here. But, while this is true of one's *individual* experience, it is also true that we are *social* beings and, in that sense, this story has elements common to many others. There are tens if not hundreds of thousands of Argentine professionals like myself dispersed around the globe; there are millions of professionals and scientists from Latin America, Asia, and Africa who have found a niche in the advanced capitalist countries. My experiences are far from random; the content of the choices I made and the choices themselves were in a sense imposed on me by macro-level national and global processes of which I was unaware at the time. On the other hand, despite the social nature of my experiences, choices, and consciousness, there is also that which makes this tale my own. As Jean-Paul Sartre (1968) once said, "Valery is a petit bourgeois intellectual. . . . But not every petit bourgeois intellectual is Valery" (56). Likewise, not every migrant intellectual worker is like me.

It was difficult to write this chapter, but I am glad I did it; it forced me to spend time on self-reflection, something that our way of life seldom allows us to do because of all the pressures under which we work. Among the things I learned from this exercise there are two that serve as a fitting end to these reflections. I have trusted the implications of my experiences more than I had realized, and that is good, for it allowed me a degree of originality in my work that I may not have otherwise attained. And, despite the many difficulties and frustrations, I have had a great life.

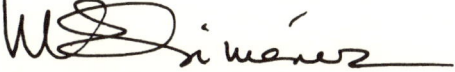

NOTES

Acknowledgements: I thank Benjamin F. Hadis, Gary T. Marx, and Don Roper for their useful suggestions.

1. Literally, it was "The Sociology of Right," in the sense of the French *droit*, meaning the study of the universal principles of law as a social phenomenon, rather than concrete legal systems.

REFERENCES

Gimenez, Martha E. 1975. "Marxism and Feminism." *Frontiers: A Journal of Women Studies* 1:61–80.
Hollander, Nancy C. 1973. "Women: The Forgotten Half of Argentine History." Pp. 141–58 in *Female and Male in Latin America: Essays*, edited by Ann Pescatello. Pittsburgh, Pa.: University of Pittsburgh Press.
Kinzer, Nora Scott. 1973. "Women Professionals in Buenos Aires." Pp. 159–90 in *Female and Male in Latin America: Essays*, edited by Ann Pescatello. Pittsburgh, Pa.: University of Pittsburgh Press.
Sartre, Jean-Paul. 1968. *Search for a Method.* New York: Vintage Books.
Sorokin, Pitirim A. 1956. *Fads and Foibles in Modern Sociology and Related Sciences.* London: Vision Press.

Ten

The Life Course of a Sociologist

Helena Znaniecka Lopata

October is my birthday month. I am now sixty-eight years of age and in a very good stage, phase, segment . . . of life. Dick, my husband of forty-eight years, is retired except for some occasional advising. The children (aged forty-three and thirty-nine) "turned out fine," and our grandchildren are, of course, beautiful and "above average." We live during the week in a condo right on Lake Michigan with a lovely beach below and on weekends in the woods at Delavan Lake. I can now think, research, and write what I want. And I am particularly pleased to no longer be writing from statistical tables. I hated that kind of writing. This chapter was fun to write—analytical reflections that Ann and Sarah call our contributions. I do not plan to retire for years to come; I like Loyola's environment and see no advantage to leaving it. So, the question to which I want to address myself now is: How did my intellectual life lead to these creative endeavors at age sixty-eight?

I was a poor student in Poland. I finished the first year of high school winning a bet about grades with my best friend: I had worse grades than she. The Nazis invaded just as school was supposed to start in September 1939;

Those colleagues and readers who have known me for some years may consider the Znaniecka to be a mistake, since my earlier writing used Znaniecki. Let me explain the change. The Polish language is gender restricted. An "i" ending is masculine, while an "a" ending is feminine. I am a woman. A second change I have tried to introduce has been harder, and even Dick forgets to use it. Americans have always mispronounced my first name, Helena. I have tried to correct this in the last few years by using the Polish pronunciation. This works when I meet new people, but with older friends even I sometimes slip into the prior sounds. For some reason, the Polish way is very difficult for Americans, and they often express irritation over my effort to make them say it.

This essay was written in 1993. Richard Stefan Lopata died July 13, 1994.

all formal education was shut down. I have written elsewhere (Lopata 1975, 1991) and I have been interviewed by David R. Maines (1983) and Barbara Ryan (1991) about my mother's and my experiences, and those of other Poles under Nazism, so I will skip now to Champaign High School. (One of the advantages of being an older "pioneer" is that people want to know "how it was in those dark days".) Mother and I were caught in the war in Poland, but Daddy had taught at Columbia University that summer and was on his way back home when war broke out. The ship was finally returned to America, which was fortunate, because he was on both the Nazi and the Soviet blacklists, simply for being a sociologist. Daddy was offered a position in the sociology department at the University of Illinois, which explains why I went to high school in the center of Illinois after we escaped from Poland in 1940. I hated the place, and America in general, during the first couple of years. The audiences within the four-state region in which mother and I made speeches in order to collect clothing, medicine, and money to send back to Poland had not even heard of the war, nor did they know anything about my country.

I was put ahead in school in spite of having missed all but the last two months of my sophomore year and my poor knowledge of English, but the kids, mainly the girls, were mean. They had never seen a foreigner before, and they did not make my stay at all pleasant. I made the National Honor Society and decided that learning was not so bad after all.

Daddy's position at the university could last only ten years because of mandatory retirement, so my parents had to establish themselves financially in America for the rest of their lives by a wise use of his salary. My mother managed that. The expenses of sending essentials to Poland were high, so it was impossible for me to go away for higher education. I had a scholarship to Smith College, where mother had gone—she was an American—but just going and living there was out of the question. I went to the University of Illinois. Daddy convinced me to join a sorority, a rather undemocratic suggestion coming from a socialistically oriented man. The idea was good. I got Americanized within the pledge year and enjoyed myself as soon as the foreignness wore off. I decided to major in chemistry to get as far from sociology as possible. The trouble was, I did not like it, and after tries at rat psychology and philosophy, I finally ended up in sociology.

Dick and I married at the age of twenty, and my parents kindly rented us rooms and fed us dinner. There were only six graduate students in sociology when I finally got to that level at the University of Illinois, the others being men, but the atmosphere was much better than at Champaign High School. The faculty was also all male. Each was working in his own field, so we did not get general theory from them, but instead acquired it on our own. The library was great, and I never left it when doing my master's thesis on international cooperation in medicine.

The European intelligentsia orientation continued in my post-master's work at the University of Chicago (known to all of the alumni ever since as U of C, so I will use this form throughout). I went there with a theoretical dissertation in mind, but my committee of Everett Hughes, Louis Wirth, and Herbert Blumer insisted that I study Polonia (the Polish American community) to find out why the predictions of its demise by W. I. Thomas and my father, Florian W. Znaniecki, were wrong. W. I. and Daddy had published the five-volume work, *The Polish Peasant in Europe and America,* in the years from 1918 to 1920. They predicted personal, family, and community disorganization due to the weakening of the norms of village life.

I had to work on the dissertation alone for a great deal of time because Dick was called into the armed service at Langley Air Force Base during the Korean War. He had been disabled from the Marine Corps during World War II, but he joined the Air Force just before Korea in thanks for all the education he got on the GI Bill. I joined him there and I developed most of the historical and analytical foundation for my dissertation with the help of interlibrary loans at Hampton Institute, which was all-black at that time. This was my first lesson in racism. Langley is in Virginia, and the white community and Air Force officers did not take well to my going to Hampton, more and more obviously pregnant as time went on. Teddy (Theodora whom I wanted to call Theo, but never got there) was born in Dixie Hospital, Hampton, Virginia, in the middle of July 1951: It certainly was hot!

In the meantime, Blumer went to California, and Wirth died. Hughes and others in the department insisted that I supplement by library and newspaper work by going out to Chicago's Polonia to talk to people, attend meetings, and do "field work." Actually, I had been somewhat hesitant to go into the community, fearing that my name would bring instant door-closing. After all, the *Polish Peasant in Europe and America* had not presented a very positive picture of the Polish Americans. Luckily, people remembered that Florian Znaniecki was a famous person and not the reason for his early fame. My contact with Polish Americans was made difficult, however, by the fact that much of Polonia was composed of the first cohort of pre– and post–World War I immigrants and their descendants, while I was part of the second cohort, which was forced out of Poland by World War II. Polonia was and still is divided by immigration (called there emigration by time of leaving Poland) cohort. The first cohort consisted of economic immigrants, mainly from villages and with agricultural skills, coming from a Poland occupied from 1775 to 1918 by Russia, Prussia, and Austria. My cohort came to America as refugees from World War II. The Poland of the interwar years in which we grew up was very different from that under the three occupying powers. It had regained independence and become more urbanized, and the population was much more educated. Many of the refugees had lived in other countries during the war and its aftermath before coming to America, and they considered themselves much more sophisticated than the first cohort and its descendants. There was strong antagonism on both sides of the cohort fence. After all, I was told, we who came recently must have been "dehumanized" by the experiences of the war. The second cohort was shocked by the poverty of language and lack of knowledge of Polish culture and history on the part of the first cohort. My most recent study of Polonia (1994a, the revised edition of *Polish Americans*) found a third cohort who left Poland at the last years of the communist rule, were Solidarnosc refugees, or entered as vacationers who continue to stay as illegal workers. The hostility between these Poles and the established Polonia is again strong.

My dependence on published sources about Polonia could have resulted in serious mistakes. Luckily, Dick's family is Polish. (They are also Lithuanian and German, but those nationalities did not influence them very much.) His mother had been very active in Polonia and was willing to talk of its life with all its complexities and excitements. What was known in English in the 1950s about Polonia was restricted mainly to what was found in *The Polish Peasant in Europe and America*. Thomas and Znaniecki had planned two other works on Poles in America: one on the intelligentsia and another on the bourgeoisie (Orbach 1993). Unfortunately, Thomas was fired from the University of Chicago in a very unpleasant and unacademic manner, and, in disgust, Daddy accepted a chair of sociology and philosophy of culture in Poznan, Poland. His Ph.D. from the Jagiellonian University in Krakow was in philosophy, and he had previously studied at the Sorbonne and Geneva University in Switzerland [Dulczewski 1992]). Had they completed the other two studies, both Polonian and other scholars would have had a broader picture of Polish Americans. Personal contact with Polonians through my field work made me realize how distorted was the picture in the social science literature, assisted by the highly developed American prejudice against all immigrants.

I have stuck with fieldwork over the years, although I have turned to large samples and quantitative data on several occasions. In each case, however, I first immersed myself in qualitatively obtained knowledge in order to understand what it was that was distributed in a select population.

I ended up with a dissertation entitled "The Function of Voluntary Associations in an Ethnic Community: Polonia" and a Ph.D. in 1954. Hughes suggested that I get someone who knew English to proofread the manuscript, since one does not write "of course" as "off course." Mother did that. (She was a Connecticut Yankee and a lawyer with Chicago's Legal Aid when she married Daddy. Where do you think all the legal data in *The Polish Peasant* came from?). However, after receiving the degree, I lost all confidence in being a sociologist. Getting the Ph.D. had been too easy, and I was convinced that everyone was just being kind to me to let me finish. I believed Blumer must have given me honors in social psychology to make up for being so critical of the *Polish Peasant* and for not giving Daddy sufficient credit for his contribution. I could not get a job in or around Chicago. Dick had joined the business world as a management consultant and would not leave this metropolitan area. The business community did not approve of wives who were scientists or who "worked," meaning those who got paid for the work they did. We moved to Skokie, a Chicago suburb, and Stefan was born in 1955. I was surrounded by anti-intellectual America. We even got a dog. I became a housewife; I did only one study in ten years; I finally began teaching, one course at a time, between 1962 and 1965, evenings and later during the day at Roosevelt University.

Two events pulled me back into academia. Daddy died in 1958, leaving behind an unfinished magnum opus. By the early 1960s, I took it upon myself to prepare this manuscript for publication. It covered only half of his full theory on the content of sociology: social roles and social relations. He had already delivered papers and published articles on the next two divisions, social groups and societies, but he had not reached these segments of the planned *magnum opus,* to be called *Systematic Sociology,* when he died. The manuscript also lacked footnotes and references. I worked hard to prepare what was there for publication. I supplied the missing references, compared his theory of social roles to the use of that concept by other sociologists, and located the resulting volume, titled *Social Relations and Social Roles,* in relation to my father's other work. The reviewers for the publisher with whom I had a contract did not like my additions, wanting only the Florian Znaniecki segments. I was devastated: all this work and no result. I sought advice from Erving Goffman, who had been in my U of C graduate school cohort and who was already a published author. He suggested that I turn what I had written into articles. I did, and my work was finally published as "A Restatement of the Relation between

Role and Status" (1964), "The Secondary Features of a Primary Relationship" (1965), and "The Life Cycle of the Social Role of Housewife" (1966).

The students at Roosevelt petitioned for me to get a full-time position, because they assumed that sexism kept me at a part-time level. In actuality I had not even asked to go full-time. Anyway, I was then in an academic setting, leaving the values of suburbia and the business community behind.

Preparing Daddy's manuscript for publication really galvanized me. This is not unusual. Many sociologists have equipped themselves with strong theoretical foundations by translating the work of famous European scholars. For example, Talcott Parsons and A. M. Henderson translated and edited *Max Weber: The Theory of Social and Economic Organization* (1947). Parsons also translated and prepared for publication *Max Weber: The Protestant Ethic and the Spirit of Capitalism* (1958). Reinhard Bendix (1960) wrote an intellectual portrait of Max Weber. Tom Bottomore translated and edited *Karl Marx: Early Writings* (1963). Europeans tend to be more theoretically oriented than many American sociologists, so their work provides a solid foundation.

Although many reviewers, and Robert Bierstedt in particular, did not like the role theory in the Znaniecki *Social Relations and Social Roles* (1965). I have found it extremely useful and have used it, with modifications, in much of my work since then. It is especially valuable to me in that it can be fitted into the symbolic interactionist framework that I had acquired from Herbert Blumer. Briefly, it defines a social role as a set of patterned, interdependent relations between a social person and a social circle, which involve duties and obligations, rights and privileges. It thus shifts the emphasis from Ralph Linton's definition of social role as behavior activating a position, to the interrelationship between the person and the circle. It is also dynamic, rather than static, in that I stress the negotiated aspect of these relationships. I do not conceptualize the person as having to perform duties of an established office. The person has obligations to all the members of the circle who grant the person rights and carry forth their part of the role.

The second impetus to my becoming a full sociologist was less pleasant. I finally got a visa to visit Poland in 1966, and I went with Dick, Teddy, and Stefan. This was a mistake for several reasons. First, I should have returned to Poland alone the first time because all I and my relatives and friends did was talk Polish and cry. My children were totally disgusted. Second, I found myself immersed in guilt for having survived. The girl whose parents gave me the *auswise* (permission) to leave the city had died in Warsaw. Many of the people we knew ended up in labor concentration camps. My half-brother, Julek, spent time in Dachau. Particularly difficult was Julek's situation. Seventeen years older than I, he had been raised in Poland by his mother's family. His mother died in America after coming with Daddy in 1914. The family did not want my American mother to educate him. He was a poet and novelist, having won the equivalent to the Pulitzer Prize for a novel in Poland. After being freed from Dachau by the American forces, he came to the United States and worked for the Voice of America. He continued to write, but he could not do so in English. Even the Polish-language press abroad did not want to publish his work because it was full of the war and the concentration camp. In those years, no one wanted to be reminded of the horrors. Poland under communism was not a viable alternative. Julek finally committed suicide just before I went to Poland. What happened to him was considered a terrible waste of life and talents by the Poles, making my survival guilt even harder. Here I was, an American housewife not doing anything to help the world. Polish history has created a strong noblesse oblige determination on the part of its intelligentsia to contribute to knowledge and art. I had a great background, but I was not using it.

Equipped with the role framework and spurred by the guilt, I turned back to the interviews with suburban and urban women that I, interviewers, and students had been gathering since 1956, and I started the analysis for *Occupation: Housewife*. It was a hard book to write, since there was no model at that time. First books, as I indicated in its preface, are hard to write anyway; the thought part is no less difficult with later ones, but the actual writing becomes easier. A typical analytical problem that I faced immediately was the question: Is "housewife" an independent social role or are the duties and rights simply part of the roles of wife and mother? I finally decided that "housewife" is a role, and I have been able to see it as such in several other studies. For example, Debbie Barnewolt, Cheryl Miller, and I treated it as an occupation in *City Women: Work, Jobs, Occupations, Careers* (1984, 1985).

Occupation: Housewife sat for almost two years with the publishers before it saw the light of day in 1971. However, it was well received, and I regained some of the self-confidence of earlier years. I began to move my main identities fully into the cluster of sociologist-wife-mother. My mother had been right, as she usually was, in suggesting that I focus on subjects with which I was personally familiar. However, *Occupation: Housewife* did not help much with my guilt, which had become a terrible burden. I felt I had to do something meaningful that could help people, and I finally hit on the idea of studying widowhood. This choice was logical. After all, my homemakers had all been married with children. What happens when these roles are modified by age and death? It was not, I knew, a pleasant subject, so I would be paying back part of the debt. I did not realize how unpleasant it was until I found myself sitting for months in libraries rather than going out and talking with widows. I did not want to see people cry, and everyone around me thought I was crazy to start such a subject. Prejudice and stereotyping of everything surrounding death, including widowhood, was strong then and I had absorbed it. It took me a year of exploratory research before I felt ready to apply for a grant. The funding came, and I used the National Opinion Research Center for interviewers who were experienced and thus able to deal with any emotion-related problems. I turned to Eric Lindemann, who was noted for studies of death and bereavement, to ask if it were all right to interview women widowed less than six months. The Administration on Aging, my funding source, had set such a time limit for the interviews. Lindemann explained that this was exactly the problem women faced early in widowhood—no one wanted to talk with them about the death. I used his advice to change the grant to remove any time restrictions and interview women regardless of length of widowhood.

The social role framework was very useful as I traced the modifications in the roles of wife, mother, neighbor, friend, and so on brought about by the death of the husband. Hank Brehm, head of the Social Security Administration's (SSA) "outhouse" research, approached me when that study was finished to ask if it raised any questions that another study could answer. Of course it did. My prior work, *Widowhood in an American City,* was limited to the United States. I had become increasingly interested in how widowhood is experienced in other societies and life circumstances. SSA had rights to use of U.S. counterpart funds. This is money that stays in a country that buys our wheat whose currency we do not want. It can be used for embassies, research, and related activities. I wrote a proposal that went through peer review and resulted in a contract. Hank, who became the project officer, knew of an anthropologist from Egypt, and I of sociologists in Iran, Poland, and Yugoslavia. We met in Chicago, Zagreb, Warsaw and, later, in Cairo and Tehran, a very interesting combination of cities. However, the social role framework was too complicated for comparative research. Finally, during one of those terrible conferences where nothing seems to work, I had a brainstorm. Why not break up the duties and rights into sets of supports? At that time there was a great deal of talk on television about the support system of the astronauts, so support systems became our framework. Our multinational team developed four systems: economic, service, social, and emotional. We jointly worked up sixty-five separate supports that could be studied in a variety of countries. In fact, people later used this framework, or parts of it, in looking at widowhood in Korea,

Australia, India, and several locations in the United States. The project met with new difficulties as governments got involved in having to approve it. The Yugoslav version was sent—for who knows what reason—to the department of war, which nixed the whole thing. The Polish government stopped that segment at the last minute. The anthropologist in Cairo quit her position at the American University, and so the study never produced results, although it was conducted. Fortunately, despite the revolution in Iran, Jackie Touba left in good health and with the data. Anyone interested in the results of all this comparative effort can read *Widows: The Middle East, Asia, and the Pacific* (1987a) and *Widows: North America* (1987b). My part of the study was published as *Women as Widows: Support Systems* (1979). Hank and I used some of the data for *Widows and Dependent Wives: From Social Problem to Federal Policy* (1986). The concept of support systems has been so deeply integrated into sociology that my name is no longer identified with it.

While all this was going on, I returned to Polonia. (Remember when dissertation advisers suggested that we select our topic carefully, for it would form a rut in which we would remain forever?) As I mentioned above, I really did not have much confidence in the dissertation, since it passed by the U of C faculty so easily. In fact, when Ernest Burgess and Donald Bogue (1965) asked me to write a chapter from it for their *Contributions to Urban Sociology,* I begged off, saying I could not do it. Someone else condensed my dissertation into that chapter.

My increasing self-confidence pushed me back to Polonia in the 1970s to see again what kept it going twenty years after the prior study and about sixty years after the *Polish Peasant* research. We were living in metropolitan Chicago, where most of the major associations, their libraries, and their publications were located, and I had access to all the records. The fact that Prentice-Hall was publishing a series on ethnic groups in American life facilitated my getting a contract. However, there is a disadvantage to being part of a series, since each work must conform to a common format. Many of the details of life in Polonia were cut by the editors. Of course, there is always the possibility that the editors were right, that I was much more interested in the details than would be the audience. Milton Gordon, the series editor, was very helpful. The result was *Polish Americans: Status Competition in an Ethnic Community* (1976).

The interest in this ethnic community has not died down even now. I gave a speech on Polish Americans a couple of years ago at the Copernicus Center in Chicago; Charley Moskos of Northwestern University was the commentator. Charley suggested that I revise my *Polish Americans* (1976) in view of the recent events in Poland and Polonia, much as he had revised his *Greek Americans* that had also been part of the Prentice-Hall series. The fact that Michael Dukakis was running for president reactivated interest in that ethnic group. His suggestion sounded like a pretty good idea, easy to accomplish since I needed only to add a few chapters—or so I thought. Prentice-Hall was not interested, as they had not been in Charley's second edition, but I turned to Irving Louis Horowitz of Transaction, who published Charley's second edition.

Contract in hand, I turned again to the Polish American community. I relearned my spoken and reading Polish. I gathered newspapers, magazines, books, and anything I could get my hands on. I went to meetings, Polish Catholic mass, restaurants and "night clubs," I talked with many people of the "old emigration," my cohort of World War II refugees, and the newest cohort from communist and independent Poland. To my dismay, I found a mushrooming explosion of literature about Polonia, not only by American social scientists, but also by Poles. This meant much more work than I had envisioned. Two Polish universities have developed research centers focusing on the emigrants and their Polonias all over the world, but especially in the United States. Historians have formed a Polish Historical Association with a journal and annual meetings with papers on various aspects of this life. The newest wave of Polish émigrés has started its own press with slick magazine and "modern" language with a great deal of political and social humor. Instead of producing a second edition with great ease, I labored for months, rewriting practically everything from the first edition. However, the work has been fascinating. My interest in symbolic interaction has been enhanced by having to grapple with the concept of ethnic and national identity. The three basic concepts that helped the analysis of Polonia for the first edition of *Polish Americans*—status competition, organizational complexity, and belief in national character—proved very useful. These aspects of community life are quite alive among all three cohorts. The subtitle of the 1976 edition was *Status Competition in an Ethnic Community*. I am not claiming that these three characteristics are unique to Polonia, only that they are dominant in this ethnic community and very useful as a framework for analysis. I was also lucky to meet Mary Erdmans, who had studied the newest cohort for a dissertation at Northwestern University. She contributed a chapter to the revised edition on the third cohort's political activity toward Poland in cooperation with, or in contrast to, that of the established Polonia.

My interest in community life has persisted in both its ethnic and suburban forms. It was a combination of that and my surprise at seeing very competent and creative suburban women call themselves "just a housewife" that spurred the *Occupation: Housewife* (1971) studies. In recent years, Judith Levy and I planned a large study of social integration of women in suburbia. We would return to the same homes in the same twelve suburbs in which the initial interviews took place. We did not get funded. I may return to that project on a smaller scale in the future. Judith is now involved in an enormous project on drug intervention and AIDS.

All the excitement of the last few decades in changing women's roles and feminist approaches to sociological theory could not help but attract me. The social role framework, as seen through the interactionist prism, is a helpful tool for analyzing these charges and theories. One aspect of all this bothered me: the concept of "sex role." No matter how I tried, I could not visualize such a thing, any more than I could see race roles or class roles. Barrie Thorne and I (Lopata and Thorne, 1978) put together a small piece on this for *Signs*. I believe that the sex roles section of the American Sociological Association changed its name to sex and gender as a result. In my view, gender becomes a pervasive identity of an individual, entering more or less significantly into the package of the social person who is involved in a social role within the social circle. Gender is a very important characteristic in the roles of father, husband, wife, mother, lesbian, and so forth; it is much less important in the roles of professor or artist, for example. The same can be said of other pervasive identities, such as race, in American society. Ethnic identity can enter into relations with members of an ethnic organization or into discussions between Polish Jews and Polish Catholics. Being a Pole should not affect my role of sociology professor unless I bring it in for some academic reason.

The studies of widowhood, and then of changes in the roles of American women, have led me back into more general theory (1993, 1994b). Changes brought about by what is called modernization, social development, or complexity of scale are too often inadequately understood in the lives of most people. High-powered male sociologists complain about being oversaturated or beleaguered by societal complexity and technology, while most women and men are only now beginning to expand their social life spaces with the help of opportunities provided by modernization. The antifeminist backlash builds on the image of the modern person as unable to meet changes in life (remember the popularity of Alvin Toffler's *Future Shock* [1970]). The backlash is an attempt to convince women that they should reduce role conflict and that all the stress they are experiencing is a result of movement from a traditional to a more modern world (read, "go back home"). I agree with Rose Coser's (1991) assessment that recent changes in the world toward mass education and the breakdown of the ideology of two spheres, away from "gemeinschaft" restrictions, are positive aspects of modernization.

Social role theory has also directed me to the study of occupations. The results of this work are found in the *City Women* (1984, 1985) volumes. My colleagues and I have also edited a series of books that are published by JAI Press. I first called the series *Research on the Interweave of Social Roles,* but no one was quite sure what that meant, so I finally narrowed it down to *Current Research on Occupations and Professions*. In these I have worked with Judith Wittner (my constant help with ideas as well as resources), Nona Glazer, David Maines, and Joseph Pleck. Judith Levy edited volume six; Gale Miller, seven; and Muriel Cantor, eight. I am now putting together volume nine.

My theoretical interests have troubled various publishers on several occasions. I decided a few years ago, while recovering from two operations within two weeks, to pull together all I know on the changing roles of American women. I used role theory again. One reviewer stated that he (I think from the tone that it was a he) did not want to read theory when reading about women! Another publisher tried to get me to cut out all the "generalizations," which meant the role theory. Anyway, I finally have a home for it with SUNY, Albany, thanks to three very helpful and positive reviewers and Richard Hall's encouragement. I have called it *Circles and Settings: Role Changes of American Women* (1994b). The circles are part of roles and roles are always in settings.

It is interesting, however, how pervasive is gender identity. I am not sure how much my being a woman now affects my relations with sociology colleagues, but I do know that my reputation for often focusing on women as the subject of analysis does affect them. Sexism rears its ugly head when male colleagues latch on to the subjects of my work as "women" rather than as social roles, identities, communities, symbolic interactionism, and so forth. It is the theoretical framework that is sociologically significant, not the subject that is studied through that prism. Labeling theory is still labeling theory, whether applied to juvenile delinquents or women scientists. One can apply the conflict perspective to the study of organizations or husband-wife relationships. The effects of modernization can be studied among various classes of women as well as among men. However, some sources of knowledge are more prestigious among sociologists than are others, and women are not high on that hierarchy. Suffice to say that most of my male colleagues are not familiar with my writing on social roles or identities when these concepts are applied to women.

Returning, for a moment, to my development as a sociologist, I must pause to acknowledge the contributions of other sociologists, friends from the U of C days, as well as colleagues at Loyola, SWS (Sociologists for Women in Society), and the various groups with which I have been involved. It is hard to work alone, which is what we do most of the time unless we are teaching or when we are part of research teams. I could not write sociology when I was a full-time homemaker. I did write, but nothing came of it. I did not attend sociology meetings for fear that someone would ask me what I was doing. I could not be Znaniecki's daughter as my only identity at such occasions. Scholars must be able to talk with others about general ideas or specific theoretical, methodological, or even technical (the computer) problems. I enjoy working with graduate students, or even undergraduates, in seminars where they can study some sociological problem in depth. I only wish that more of our students were imbued with the imagination of which C. Wright Mills (1959), so eloquently wrote. The worst are our premed, predental, and prenursing students, who do not want to play with ideas. I encourage my students to go to sociological meetings and congresses, where they meet others with different perspectives and academic lives. This is why regional, national, and international conferences are so important.

My interest in the world scene is the result of my background, of living in several countries, of visiting many lands, and of friendships with sociologists around the globe. The whole atmosphere of family and home was cosmopolitan. My mother, a nice American lady, graduate of Smith College, Columbia University and the law school at the University of Chicago (the only one that would admit a woman at that time) gave up all that and moved to war-torn, poor Poland just because she had married a Pole. There were people from countries all over the world in our home, and an international perspective pervaded throughout. Dick has also been interested in the world from a historical and also a management-consultant viewpoint. He has traveled often to Poland and has contracts in France, Mexico, and Italy.

In looking over this chapter, I am struck by the lines of continuity of my work, in spite of the different directions it has taken. As C. Wright Mills (1956) convinced us in *The Sociological Imagination,* individual biography is tied into societal history. I have been living in historically fascinating times and have been lucky in experiencing many of its events. It is not surprising that I believe very strongly that good sociology must include comparative and historical knowledge and perspectives.

Helena Znaniecka Lopata

REFERENCES

Bendix, Reinhard. 1960. *Max Weber: An Intellectual Portrait.* Garden City, N.Y.: Anchor/Doubleday.

Burgess, Ernest, and Donald Bogue. 1965. *Contributions to Urban Sociology.* Chicago: University of Chicago Press.

Coser, Rose Laub. 1991. *In Defense of Modernity: Role Complexity and Individual Autonomy.* Stanford, Calif: Stanford University Press.

Dulczewski, Zygmund. 1992. *Florian Znaniecki: Life and Work.* Poznan: Wydawnictwo Nakom.

Lopata, Helena Znaniecka. 1954. "The Function of Voluntary Associations in an Ethnic Community: Polonia." Ph.D. diss. University of Chicago.

———. 1964. "A Restatement of the Relation between Role and Status." *Sociology and Social Research* 40 (October): 58–68.

———. 1965a. "The Secondary Features of a Primary Relationship." *Human Organization* 24(2): 116–23.

———. 1965b. "The Function of Voluntary Associations in an Ethnic Community: Polonia." Pp. 203–23 in *Contributions to Urban Sociology,* edited by Ernest Burgess and Donald Bogue. Chicago: University of Chicago Press.

———. 1966. "The Life Cycle of the Social Role of Housewife." *Sociology and Social Research* 51 (October): 5–22.

———. 1971. *Occupation: Housewife.* New York: Oxford University Press.

———. 1973. *Widowhood in an American City.* Cambridge, Mass: Schenkman.

———. 1975. "The Life Record of an Immigrant." *Transaction/Society* 13 (November/December): 64–77.

———. 1976. *Polish Americans: Status Competition in an Ethnic Community.* Englewood Cliffs, N.J.: Prentice-Hall.

———. 1979. *Women as Widows: Support Systems.* New York: Elsevier.

———, series ed. 1980–1994. *Research on the Interweave of Social Roles,* vols. 1–8. Renamed *Current Research on Occupations and Professions.* Greenwich, Conn.: JAI Press.

———, ed. 1987a. *Widows: The Middle East, Asia, and the Pacific.* Durham, N.C.: Duke University Press.

———, ed. 1987b. *Widows: North America.* Durham, N.C.: Duke University Press.

———. 1991. "Occupation: Sociologist." Pp. 191–208 in *Lives of Career Women: Approaches to Work, Marriage, Children*, edited by Frances M. Carp. New York: Plenum.

———. 1993. "The Interweave of Public and Private: Women's Challenge to American Society." *Journal of Marriage and the Family* 55 (February): 176–90.

———. 1994a. *Polish Americans*. 2d rev. ed. New Brunswick, N.J.: Transaction.

———. 1994b. *Circles and Settings: Role Changes of American Women*. Albany: SUNY Press.

Lopata, Helena Znaniecka, Debra Barnewolt, and Cheryl Allyn Miller. 1984. *City Women: Work, Jobs, Occupations, Careers*. Vol. 1, *America*. New York: Praeger. Reprinted as *City Women in America*. New York: Praeger, 1986.

Lopata, Helena Znaniecka, and Henry Brehm. 1986. *Widows and Dependent Wives: From Social Problem to Federal Policy*. New York: Praeger.

Lopata, Helena Znaniecka, Cheryl Allyn Miller, and Debra Barnewolt. 1985. *City Women: Work, Jobs, Occupations, Careers*. Vol. 2, *Chicago*. New York: Praeger.

Lopata, Helena Znaniecka, and Barrie Thorne. 1978. "On the Term 'Sex Role.'" *Signs* 3 (Spring): 718–21.

Maines, David R. 1983. "Coming to Grips: Aspects of the Life History of Helena Z. Lopata." *Midwest Feminist Papers* 4:112–24.

Marx, Karl. 1963. *Early Writings*, translated and edited by T. B. Bottomore. New York: McGraw-Hill.

Mills, C. Wright. 1956. *The Sociological Imagination*. New York: Oxford University Press.

Moskos, Charles. 1977. *Greek Americans*. Englewood Cliffs, N.J.: Prentice-Hall.

———. 1990. *Greek Americans: Struggle and Success*. New Brunswick, N.J.: Transaction.

Orbach, Harold. 1993. "Znaniecki's Contributions to *The Polish Peasant*." Pp. 142–58 in *The Contribution of Florian Znaniecki to Sociological Theory*, edited by Renzo Gubert and Luigi Tomasi. Milan: FrancoAngeli.

Ryan, Barbara. 1991. "Helena Znaniecka Lopata." Pp. 263–72 in *Women in Sociology: A Bio-Bibliographical Sourcebook*, edited by Mary Jo Deegan. New York: Greenwood Press.

Thomas, W. I., and Florian W. Znaniecki. 1918–1920/1927. *The Polish Peasant in Europe and America*. New York: Alfred A. Knopf.

Toffler, Alvin. 1970. *Future Shock*. New York: Random House.

Weber, Max. 1947. *The Theory of Social and Economic Organization*, translated by A. M. Henderson and Talcott Parsons. Glencoe, Ill.: Free Press.

———. 1958. *Max Weber: The Protestant Ethic and the Spirit of Capitalism*, translated by Talcott Parsons. New York: Charles Scribner's Sons.

Znaniecki, Florian. 1965. *Social Relations and Social Roles*. San Francisco: Chandler.

PART IV

Isolation, Marginality . . .

Eleven

Discovering Gender
My Paths to a Feminist Sociology

Elaine J. Hall

An Unwomanly Choice

One day in the late 1950s when I was in high school, I made a conscious decision about being a woman that was one of my first steps toward becoming feminist sociologist. I don't remember exactly what prompted my thoughtful mood, but I remember the curtains moving in a gentle breeze and the shadows of the walnut tree dancing on the walls as I sat on my bed thinking about the women in my life—my mother, a few cousins, a couple of aunts, and a neighbor woman. Some of them were better off than others, but as a group these women had neither the best nor the worst lives of middle-aged women with families. It is important to emphasize that none of these women was unusual: the group of women included a woman who was beaten by her husband, a woman who labored at a physically demanding, poor-paying job as a housekeeper because her husband's drinking kept him from holding a steady job, a woman who unwillingly submitted to her husband's demands for sexual intercourse, a woman who wanted to hold a paid job but whose husband forbade it, and a woman who wanted to leave her husband but stayed with him because she couldn't support her three children.

These women, believing their lives to be ordinary, did not complain about being oppressed. Accepting their self-descriptions, I saw them as representatives of the "marriage road." After all, they were my only example of what acting out the conventional gender script might be like for me. I had no contrary image of self-actualized women from television or books or teachers or movies, no alternative role model of career fulfillment from the mothers of my peers. For us, coming of age in the 1950s, a generation before "the women's movement," before sociology or any academic discipline "discovered" gender research, before the first women's studies class, no alternative visions existed.

And so one day in high school I decided I would never marry. More correctly, I vowed, "If that is what it means to be a wife and mother, then I will never be one. If that is what being a 'woman' means, I will not be feminine. Even if it means becoming an 'old maid,' I will not be trapped like they are."

I did see them as victims, as women caught in situations that they somehow let happen and from which they could escape if they tried hard enough. Like most young people then and now, I believed that if you were smart and worked hard enough, you could accomplish whatever you desired. I failed to understand the courage my mother demonstrated in leaving her family and migrating to New York City, in marrying a man outside her religion and her Polish heritage, and in following that man with two children across the country in hopes of a better job to insure that her children would not live in the poverty she had experienced. I failed to acknowledge the fear she experienced when my father drank, when he forced himself on her, and when his "spankings" of the children turned into angry beatings. Because at age sixteen I already had more schooling than she had, I could not comprehend how mystified she was about the books I read and the science courses I took, or how intimidated she was by "educated folks," even when they were half her age. Looking at my mother through the lens of my own dreams, I saw only the limitations, the pain, and the loneliness of her life. Because I did not acknowledge her struggles to make a better life for herself and her family, the gentle ways she encouraged her children to dream big dreams, or the denial of her own needs to meet ours, I saw my mother as a victim who was trapped and I vowed, "No, not me." My mother died long before I learned how foolish my judgment was, and before I had lived long enough to recognize the constraints that life imposes on all women.

Several aspects of my decision seem typical of the way young white women saw their lives in the 1950s. I individualized the problem, seeing it as the particular incidents in only one woman's life. I did not situate her struggles in the context of other working-class women migrating to the big city or of the sacrifices of other upwardly mobile families relocating in California's land of golden opportunity. Because my mother and her peers lacked knowledge about sexism and patriarchy, the gender inequality they experienced was reduced to the life-styles of particular women for whom individual coping mechanisms were the only solutions.

Blaming my mother was beneficial, and maybe even necessary, for my own survival. Only if I believed my mother and her peers had let themselves be trapped could I believe that I could choose to escape. I didn't escape, of course; regardless of our personal decisions, none of us escapes what happens to all women in one form or another. Choosing not to marry did not protect me from being battered, from being forced to perform sexual acts against my will, or from going through an abortion alone. I may have chosen not to birth a child, but I was treated as a woman who *should* bear children, who *should* want to have and to rear children. Denial did not change the fact that everyone treated me as a *woman first*, or at least as a *woman and*. Regardless of my hopes or achievements or fears, I was always a woman and a student, a woman and a worker, a woman and a sociologist.

I did not question the two choices before me that afternoon in high school. By the late 1970s, other options were possible, such as an androgynous mix of masculine and feminine characteristics (Bem 1974) or the role models of women scholars and artists finding their own work (Ruddick and Davis 1977). But for me, in the late 1950s, only two incompatible options existed: the private domestic world of a heterosexual marriage with emotional, if not financial, dependence, or a life of paid employment, single apartments, solitary vacations to exotic lands, and eventually old maidism. It was not a question of "acting like a male." I was not a tomboy, and somehow knew I wanted the freedom and power of men without being like them. It was not a question about my sexuality. I knew gay men existed, but I do not recall knowing about lesbians; I never considered rejecting the hegemonic heterosexuality of my world. The dilemma for me was not whether to be a feminine or an unfeminine woman; rather, it was whether to be a woman or some unwomanly entity defined as the opposite of that "feminine thing." Rejecting my model of a feminine woman, I chose to be an Unwomanly Person.

I recall this choice each time I teach a course called sociology of women, in which we talk about the implications of dividing gender and society into men who live in the public institutions of work and politics and women who live in the private world of family and home. The divisions still exist, though perhaps they are less starkly drawn. To many of my students, being a superwoman (Shaevitz 1984) who strives to "have it all" or "choosing" a less demanding speciality as a doctor or a lawyer (the "mommy track") are seen as desirable options for juggling the overload and conflicting demands of wife, mother, and career. Mirroring the curriculum's separate courses on work and family, sociological research still utilizes a "job model" to explain men workers and a "gender model" when studying women workers (Feldberg and Glenn 1979). In my classes, I describe it as one foot on the dock and one foot on the boat, and ask why only women stand (stretch?) so precariously between divided worlds. Back when I was in high school and took the separation for granted, I decided between them by firmly placing both feet on the dock of career person and walking away from the boat of married woman.

Becoming a Sociologist

Living at home to save money, I enrolled in 1959 at Mt. San Antonio Community College (Mt. SAC) in southern California as a biology major. My interest in science was the legacy of an empowering science teacher in high school. One year of the "chilly climate" (Hall and Sandler 1982) in my college science courses, including a lab assistant who with the knowledge of the male students sabotaged my organic chemistry experiments, left me discouraged and wondering how I would survive another three years. The door to sociology was opened when I took the required social science course and when I worked as a reader for the nine male members of the sociology, psychology, and philosophy department. Like many students today, I changed my major to sociology not only because the course content focused on my life but also because caring professors treated me as a competent student who could teach one day. The educational experience at Mt. SAC was intoxicating. For example, in the Last Lecture Series, professors from every department identified what they considered important "life lessons" to share with their students. In monthly meetings of the psychology club, professors and students read their poems, debated the pros and cons of the new gestalt therapy, or interpreted piano concerti. Graduating with an associate of arts degree in 1961, I left Mt. SAC for the University of California at Santa Barbara (UCSB) on the path toward becoming a professor of sociology.

In the early 1960s, UCSB was a small college of about five thousand students, as yet untouched by violent student protests. I lived in the dorms, as did many young women, because our parents favored the structured environment of curfew hours, locked doors, and parent-controlled overnight passes; men's dorms did not have these restrictions. My courses in sociology were challenging and engaging. In research methods we completed surveys by coding each case on an index card and calculating statistics by hand, and in small group behavior we participated in and analyzed our own learning groups. Whether studying the sociology of art or the mass communication techniques used to brainwash soldiers in the Korean War, I believed the sociological knowledge in my classes applied as much to me as to the men in my classes.

What I remember most about UCSB, however, is that I became a loner. Tired of missing plays or gallery openings because no one wanted to go with me, I made myself go alone until it stopped bothering me, and until I enjoyed being among strangers as much as being with friends. I lived away from home for the first time, and I learned the difference between being alone and being lonely when I discovered the sea. Sun-bright walks between classes, fog-drenched strolls after dinner, moonlight hikes scalloping the florescent greenwhite waves—this is where the poems filled the pages, where I learned to "zen see" (Leverant 1969) through the lens of a camera, where I wrote long letters to friends and lovers. I graduated with my bachelor's degree in sociology in 1963. I knew I would continue sociology in graduate school, and I knew I would always be drawn to the sea.

For the next two years I lived like a "normal" nonacademic person. I worked as a social worker in the Aid to Families with Dependent Children program in Ventura County, California, in order to become financially independent. My clients taught me how much people can achieve even when I, with all my privileges (McIntosh 1988), saw them as oppressed and limited. My friends who were painters and my solitary times on sandy shores taught me to see myself as someone who creates word pictures.

Grad School B.F. (Before Feminism)

In 1965 I entered the master's program in sociology at the University of Washington, a large school of approximately thirty thousand students located in Seattle. Computers were just becoming available, and the sociology department was building a reputation in macrosociology and empirical research. The rigorous master's program included an eight-hour comprehensive exam, an empirical thesis, and a language requirement. Each new cohort took a one-year "orientation" course in which students wrote their thesis proposals and after which students were automatically scheduled for the master's exam at the beginning of the second year. Ranging from the behaviorist Robert Burgess to the anthropology-trained Pierre Van den Berghe, the faculty provided some diverse viewpoints, but the content of sociology in the 1960s was primarily functionalism. The Marxist and/or conflict theories that are currently included in our introductory sociology textbooks (Wells 1979; Villemez 1980) were not even taught in graduate seminars in the 1960s. Without xerox machines, graduate students spent hours typing notes in their offices or handwriting notes in the reserve stacks of the library. Most of us were young (late twenties as I was), and many of the men were married, often with small children.

It was a very political time for all of us. Whether we marched with signs, circulated petitions, or wrote letters against the Vietnam War to the campus newspaper, we shared the belief that somehow our generation would make things better. The flower children were everywhere. We called them "fringies" instead of "hippies" because they frequented the bookstores and coffeehouses along the west side of campus. I was a "spiritual fringie" who identified with the philosophy of personal growth and the creative life-style; I occasionally participated in political demonstrates, such as a Poor People's March in downtown Seattle, but I rejected the drug scene. I was more likely to participate in the efforts by the graduate students to be taken seriously within the department, such as opening the faculty lounge to graduate students. I wrote petitions and letters, and I went with other students to see the department chair; initially they opened the lounge only one afternoon a week, but in time the department lounge was opened to all graduate students and faculty. Although they may seem like small victories, in hindsight the "lounge" and other incidents were important advances that empowered us as sociologists within paternalistic academia.

Considering the political landscape that permeated our lives and our campus, it seems amazing that we never organized to combat the sexism that daily impinged on our lives. Blatant, overt sexism was commonplace and openly tolerated. As women students, we could identify the faculty who just happened to brush against you in their office, or who turned the "few beers with the students on a Friday night" into a sexual harassment ritual. We helped each other struggle through the statistics course in which we were told women couldn't do mathematics. The women competed hard for funding even though we were treated as second-class students. I recall one (outside) fellowship in which all male students with a 3.5 GPA were considered first; then, if money was still available, women who had a 3.8 GPA were considered. Women students were considered bad investments because we would marry and choose to leave our jobs; individual protests denying any intentions to marry went unheeded. After all, women were women, which meant we were categorically different from all men.

Covert, systemic gender discrimination (Benokraitis and Feagin 1986) also existed, but was harder to see because it was built into the curriculum and the discipline of sociology. Half of the graduate students in the sociology department were women, but all of the faculty were male. We never had a woman sociologist as a role model; we never saw a woman as the professor, the researcher, and the scholar we were studying to become. We studied all aspects of society in our courses, except gender. In the mid-1960s not a single course focused on women or gender issues. We could study, even specialize in, the subject matter of race or class, but we could not take *one* course on women or gender. If, for some strange reason, any of us wanted to focus on "women's issues" (a term we had not yet invented), we could concentrate on the sociology of the family. We all knew it was a less prestigious area, a cut below the important topics of real sociology. How could it be otherwise when we could pass the master's exam and complete our degree without ever studying family sociology?

Our lack of outrage at the omission of courses on gender is unsettling because we did demand other forms of relevance in the sociology curriculum. For example, when the undergraduate students challenged the outmoded theories and research about drug use, the graduate students who taught deviant behavior struggled to find something more than Howard Becker's (1963) study of marijuana to use in class. Graduate students involved in the student movement also openly questioned the established knowledge about social movements; theories about "rabble rousers" or a contagious "group mind" did not explain their participation in the antiwar movement. Some of us even extended the mainstream curriculum by participating in the Free University where we studied the Vietnam War, the Taoist way, or the poetry since the beatnik period. But for all our demands for personal relevance, we neither grasped nor collectively challenged the exclusion of women and gender from our curriculum.

Occasional personal acts of defiance did occur, such as the day I violated the unstated appearance norm for women (no one yet knew about the concept of gender norms). My decision was not precipitated by a group conspiracy or traumatic event; I was just tired of "dressing up" in nylons, girdle, and skirt or dress to attend classes. So one day, without warning, I wore a tailored, polyester, tan pantsuit with matching blouse and costume jewelry—something I wouldn't even own today. I held my office hours, attended graduate classes, and taught my discussion sections in a nondescript pantsuit that a middle-aged woman might have worn. I felt very conspicuous as students and faculty made negative comments; I heard "tisk tisk" as I walked down the hallways, and I saw the stares when I walked into my classes. Did the gender norm magically dissipate? No, but I had crossed over a line, which eventually led me to teach classes in bell-bottomed jeans and turtleneck sweaters. Learning that you can violate an unspoken taboo and live in dangerous knowledge; the power of outrageous acts (Steinem 1983) is not easily forgotten.

Even though we complained about everything from uninspiring teachers to irrelevant assignments, we women students never talked about sexism or patriarchy or gender exploitation. We experienced sexism daily and we resented it, but we did not have a consciousness or the language to interpret it as something other than individual behavior. It was our "problem with no name" (Friedan 1963). Until we could name it as something beyond ourselves, we really could not see it; until we could recognize it as a problem shared by the women students, we could not collectively challenge it. Without the larger picture, the chauvinistic behavior of individual men, the sexism built into our academic procedures, and the androcentric nature of the theories, research procedures, and content areas of sociology remained *my* problem, or Sue's problem, but never *our* problem. In the end, we coped with it all as individual women, usually choosing to leave the hostile environment by quitting school or abandoning the unfriendly discipline of sociology that did not even recognize women's experience as a legitimate topic of knowledge.

After two rejected thesis proposals, I spent a year trying to find a thesis topic that both they would accept and I could live with; I never found it. I became increasingly intolerant of course materials that did not resonate with my life. Eventually they cut my funding because I wasn't making "satisfactory progress" toward completing the master's degree. After three years of work and successfully passing the comprehensive exam, I made a tortured decision to leave graduate school without the degree. My father never forgave me for "throwing it all away," and I considered it *my failure* for years. "Dropping out" confirmed the faculty's perceptions of my incompetence, and reinforced their rationalizations that women students lacked the motivation and scholarly abilities to become competent sociologists. Yet, it was the only decision possible for me. Knowing my decision was right, however, did not prepare me for the road that lay ahead or the adventures that were to come.

Gypsying into Myself

I left for one year "on the road" to figure things out, to give myself a break, and to put grad school and sociology into perspective. My one year turned into more than fifteen years of roaming free as I meandered through the redrock country and the desert land of the west, wandered across the Mississippi and into the hardwood tangles of Appalachian forests, and gypsyed my way from the stony cliffs of northwest shores to the coral sands of the Gulf coast. Looking back, I know I needed this time to come into myself. For all the seeking and writing and reflection throughout my early twenties, I needed a space away from outside demands and schedules, away from shoulds and don'ts, and away from other people, even friends. I needed time away to develop my own voice, to enjoy my own company, and to discover how I would spend my days when I did not HAVE to do anything.

Traveling without an agenda, my late twenties and thirties were folded into the creases of state maps, the pages of journals, and the frames of film in my camera. Driving down roads to see the next town, hiking trails to see the next waterfall, crossing lakes to see the next shore, or walking along beaches to see the next wave, I stopped wherever something caught my attention and stayed as long as there was something new to see. I gave a day to following the sun's path down one side of a mountain valley, across the Mad River, and up the other side. I discovered the smell of rain on cactus in Arizona, on sweet gum leaves in Kentucky, on hemlock needles in the Smokies. I learned to identify the songs of birds in New Mexico, and to map the stars while floating on a lake in the Okefenokee Swamp in Georgia. City-born and housing tract–bred, I lived for a while on earth time instead of calendars, on daylight and darkness instead of clocks, and it filled my soul and nourished me in a way that was never faded.

When my funds ran low, I worked at odd jobs, mostly doing resort work of one kind or another. Waiting tables or cleaning rooms, I performed the traditional "women's work" of server and maid. Like women before me, I discovered these jobs were easy to find and easy to leave; like women after me, I needed the coins in my pocket each day to buy gas, the lunch they fed us, and the occasional room that saved me from paying rent. Sometimes the work was empowering; once I worked as a "handyman" at a resort in the ponderosa pines of Arizona in which women did most of the work. We pumped the gas, ran the store, cooked the meals; we painted the cabins, repaired what was broken, hauled whatever needed to be moved. We held "men's jobs," and we took pleasure in our strength and our abilities.

But most of the time, performing personal service work was a primer on the gender inequality built into "women's work," a primer I lived but lacked the consciousness to fully comprehend. I learned to banter the sex talk from customers and evade the groping hands of cooks, but I did not protest the sexual harassment that pervaded my work site. I resented wearing degrading uniforms as a waitress and being fired because I did not wear lipstick, but I failed to identify it as being treated as a sex object. I argued against the policy that hired women to serve breakfast and lunch, and limited them to "waiter's helpers" on the dinner shift because "it was classier," but I did not understand it as occupational segregation. I even complained about the uniforms required for the "men's" job as a naturalist that did not fit my woman's body, but I did not recognize the message that women did not deserve this job.

Throughout the 1970s, I encountered discrimination on every job, in every town, and in most of my relationships; I did not see the sexism, but other women did. While I was off banding birds in the mountains of West Virginia, women all over the country shared the kind of experiences I have described, and they discovered that those experiences derived from patriarchy and not from their individual strengths and weaknesses. While I was photographing carnivorous plants and alligators in the Okefenokee Swamp, women's studies programs washed across the country in that first wave of studying everything with new eyes and ears to reclaim the lost and ignored voices of women. The ideas of sexism and the women's movement became part of the public discourse; I agreed with them but, like many of my students today, I did not consider myself a feminist. My decision to return to graduate school came from an internal gyrocompass, without any knowledge that new paradigms had been developed in sociology, particularly gender studies.

Encountering a Feminist Sociology

I entered the master's program in sociology at the University of Connecticut in 1983. One night during the spring semester of my first year back in grad school, I was sitting in a class listening to six students discuss the assigned readings. It may sound ordinary, but this scene was truly remarkable because we all were women—students and professor—and the readings were about gender inequality. Specifically, we were studying how gender bias permeated the foundation of knowledge and science, and how women and their lives were kept invisible in sociology.

Suddenly, I was deeply angry; I put down my pen and silently sat there, trying to control the rage that swelled within me. After a while, the professor, Myra Marx Ferree, asked me what was wrong. "They ripped me off!" was all I could say, all I felt. Five years of studying sociology, all those classes I took, and all the books and articles I had read—all of it had been a hoax. I was drawn to sociology because I thought that it was about me, but in that one moment, I *saw* for the first time that sociology never really had included me because I am a woman. All of the sociological knowledge I had worked so hard to learn was biased from the white, middle-class, male point of view. And to make matters worse, this knowledge that ignored gender and made women invisible had been presented as an objective reality supposedly including everything that one needed to understand social relations and society.

There it was—the click as the blinders fell, the seeing clearly through the fog. Those of us who have been fortunate enough to teach women's studies courses know the look, a sudden "ah . . . I see" that comes when the lived reality of this incident and that event come together into a pattern that can be named and understood. It clicked for me that night and never again would my vision be as simple, as surface-bound, as segregated from my inner knowledge.

Instead of seeing a single barrier here and another one there, finally I saw the whole cage of oppression (Frye 1983), the macrostructure of patriarchy and inequality. Grounded in my own direct experience yet extending to the lives of other women, I now had a way of understanding, thinking, and discussing the multiple ways our society structured gender inequality into my life and into our lives. Now I could name it, and in the naming, I could know it in a manner very different than before.

At first I felt cheated by the discovery that sociology had presented an androcentric, and therefore partial, knowledge about society, about people, about me. But after the initial shock and rage diminished, I came to feel empowered. After all, enough feminist scholarship existed to take an entire seminar on gender, and some battles had been won. Ann Oakley (1974), to cite just one example, had successfully convinced mainstream sociology that her research on housework was legitimate by challenging the definitions of work and family. And I believed that some of the conceptual tools needed to undo the bias already existed within sociology, namely, the premise that all knowledge is socially constructed and socially located. If knowledge were socially constructed (Berger and Luckman 1967) instead of an objective "truth," then a new gender-inclusive knowledge could be created. If the traditional sociological knowledge manifested the particular social positions of its producers, then sociology could become inclusive by bringing in the voices of "knowers" with different race, gender, and class locations. We could rebalance the "view from the top" in mainstream sociology by researching and theorizing from the perspectives of people who lived and resisted the multiple forms of race, class, and gender inequality that are the central structures of society.

Later I would realize that sociology also has the tools to ghettoize the feminist revolution (Stacey and Thorne 1985), and I would understand the power that paradigms have to define what constitutes "normal science" in sociology (Kuhn 1970). But back in 1984 when the vision of a feminist sociology was brand new to me, it was enough to be lifted up by the feminist sociologists who had come before me, to accept the feminist legacy, and to believe that a revolution from within was possible. If this was one of few situations in which the tools did exist to dismantle the master's house from within (Lorde 1984), then at least I could complete graduate school; I earned my long-delayed master's degree in 1985 and my doctorate in 1990. My master's thesis compared a demographic and a feminist explanation of the race differences in abortion support (Hall 1985); my dissertation on the gendering of waitress work (Hall 1990) examined topics that I could not have studied in the 1960s when I began grad school. Now I could "do sociology" in a inclusive way in my teaching and my research.

Praxis: My Research on Waiting

After working as a waitress in family restaurants from coast to coast, I "naturally" chose to do a dissertation on the work experience of table servers. Research about waiting would allow me to document my experience, to give voice to the working-class women who seldom are studied by sociologists, and to debunk some of the myths about the "semi-skilled" personal service jobs that supposedly manifest women's feminine "nature." Equally important to me, research about table servers offered the opportunity to examine the many ways that gender is constructed and reconstructed through work.

One of the ways that work creates gender relations is by the sex/gender category of the worker. Having always worked with other women in coffeeshops and family-style restaurants, I had avoided the upscale restaurants that hired only waiters. I had served breakfast and lunch with the other waitresses in a hotel restaurant in Florida, while the men performed gourmet table-side cooking for dinner customers. I expected to find this historic pattern of firm-specific segregation, but my research in Hartford restaurants showed that extensive integration had occurred. Two out of three Hartford restaurants had integrated wait staffs consisting of men and women coservers.

The extent of integration posed new research questions. Did gender lose its salience when wait staffs were integrated, or were gender processes merely shifted to the arena of the kind of service that integrated staffs perform? Did the men and women in integrated staffs give different kinds of service in the same restaurant, or did everyone in an integrated staff perform a single style of service deemed appropriate for that kind of restaurant? Because I didn't know they existed, I had not designed my research to find gendered jobs. But the existence of gendered work roles is exactly what my research uncovered. The women who waited with men at the Elegant Nouveau, for example, consciously and actively enacted a masculine-defined formal style of service that was deemed appropriate by this three-star, fine-dining restaurant.

I discovered gendered work roles in the language women servers used to describe themselves and in their politically conscious attitudes about their uniforms. As gender-atypical workers in this formerly all-waiter restaurant, women servers at the Elegant Nouveau called themselves "waiters," or sometimes "servers," instead of "waitresses." What really caught my attention, however, was their usage of the term, "male waiter." When I first heard the term, I was startled by its redundancy, but the term "male waiter" was not redundant to the servers at the Elegant Nouveau. For them, the "male" in the term "male waiter" referred to the sex/gender category of the server; the term "waiter" referred not to the person doing the work but rather to the kind of work being done. Thus, both "male waiters" and "female waiters" were possible because both male and female servers at the Elegant Nouveau were doing *waitering,* a kind of service loaded with masculine gender meanings (Hall 1993a).

The importance of performing *waitering* was also evident when the women servers talked about their tuxedo-style uniforms. In response to a simple question about how they liked their uniforms, all of the women servers interviewed but none of the men servers at the Elegant Nouveau gave lengthy stories about the meaning of their "unisex" uniform and the significant role it played in maintaining gender equality among the integrated wait staff. If they did not dress in pants exactly like the male servers, the waitresses said customers would treat them differently or ask for a "real" waiter. If they wore skirts, male servers would once again take advantage of them as coworkers by dumping their clean-up tasks or taking the better-tipping tables. To the women at the Elegant Nouveau, gender had more to do with the style of service and the meanings embedded in their work tasks than with the sex/gender category of the workers.

I also interviewed male and female servers who worked at a franchise coffeeshop, which I called the Sandwich Shop. Here the women wore dresses and called themselves waitresses; they performed a casual, friendly, almost familial, style of service. During my observations of lunch service, I was intrigued with "sexy" inflection of a greeting, the body language signaling prowess or accessibility, and the flashy smile that indicated the way male customers and female servers flirted with each other. Most table servers used flirting as a standard technique for getting good tips; the waitresses at the Sandwich Shop were no exception. Openly admitting they flirted, the waitresses of the Sandwich Shop wanted me to understand the difference between the flirting they did on the job and the "real" flirting that occurred when they were off duty. Some waitresses even wanted two terms, one to describe personal flirting, and one to name the flirting that was built into their jobs and encouraged by their manager. I remembered the feeling from my own waitressing jobs—acting extra friendly to get larger tips while resisting the appearance of being sexually available to my customers. I had not been "available" and neither were the waitresses at the Sandwich Shop; we were performing a "job flirt" (Hall 1993b). These servers in the fast-paced, no frills Sandwich Shop clearly understood that gendered encounters with their customers were created when restaurants structured a ritualized "job flirt" into the script for "good service."

Conclusion

This has been my journey: from someone who rejected her own womanhood to a researcher using a womanist perspective, from a diligent undergraduate student who uncritically accepted the knowledge in journal articles to a professor evaluating textbooks with a race-gender-class lens (Ferree and Hall 1990; Hall 1988), from a graduate student gratefully absorbing the woman-centered research of our "fore-mothers" to a copresenter on panels with women whose books I have read and a colleague who is amazed that others take notes of my "off the cuff" remarks as I did with my mentor. Traveling the three paths of a personal consciousness, the women's movement, and an inclusive sociology, I learned a gender consciousness that is part of who I am as a woman, a teacher, and a sociologist. Having discovered gender, I can never unsee it. Whether teaching in a classroom, watching television at home, or eavesdropping on conversations in a restaurant, I experience the activities of my daily life as the process of "doing gender." Even the women of my past—my mother and the women of her generation who are frozen in a snapshot in my mind from my high school days—are seen anew through the gender lens.

If my mother were alive today, I would tell her how much I now understand about her life and her struggles. I no longer consider her a victim any more than I blame myself for the sexual harassment I experienced or judge the student who struggles to end an abusive relationship. Where once I misjudged her choices as "inadequate," I now see her sustained efforts to keep her family afloat despite a system of gender and class oppression. I understand because I, too, have made "choices" that reduce the suffering of others at my expense, or I have selected the lesser of two evils while raging against the limited options available to me. But it is more than humility that I have gained from living a life full of compromises. Regardless of the "choices" either of us made or did not make, I know now that it is not a matter of making "choices" and it never was.

Most of all, I want my mother to know that she has been with me all these years. Her gypsying spirit lived within me as I hiked the craggy trail to a misty Appalachian waterfall, photographed columbines blooming beside a snow-fed Colorado lake, or collected bits of coral along the Florida keys. I carried her dreams into every classroom whether I entered to study, to learn, or to teach a discipline whose name she practiced pronouncing and spelling one night at the kitchen table in order to "brag on me" to her family. My mother informs my research on working-class women, such as waitresses, by reminding me of the many skills required to perform "unskilled" jobs and the sense of accomplishment women achieve from traditional "women's work." My efforts to theorize gender as a process people do and a structure that presents gendered options arise in part from a need to have my discipline avoid victim-blaming "choice" explanations based on a definition of gender as a characteristic of individuals acquired through socialization. My mother was a presence with(in) me as I wrote this essay. From the first sentence to the final editing, our voices mingled as we told the story of the gendered journeys we have traveled—one from a poor, immigrant family to a comfortable tract house and a small business in southern California, and the other from a working-class woman unconscious of gender to a feminist sociologist seeing the world through a gender lens.

Elaine J. Hall

Acknowledgments: An earlier version of this essay was given as a talk at the 1992 International Women's Day Celebration at Old Dominion University, Norfolk, Virginia. I wish to thank Sarah Fenstermaker and Ann Goetting for their editorial assistance as I revised a talk into a book chapter.

REFERENCES

Becker, Howard. 1963. *Outsiders*. New York: Free Press.
Bem, Sandra. 1974. "The Measurement of Psychological Androgyny." *Journal of Consulting and Clinical Psychology* 42(2): 155–62.
Benokraitis, Nijole V., and Joe R. Feagin. 1986. *Modern Sexism: Blatant, Subtle, and Covert Discrimination*. Englewood Cliffs, N.J.: Prentice-Hall.
Berger, Peter, and Thomas Luckman, 1967. *The Social Construction of Reality*. Garden City, N.Y.: Doubleday.

Feldberg, Roslyn, and Evelyn Nakano Glenn. 1979. "Male and Female: Job Versus Gender Models in the Sociology of Work." *Social Problems* 26(5): 524–38.

Ferree, Myra Marx, and Elaine J. Hall. 1990. "Visual Images of American Society: Gender and Race in Introductory Sociology Textbooks." *Gender & Society* 4(4): 500–533.

Friedan, Betty. 1963. *The Feminine Mystique.* New York: W. W. Norton.

Frye, Marilyn. 1983. *The Politics of Reality: Essays in Feminist Theory.* Trumansburg, N.Y.: Crossing Press.

Hall, Elaine J. 1985. "Determinant of Abortion Attitudes: Social Location or Attitudes." Master's thesis, University of Connecticut.

———. 1988. "One Week for Women? The Structure of Inclusion of Gender Issues in Introductory Textbooks." *Teaching Sociology* 16(4): 431–42.

———. 1990. "Waiting on Tables: Gender Integration in a Service Occupation." Ph.D. diss., University of Connecticut.

———. 1993a. "Waitering/Waitressing: Engendering the Work of Table Servers." *Gender & Society* 7(3): 329–46.

———. 1993b. "Smiling, Deferring, and Flirting: Doing Gender by Giving 'Good Service.'" *Work and Occupations* 20(4): 452–71.

Hall, Roberta M., and Bernice R. Sandler. 1982. *The Classroom Climate: A Chilly One for Women.* Washington, D.C.: Project on the Status and Education of Women, Association of American Colleges.

Kuhn, Thomas. 1970. *The Structure of Scientific Revolutions.* Chicago: University of Chicago Press.

Leverant, Robert. 1969. *Zen in the Art of Photography.* Berkeley, Calif.: Images.

Lorde, Audre. 1984. *Sister Outsider.* Trumansburg, N.Y.: Crossing Press.

McIntosh, Peggy. 1988. "White Privilege and Male Privilege: A Personal Account of Coming to See Correspondences through Work in Women's Studies." Working Paper No. 189. Center for Research on Women, Wellesley, Mass.

Oakley, Ann. 1974. *The Sociology of Housework.* New York: Pantheon.

Ruddick, Sara, and Pamela Davis. 1977. *Working It Out.* New York: Pantheon.

Shaevitz, Marjorie Hansen. 1984. *The Superwoman Syndrome.* New York: Warner.

Stacey, Judith, and Barrie Thorne. 1985. "The Missing Feminist Revolution in Sociology." *Social Problems* 32(4): 301–16.

Steinem, Gloria. 1983. *Outrageous Acts and Everyday Rebellion.* New York: Holt, Rinehart, and Winston.

Wells, Alan. 1979. "Conflict Theory and Functionalism: Introductory Sociology Textbooks, 1928–1976." *Teaching Sociology* 6(4): 429–37.

Villemez, Wayne. 1980. "Explaining Inequality: A Survey of Perspectives Presented in Introductory Sociology Textbooks." *Contemporary Sociology* 9(1): 35–39.

Twelve

Isolation and the Woman Scholar

Diane Rothbard Margolis

As a young girl, I read Madame Curie's biography. I must have done so more than once; I remember it well. I also saw the movie with Greer Garson. I wanted to be just like Curie. She was brilliant. She was gutsy enough to succeed in the face of an isolation that would have made others run for the shelter of an ordinary life. She rose to the top at a school where there were no other women. She fought for and won the support she needed to complete her experiments and prove her discovery of radium. Day after day, year after year, she was there, alone in her laboratory, endlessly distilling. That isolation—forced on her both by a career denied almost all women and by ideas beyond anything most colleagues could imagine—was not a pathetic isolation. She was brave. And she was lucky. She had Pierre, her colleague, companion, and partner. And she had two daughters. (One of them, Eve, would be her biographer.)

Marie Curie was a woman who had it all and did it all before such goals were even imagined. She was my model, my idol. But I was not Polish, I did not go to the Gymnasium, I did not rise to the top of my class. And I most assuredly did not have the guts as a young girl to go it alone. Like most of my peers, I went to grade school, then to high school, then to college, and then I married. It would take years and the reassurance of a women's movement before I would experience the satisfactions—and the isolation—of a woman scholar.

In this essay, I want to reflect on those years. I begin with my college days, then I tell about life as a suburban housewife and mother. My sons were almost ready for college at about the same time the women's movement was reawakening; that is when I resumed my college career. As I drifted into my current position as a professor of sociology, doing the research that is the most engrossing part of this work, I was struck repeatedly by disjunctions between the life I was experiencing and the theory I was teaching. So I started revising the theory. Challenging current beliefs is one way to learn the discomforts of isolation. But the isolation I experience as I reweave some basic sociological beliefs is not the first or the only kind of isolation I have experienced. Suburban housewifery has its own brand of isolation.

Let's begin, not at the beginning, but when I was eighteen and I had just arrived in Ithaca, New York. I have four memories from my days at Cornell University that reflect the choices young women had to make in the mid-1950s. The first comes from orientation week. I had chosen Cornell over the Seven Sisters because I wanted a coed school. There, I thought, I would receive an education equal to any man's. At first it seemed I had come to the right place. I had been educated in New York City public schools. I knew about Horace Mann and Fieldston and other private day schools where youngsters went whose families had more money than mine; but I knew nothing of prep schools. Cornell's entering class must have had a large contingent from prep schools because during orientation week, as we went from one assembly to another, we were told about how college life would be different from our prep schools; high schools were less often mentioned. Frequently, the deans and others who spoke to us used a phrase I had never heard before: "You are the leaders of tomorrow." That was heady stuff; I had arrived; I loved it.

But on the last day of orientation week, they separated the boys from the girls—or the "men from the women" as they called us. I'm not sure what the dean of men told them, but for us there was no more anticipation that we would be "leaders of tomorrow." Instead the dean of women explained that we were attending Cornell to become fit companions for the leaders of tomorrow. What a downer! There I was, all ready to become a leader of tomorrow, and now all I could look forward to was companion status. It wasn't the first such disappointment. Lots of times as I was growing up I noticed that the boys got to be and do things that made it seem as though they were having a better time of it than the girls. They went to shop, and we had to go to cooking and sewing; they could yell and shout and get all muddied up, and we were always being told to "act like a lady"; they could play real basketball, and we had to play by "girls' rules" and stay within our assigned boundary lines on the court. Girls' basketball rules seemed a perfect metaphor for the differences. It wasn't as much fun, but I was used to it.

At Cornell, I quickly learned that a "C" or even worse on an exam felt bad but was a private matter. Being alone in the dorm without a date on a Saturday night was a public humiliation, impossible to hide. So, if nobody had called by Wednesday or Thursday night, I'd put my books and papers aside and get myself over to Straight Hall, the student union, to circulate. The dean of women had told us the score, and I was going to get myself one of those leaders of tomorrow.

My second Cornell story is about Roberta, who was a lesson to us all. She was a premed, the only woman in the class I knew who was planning a professional career. (There was one woman in the engineering school of whom I heard, but I never met her.) Roberta was a grind. I saw her at meals and that was it. The rest of the time she was studying—getting her "A"s. She never had a date. The rest of us would giggle about the pale blue nail polish she wore and the boot marks on the back of her calves during finals week in May, when it hadn't snowed for months. In those days, girls wore black rubber boots, shaped like toddler's boots that came up to mid-calf. Hitting against the back of your leg as you walked, they left a black mark. Boot marks in May said something rather shameful about your grooming habits.

Years later at a small reunion in New York City, I saw Roberta again. The rest of us looked like the bedraggled mothers we were. Roberta sparkled: hair done, nails polished (red), clothes in perfect press. It dawned on me then that the blue nail polish and the boot marks that made her so unlovely, saved her the time the rest of us spent on dates. She used that time to become a doctor. But we didn't know that then.

The third memory, like the first, began during orientation week. I had been very good at math in high school. I hadn't taken philosophy because it wasn't offered, but I thought I might like it—abstractions came easily. So at Cornell, at the only meeting I ever had with my advisor, when he asked what I would like to take, I said, "I think I'd like logic, I think I'd like symbolic logic." I had no idea what symbolic logic was, but it sounded as though it would be a nice combination of my grasp of symbols and my enjoyment of ideas and abstract concepts. I tried to strike up a conversation about that choice, but all my advisor said was, "You'll have to take calculus first." I didn't know what calculus was either.

Calculus was taught in the largest lecture room I had ever seen—tiers and tiers of seats rose from the fluorescently lit well in front. The doors were up front too, and when I entered what seemed to me like a stage, I searched for a familiar face. Like Marie Curie, I was the only woman in the room. As it turned out, they were not only all men, but all, or almost all, of them were engineering majors, and all, or almost all, of them had taken solid geometry. Math education at Music and Art High School, where I had gone, had stopped at trigonometry.

I did okay, until one day, at the blackboard, the professor flipped an eight on its side and started talking about "infinity." Now there was a concept worth grappling with! I was captivated. No one else seemed to be. They just kept slotting their numbers into their formulas, and every now and then there was an infinity sign at the end of a problem. Meanwhile, I thought about infinity and lost my way. At the final, I tried to make a deal with the instructor: pass me and I'll never take another math course as long as I live. I got a passing grade and, strictly speaking, if you don't count statistics as math, I never did take another math course. I'll never know whether it was the deal or getting a few infinity signs in the right place that won me the passing grade. In any case, I switched my major to English: There were lots of other women there!

But women were not among the faculty. The only time I ever saw a woman teaching at Cornell was in an astronomy course. She was a teaching assistant, and she was almost as telling an object lesson as Roberta. I was fascinated by her as she stood at the board writing her formulas with a hand and an arm that were thin but as muscular as a man's. Nobody else seemed impressed. Nor did anybody else have a good word for her. Whenever I tried to find out more about her, I'd hear damning stories: she was engaged to a fellow student, but he had broken it off; she was divorced; who would want her anyway, she was as feminine as an ox. The men were even more disdainful than the women. I lost interest.

Onward to Marriage and Motherhood

By the time I left Cornell, I had lost interest in Marie Curie, too. I had met Dick. Maybe he would be a leader of tomorrow. He was a journalist; he came from Saint Paul, Minnesota, just like F. Scott Fitzgerald; he had been an editor at the University of Minnesota *Daily*, where he even had a humor column of his own; he had published an article in a Chicago magazine; and he was in New York City working for *Redbook*. We fell in love, we married, we moved to Brooklyn Heights, we had a son, we decided the *Brooklyn Heights Press* was nothing but a gossip sheet when it could be much more, so we brought it for a song. I worked at the *Press* during the day while Dick stayed on at *Redbook*.

Our first big moment came when we found out that Robert Moses, the great developer of parks and roads and bridges in the tristate area, had plans to tear down and rebuild the southern end of Brooklyn Heights. With the *Press*, we encouraged a group that was fighting the plan. They won a compromise, and the *Press* won a prestigious Polk award for community service.

By then the sixties were upon us. The *Village Voice* was edging out the stodgy *Villager* in Manhattan; a reform Democratic movement was fighting and winning primary elections against party bosses, and, on the Heights, some young lawyers and others had formed the West Brooklyn Independent Democrats. Naturally, the *Press* championed them. And naturally, it lost all of its legal notices, the economic lifeblood of most community weeklies in New York City in those days. When the *Press* seemed on the edge of bankruptcy, members of the community rallied to it; they bought shares in the corporation, trying to shore it up. But there was not a large enough friendly business community to support it with advertising, and in 1960 we had to sell it. We went to Chicago, where Dick became editor of the Lerner chain of newspapers in the Chicago suburbs. Leo Lerner and his newspapers had been the subject of Morris Janowitz's study, *Community Press in an Urban Setting* (1952), but it would be several more years before I would discover that connection or sociology.

Awakening from the Suburban Dream

In 1962, Dick decided to try his hand at free-lance writing, and we moved back East, this time to Connecticut. There began my suburban years and an exhaustion I could not understand until I read Betty Friedan's *The Feminine Mystique* (1963) and discovered that I was suffering from "the malaise without a name." Previously, I had managed a newspaper, two children, and a Brooklyn Heights brownstone with four tenants. Now, in idyllic Connecticut with a house by a pond, my children in school, and my husband in his studio writing, I had barely the energy to get dinner on the table each night.

For suburban wives, isolation and loneliness were the price of success. There we were, each upper middle-class mother working alone in her perfect house with its three or four bedrooms, its modern kitchen, and its family room. Solitary in our little castles, each of us took care of husband and 3.7 children. The closer our husbands came to being a leader of tomorrow, the richer we would become, the more land we would buy, and the more isolated we would become. We even went to town meetings and passed regulations to zone ourselves into greater isolation. My town, Wilton, Connecticut, required each house to sit on two acres; some suburbs, Greenwich, for example, demanded four.

Middle-class women had achieved the American dream and it had turned out to be a nightmare. Marie Curie's isolation may have been the lot of any woman who departed the normal path. But as I review my years in suburbia, I realize that Americans' dreams were very like the hero's wishes in that W.

W. Jacobs story counselors used to tell sitting around a camp fire on summer nights. In "The Monkey's Paw," all the hero's wishes are granted, and each turns out to be a curse. Because each of us had her private park, we did not build playgrounds where we and our children might find companionship. Instead, mothers became chauffeurs carting children to dancing, music, and sailing lessons, or to doctors' and orthodontists' appointments. Every afternoon the yellow school bus would drop off our young and we mothers would set out, each in her shiny car with her one, two, three, or four children. The best escape most of us could manage was a car pool. Then there would be more kids in each car, but still just one lone adult.

I even bought a convertible so at least I could sun myself while I waited for the sailing lessons to end. But that hardly helped in the wintertime, and it did nothing to dispel the isolation. For that, mild social activism came in handy. Once a bunch of us decided that Wilton was too white and too upper middle class. So we set to work opening it up: an integrated day camp with kids from nearby Norwalk, a program to bus kids from the inner city of Bridgeport to our schools, a program to build subsidized integrated housing in town. This last was my special project. I organized support for it, got some lawyer friends to draw up the corporation papers, and held its first incorporation meeting, assuming I'd be elected its president. Instead, a male architect who didn't even seem interested, became president. It was a familiar pattern: I would get a project off the ground and then some man would take over.

That night, I reasoned that I needed professional credentials, and I decided to go back to school. It took a while for me to choose a field. I did some looking around. Architecture would have been my choice, but most nearby schools had an age cutoff that I exceeded. I tried the nearby Silvermine Guild of Artists' School, but, after a year it didn't seem as though I had the stuff to work on my own in a lonely studio hoping for notice from what seemed a capricious world of dealers and critics. Finally, I talked to a friend in the psychology department at New York University (NYU). He asked a simple question: What do you read? I looked at the short bios on the jackets of the books I had especially liked over the previous few years, and it turned out the authors were all sociologists. Sociology, then, would be my field.

School Days and Nights

Returning to school, I once more learned the lesson of "The Monkey's Paw." Although my return was motivated in part by a desire to escape isolation, graduate school brought a new kind of isolation—the kind accorded anyone who departs the normal path. Until then, I had stayed in groove and had been rewarded with acceptance, what I would learn to call a "positive sanction." Now, as I began to step out of line, I found myself having to explain again and again what I was about. "Why are you getting a Ph.D.?" some man would challenge at a dinner party, insisting that I was frivolously wasting my husband's money and a place in graduate school that a young man should fill.

Because, in those days, women raising families were odd types at graduate schools, there were not many I could attend. NYU was the only school I could find that allowed me to study part-time, which was all I thought I could handle with young children and a budget that couldn't cover tuition and baby-sitters. Years later, I learned that most graduate students were supported to some extent by their departments, but that was not the kind of information likely to be passed on to a suburban matron whose only connection with academia had been as a coed being groomed for companion status.

NYU was a commuting school. Students attended at night and they didn't have much time to build up the kind of esprit that graduate students at other schools sometimes have. (The NYU table on Departmental Alumni Night at the American Sociological Association meetings reflects the department's ambience: It is empty.) Fortunately for its students, NYU's graduate school offered an opportunity, not available elsewhere, for students in "unusual" circumstances. Unfortunately, those circumstances often precluded time for casual socializing. I didn't have much to do with fellow students; I keep up with only a couple of them now.

My biggest problem, I think, was that I was too old to be doing what I was doing. That tended to make for awkwardness in relationships with possible colleagues or mentors. By the time I got around to writing my dissertation, my sons were in college and junior faculty at NYU weren't much older than they were. My advisor was several years my junior, and in some ways, I might have put him off a bit. There I was, completely grown up in one sense and an absolute baby in another. Because I was used to running things at home and in my community, I probably wasn't able to act in ways that might have encouraged someone to be my mentor.

My timing wasn't very good either. I haven't seen any research to substantiate this, but my sense of it—judging from the women academics and professionals I know and know of—is that my cohorts, the women of the Silent Generation, are not much represented in academia. We came of age during the 1950s, probably the most pronatalist time of this century. Our older sisters were the Rosie the Riveters who had kept the home fires burning while their male cohorts were off fighting World War II. We joined them in mothering the baby boom and settling the suburbs. When the women's movement began its second wave, they already had experience and training to return to; we did not.

By the time I got my degree and went looking for a position, the 1960s were over and we were well into the 1970s. The academic market had tightened up. And then there was my age. I heard in one case that I had been turned down as a "favor." It was one of those elite schools that do not usually tenure their junior faculty, and the search committee worried that if I were thrown out of a job in my fifties, I might not be able to get another. They may have been right. But the only position I was able to get, the kind of position most women academics land in, perhaps because of similar acts of kindness, was at the University of Connecticut (UConn) at Stamford. There my teaching load began with four courses and three new preparations each semester. Evaluations for merit increases, tenure, and promotion, were made by the faculty at Storrs, the main campus. Regional campus faculty were held to the same standards as Storrs faculty, but at Storrs, teaching loads were lighter, more like the normal load for a university with research expectations.

Survival at regional campuses thus demanded many hours spent researching, writing, preparing classes, and grading student papers. By that time, the nest had emptied at home, so I did not experience the overload of housework, child care, and employment that plagued so many other women. I was able to concentrate on the tasks my position demanded. But it was solitary work. Whole departments at regional campuses have only one or two faculty members, so there is none of the casual communication through which younger faculty learn the ropes and become part of a department. Mail, telephone, and occasional meetings at national conventions are the only way regional faculty might find others with overlapping research interests.

My research focused on the world I knew before I became a sociologist: the political sociology of suburbia. My dissertation and first book were about corporation managers and their families. The focus was on the way the demands of large corporations prevented political participation among this new middle class. Paradoxically, my university job was having the same effect on my own political participation. I had heard about the offer from UConn while I was attending the 1976 Democratic National Convention as a delegate. Once I took the position, I seldom had time even to attend town meetings; my participation dribbled almost to the level of the corporation managers I studied. (Unlike most of them, I still vote in primaries.)

New Observations Spur New Theory

Right after earning my Ph.D. I was awarded a grant from the Center for the American Woman and Politics at Rutgers University to compare women and men in local political parties. To my surprise, that study set me to work remodeling some basic sociological theory. Increasingly, as I examined the lives of other women and my own life, I noted that the theories I had been taught—and was teaching—could not explain the world I studied and experienced. Janet Saltzman Chafetz uses the metaphor of tools to describe sociological theory. Theories, she says are abstract general ideas that can be used to help answer important questions about the social world.

After more than a decade spent trying to apply the standard sociological toolkit to women's experience, I concluded that using most social theories to answer questions about women's lives is like trying to sink a nail with a screw driver. Either explicitly or metaphorically, social theory takes market relationships as the model of all relationships; it presupposes self-interest as the basic motivation and exchange as the basic action in social life. Although self-interest can explain some things women do—for instance, why, given the chance, middle-class women eagerly set about getting themselves careers—it cannot explain others—for instance, why women continue to shoulder the major burdens of care for children, the elderly, the sick, and the infirm although it is not in their self-interest to do so. To say, as many people do, that women are instinctively nurturant doesn't hit the nail on the head. Lots of women do not take easily to care giving and lots of men do. Moreover, class appears to have more than sex to do with who gives care. Rich women do a lot less care giving than poor women. Care giving is not like breathing. It is something some people do because they are obligated to do it. It is learned, not reflexive, behavior.

To explain why women still meet care-giving obligations, and to explain also such apparently irrational behavior as discrimination, I decided to try to construct a theory that could bridge the chasm between concepts on either side of such dichotomies as private/public, gemeinschaft/gesellschaft, household/market, and reproduction/production. As an alternative to these one-sided and dichotomous either-or theories, I postulate that the two sides of those dichotomies operate simultaneously and that, like colors when they are mixed, they can produce an infinite variety of social shadings that can, again like colors, be named. Market-like interactions represent only one pattern of contemporary social action. I have identified five others. Here, to help analyze the isolation I experienced as a suburban housewife and later as an academic, I will introduce one of them.

Standard, market-oriented social theory assumes that social action takes the form of tit-for-tats. It presupposes two sides, a kind of equality between the sides, and the power to possess and trade alienable property. Actors self-interestedly compete for and accumulate resources. Most of men's experience reflects that pattern. As markets came to dominate modern economies, men were released from their feudal obligations and were thus freed to compete in labor markets. Markets require isolated individuals who can sell their labor as freely as they can sell any other commodity. But markets are unsteady, they fluctuate, and they presume possession of commodities by both partners to a trade.

The problem is, most of those who need care, babies, for instance, have nothing to trade. To ensure that care would be given to them, some people had to consider that care an obligation, even a sacred obligation, something that came before self-interest. Thus, as men became subject to a market morality and were required to sell their labor power, women, along with people Rudyard Kipling called "lesser breeds," continued to perform obligatory labor. Many were also confined to the lowest paid work in markets. Ideas like "the white man's burden," the conception and social construction of woman as the bearer of a finer sensibility, and the notion that nurturing is women's "natural" work formed the underpinnings of a social system that made markets possible by ensuring that work essential to life would be performed no matter the fickle fluctuation of markets. I call this a placed person system. We see the term commonly used in phrases like "he doesn't know his place" or "I put her in her place."

Placing presupposes difference, not among things that may be equated in a market as commodities, but of persons and social positions. In this system, people are described as naturally suited to certain work in a hierarchy of functions. You know a placing system is operating when you hear phrases like "blacks have natural rhythm," "the man should be the head of a household," "boys will be boys," and "maternal bonding." Some categorical assumptions about people seem discriminatory now. All seemed to reflect a simple truth once, but probably they will all seem foolish and discriminatory when we find other ways to take care of people who cannot buy the care they need in markets. Meanwhile, ideas that different kinds of people are naturally nurturant or subservient construct reality so that life's necessities can be met by obligatory daily toil in market-oriented societies just as vassalage guaranteed labor in feudal societies.

Using the New Tools to Make Sense of Women's Isolation

The isolation I escaped when I switched my major from math to English was the isolation anyone encounters when she or he steps out of place in a social order. It was different from the isolation I encounter when I stand alone in front of a classroom, when I struggle to write publishable papers and books, and when I review my efforts of the past year to write a merit report. In these, I suffer the aloneness of a solitary competitor. When things are going well, it is invigorating; you forget yourself in your work, all energies are concentrated on doing your best; winning is a thrill. Losing is a disappointment, but in the world of market exchange, losing is part of the game. Seldom does a single loss shape a career or a reputation.

Loss in the world of placing is different. Here, whole identities are at stake. Single mistakes can ruin reputations; it is not single performances but entire persons that are accepted or rejected. That is because the places a person may fill can be determined on the basis of a single characteristic. These are usually ascribed characteristics such as gender, age, family status, religion, race, and ethnicity. But attributes that place a person are not limited to ascribed characteristics. Vide virginity. In many cultures, an unmarried woman is defined either as "pure" or "impure." If she is impure, no matter how her virginity was lost, she is no longer marriageable. In such cultures, there usually is no other honorable place for a woman. Many definitions are not so absolute. There were women sociologists when I was at Cornell. But there were not many, and the few there were suffered an isolation more acute than any I could bear.

I did not become a sociologist until the women's movement had so altered the United States' placing order that my isolation would not be unbearable. The movement had changed the world in two ways. First, I did not have to make the choice most nineteenth- and early-twentieth-century women academics had to make: I did not have to choose between family and sociology. Here, too, it is a matter of degree. There is evidence that women are still being forced to choose between career and family. The fact that a larger proportion of women, compared to men, who have successful careers in academia, the professions, and business are single or childless suggests that although women are being admitted into places from which they have previously been barred, placing barriers have not completely fallen.

The second and perhaps more important change that permitted me to become a sociologist was that by the time I had my Ph.D., many other women had theirs, and an organization existed where we could meet. Sociologists for Women in Society (SWS) was formed to ward off the isolation suffered by women who were sociologists. It was one way women sociologists could make a place for themselves in the world of sociology. To some degree it worked. SWS provides a hospitality suite at ASA meetings; it is a place of refuge that cuts into the isolation so many of us feel at meetings. SWS has also helped to prepare places for women in the field.

Looking back, I feel lucky that I formed my family and raised my sons before there was a women's movement. When they were young, I was not torn between two greedy institutions. I could enjoy them seriatim. Through all of the changes, my husband was an anchor. If a paper had been accepted he cheered with me, and when one was rejected he was there to commiserate and spur me on. My two worlds supported each other enough to sustain me through the isolating forces of each.

But Dick died three years ago. Friends often say I am lucky in these, the most lonely and isolating years I have ever experienced, to have my career and sociology. They are right. My place at the University of Connecticut and in sociology offers some community, some diversion, and, of course, a necessary income. But still, most of my life had been spent caring for others, three men as it happens, my husband and my two sons.

And there is the rub. Women are raised in ways that men are not, even men who are sons of feminist mothers. Women are taught to make sure that everyone in the family is watched over. Often I grouse with my friends about the care my sister and I give my aging mother as she heaps complaints on us and praise and adoration on my brother, who visits less than once a year. Now, as I note that my sister checks to see how I am doing and that my widowed friends usually see more of their daughters than their sons, I regret that when Dick and I were trying to decide whether to have another child, we didn't do it. We used to joke that it would be "just another boy"; but it might have been a girl. Then I remember that one reason we decided to be satisfied with two children was that I wanted a career.

Because my marriage was such a haven, I sometimes dream that I might get lucky again. Toward that end, I occasionally peruse the personals in the *New York Review of Books*. Most men are looking for women five to twenty years younger than they are. I contacted one who didn't state the age of the woman he sought. We seemed well matched: both professors, both widowed, both tall, both in our fifties. After a while, he asked the ages of my children. When I told him, the conversation took a turn toward cutoff. It was his indirect way of finding out my age.

No point telling him that the woman I hike with twice a week thinks I'm still in my forties. We were not in the world of market rationality where capacities may be matched to needs; we were in the world of placing where ascribed characteristics, such as age, race, sex, and not capacity, determine what someone may do and be. Once again, because I am female, I am being placed in a confining social position: sewing instead of shop; basketball by girls' rules instead of being able to run down the court; housekeeping and child care instead of a career; and now, singlehood instead of companionship. The belief that as I age, I will loose my sexual value while my male cohorts will become more attractive is as absurd as the Victorian notion that intellectual work would cause women's wombs to wither. But, like any bigot's myth, it serves the mythmaker. As long as men can perpetuate the illusion of increasing appeal, they can hide from themselves and others the fact that men do age faster than women—on average, they lose their sexual potency, their health, and their lives at a younger age than women.

Once marriages between younger women and older men made some sense. If the man was to be the chief or only breadwinner, he needed time to establish himself. Moreover, his greater maturity helped establish a patriarchal household. But with today's ideal of egalitarian marriages, the older man–younger woman ideal makes no sense. I wonder at widowers, men who know loss and grief as well as I do, when they set age conditions before even meeting a woman. Those conditions virtually guarantee that the price of the love that might grow between them will be her almost certain widowhood. Young women who seek out men older than themselves are probably just ignorant; they would probably not knowingly guarantee themselves years of playing nurse and widow.

I have little doubt that sometime in the not too distant future ideas about beauty, age, and sex will come into line with new realities. As I tell my students, humans are flexible creatures, free of instincts, a species that socially constructs its beliefs to adapt to changing environments. We have changed the world of market exchange and reduced the isolation women scholars once endured. There are not many classrooms where budding Marie Curies must sit alone. But the values of placing orders respond less quickly to change. If we continue to believe that women are better suited than men to be housekeepers and care givers, then women will work a double shift. To avoid that, some women will choose not to have children, and they will miss the joy and companionship of parenthood. If we continue to dream of living in nuclear families on private two-acre parks, then we will add long commutes for both spouses to the nightmare of isolation and loneliness the suburban house enforces. If we continue to believe that as they age women lose and men gain attractiveness, then women will spend the last period of their lives alone and isolated—divorced by husbands who try to regain their youth with younger women or widowed by husbands who die. It is not a happy prospect, but it is avoidable. Looking back, I have seen ideas change about what women are. The isolations women endure are matters of cultural values that women themselves share and can therefore change.

Thirteen

Slouching toward Sociology

Helen Mayer Hacker

I never travel without my diary. One should always have something sensational to read on the train. —Oscar Wilde, *The Importance of Being Earnest*

Family of Orientation

Four things no one ever told me I have always known: there is no God; the world is full of injustice; babies don't come from heaven; I was an adopted child. I *was* told, however, that I was Jewish. All the foregoing, I believe, conduced to a sociological orientation.

The adopted child receives a double message. You belong to us, and yet you don't. You were chosen by us, but you were rejected by somebody else. Early on I formed the concept that my origin was lowly and that my adoptive parents were constantly assessing what about me could be attributed to their benign upbringing and what to inheritance. They were third-generation German Jews who clung to a social status not matched by their financial means. My mother never actually used the work "kike" in reference to more recently arrived Jews from eastern Europe, but rather the patronizing expression "first generation." As an amateur Lady Bountiful, she regularly visited several poor immigrant families on the near north side of Minneapolis, bringing care packages and counsel. I was her unwilling companion on these social work calls, hating the smell of poverty and suspecting that my birth family was their kin. "Where does Helen get her love of books from?" my mother often mused. "Sidney [my father] and I are no intellectuals." Again, although she never came out and said it, I felt she was alluding to some gender-misplaced, Talmudic, stetl background. Just before my sixteenth birthday, I was rushed by a sorority that pledged only German Jews, and although my best friends were of Russian provenance, I joined, under extreme pressure from my mother, and felt like both a traitor and an imposter.

Our family was a matriarchy. My mother's dominance was reinforced by her husband's financial failure; thus our household had to be partially subsidized by my mother's sisters, who had had the wit to marry men who were already rich or who became so. My father began as an optometrist, but my mother's prodding forced him into business first with my maternal grandfather and subsequently on his own. He went bankrupt when I was five, and from then on penny-pinching became my mother's occupation.

To reduce expenses, we moved in with another family when I was ten. As an only child, I was delighted to acquire siblings so easily. They were two brothers a few years older than I who taught me how to play football and baseball with a hardball. Perhaps this experience helped consolidate my feelings, an outlook not widely shared, that girls could play the same games as boys.

As I mentioned, I do remember being told that I was Jewish. It was after school one day that I asked my mother where I should be going on Sunday mornings, a question I had been unable to answer when my classmates put it to me. Her reply was an offer, which I eagerly accepted, to join Temple Israel, a reform congregation. During that summer vacation I was tutored in Jewish history and Bible in order to enter the preconfirmation class in the fall. The following year, each member of the confirmation class was asked to participate in an essay contest on "What the Synagogue Means to Me." My entry, under the pseudonym "Faith Ascendant" won the prize—probably because of my research on the synagogue as a house of prayer, house of meeting, house of study. But the nascent sociologist was betrayed in the first paragraph in which I said that when I entered the synagogue on Friday night I felt like more of a Jew and less of a Jew than at any other time. More of a Jew because I was with my own people, suffused with a "consciousness of kind"; less of a Jew because I did not have "to prepare a face to meet the faces" that I met. (During the time that I attended West High School there were only a dozen or so Jewish students, and, in general, Minneapolis was an anti-Semitic town.) Since Rabbi Minda did not take my confession of atheism seriously, I was confirmed in the Jewish faith and became a member of the junior congregation. As such, I was asked to give a talk at a Friday evening service. I chose to discuss a book I had just read, Vera Brittain's *Testament of Youth* (1933), and I quoted her goal of "knowing something about everything, and everything about something." I think I have fulfilled the first half of this aspiration.

My parents subscribed to *The Nation,* wherein I read articles assuring me that unemployment insurance, health care for all, and other social welfare proposals were not socialistic or communistic. Why would that be so bad, I wondered, and at age thirteen set off for the public library to find out. Under the heading "socialism" I found Morris Hillquit's *History of Socialism in the United States* and Friedrich Engels's *Socialism: Utopian and Scientific.* I immediately became a convinced Marxist, and I passed up a chance to hear T. S. Eliot in favor of one Sam Davis who was running for governor of Minnesota on the Communist party ticket. At party headquarters I picked up a slew of pamphlets like "A Noon Hour Talk with the Communist Party." I wrote a paper on American radical movements of the nineteenth century for a high school history class, but it got lost after the teacher lent it to a fellow student. I dropped out of high school at the end of my junior year and applied for admission to the University of Minnesota.

Education: Formal and Informal

Although my parents were in straitened circumstances, there was never any doubt about my attending the university. In the 1930s, residents of Minnesota paid only about twenty-five dollars a quarter, so tuition was not a hardship. The real problem in those depression years was that families needed the help of their children to keep from going under financially. My father, who saw me as another Walter Lippmann, accompanied me when I visited the campus. The university administrators were taken aback at my request to enter the university without graduating from high school but admitted me on probation. My first year was filled with intellectual and social excitement, engaging with able, provocative teachers: Benjamin Lippincott in political theory, who assigned books like Richard Henry Tawney's *The Acquisitive Society* (1920) and Beatrice Webb and Sidney Webb's *Industrial Democracy* (1897); Castell in philosophy and logic; Minnich in zoology; Charles Bird in abnormal psychology; and Eugen Altschul in socialist economics. Somehow I got turned on to Thorstein Veblen, peppering my conversation with "pecuniary emulation," "invidious comparison," "vested interest," "conspicuous consumption," "idle curiosity," and the rest of his catchy concepts. I read all his books and toyed with the idea of writing a biography of him, but Joseph Dorfman beat me to it. I also made the varsity debate team, a learning experience in how to take any side of a question. Encounters with more sophisticated students from Saint Paul were also stimulating. I was aware that there were a few feminists around, but I dismissed them as oddballs who insisted on racing men to doors and windows. I also disdained women's organizations, like the Women's International League for Peace and Freedom, and the National Council of Jewish Women, as bourgeois and supportive of the status quo.

During my first year at the University of Minnesota, I went to hear Lucian Koch, the director of Commonwealth College, a labor college in Mena, Arkansas. The notion of becoming a labor organizer began to germinate. But there were other notions, too. A year or two earlier I had become friendly with a literary young man who introduced me not only to T. S. Eliot, Restoration comedy, and other hitherto unknown-to-me English writers, but also to Proust, Rimbaud, Mallarmé, and the symbolist movement. I felt that Eliot had written Prufrock just for me, even though it wasn't coffee spoons I was measuring my life with. (Later I made extensive use of poetry in my sociology classes, especially that of the most sociological of poets, W. H. Auden. See, for example, his "Law Like Love" to spark a discussion of social control.) I also became hooked on Proust and read every word of his, mostly in translation, and everything about him I could find. Although I still have a bookcase of Proustiana, I have not been as meticulous as he in dredging up detail for this quick autobiography. Proust reappears later in my story.

After a year and a half at Minnesota I transferred to the University of Chicago to live with my parents, who had moved to Chicago. I decided to major in philosophy, especially Hindu philosophy. I supplemented my full-tuition scholarship with part-time jobs, such as cataloging the books in the personal library of a professor of public finance and catering private dinner parties. During the summer, I worked full-time as a bookkeeper in a jewelry store and as a stitcher of skirts in a cotton goods factory. This last job was taken with a view to becoming an organizer for the International Ladies Garment Workers Union, but I was fired after six weeks because I was unable to meet the piecework quota. After a quarter at the University of Chicago, only eighteen and acting on an impulse I don't fully comprehend, I applied for admission to Commonwealth College—which my father called "Commonfilth"—and was accepted as their youngest student despite telegrams from my family urging them to reject me. Tuition, including board and room, was forty dollars a month plus twenty-five hours of work a week. I was apprenticed to Willie the cook, who had been a member of the German Communist Party. Willie's other helper, Jeff, was an anarchist; listening to their arguments was instructive. (I had read with great fascination Emma Goldman's *Living My Life,* but knew I was not one "on bare knees to climb the volcanic hill.")

At that time, the college was nonsectarian and all the extant proletarian parties were represented there. I took courses called "Imperialism and Fascism," "History of Trade Unionism in the United States," and "Proletarian Literature." I prepared a genealogy of the fifty-odd proletarian parties in the United States, and I became romantically involved with a Trotskyite. On Saturday nights I square-danced with local farmers. I discovered, however, that I was an intellectual snob, like John Reed, who despised every communist who was not a Harvard graduate and every Harvard graduate who was not a communist—in the manner of Oscar Wilde's more famous statement about wits and gentlemen. Why I had expected workers from southern mills and factories to join me in contemplating the bourgeois wasteland, I don't know. Anyway, my tuition money ran out after three months, and I returned to the University of Chicago. At this time, a dissident group within the Socialist Party was flirting with a Trotskyite faction led by James P. Cannon (of Local 544 of truck drivers union fame) and Max Schachtman. In 1938, that faction became the Socialist Workers' Party. In joining the left-wing youth group of the Socialist Party, the Yipsels (Young People's Socialist League), in 1936, I was relieved of the necessity of choosing between reformism and revolution. In the Yipsels with me were such future greats as Saul Bellow, Oscar Tarcov, Herb Passin, George Reedy, Ithiel de Sola Poole, and Isaac Rosenfeld. I still remember the night a bunch of us spent at Isaac Rosenfeld's listening to De Falla's "Three Cornered Hat." I was also active in the Workers' Defense League. The C.I.O. was on the ascent, and I recall getting up very early on the morning of my final exams in order to be on the picket line of a strike by the Cap Makers' Union.

I changed my major to economics in order to find out if Marx was right and was guided through the three volumes of *Capital* by Paul Douglas, discovering the famous contradiction of how market forces were brought in "behind the backs of the workers." Our backs were sore from the whacks Douglas administered when he made an important point while pacing around the long seminar table. From Herbert Simon I learned that Marx as an economist was largely irrelevant, but that he could be admired as a sociologist. While an undergraduate at the University of Chicago, I took no course in sociology, although through independent study I did pass an examination in that subject. It was a philosophy course, "General Theory of Mind," that set me on the path to sociology. The instructor, Charles Morris, suggested that I read Karl Mannheim's *Ideology and Utopia* for the required book report. The sociology of knowledge solved a fundamental problem for me—how it was possible for someone to disagree with such a right-thinking person as myself without being either a fool or a knave. Many other remarkable professors at the University of Chicago remain in my memory:

Mortimer Adler (great books), Richard McKeon (literary criticism), Frederick Schuman (international politics), Fay Cooper Cole (anthropology), and the boy-president himself, Robert M. Hutchins. This "mountain range of Gothic," as Vincent Shean dubbed the university, was the field for the "battle of the books," which overflowed the classroom into nearby beer halls. My chief learning from the University of Chicago was that anything not in Aristotle or Aquinas was either false or insignificant.

Bicoastal Experiences

As an adolescent in Minneapolis I had dreamed of leading a bohemian life in Greenwich Village. So, armed with an A.B in economics and the social sciences from the University of Chicago and on the basis of my experience in writing for the *Chicago Daily Maroon* and *Soapbox,* I sent letters to every New York–based publication from *Boating Magazine* to the *Police Gazette,* modestly offering to serve as editor. Although hardly shaking the big city loose from its underpinnings, I finally did land a job on *The Advance,* the publication of the Amalgamated Clothing Workers. Besides reporting on labor matters, I prepared instructional materials for workers' education classes. Many evenings were spent at party meetings followed by long discussions at Life Cafeteria in the Village. I noted, without the indignation of a raised consciousness, that men did most of the talking and that women changed their political outlook with their lovers. At the behest of the party, I became a soapbox orator, holding forth on housing, unemployment, and war, and rescuing the vegetables hurled at me for the dinner stew. Late hours took their toll, and I was fired from *The Advance.* My account of my dismissal cites Trotskyism, but according to my boss, J.B.S. Hardman, it was for being late to work.

Unemployment forced a return to the parental nest, now in Los Angeles. After a series of odd jobs, including one as a hypnotist's accomplice, I went to work in 1939 as a case-aide for the California State Relief Administration. When one of my clients, angry at the cut in his check, pulled a gun on me, I disarmed him with an exhortation to join the union of people on relief. Party activities continued and Sunday mornings found me distributing leaflets to Japanese workers in Sawtelle, lecturing on the crisis of the middle class in San Diego, and, for a time, editing a publication for Mexican workers called *La Lucha Obrera.*

My sojourn in "warm Siberia" ended when, after passing a civil service exam for junior economist, I received a job offer from the Bureau of the Census. In Washington, D.C., my alienation from the party intensified. In Los Angeles, I had begun to prefer concerts over Red Card meetings. In the capital, I resented having to contribute half my salary to the party. The petty bourgeoise in me preferred spending that money on graduate study, especially since my roommate, who had left to attend Columbia with a fellowship in economics, urged me to join her, assuring me of a similar fellowship. One course in public finance was, however, enough to confirm that I had lost my taste for economics. Accordingly, I had the chutzpah to ask Robert M. MacIver, then chair of the sociology department, if I could trade my scholarship in economics for one in sociology, which I considered the last refuge of the dilettante. MacIver was agreeable to subsidizing my tuition, but I still had to work full-time to support myself and so I had little time to hang around school and network. I did, though, have flexible hours with the North American Service of the BBC, for whom I wrote reports on American reactions to their broadcasts and on the contribution of American women to the war effort. I did this in spite of my personal opposition to the "imperialist war," believing there were better ways of saving Jews and others from the Nazis.

Caste and Class in a Southern Town

In 1944, after completing the required sixty hours of course work for a Ph.D. in sociology, I registered with the employment bureau and was interviewed by Dean French of Randolph-Macon Woman's College in Lynchburg, Virginia, who confided that, never having had one, they were looking for a "nice Jew" to be on their faculty. I replied that I hoped they would find me so nice that they would hire more (indeed, Hilda Hertz succeeded me). I wasn't, however, very nice. I was horrified, I told the students, by water fountains marked "white" and "colored," at a drugstore clerk's refusing a Negro woman a drink of water because they had run out of paper cups, by the lack of a hospital where a Negro doctor could take his patients. I encouraged my students, as young women of good will, to walk rather than ride the segregated bus. With a religion instructor, Emma Lou Benignus, I took a group of students to an interracial conference in Durham, talked about the "white peril" in Lynchburg at the Methodist church, and heard that alumnae were threatening to cut off bequests to the college unless they got rid of this damn Yankee. Emma Lou and I also managed to invite a group of Negro high school teachers to the annual Greek play, where they were seated next to carefully selected student buffers. I got a firsthand lesson in caste and class when, at a tea at my house afterward, they complained about the riffraff they had to teach.

Although I was opposed in principle to marriage as an institution oppressive of women, I was married at the end of my first year at Randolph-Macon. There was no way I could "live in sin" and remain on the faculty. I should have mentioned that although I had never taken a course in the family, it was assumed that as a woman I was fitted by nature to teach such a course. Amusingly, when it came time to impart sexual facts, Donald Taylor, who also taught a family course, added my class to his. Perhaps this delicacy on the part of the chair derived from my as yet unmarried state. My husband, Emanuel A. Hacker, kept house for us while working on his dissertation on the marginal utility of leisure. When he received an offer to teach economics at Brooklyn College, I left for New York with him. I got a job at the New School for Social Research as student adviser with teaching responsibility for one course, which in those prefeminist days I called "Man-in-Relationship."

Academic Bites in the Big Apple

Permit me to backtrack a bit. Robert K. Merton and Paul Lazarsfeld supported the sociological firmament at Columbia during my sojourn there, prior to my teaching at Randolph-Macon. It was a "window of opportunity" for women, since most of the men either had been or were about to be drafted. Although Merton's lectures had the elegance of a chess game, I chose Lazarsfeld and majored in public opinion and mass communications. Regrettably, I did not have the leisure to serve an apprenticeship under his tutelage at the Bureau for Applied Social Research. I wrote, however, a paper titled "The Ishmael Complex" (1952), for one of his courses. It was based on a content analysis of popular books for boys, and, in part, it exploited the black-woman analogy in explaining the camaraderie between white boys and their colored companions. Its publication provoked a host of angry letters to the editor and attacks in the *Amsterdam News,* all based on a complete misunderstanding of sociology. For Merton I began, but never finished, a paper titled "Nietzsche's Theory of Ideology," which was finally published in an Indian journal (1970). Nietzsche succeeded Veblen and Proust as my third great hero.

Doctoral candidates were encouraged early on to give thought to their dissertations. Several of my attempts fell by the wayside. The first, "Social Structure in Proust," was salvaged for a course in the sociology of literature that I cotaught at the Columbia School of General Studies. My second try was titled "Petticoats in the Pulpit." I had fallen heir to a list of some two hundred women ministers ordained in four Protestant denominations concentrated largely in New England, and I thought I might interview them in depth about their experiences and problems. I hoped that Merton might agree that such a study would make a valuable contribution to the sociology of occupations in exploring the paradox that the ministry, stereotyped as the most feminine of male occupations, was most closed to women. He did not, however, find the suggestion interesting. Years later, after many false starts, I finally wrote a Parsonian dissertation, which was accepted without revision and will be discussed below.

I had been poised to take my orals until a fellow student told me I was sure to fail; I cancelled. I was also aware that in those years the average time for getting the doctorate at Columbia was from ten to fifteen years. I was also told that things might go faster at Teachers College–Columbia University, and so, with the aid of a fellowship, I embarked on a program of study there and received master's degree in intergroup relations in 1949. Although in the end I did return to Columbia for my orals and doctorate, it was at Teachers College that I decided that every term paper should explore some theoretical problem in relation to women in the hope that these papers in combination might constitute a dissertation. So it was for Goodwin Watson that I wrote "Women as a Minority Group" (1951)[1] and "Marx, Weber, and Pareto on the Changing Status of Women" (1953). At this time I was a non–tenure track faculty member at Hunter College, where I unsuccessfully proposed a course called "Conflicts of Modern Women." In my social problems classes, I was also pushing the "Hacker Plan for the Reconstruction of Family Life," a ten-point program emphasizing the need for part-time jobs on all skill levels and mothers' preference, similar to veterans' preference, on civil service exams. (As men bear arms for the state, women bear children.) My tenth point gave women permission to marry down: If the prince can marry a shepherdess, then the princess can marry a goatherd.

In a way, not having a Ph.D. was an advantage. In those days the operating system at Hunter was known as the "fluid bottom" in that hardly anyone on a tenure track ever achieved it. Rather, after serving for three years, instructors were not renewed. As a degree-less "temporary tutor" I could stay on indefinitely without raises or perks, but I was allowed to teach practically every course in the curriculum, including a graduate course in theory. Personal circumstances, however, impelled me to leave Hunter. My husband had been hospitalized for an indefinite period, and I needed much more money. Luckily, a friend brought me to Ernest Dichter's Institute for Motivational Research at Croton-on-Hudson and, after a trial assignment of a "think piece" on the role of barbers in selling men's hair products, I was hired. Thus began a fascinating apprenticeship in imaginative, qualitative research. Vance Packard didn't name me in *The Hidden Persuaders* (1957), but I was responsible for the suggestion made to Duncan Hines that women should be asked to add their own egg to the cake mix. From the Institute I graduated to Young & Rubicam, an advertising agency, where the conversational level surpassed that on most college campuses. There I supervised a series of special market studies on Negroes, farmers, adolescents, and, most significantly, working wives.

I was permitted to add a page of my own on working wives to the agency's Consumers' Poll, with its national probability sample of four thousand men and women. These data served not only as the basis for advertising strategies but also provided the material for my dissertation, "A Functional Approach to the Gainful Employment of Married Women." My study purported to explain why the large-scale employment of married women outside the home, like woman suffrage, had had so little impact on the relations between men and women and the status of women in our society. It demonstrated that women's attitudes toward work served to obviate any potential conflict between their jobs and the primacy of their family roles. I found that the majority of working wives did not seek to compete for jobs on an equal basis with men, but were satisfied with the connotations attached to merely holding a job.[2] At last in 1961 (and aged forty-something) I became in my eyes the world's oldest newly minted Ph.D.

The acquisition of a Ph.D. did not help to overcome my growing dissatisfaction with Young & Rubicam, but would, I hoped, provide a springboard for reentry into college teaching. Letters of application to Queens College and other schools, however, netted nothing. Women in their forties and lacking a male patron were not hired as assistant professors, or even instructors. I was taken on, however, by Ed Suchman as a resident in accident research for the New York City Department of Health. Among my duties was the ghoulish task of watching for near-accidents in playgrounds, schools for the deaf, and tunnels under the Hudson as background for writing research proposals. Although none of the proposals got funded, I did publish a theoretical article (1963). Concurrently, I conducted a research seminar and served as adviser on doctoral dissertations in the Teachers College department of home and family life. In this capacity, I helped policemen, rabbis, social workers, and others who had mindlessly collected data to ferret out questions that their data might answer. Gertrude Stein would have been pleased!

My Not So Dolce Vita in Italy

I had always dreamed of living in Italy: *Bell'Italia, amate sponde, pur vi torno a riveder!* I still have a postcard from my childhood sent to me by my Aunt Ada, who had been a friend of the Italian novelist and poet D'Annunzio, exhorting me to come to Italy even on my hands and knees like the pilgrims of old. So shortly after I had my Ph.D. and freed by divorce from marital responsibilities some years earlier, I applied for a postdoctoral Fulbright to conduct research on the family life of working mothers in northern Italy. Thus, in 1962 I traveled blissfully by freighter to Genoa. Random sampling was out of the question, but I gained access to *operaii* (blue-collar workers) and *impiegati* (white-collar workers) through personal contact with several important employers in Genoa. I was probably in more Italian homes than most Italians, and I quickly learned to plead *fegato* (liver trouble) to fend off repeated offers of sweet vermouth. Findings from intensive interviews with over a hundred husbands and wives in which I employed a Rashomon-like technique have been reported to various international conferences, but nothing ever found its way into print.

I spent a second year in Italy doing consumer research for several advertising agencies in Milan. One of my projects uncovered an interesting relationship between technology and the household division of labor. With the acquisition of a washing machine, the wife became the laundress because she didn't trust the maid with the machine. Similarly, with the acquisition of a dishwasher, the husband took over from the wife. Of course that was thirty years ago, and I haven't had a chance to check on more recent appliances like the microwave. I had obtained these assignments through the good offices of Francesco Alberoni, a Milan-based sociologist who also published several of my reviews and articles in the journal he edited, *Studi di Sociologia*. One of them, which attempted a definition of role conflict in modern women, paralleled to some extent Merton's concepts of role-set and status-set (1965).

In 1964, I reluctantly returned to New York from Italy after receiving notice that carrying charges had begun on the co-op apartment that I had purchased in the blueprint stage. After another stint in motivational research, in 1966, I obtained a position as associate professor at Adelphi University through the then-chair of the department of sociology, Robert Endleman, whom I had met at a cocktail party.[3]

Song of India

The fall of 1969 found me, on leave of absence from Adelphi, at the University of Bangalore in South India on another Fulbright fellowship as a visiting professor. I taught graduate courses in the family and field research methods, and it is not altogether complimentary to my students that I learned much more from them than they did from me. While I tried to encourage them in sociological ways of thinking about the social problems that beset India, they were orienting me to India in matters small and large. In the beginning, there were lessons in sari-draping before class; my highest mark in this endeavor was B+. Then I was invited to weddings, dance recitals, religious lectures, tabla (drum) and sitar concerts, picnics, and above all to their homes. (When they came to mine, I escorted the women home in an auto-rickshaw.) Perhaps it was the eager hospitality and openness of my students that gave me the illusion that I shared in their world. Indeed, it seemed that time past and time future were present in India. Strangely, it was my very immersion in Hinduism—I spent some time at the Pondicherry ashram—that brought me to a new appreciation of Judaism. Acres of diamonds in my own backyard!

Although my primary purpose in India was to teach, I also engaged in research, both planned and serendipitous. The former was an adaptation to the Indian scene of my Italian questionnaire. English is the language of instruction in Indian universities, so my students were able to translate the questionnaire into whichever of the some twenty-six languages they also spoke and to conduct interviews in it with Indians who did not know English. After I resumed my duties in the States, the data were farmed out to Adelphi students for master's essays.

I have already hinted at the pervasive sexual and nonsexual harassment of Indian women called "Eve-teasing." Women students were afraid to go alone to the library at night. After graduation, they were escorted to and from their jobs by male relatives or husbands. I sent a letter protesting this situation to the local paper, the *Deccan Herald,* signed only H. Hacker, which provoked a prolific, largely negative response. Many of the letter-writers assumed I was a foreign man seeking to corrupt the purity of Indian womanhood. The letters editor of the *Deccan Herald* gave me all the letters and subsequently published my content analysis of them. The whole exchange became a minor cause célèbre that outlasted my stay in India as indicated by the headline "WOMAN: DEVI [goddess] OR DOLL: Hacker and After." On my lecture circuit in India, Pakistan, and Bangladesh, sponsored by the U.S. Information Service, many women expressed appreciation of my modest efforts on their behalf. For me, India abounded in wondrous experiences, but the most enchanting was hearing a nightingale outside my mission window in Rajshahi just before dawn.

At the end of my Fulbright year, and somewhat unwillingly, I returned to New York via Indonesia and Japan just in time for the mighty march celebrating the fiftieth anniversary of the woman's suffrage amendment. In consonance with my long-time interest in the study of women and my commitment to the women's movement, I had joined NOW in 1966 in response to an invitation from Pauli Murray, a founding member and the first African American woman to be ordained a priest of the Episcopal church. She had previously been a lawyer for the American Civil Liberties Union (ACLU), and our friendship had begun after she had telephoned me out of the blue to say that she had used my "Women as a Minority Group" in a brief before a federal court contesting the exclusion of women from jury duty in three southern states. I had also gotten in on the ground floor of Sociologists for Women in Society. In fall 1970, I offered a course in "Women's Liberation" at Adelphi, which elicited long and impassioned term papers from the women students. In subsequent years, in order to bring men in, the title was changed to "The Social Roles of Men and Women"; ultimately it became "The Sociology of Gender." I also pioneered a course named "Sexuality in Sociological Perspective."

A sabbatical from Adelphi in 1974 provided an opportunity for visiting Israel, where I substituted for Dorit Padan-Eisenstark at the University of the Negev in Beer Sheba while she was occupied with a project in Jerusalem. We were collaborating on a pilot study of marital power in four Israeli institutional frameworks: the kibbutz; the "regular" *moshav*; an intermediate form known as the *moshav shitufi,* which combined equality of income with traditional family patterns; and the private sector. These four structures constituted a continuum along which the key variables of family and work arrangements varied systematically. For purposes of observation and interviewing, I was invited by Menachem Rosner, a noted Israeli sociologist, to spend a week at his kibbutz, Reshafim. I then moved on to Regba, as representative of the *moshavim shitufim* (small landholders collective settlements) for another week.

Our conclusions included two propositions: First, until men are drawn into child care and service occupations, job segregation, with lower prestige for women's work, will persist; and, second, even when wives are not economically dependent on their husbands, they retain an inferior social position in a male-dominated community. Back in the United States, I devoted months to grant applications to the Ford Foundation and the National Institute at Mental Health (NIMH) for a research project based on our pilot study. It was never funded, possibly because of the modesty of the request and the evaluators' lack of sympathy for Israel. Amusingly, the first proposal I wrote, "The Socio-Economic Context of Sex and Power: A Study of Women, Work, and Family Roles in Four Israeli Institutional Frameworks," was published in an anthology edited by Florence Denmark (1976). A paper, "Cognitive Dissonance and Choice of Reference Group: The Case of Women and Work in the Moshav Shitufi," was rejected by the *American Sociological Review* with the suggestion that I submit it to a journal dealing with sex roles, perhaps indicating minimal mainstream interest in integrating studies of women's experiences into sociological theory.

Finding My Birth Family

In March 1969 I went to my hometown of Minneapolis as a delegate to the annual meeting from the Adelphi chapter of the American Association of University Professors. There my research skills paid off: I found my birth family. The high drama of that encounter I reserve for another context, and I say here only that suddenly I acquired four brothers and four sisters, all but one older than I. It saddens me that I missed meeting my birth mother by only two years. My father, though, had been long dead. Both had been born in Odessa. Poverty had forced them to give me up, but the trauma had been so great for my mother that they kept my youngest, equally unwanted, sister. Over the past twenty-some years, I have formed strong bonds with this second family and am continually celebrating birthdays, anniversaries, Bar and Bat-Mitzvot, weddings, and so on. In 1977, I led a workshop on the adoptee experience at the Groves Conference on Marriage and the Family. At present I am involved with three families, since even though I am divorced from his uncle, Andrew Hacker continues to regard me as his favorite aunt.

The Recent Past

In 1984 I took early retirement from Adelphi. Since then I have been teaching one course a semester at the New School for Social Research, alternating among my current interests in religion, sexuality, and the impact of feminist scholarship on the social sciences.

In my end was my beginning. I seem to have returned to my early concern with philosophy, and I now regularly read *Hypatia* and similar journals. It was at the Non-Governmental Organization Forum before the UN Decade for Women Conference in 1985 in Nairobi that I first heard myself say that my current interest was feminist epistemology. I now have a formidable library on the subject. At an International Sociological Association conference in Trento, Italy, in June 1992, I made a presentation on feminist methodology. Then there are lesser flights of fancy, like my frequently given talk with musical illustrations, "Women's Plights in Opera Plots: Fantasies of Male Librettists."

Apologia pro Mea Vita

Shall we look at my story as oral history, cautionary tale, or just personal memoir? In reflecting on my sociological career, what can I say I have accomplished? Like most teachers, I have spent hours in student hand-holding; have recruited young people into sociology, most notably, Bennett Berger, who has often told me that I "turned him on to sociology"; and have labored interminably with graduate students. I have written countless letters of recommendation, marched and demonstrated for women's and other worthy causes, testified in Albany and Washington, D.C., about discrimination against women, acted as outside reader for dissertations written both in the United States and in India, served on professional committees, written dozens of painstaking critiques of papers submitted to professional journals, done duty as reference librarian for friends and colleagues on a wide range of subjects, addressed graduate colloquia, participated in radio and television programs, and more.

Although I have contributed chapters to several books, in one case amounting to half the volume, I have not published a book. (The covers of *The Social Roles of Women and Men* (1975) were too close together to merit that designation.) My vita is eclectic as well as hectic. The articles (twenty-one), book reviews (sixteen), and presentations at professional meetings (thirty) roam the sociological spectrum rather than mining one vein. In the main, my sociological work bears witness to my lifelong interest in the problem of redefining gender roles and restructuring the power relationships between women and men in a manner to maximize human potential. I have addressed this question on both the social and the psychological levels—that is, by investigating the interrelationships among such dominant institutions of our society as the family, the economy, legal and political systems, and the church, on the one hand, and the impact of these institutions on the motivations and self-concepts of individuals, on the other.

Although I have to my credit a few major articles, my contributions might have been much more substantial. I have always been more of a gadfly than a solid scholar. I am attracted to unpopular causes and outsiders, people on the margin (1971b). It is axiomatic to say that my paucity of publications can be attributed to an interaction of environmental, accidental, and characterological factors. I have always been out of sync: entering graduate school a few years older than was customary at the time, completing my Ph.D. as a middle-aged woman, spouting ideas whose time had not come. As mentioned earlier, in my youth, women needed male sponsors and I had neither the time nor the inclination to acquire one. I should say, however, that all my jobs and most of my invitations to present at professional meetings came from personal contacts, mostly male.[4]

On the characterological side, there was the nagging doubt as to whether what I was doing was worth any great investment. Also, I have been a peculiar combination of quick study and obsessive-compulsive attender to detail. Call it grandiosity, but there was always one more book or article to be read, one more anticipated counterargument to be taken care of, before closure could be achieved. Often it was more interesting to move on to a new enthusiasm or to throw off a think piece for others to substantiate. Brainstorming is more fun than fact gathering. Lack of discipline looms large. I never wanted to give up anything—concert, play, opera, party, lecture, seminar—because of fundamental uncertainty that the sacrifice would pay off.

Feminism has always been the beacon that I follow even as its trajectory changes. It is difficult now to recollect in tranquillity just what propelled me along different paths. Overall, like so many others, I have been concerned with the causes of women's subordination. In reflecting on the failure of those modern societies officially committed to the liberation of women, such as the Israeli kibbutzim, the Soviet Union, the People's Republic of China, Cuba, and Sweden, to implement sex equality I speculated that, in addition to their special circumstances, a pervasive traditional counterideology, stemming from religion, persisted. For the past decade or so, I have been interested in the pursuit of strategies to transform the religious substrate of primordial images of masculinity and femininity and, in addition to writing in this area (1983, 1984), have offered a course at the New School for Social Research titled "Men's Rites; Women's Rights: Sociological and Feminist Perspectives on Religion."

Quo Vadis?

What next? Shall I cultivate my garden, or which, if any, of my unfinished projects that fill ten file cases shall I try to complete? Polish the paper "Outing versus Coming Out" given at the 1992 meeting of the Society for the Study of Social Problems? Develop the play based on the life of Frances Wright? Deliver the coup de grâce in the argument about matriarchy or the best definition of marital power? Distill more articles from the in-depth interview study of same-sex and cross-sex friendship dyads that so far has yielded only one published (1981) and one unpublished paper (1978)? Revise and resubmit the analysis of the situation of women in Regba, a collective settlement in Israel? Look over the transcriptions of my

Italian interviews? Go beyond the two chapters of the update of my dissertation based on new survey data that I had completed before Harper and Row—not the first publisher to do so—canceled my book contract? Try to integrate into a book my lecture notes for the course dealing with the impact of feminist scholarship on the social sciences? "Decisions and revisions which a minute will reverse." Or shall the agéd eagle spread its wings and fly off in some new direction?

No matter. At least I have the satisfaction of knowing that under the terms of my will a fellowship will be established in my name at the University of Minnesota to provide one year, or possibly two, of subsidy to a promising graduate student, who has completed all the course requirements for the Ph.D., to work full-time on a dissertation that will contribute to feminist scholarship.

Helen Mayer Hacker

NOTES

1. A revised and updated version of this essay was published in 1974.

2. This finding is clarified and elaborated in my article "The Feminine Protest of the Working Wife" (1971a). The title alludes to Adler's concept of "masculine protest." In effect, the working wives in my study say, "Even though I work like a man, I am still a woman—and a good wife and mother."

3. It may be of historical interest to note that my beginning and continuing salary was substantially less than that of the average male *assistant* professor at Adelphi. Some years later, and without any intervention on my part, I was identified by Committee W of the American Association of University Professors as the most discriminated against woman at Adelphi and given a raise of $2,000.

4. For example, "The New Burdens of Masculinity" (1957) was originally a paper on role conflicts of men that was commissioned by Nelson Foote, a family sociologist, for a meeting of the Groves Conference on Marriage and the Family.

REFERENCES

Hacker, Helen Mayer. 1951. "Women as a Minority Group." *Social Forces* 30(1): 60–69. No. S-108 in the Bobbs Merrill Reprint Series in Sociology.

———. 1952. "The Ishmael Complex." *American Journal of Psychotherapy* 6(3): 393–512.

———. 1953. "Marx, Weber, and Pareto on the Changing Status of Women." *American Journal of Economics and Sociology* 12(2): 149–62.

———. 1957. "The New Burdens of Masculinity." *Marriage and Family Living* 19:227–33.

———. 1963. "A Sociological Approach to Accident Research." *Social Problems* 10(4): 383–89.

———. 1965. "Verso Una Definizione dei Conflitti di Ruolo nelle Donne Moderne." *Studi di Sociologia* 3(3): 332–41.

———. 1970. "Nietzsche and the Ideology of Greek Tragedy." *Daystar: Social, Cultural, and Literary Magazine* 2(4): 17–30.

———. 1971a. "The Feminine Protest of the Working Wife." *Indian Journal of Social Work* 31(4): 403–6.

———. 1971b. "Homosexuals: Deviant or Minority Group?" Pp. 65–92 in *The Other Minorities*, edited by Edward Sagarin. Waltham, Mass.: Ginn and Company.

———. 1974. "Women as a Minority Group: Twenty Years Later." *International Journal of Group Tension* 9(1): 122–32.

———. 1975. *The Social Roles of Women and Men: A Sociological Approach*. New York: Harper and Row.

———. 1976. "The Scio-Economic Context of Sex and Power: A Study of Women, Work, and Family Roles in Four Israeli Institutional Frameworks." Pp. 579–600 in *Women, vol. 1: A PDI Research Reference*, edited by Florence L. Denmark. New York: Psychological Dimensions.

———. 1977. "Problems in Defining and Measuring Marital Power Cross-Culturally." *Annals of the New York Academy of Sciences* 285:646–52.

———. 1978. "The Influence of Gender Roles on Reciprocal Ratings in Same-Sex and Cross-Sex Friendship Dyads." Paper presented at the Ninth World Congress of Sociology, Uppsala, Sweden.

———. 1981. "Blabbermouths and Clams: Sex Differences in Self-Disclosure in Same-Sex and Cross-Sex Friendship Dyads." *Psychology of Women Quarterly* 5(3): 385–401.

———. 1983. "Women and Islam: Dilemmas of Muslim Feminists." Paper presented at the annual meeting of the Society for the Scientific Study of Religion, Knoxville, Tenn.

———. 1984. "Towards a Feminist Reformation of Biblical Religion." *New England Sociologist* 5(1): 23–36.

Fourteen

Working the Third Shift

Lynda Lytle Holmstrom

"Unfortunately, there's no place for women in sociology," replied the professor matter-of-factly when, as a recent college graduate, I inquired about the possibility of becoming a sociologist. "Well," I thought to myself, "I'll make a place!" Thus began my journey from anthropology, a field where I had been invited to attend graduate school, to sociology where apparently, to use a familiar phrase, "no women need apply" (Walsh 1977).

Whatever gave me the audacity to think I could make a place for myself as a woman in sociology, I'll never know. Nothing in my background suggested such a course of action. Like many women, I got there by a circuitous path. The three questions posed by my story are: Why a career? Why sociology? and, Why with a feminist, activist orientation?

Roots in the Pacific Northwest

Two of my ancestors, and maybe more, arrived in the New World in the 1700s; by the time of the Civil War, all branches of my family had arrived. My more immediate roots, however, are in the Pacific Northwest, where my four grandparents moved around the turn of the century. I was born in Seattle in 1939 on the eve of World War II. I was raised there as well, although with early sojourns in Milwaukee and Chicago. I was an only child. And I was from a "broken" home, an oddity then; the term "single-parent" was not yet in use. The divorce occurred in Illinois in 1946 when I was six or seven. It was long before no-fault changed the rules of the game and wreaked its havoc with women's lives (Weitzman 1985). In the custom of the day, the court awarded me to Mother, and we moved back to Seattle. Father, a businessman, soon moved to San Francisco, where he became president and principal owner of the Lytle Buick Company at the corner of Van Ness Avenue and California Street, thus achieving his version of the

American Dream. He saw himself in the good-provider role (Bernard 1981) even after the divorce, and he dutifully paid regular, albeit modest, alimony and child support.

Memories from my early years often are associated with the places to which I moved because of the stage of Father's business career and the state of my parents' marriage. I remember World War II blackouts in Seattle, with blankets over the windows in case Japan might bomb there, too; neon lights of Chicago nightlife outside our Rush Street apartment near Michigan Avenue where, reunited with Father, we lived close to his General Motors' office in the Loop; and our postwar home in then-rural Barrington, Illinois, surrounded by twenty acres of woods in which I wandered freely and alone. The postwar nation focused on the family, created the baby boom, and moved to the suburbs; in contrast, my family fell apart, I remained an only child, and we moved back to city life.

I remember the long train trips with Mother back and forth between the Midwest and Seattle as my parents separated, reunited, and then divorced. No one bothered to tell me they got divorced until one day Grandmother mentioned it. My parents' divorce, when I learned of it, seemed like a nonevent since Father seldom had participated in family life. But in retrospect, the divorce, which Father wanted and Mother did not, changed every aspect of my existence and was one of the defining moments of my life. Years later, it propelled me toward a career.

Female Role Models

Nothing in my background suggested one could "have it all"—career, marriage, and motherhood—although the women in my family were well-educated for their times. Several attended college when few women did, and many were adventurous and accomplished in various ways.

Grandmothers Mayme and Jennie both were pioneer women, part of the white migration to the Pacific Northwest around the turn of the century. Grandmother Mayme, on my father's side, studied music in Lindsborg, Kansas. Later, thinking it would be better for her health, she and her pharmacist husband moved to a homestead in Idaho, taking her piano along. She had four children, and she played music in the northern Idaho wilderness near Coeur d'Alene.

Grandmother Jennie left a farm in upstate New York for a pioneer life in British Columbia and later in Bellingham, Washington, on beautiful Bellingham Bay near the Canadian border. Jennie had two children, did some sort of work at the courthouse (I am hazy as to what), and collected cut crystal.

Mother, whose name was Dorothy, was born in Bellingham in 1905; she grew up there riding her Shetland pony and playing the flute, often giving concerts. The family later moved to Seattle. She attended the University of Washington for three years, but she switched to work and marriage before completing her degree. The bank where she worked fired her when they found out she had married. She got another job doing administrative assistance work and did that for a number of years until she was forced to quit. Her husband suddenly had decided to move to California. She never returned to the paid labor force, instead spending her time on hobbies (equestrian and musical), motherhood, and volunteer work (Red Cross during World War II).

Aunt Nellie, Mother's much-older sister, studied piano in Rochester, New York, and she had a music studio in Bellingham in the early 1900s. At some point, she retired from teaching piano and although she married, she had no children.

Nor did any of Father's three sisters "have it all," although Aunt Mev, remarkable for her generation, came very close. Born in 1909, Mev became "Dean of Women" (associate director of student affairs) at the University of Washington as a young widow with a small child to rear. After her remarriage, to Uncle Gordon, dean of forestry at the University of Washington, nepotism rules led to her resignation. She returned to the paid labor force about nine years later when her youngest child was in kindergarten. She often referred to herself as a "dean's wife" and was pictured in the Seattle papers hostessing wives of visiting dignitaries.

Aunt Jane married, but quickly and wisely divorced when, on her honeymoon, her new, well-to-do husband talked of driving her over a cliff. I never knew Aunt Betty. She graduated from the University of Washington, married, and immediately contracted Hodgkin's disease and died.

Neither of Father's other wives combined career and family. Father's second wife, whom I met only a few times, was chronically mentally ill and later, after divorce proceedings, hanged herself while in a mental hospital. Father's third wife, a San Francisco socialite to whom he remained married the rest of his life, was an astute businesswoman who had no children by any of her several marriages and whose interests were in finance and the social scene.

The strengths, adventures, and achievements of the women I knew best growing up became apparent as I gained distance from them and learned more about what they had done over a life span. Growing up, however, I saw them primarily in domestic and auxiliary roles. I wanted something different.

Coming of Age in Seattle in the 1950s

My school years, from second grade through high school, were spent in Seattle, a city set between Puget Sound and Lake Washington. Framed by the snow-clad Olympics and Cascades, the city is filled with evergreens and linked to myriad islands by ferryboats. We lived in Aunt Nellie's house on Capitol Hill, close to downtown, in a predominantly middle-class neighborhood adjacent to Volunteer Park. I was raised primarily by my mother, although with considerable input from her relatives who took us in: Aunt Nellie (Mother's older sister), her much older husband, and Grandmother Jennie, born in 1889, 1876, and 1870, respectively, and thus with notions formed in the nineteenth century. Mother was very nurturing and patient, and she had high expectations for my education, the purpose of which was never discussed. Good grades were expected, I dutifully complied, and college was assumed.

I spent much of my childhood reading. Our home was filled with books that belonged to Mother or my aunt. I also borrowed books from a nearby library and the parents of my second-grade friend, Coppélia. Some books, like *The Scarlet Letter* and *Of Human Bondage,* I first read at an age when they did not make too much sense to me. My favorites were *The Bounty Trilogy,* especially *Pitcairn Island,* and *Gone with the Wind*. Intrigued by Scarlett's adventures, I decided to go on to *Forever Amber,* but the librarian, a prude I thought, disapproved, and I had to buy a copy at the drugstore. I also liked Halliburton's *Complete Book of Marvels,* especially the photos of Machu Picchu; a sex manual, obtained clandestinely by my friend Coppélia in the fifth grade; and *Mad* magazine.

Mother's notion of childrearing included numerous doses of culture. I spent many hours in the Seattle Art Museum in Volunteer Park. She took me to classical concerts and plays. Piano and ballet lessons were required. I traveled just enough to whet my appetite. In high school, I visited my father in California. This trip started the jarring process of going back and forth more frequently between my parents' separate social worlds, with their disparate values and economic resources. Newspaper clippings in my scrapbooks tell the tale—snippets about Father and his third wife from Herb Caen's *San Francisco Chronicle* social column; photos of Mother were more cultural and educational in tone.

High School, 1954–1957: The Smart-Girl Problem

I attended Garfield High, a centrally located Seattle public school whose enrollment, long before busing, included a goodly mix of white, black, and Asian students and a socioeconomic range from the affluent to the poor. Seattle students sometimes did attend private school, but in the Pacific Northwest, private school did not have the same cachet it has in other areas of the country. I attended high school during the era of the feminist doldrums (Rupp and Taylor 1987). Except for Coppélia (now a professor at Brown University), I do not recall any of the girls discussing career goals, although later a handful did have careers. We were raised on movies like *The Red Shoes;* there is not even a "mommy track" option in that tale, only the heroine's fatal leap onto the train track. "I Love Lucy" reigned on television.

My strongest high school memory is the schizophrenic split between academic and social life. It was not a good time for smart girls (Komarovsky 1950; Breines 1992). Only one girl, who later became a physician, managed to be both a "brain" and popular in the teenage sense. I was friends with other good students, both boys and girls. And I was friendly with many of the socially popular girls, but I was never a core member of the social set.

I solved the "smart girl" problem by developing a social life outside the school. This segmentation by time and place perpetuated the academic/social split, but it led to many happy times. As long as I was with kids from other high schools, no one cared about my high grades. First, several girlfriends and I joined the Seattle Mountaineers. It was fun and an empowering gender experience. On winter weekends, we took the ski train to Stampede Pass. After the snow melted, the focus turned to mountain climbing, and some of the strongest climbers were girls. We trained with ice axes, ropes, and crampons, and we practiced belaying, glissading, and camping in the snow. I climbed Mount Saint Helens before the top blew off.

Second, I mentioned my religious doubts to my friend, Elaine, who whisked me off to her Methodist Youth Fellowship (MYF). I never got the religious issue answered and thus remain a staunch agnostic. I think about this issue now and then, when a flower opens in my garden or Orion moves across a clear New Hampshire sky. The answer seems no closer now than then, so I always come back to agnosticism. But in my high school days, the MYF is where I met boys and girls from other high schools.

Better yet, and further removed from the Garfield scene, at MYF I also met a college junior named Ross who seemed smart and who rowed varsity crew for the University of Washington, a school that took its crew seriously. He asked me out to see *War and Peace,* and he did not seem to mind female intelligence. He was good at math and helped me with Algebra III, and we have been discussing ideas ever since. He introduced me to his family in their Seattle home—his father, a businessman; his mother, a kindergarten teacher; and his younger brother and sister. We continued dating during my senior year. Years later, reminiscing, I asked him, "Why me?" Somewhat to my surprise, he said that my intelligence, rather than being off-putting, was part of the initial attraction. He had tired of "Sally Sorority" and "dumb clinging vines."

High school graduation was approaching and because of the highly gendered and confining social scene on the University of Washington campus, I was hell-bent to get out of town. Most college-bound Garfield graduates in this state of land-grant higher education would go on to the University of Washington (U of W). My aversion to attending the U of W was so great that I took no notice of its highly competent faculty or its beautifully landscaped campus with a vista of Mount Rainier. I feared I would have the "smart-girl problem" all over again. Women's social life was dominated by the sororities on Greek Row, and I thought I would be on the fringes.

I applied to Stanford, Berkeley, and Whitman, although I do not remember any rational process in selecting these three. I decided on Stanford, not for any compelling academic reason, but because it was near San Francisco, where my father lived; because it did not have sororities then; and because my cousin Lois was a student there. I became the indirect beneficiary of the fact that her parents, my Uncle Gordon and Aunt Mev, knew their way around the academic scene. I never gave much thought then to the cost of tuition. Money for college was not mentioned in the divorce decree, but it always was understood that Father would pay for college wherever I wanted to go. Autumn arrived. Coppélia went East to Barnard, and I flew off to "The Farm."

The Stanford Years, 1957–1961: Undergraduate Life

Stanford, founded by the senator and his wife in 1885 and designed in collaboration with Frederick Law Olmsted, was built on the Stanfords' eight thousand–acre Palo Alto farm. Past the main gate, the long, straight driveway is lined with rows of palms. The gracefully arched sandstone buildings come into sight and in the center of the Quad sits Memorial Church. Presidents such as J. E. Wallace Sterling put Stanford on the academic map. The fact that the university survived the senator's death, however, is because his astute, iron-willed, widow—Jane Lathrop Stanford—shepherded the institution through the financial chaos associated with the settlement of her husband's estate (Allen 1980; Nagel 1985).

I arrived on a hot September day in 1957, eighteen years old, shy and nervous, but determined to succeed. I knew being there was special—not every one got in—and it was harder for girls than boys. The school had been open to females since its founding, but the gender ratio of students on campus was not in the girls' favor. Dwight D. Eisenhower was president and politically it was a quiet period on campus, the calm before the storm. The student body was "lily white," but I cannot say I noticed then. Rules for women were minimal, compared to other institutions of the time, but we did have a curfew, sign-out sheets, dress-up dinner once a week, and a rule to wear skirts when on the Quad. Dorms were single-sex, not coed. I was shy around the boys on campus and at the awkward "mixers" for boys and girls to meet each other that were one of the social fixtures of the time. Long-distance phone service was for emergencies, and no one used it just to chat. I was lonely at times, but Ross's letters from Seattle cheered me up. I never understood why anyone cared who won the football game, but I liked the ski club. When I got too stuck interpreting a poem by T. S. Eliot, my cousin Lois (now a vice-president at the University of Alberta) helped me out.

I zeroed in on my studies. The freshman curriculum included the famous Western Civilization course that has been the focus of national controversy in recent years as Stanford dared to change the canon. I slaved to get through that canon, ever the more so because of my high school sin of avoiding history. It was only later after graduation, however, that I thought about the biases, including the male bias, in the reading list. Likewise, only later did I ponder the fact that Mrs. Stanford, as she always was called, was the butt of campus jokes about the allegedly dour will she wrote, and students never heard of her stunning success in fiscally rescuing the university.

My life improved sophomore year. Ross joined me at Stanford, pursuing his graduate studies in electrical engineering. I had a bright and adventurous roommate, Marilyn Carlsmith (who became a lawyer and judge in Honolulu). I liked the girls in my Faisan wing of Flo Mo dorm. Most took their studies seriously. I do not recall career talk in any of the dorms, but later a number of the women in my graduating class had ambitious careers and made their marks in medicine, law, motion picture production, the arts, engineering, government, the academy, and as entrepreneurs.

The expectation I internalized from the broader 1950s society was that I, as a girl, should do well in my studies, but not for any particular reason. The problematic side of this lack of a goal was a lingering sense that perhaps there still was something incompatible between overt intellectual success and femininity. An old joke—"Nine out of ten women are beautiful and the tenth one goes to Stanford"—captures that sense. It was the only negative reference I ever heard in regard to women at the school and one clearly belied by yearbook photos.

The positive side of this lack of a goal is that I did as I pleased. I discovered I could get course credit for reading novels, which I liked to do anyway, and I enrolled forthwith. I spent hours at Lake Lagunita, lost in the worlds of Flaubert, Zola, Kafka, Shaw, Mann, Goethe, Faulkner, Joyce, and Lawrence.

I became an anthropology major, as did my roommate Marilyn. Felix Keesing, a specialist in peoples of the Pacific, was supportive of my studies. The anthropology department had only a few majors, which made it a cozy place. Professor and Mrs. Keesing sometimes entertained students in their home. He invited me to do a senior honors thesis. Suffering temporarily from academic burnout, I declined, obviously making the wrong decision. Keesing invited me to go on for graduate work in anthropology at Stanford. The department did not like to take its own students, believing it too intellectually incestuous, but he knew Ross still would be at Stanford and he suggested that I stay on to get a master's degree. I was not sure that was what I wanted, and I sought employment instead. Keesing died suddenly of a heart attack while playing tennis that spring. One of my few regrets is that I never had a chance to tell him that I eventually had a career and that his belief in my abilities was not misplaced.

I had my first fieldwork experience as an anthro major, excavating Native American burial mounds near a big patch of the world's most delicious tomatoes in the Fremont, California, farm fields. Marilyn, Mary Sanches (who later completed her doctorate in anthropology), and I dug up graves and ate tomatoes together. It is hard, tedious work—one moves lots of dirt with extreme care to avoid damage to skulls and artifacts. Excavating burial mounds is fieldwork that simultaneously is the most distant (no rapport required) and the most intimate and invasive (disturbing without consent a person's physical remains and final resting place). The ethical implications of excavation were not discussed by the professor. The course predated that line of thought. More recently, Native Americans, not all in agreement themselves, have been involved in discussions with Stanford about the appropriate disposition of these remains (Bartholomew 1990).

I had my first and only factory-based work experience during a summer vacation from Stanford, working as a file clerk. Father was nudging me toward financial independence. He would say, "It's good to have money in your pocket," by which he meant, "It's good to *earn* money and have some in your pocket." I learned the lesson well when he declined to finance my desired trip to Mexico. Summer jobs were hard to come by with no marketable skills, but I got a clerical job at Boeing Airplane Company in Seattle. I worked swing shift and spent a summer with hands purple from filing ditto masters in an office adjacent to the shop floors. One day my boss walked by the shops with me and he said, "You be sure to finish your college education so you don't have to do this all your life." I did not need to be persuaded. The boredom of the work—and that of my prior summer's work sales clerking—was excruciating, but the experience has been useful in thinking about occupations, opportunity structures, and gender. Father also insisted that I learn shorthand, a demand symptomatic of his "in case you have to support yourself" mentality. I resentfully complied. I swore I would not use this occupationally limiting skill and I did not until years later when I turned it to my advantage taking sociological fieldnotes at rape trials and hospital rounds.

I had my first in-depth, cross-cultural experience after my sophomore year. At age twenty, I went off by myself to see Mexico, financing my adventure with savings from my prior summer's job at Boeing. It was the Mexico of 1959: Men harassed every woman on the street. An unmarried Mexican woman even in her twenties was not supposed to date and did so only clandestinely. Throngs of impoverished worshipers stood on the Zócalo outside the gold-ornamented cathedral. Specialty shops were filled with silver, but beggars with crooked eyes rode on every bus. The starkness of stratification by gender and class stood out unlike anything I ever had seen. I lived with a middle-class Mexican family who spoke no English and thus I learned the excitement and exhaustion of having to express oneself in a second language.

Stanford campus life provided another set of experiences—some cerebral, some otherwise. Margaret Mead came to speak, Louis Armstrong played, and diva Anna Moffo sang. Film series were in process everywhere. On Wednesday evenings, the City beckoned us for the San Francisco symphony. There were lighter moments at Rossotti's Alpine Beer Garden. Marilyn and I went off on adventures whenever we could—to the Territory of Hawaii to visit her family (overnight on a propeller plane), and on escapist trips to ski at Sun Valley and Squaw.

The institutional feel of dorm life and the food, mystery meat and hash, nearly drove me mad. Housing policy differed by gender. Boys who were upperclassmen could live off campus, but girls, unless married, had to be in the dorms all four years. I escaped to the City when I could, visiting Father and his wife in their apartment overlooking the Presidio with its eucalyptus trees. There were no books to read, only *Vogue* magazine, but I enjoyed the respite, and I liked looking out over the Golden Gate and, at night as I fell asleep, hearing the foghorns' lonesome cadence.

I completed my undergraduate studies in March 1961, and I started working right away. The graduation ceremonies were at the end of the academic year, and the man who spoke at my Phi Beta Kappa initiation said it should be just the beginning. Ella Fitzgerald sang at the Senior Prom at the Mark Hopkins on Nob Hill. Ross and I concluded our on-again, off-again, five-year courtship, and married.

Stanford overall was an empowering experience for me. The faculty took me more seriously than I took myself at the time. The institution instilled a notion of self-confidence—the idea that "If I can graduate from Stanford I can do anything." The career office, however, was "out of sync" with that institutional message.

March 1961 to September 1964: Three and a Half Years in Limbo

What could a woman with a bachelor's degree in anthropology do in 1961? Not much. The Stanford career office woman suggested I work as a telephone company representative dealing with customers. I resisted and wondered if she advised such a fate for the male graduates. Ever determined, I landed a job in the Stanford sociology department as a research assistant—a coup since those jobs usually went to their own students.

W. Richard Scott and Edmund Volkart were editing a book on medical sociology. I worked for them surveying journals, selecting and abstracting articles that might be appropriate to include. Various graduate students, on learning what I was doing, responded saying that that was considerable responsibility. Dick Scott's Ph.D. was from the University of Chicago and he was an admirer of Everett Hughes—a fact that became relevant later in my career. One day Dick suggested I read Erving Goffman's *Asylums* (1961). Having just escaped from dorm life, I was captivated by Goffman's analysis of total institutions. The assistantship job ultimately led to my becoming a sociologist, although not in the stochastic theory mode common in the Stanford department of that era.

Ross meanwhile was progressing with his doctorate, and I learned what it was like to be married to someone working the unconscionably long hours of a graduate student. I amused myself doing other things—studying calculus and Russian literature, going to the Monterey Jazz Festival, reading *Sight & Sound* film reviews.

We lived on Ross's fellowship and my research assistant salary and had a small duplex near San Francisquito Creek, halfway between The Oasis, a popular college hangout, and the Stanford Shopping Center. We continued to lead a student life-style, including Soc Department parties at Big Basin and browsing for books at Kepler's. We had our favorite San Francisco spots, too: The Actors Workshop, where we ushered to get free tickets to plays by Pinter, Beckett, Albee, Genet, and others; The Jazz Workshop and The Black Hawk with John Coltrane, Miles Davis, and the Modern Jazz Quartet; and the Surf Cinema with its "art" films.

Our time to leave Stanford was drawing closer. My work for the edited reader was concluding. The book was published eventually as *Medical Care* (1966), and the phrase, "with the assistance of," acknowledged my contribution. My name was listed as Lynda Lytle Holmstrom and that became my professional name. In keeping with the times, I did not consider then the option of using only my maiden name.

I got another research assistant job at the medical school. About 11:30 A.M. November 22, 1963, my boss walked in and told us, with sadness, that President Kennedy had been shot. The nation stopped to mourn.

Ross's college studies had begun shortly after the Korean armistice and were undertaken in the era of the draft. Like many undergraduates, he had coped with the situation by obtaining an ROTC commission. Several years later, in 1963, a nearly complete doctoral dissertation meant orders for Ross to report for officers' basic training at Aberdeen Proving Grounds, Maryland. I learned what it meant to be an army officer's wife, albeit in peacetime. I never want to do that again! We drove across the United States in our '54 Chevy and arrived at the Aberdeen ordnance base, a flat wasteland for testing tanks and artillery, to face massive culture shock. The general's wife told the distaff side it was a man's world, as if we could not tell. The military controlled the wife by explicitly saying inappropriate behavior by her would harm the husband. Korea was still a focus of military attention, but Vietnam was becoming an American concern. The attitude of the career officers was, "Vietnam may be a dirty little war, but it's the only war we've got."

The army stint was a nadir for us, not ideologically because the Vietnam buildup was yet to come, but regarding orders about where to live and the difficulty of making egalitarian decisions under such a regime. It meant I was ordered about, too, unless we split up geographically. Fortunately, the army did not need a lieutenant with a Ph.D., and Ross was lent to NASA headquarters in Washington, D.C. There I learned how much effort it takes to find a job in a new town without contacts. I also learned what it is like to do editorial work for a contract research firm that scrambles for government money. I never want to do that again either! Furthermore, I also learned about sexist attitudes more conservative than I ever had encountered before; army-base male employees from physicians to shoe repairmen felt free to tell me that a woman's place was at home having babies.

The army moved Ross from NASA headquarters to the new Electronics Research Center in Cambridge, Massachusetts. I had been thinking about my future. As I reflected more on Mother's life, I saw how Father had made the crucial decisions. It was clear to me that control of women by others was facilitated by women's economic dependence. I decided to become economically independent, an atypical motivation for career women of my generation· (Deitch 1992). I liked working with ideas, so doing something intellectual seemed to be the way to go. I also had tired of working on other people's projects. The pay had been low, but, more important, I wanted to call the shots and work on what I deemed important. I decided to become a sociologist. Ross said, "Fine, go ahead!" and has been unerringly supportive of my career ever since.

The sociologist who had said there was no room for women wrote a letter of recommendation. It was midsummer—far too late for a regular application. I applied anyway. Brandeis said no, but Boston University said yes.

Becoming a Sociologist

Boston University, 1964–1965

Boston University (B.U.) is a university with a noncampus. Marsh Chapel notwithstanding, B.U. is a string of dingy buildings along Commonwealth Avenue, with the MTA clattering noisily outside. Mugar Library tower was yet to be built, and President John Silber, with his authoritarian and sexist statements, was not yet there.

The academic year, in contrast to the drab surroundings, proved exhilarating. Rose Laub Coser, with charismatic style, led us on an exciting journey through Vico, Condorcet, Saint-Simon, Comte, Spencer, Sumner, Ward, Marx, Pareto, Durkheim, Weber, and many others. Mark Field, able to toss out concepts at a fast pace, taught medical sociology. Julius Roth encouraged us to actually *do* sociology, and I wrote two "mini" projects under his supervision, one of which analyzed my army base experience. I made friends with a few of the students. Jeff Salloway was witty and fun. And in Natalie Allon I found a scholastic soul mate. On Friday nights I hopped on the MTA to Harvard Square, met Ross at the Wursthaus, and caught a Bogart or foreign film at the Brattle.

I began to attend the American Sociological Association (ASA) meetings, and I actually went to my first meeting before starting B.U. Ever the travelers, we moved to Boston by way of Montreal, and I went to the 1964 Montreal ASA annual meeting. There was no Sociologists for Women in Society (SWS) room in those days, and I felt a bit lost wandering around. However, I knew some people from Stanford, and I went to sessions. A man reported demographic research on the expected death toll from a nuclear strike, and Elise Boulding cogently explained the immorality of his position.

The B.U. master's program was exciting, but I wanted to move on. I applied to Harvard and to Brandeis. I arrived at Emerson Hall in ivy-covered Harvard Yard for my interview with Talcott Parsons. He made it clear that *married* women were not welcome—not a surprise for anyone who knew his writings. He said there were some strong points in my application. He liked the fact that I had studied with Rose Coser—undoubtedly both for professional reasons and because of her kindnesses to his troubled daughter, Anne; Natalie Allon had told me the story and it since has been written about (Breines 1992). My chances of the strong points overcoming my marital status deficit did not look promising.

I drove to Brandeis for my interview. Things went a bit better, although I still was asked questions about my husband, his career, and how would he handle my potential future success. I walked back to our '54 Chevy, which was parked by Goldfarb Library, feeling defeated. Both institutions looked like they would judge me by my marital status rather than my accomplishments—the same thing that happened to Mother a generation earlier at the bank.

Career discrimination hit me solidly for the first time. Always there had been gender differences in socialization, expectations, and rules of behavior. But this brick wall was blatant. How was I ever going to get anywhere? Outraged, I took off my wedding ring—the only visible sign of what others saw as my problematic married status—and I have not worn it since. It did not change which box was checked off on those bureaucratic application forms, but at least in most interpersonal encounters my married status would not be visible to dominate people's first impressions.

Harvard said no, and Brandeis said yes, complete with a tuition scholarship. Harvard's rejection, in retrospect, was lucky for me. Who knows? I might have gone there and been mired in Parsons's "pattern variables" for years! Brandeis turned out to be electrifying, and in my judgment, clearly the place to be.

Brandeis University, 1965–1970: The Vietnam Sixties' Era

Brandeis University sits high on a hill eight miles west of Boston. The Castle dominates the scene as one approaches, and further on stands Robert Berks's statue of Justice Brandeis, with his robes flowing in the wind. Jewish-sponsored but nonsectarian, Brandeis University was "the gift of American Jewry to higher education" (Pasternack 1988, 1). Founded in 1948, Brandeis surely must hold a world record for the rapidity with which it established its reputation of academic excellence. The list of superstars associated with Brandeis's history includes Eleanor Roosevelt, who was one of the early trustees and who later commuted from New York to teach a course on the United Nations (Lash 1972; Pasternack 1988).

Exciting, intense, challenging, unusual, chaotic, and caring are the adjectives that come to mind as I think about the graduate school environment I experienced at Brandeis in the sociology department. Theoretical sociology, including strong ties to the European traditions; field methods and qualitative research; a critical perspective; and political activism/social change were hallmarks of the department. In short, this was a different and special place to be. Not surprisingly, several students were refugees from other academic programs that they had found to be less congenial.

Civil rights, Vietnam, draft resistance, the feminist second wave, and students' rights were the issues of the day. One did not have to be a politico, although there was support for those who were and some pressure to go in that direction. C. Wright Mills was esteemed for his advice to see connections between personal troubles and public issues, between biography and history. It was a heady environment, perhaps especially so for a student like me who came to sociology via anthropology and literature, rather than by way of political concerns.

The Brandeis department imparted a schizophrenic quality to life. The lofty and mundane coexisted; despite idealism and activism, exams had to be taken, papers had to be written. My doctoral defense was scheduled on a day when Pearlman Hall was headquarters for the national student strike that occurred after the Kent State murders. One learned to work through chronic chaos.

Our training at Brandeis was deviant methodologically as well. A year-long fieldwork course was required of all graduate students—even those most theoretically or historically inclined. Gordy Fellman, Everett Hughes, Phil Slater, Sam Wallace, and Irv Zola team-taught the fieldwork course I took. Notebooks handy, we students invaded Charlestown's streets, bars, churches, and housing projects. I decided to study high school girls—their life-style, and ambitions. Through a snowball sample, I interviewed seven girls, ambitious by local standards. I wrote about their expected futures as white-collar workers (secretary, typist, teacher) and the ways their lives might follow and differ from their mothers' lives.

Lewis Coser taught a stellar theory course on Durkheim, Simmel, and Mannheim. Kurt Wolff led us on an exploration of pretheoretical problems of sociology, emphasizing the work of Alfred Schutz. Robert S. Weiss had us analyze a multiplicity of methods by reading and evaluating classic works in each genre. A statistics course was not offered, and I trudged over to Harvard to learn the techniques. Two foreign languages were required, although that soon changed. I already had studied Spanish, but I went to summer school at Harvard to learn enough German to translate a page or so of Weber. This linguistic endeavor never helped my sociology, but it later proved useful when traveling in Eastern Europe where German was often a second language.

The admission policy at Brandeis was unusual, or I never would have gotten in. A number of female graduate students, including a few *married* ones like me, were permitted to enroll. A few older women, such as Ruth Jacobs, switching from earlier careers in journalism or nursing, also were admitted.

Among the many professors at Brandeis who were supportive of women's careers, Everett Hughes stands out. Everett both saw the conceptual importance of studying women's careers and was helpful to female students and colleagues (Holmstrom 1984). His early article on contradictions of status, which includes an informative vignette about his sister-in-law who was an aeronautical engineer, remains a classic (Hughes 1945).

A critical mass of intellectually exciting female students existed at Brandeis in the 1960s (Thorne 1987). The second wave of the feminist movement hit Boston roughly around 1968, and I, like many of the women, was active in various feminist arenas including a consciousness-raising group in Cambridge. I began taking fieldnotes, with permission, but then I decided to just participate rather than simultaneously participate and study the movement.

Numerous female careers, including many with a feminist bent and those of a number of women of color, were launched from the Brandeis sociology department starting in the 1960s. My work on two-career families is based on my doctoral dissertation done at Brandeis. Female sociologists whose graduate student years at Brandeis overlapped considerably with my own include Barrie Thorne, Gaye Tuchman, Nancy Stoller Shaw, Barbara Carter, Marcia Millman, Natalie Allon, Rachel Kahn-Hut, Judith Adler, Janet

Mancini Billson, and Shulamit Reinharz. The list of notable women graduates also includes, among others, Jeanne Guillemin, Fatima Mernissi, Nancy Chodorow, Tahi Lani Mottl, Karen E. Fields, Marilyn Rueschemeyer, Judith Stacey, Wini Breines, Elizabeth Higginbotham, Donna Huse, Lise Vogel, Diane Balser, and Patricia Hill Collins.

Departmental enlightenment on women's issues was uneven, however, at the time I was there. A departmental colloquium on "The Woman Question" was held, and the remarks of one young male professor were embarrassingly archaic. I also remember a day when the corridors of Pearlman Hall reverberated with the hostile shouts of a male faculty member upset about the "ambition" of the newly hired female scholar. Nevertheless, overall, I experienced the Brandeis sociology department as a congenial place. Everett Hughes, Phil Slater, and Irv Zola, an unlikely assemblage I was told, made a fantastic dissertation committee. Many others helped, and I always was learning things from my fellow students, often over lunch at the Castle.

My dissertation eventually reached a stage where I could at least see that the end was in sight, and my thoughts turned to getting a job. Fortunately for me, by this time Everett had retired from yet another university, and he moved from Brandeis to Boston College. Ever proper, Everett would never even think of intervening in a hiring appointment. But when a tenure-track position opened up for September 1969 at Boston College (B.C.), it certainly did not hurt that he wrote a letter of recommendation for me. Nor did it hurt Jeanne Guillemin a few years later when he recommended her for another tenure-track position at Boston College. I thus joined the faculty at Boston College without going on the job market in any systematic way. Ross remained at NASA in Cambridge, and we jettisoned the complicated plan we had developed for seeking employment in various metropolises throughout the United States.

Boston College: The Professorial Years

Boston College sits on the Heights, and from its suburban vantage one can see downtown Boston in the distance. The main drive off Commonwealth Avenue leads to our totem, The Boston College Eagle, perched high on a marble column. Gasson Hall's Gothic spires and our state-of-the-art library—symbolizing religious and intellectual elements—are just beyond. Down the hillside sits the Stadium, representing athletics. Earlier, Boston College served urban, male, working-class commuters, but the current student body, recruited nationwide, is coed, affluent, and suburban. This conservative, male-dominated, Jesuit-sponsored, Irish-Catholic, sports-oriented campus is an odd place to have landed for a woman who is a feminist Protestant agnostic of WASPish origin, with an interest in participatory rather than spectator sports. It is like visiting a foreign country for me each time I drive through the gates.

Jokes abound that the term "Catholic University" is an oxymoron, but in truth there is more academic freedom at Boston College than at many secular universities. Feminist women's studies and gender courses have been taught in the sociology department since about 1968, with Kay Broschart (now of Hollins College) doing some of this pioneer teaching.

BC has treated me well for the most part. Hired in 1969, I went quickly from instructor, to assistant, to associate, to full professor in ten short years. I did so while teaching and researching in areas related to feminist issues, most notably research on careers and then later on rape. Space precludes commenting in detail on my BC career, but let me mention in passing that I was chairperson for six years. There are some amusing stories about what such a formal position does and does not bring to women. One male assistant professor I hired later mistook me, as I was sitting at a typewriter, for a secretary. Another male assistant professor stormed into my office like a two-year-old having a tantrum, ranting and raving that I had not answered his memo.

During my early professorial years, SWS and also the International Sociological Association (ISA) Research Committee 32 on Sex Roles were established, and I was at the informal dinner in Bulgaria in 1970 when this ISA undertaking began under the able leadership of Elise Boulding. I was not present at the initial SWS founding meeting, but I began participating very soon thereafter, most notably on the discrimination committee and the social issues committee. Highlights of the early sociological feminist endeavors include a 1969 Women's Caucus in San Francisco, Alice Rossi's daring polemical speech at the ASA business meeting (Rossi 1970), and the sit-in at the Men's Grill in 1972 at a New Orleans ASA hotel (Roby 1992).

SWS was and is an important aspect in my own career. It provided professional connections across generations, practice in various skills, networking opportunities, encouragement for applying one's ideas, and an oasis of hospitality at annual meetings. SWS members such as Pauline Bart, Jessie Bernard, Rose Laub Coser, and Suzanne Keller have helped me at crucial junctures in my career.

I also had two children during my years at BC. Their arrival predated any official parental policy by BC, but my colleagues were supportive of this endeavor. It certainly did not bother the undergraduates, most of whom are Catholic and enjoy children.

The Second and Third Shifts

Arlie Hochschild (1989) has called attention to the second shift, the domestic and family work that occurs in addition to one's job and that, although it sometimes is shared equally, more often than not falls disproportionately on women. Ross and I have solved our own second shift by dividing it fifty-fifty, albeit with help for child care.

I believe there is another shift, which I call the third shift, that falls overwhelmingly on women. It consists of all the work that women do—both tasks and emotional work—to manage the effects of sexism on their daily lives, as well as the more voluntary efforts many women make to counteract and fight sexism more broadly. The third shift includes the added layer of effort women have to make, because of pervasive sexism, to carry out their occupational tasks, their family tasks, and to survive in every other realm of their lives—from walking down the street to dealing with health care to housing to family law to pension policy. While other disadvantaged groups may have a third shift (for example, black men have one regarding racism), what is peculiar to women is that their third shift is added to the second shift of domestic and family work that also falls overwhelmingly on women.

We work the third shift in part just to get through the day, and perhaps to advance ourselves a bit. When doing it on behalf of others, we do it out of altruism and outrage at the injustices.

The academy is no exception in causing the third shift. Female faculty face many special barriers, as do females in other university roles such as secretaries, graduate students, and undergraduates.

Gender issues have surfaced more in our department in recent years than before. As a result of this increase, not long ago the men in the department asked the female faculty what bothered them. The five women do not agree among themselves about what is fair. What bothers me the most—aside from the concrete issues themselves such as salary discrimination and exploitation of minority women—is that they all cost me time. The bottom line is that the men make more work for the women. The male faculty in our department, like the men in our society, create the woman's third shift.

The third shift is extant in other departments as well. A faculty man in the political science department was accused of sexual harassment, and it was reported (Finch 1990) that administrators gave him a medical leave, an outcome seen by many women on campus as a reward for bad behavior. A female professor in the political science department, on a research leave, voluntarily gave up considerable research time coming to campus to help draft the new sexual harassment policy for the university. Regarding time, he gained and she lost, although regarding principled behavior, the matter is reversed.

The positive side of women working against sexism—above and beyond the concrete progress they may achieve—is that it often leads to a sense of camaraderie with like-minded people and of being part of a larger cause. The problematic side is the cost in time, energy, and emotions.

Is it worth it? Yes, if for no other reason than that there is no reasonable alternative if one wants to have economic independence and a reasonable amount of control over one's life. Betterment of women's lives will, I believe, occur in a glacial manner. As anyone knows who grew up mountain climbing in the glaciered terrain of the Pacific Northwest, glaciers move slowly but ultimately they push aside all barriers in their path.

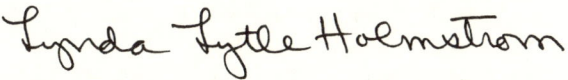

Acknowledgments: I wish to thank Jeanne Guillemin, F. Ross Holmstrom, and David A. Karp for reading and commenting on this essay. The discussion of my years at Brandeis is based partly on my statement in a booklet printed by the Brandeis University sociology department in honor of the twenty-fifth anniversary of its graduate program. The booklet lists Brandeis Ph.D.s, and it includes reflective statements from about fifty of them.

REFERENCES

Allen, Peter C. 1980. *Stanford: From the Foothills to the Bay.* Stanford, Calif.: Stanford Alumni Association and Stanford Historical Society.

Bartholomew, Karen. 1990. "Tribal Discord over Reburial." *Stanford Observer,* April–May, 3 and 17.

Bernard, Jessie. 1981. "The Good-Provider Role: Its Rise and Fall." *American Psychologist* 36 (January): 1–12.

Breines, Wini. 1992. *Young, White, and Miserable: Growing Up Female in the Fifties.* Boston: Beacon.

Deitch, Cynthia. 1992. "The Construction of Gender and Class in the Narratives of Women in Dual Career Marriages." Paper presented at the annual meeting of the American Sociological Association. Pittsburgh, Pa., August.

Finch, Rick. 1990. "Administration Saw the Writing on the Wall." *The Heights* (Boston College), November 26, 10.

Goffman, Erving. 1961. *Asylums.* Garden City, N.Y.: Anchor/Doubleday.

Hochschild, Arlie, with Anne Machung. 1989. *The Second Shift: Working Parents and the Revolution at Home.* New York: Viking.

Holmstrom, Lynda Lytle. 1984. "Everett Cherrington Hughes: A Tribute to a Pioneer in the Study of Work and Occupations." *Work and Occupations* 11 (November): 471–81.

Hughes, Everett. 1945. "Dilemmas and Contradictions of Status." *American Journal of Sociology* 50:353–59.

Komarovsky, Mirra. 1950. "Functional Analysis of Sex Roles." *American Sociological Review* 15 (August): 508–16.

Lash, Joseph P. 1972. *Eleanor: The Years Alone.* New York: W. W. Norton.

Nagel, Gunther W. 1985. *Iron Will: The Life and Letters of Jane Stanford.* Rev. ed. Stanford, Calif.: Stanford Alumni Association.

Pasternack, Susan, ed. 1988. *From the Beginning: A Picture History of the First Four Decades of Brandeis University.* Waltham, Mass.: Brandeis University.

Roby, Pamela. 1992. "Women and the ASA: Degendering Organizational Structures and Processes." *The American Sociologist* 23:18–47.

Rossi, Peter H. 1970. "Minutes of the 1970 Council Meeting" and "Minutes of the First Business Meeting." *The American Sociologist* 5 (February): 59–68.

Rupp, Leila J., and Verta Taylor. 1987. *Survival in the Doldrums: The American Women's Rights Movement, 1945 to the 1960s.* New York: Oxford University Press.

Thorne, Barrie. 1987. "Feminism and Sociology." Paper presented at the Twenty-fifth Anniversary Celebration of the Brandeis Sociology Graduate Program, Brandeis University, Waltham, Mass., April.

Walsh, Mary Roth. 1977. *"Doctors Wanted, No Women Need Apply": Sexual Barriers in the Medical Profession, 1835–1975.* New Haven, Conn.: Yale University Press.

Weitzman, Lenore J. 1985. *The Divorce Revolution.* New York: Free Press, Macmillan.

PART V

. . . and Community

Fifteen

Seventeen White Men and Me

Coramae Richey Mann

I am constantly aware of my racial status and gender—in that precise order—but it was not until I began to outline this essay that I realized how much these two characteristics have influenced my life. Like breathing, being black and being female are features about which I am always subliminally cognizant. Like gasping for breath when you are drowning, my skin color and gender have become painfully familiar constants in my life. It wasn't always that way.

The Author as a Chocolate Drop

I was born in the largest African American hospital in Chicago. My mother, who had been out playing poker all of that night, was pronounced dead as I came into existence at 7:13 A.M. on a cold Sunday in January; raising "holy hell," so they said. My mother was miraculously saved. I continue to raise holy hell, for, after all, it was my destiny.

We were in Chicago because, as was the tradition in those days, my mother wanted to be with *her* mother for the birth of her second child. It also was helpful that her father was a physician on the hospital staff. My parents lived in Dayton, Ohio, where my father taught at a segregated black high school; he was also the basketball, football, and baseball coach there. My mother was a homemaker and had given up a potential career as a concert pianist for the love of my father. When she died in 1987, they had celebrated sixty-three years of marriage. In fact, they married twice. Her father had not approved of her wedding my father, the "jock," so they eloped, but since she was only sixteen, my grandfather had their marriage annulled. Mother was sent to France to a private girls' school for two years; she returned speaking fluent French, and she married my father again. They always celebrated both anniversaries.

My mother's gift for the arts influenced me deeply. Between her homemaking chores, mother played the piano or sketched. Our house was filled with music. At about the age of four I decided I wanted to be either an artist or a writer; maybe both—I could illustrate my books. I rendered my first oil painting before I attended school; it was of an Ohio cornfield: browns, oranges, and yellow ochres. Two weeks ago, after thirty years of artistic idleness, I completed an acrylic (a new medium for me); it was of my backyard: fields and bushes in multiple shades of green, and trees with vivid green foliage and dark, almost black trunks and branches. Somehow, in my memory's eye, this one seems brighter than my first effort, which was lost long ago. However, my first painting I remember as better executed. My first "publication" occurred later in grammar school when I wrote and illustrated my poem called "Rabbit Tracks."

We lived in a predominantly white neighborhood at the edge of town where, as a preschooler, I had no conception of color. Most of my playmates were white. One day, while playing some child's game, I won the game over a little boy I had known all of my four or five years. Fighting tears furiously, his face snarled into a little old man's reddened face, the boy viciously lashed out, "You . . . you . . chocolate drop!" I was hurt to my heart and ran home in tears to my mother's always waiting arms. When I told her what he had called me, she smiled and said, "Darling, he *complimented* you, don't cry." "But Tommy was so mean," I cried, "and his face was so ugly!" My mother held me closer and stroking my hair said, "Think, Coramae, think of chocolate. It is sweet and you love it. It is a rare treat in your life. That is what Tommy meant. Always think that way." I really tried to think that way, but I never could. Despite my mother's explanation, I knew something cruel and wrong had occurred. It was my first brush with the racial prejudice I face and fight to this day.

The Makings of a Juvenile Delinquent

I started public school, illegally, at the age of five. With the exception of a girl named Estella Turner, I was the only child of color in most of my classes in our integrated Ohio grammar school. Year after year, Estella and I were the brightest children in the class. Our school had a system where the child receiving the highest grades sat in the first seat near the door. The next seat was assigned to the second highest achiever, and in the last seat, in the last row, on the far side sat the poorest performer. In retrospect, I realize that was a degrading and stereotyping seating system, but at the time all I wanted was that first seat. If I did not occupy it, Estella did; in my eyes, she was my only competition. We were both straight "A" students.

My maternal grandmother died when I was about two. As a child, I never knew my paternal grandmother. She was Irish, and she had married a white man after my grandfather, who was of mixed Indian, African, and French blood, died. I could not visit her in Chicago; I was too "shady." My older brother and only sibling, Edward, died in 1943. When my maternal grandfather died in 1944, we returned to Chicago. For a long while it seemed as though there was nothing in my life but tearful people, flowers, and funerals. These last two deaths seriously changed the course of my life: I no longer had a big brother to protect me, and I could not attend school in Chicago.

At that time, as for the most part today, Chicago was racially segregated. Although my grandfather was very wealthy, he had been confined to the black ghetto, albeit the most affluent part of it. He had a live-in housekeeper, cook, and chauffeur in his twelve-room, limestone mansion. Although my mother acquired everything when he died, we were still confined to the ghetto. This urban ecology meant that I would have to attend the all-black Doolittle grammar school and ultimately the all-black Wendell Phillips High School in our neighborhood. My parents had already decided that my newfound Chicago friends were bad influences and that I had the makings of a juvenile delinquent.

I was first sent to a coeducational black boarding school, Palmer Memorial Institute, in Sedalia, North Carolina. There, under the guidance of my two teenage "big sisters," who where high school seniors, I learned a great deal about boys. When I went back to Chicago that first summer, I was "boy crazy" and a potential status offender (a juvenile who is not delinquent but who violates social rules such as curfews, truancy, and other non-crimes). After much agonizing, my parents decided to send me to Minneapolis, Minnesota, to live with the Kelleys, my father's childless older sister and her husband.

Ironically, my leanings toward delinquency were enhanced more in Minnesota than at Palmer or in ghettoized Chicago when I fell in with a youthful shoplifter who became my best girlfriend. She taught me all of the tricks of the trade. What I learned was similar to professional "boosting" as I came to know it years later when I studied criminology. We stole only the very best: cashmere sweaters, leather cigarette lighters, and jewelry. We gave away most of our "loot," a practice that made us very popular kids. By accident one day I found that some of my "loot" had slipped through a hole in my winter coat and down into the lining. Eureka! I enlarged the hole and thereafter deliberately stuffed my coat lining. That act of brilliance was my undoing, and it ended my brief shoplifting career at the age of thirteen. After one major shoplifting spree, my aunt asked me what was wrong with my coat. I did not realize that my coat was sticking out almost parallel to the ground. In fact, when I tried to turn to avoid her outreached, probing hand, the weight of the "loot" in the coat almost threw me to the ground. My aunt was not angry, but she felt hurt and disgraced. After I emptied my bountiful lining, she told me that on Monday (we shoplifted only on Saturdays) I would have to take every item back to its respective department and apologize to each sales clerk. That was a weekend from hell. After that day, I never shoplifted again. In fact, I can take nothing that is not mine.

The Temporary Color Void

During my five years there, Minnesota was reputed to have the best public school system in the nation. It was also racially integrated because of the smattering of Asian, Native, and African Americans who collectively made up less than 3 percent of the student body. Despite my brief detour into the world of delinquency, I maintained a predominantly "A" average and, as usual, I loved school and learning.

From ninth grade until my senior year of high school, I was basically unaware of racial or gender differences. Most of my schoolmates were Scandinavian, and after my shoplifting tutor and I parted ways when she viciously kicked a sweet neighborhood dog, a Swedish girl became my best friend. Those were confusing times. In Minnesota, my friends were of all colors and there was no discernible racial segregation of any kind. When I returned to Chicago for vacations, I again experienced the mindless racial prejudice and ghetto life with only faces of color and segregated beaches and other "public" facilities. One could go downtown to the movies only to hear racial epithets and see hatred-twisted white faces. Adult faces. The "chocolate drop" of Ohio became the "nigger" of Chicago. Returning to Minneapolis every fall was a racially schizophrenic experience until my senior year of high school.

I had been told by my favorite teacher, Miss Utley, a very refined English teacher, that I was to be the class book editor. This was not a matter of *racial* "firsts"; I did not even think of the assignment in terms of being the first "colored" (the term back then) yearbook editor. The honor was like sitting in that first seat in grammar school. I was number one! After school, I rushed home to call my parents in Chicago and give them the news; my dream of being a writer was more entrenched than ever. The exhilaration was short-lived. When I arrived at school the next day, Miss Utley was waiting for me, her eyes bright with tears. Apparently, Miss Utley explained, my high school was not ready for a colored editor. The original appointment had been rescinded. It had been decided that, for the first time in the history of the high school, there would be coeditors of the yearbook. Suddenly I came face-to-face with the ugly countenance of racism in what I had considered a color-blind school. This was the first of many disappointments generated by the so-called liberal population. Like most teenagers, I soon forgot the sting of pain and the embarrassment of having to tell my family and friends of the retraction. As it turned out, only I was surprised. Everyone else just shook their heads knowingly and said it was more of "the man's" chicanery and double-dealing. I did exact a modicum of revenge, thanks to the lack of resistance from my coeditor, a very nice and bookish Swedish lad: My face was the first and last one seen in the yearbook, and it appeared regularly throughout the volume.

I don't know if all of those pictures affected me, but not too long afterward, I was shopping in a black-owned department store in Chicago when a strange man approached me about modeling. I was fairly "hip" and I knew not to talk to strangers, but the man had kind eyes and I trusted him. As a result, I ended up on one of the first covers of *Ebony* magazine. Later, during my first year of college, I modeled for my second *Ebony* cover at Notre Dame. I also did *Jet* and *Tan Confessions* covers and some fashion pictures for Johnson Publications. Although the money was not spectacular, modeling was a great deal of fun and came easily to me, a natural "ham." I began to think of modeling as a part-time career, and I envisioned the trips to Europe and other exotic places where I could gather material for my future novels. But again racism entered my life equation. I had been called to do some photos for a possible series of Miller's High Life beer ads for *Ebony* magazine. The proofs had turned out fabulously and the staff was very excited about them. Unfortunately, the ad agency representative rejected them, saying that I photographed "too white"; they wanted someone closer to a mahogany color to appeal to potential black purchasers of Miller's High Life beer. Little did the ad man know that this was before "black is beautiful" and that my color appealed to both men of color and white men. That experience ended my modeling career.

My final disappointment in high school occurred when I found that I was in contention to be valedictorian of my graduating class. It was never proven that a scheme existed, although the ever-loyal Miss Utley intimated as much. I received a "C"—the only one in my life—in chemistry lab in my last semester; a very subjective decision by the male teacher. The resultant "B" for the course brought me down to fourth in my senior class of about 350. Again, the system felt the need to oppress a youngster simply because of skin color.

The Marriage/Education Correlation

After high school graduation I applied to three universities: Wisconsin, Northwestern, and Chicago. I was accepted by all three. I yearned to be back in Chicago with my family and friends and therefore entered the University of Chicago. There was an unwritten quota system at the university in 1948, which meant that there were fewer than a dozen black undergraduate students on the campus. For the most part we all stayed together, but I soon found that playing bridge and drinking beer in Jimmy's Woodlawn Tap were more challenging than attending classes. I almost flunked out my first year, but somehow I remained in good standing. To make matters worse, after completing my first year, I eloped.

The correlation between my academic achievements and marriage is inescapable, if not statistically meaningful. After each of four divorces, I returned to school and got a degree; hence, I earned a B.A., two M.A.'s, and a Ph.D. To put distance between myself and my first husband, I went to Howard University in Washington, D.C. For the second time in my life (recall the year at the southern boarding school), I had all black instructors. The three years I spent at Howard were clearly the most important in my educational life.

Our nation's capital was segregated at that time, and my friends and I did our very best to integrate it. Most of my friends were from New York or New Jersey and many of their friends were white. They quickly became *my* friends. On weekends, when we were not in New York City with them, our white friends were in Washington with us. We shocked the black community and devastated the capital as we went everywhere and anywhere, challenging white proprietors to oust a racially integrated group of fun-loving young adults. Since they did not know exactly what to do, most establishments left us alone; we were gone before they figured it all out. I can recall only one truly negative fallout of our interracial gadding about: Two of the guys were evicted by their white landlady after she saw us leaving their apartment en masse one Sunday morning after partying all night.

At Howard University I first majored in English, specifically short-story writing. I had never lost my yearning to be a writer of fiction, and I was thrilled to study under Sterling Brown, one of the foremost black poets and authors in the nation. Through his classes I stumbled onto the literary works of O. Henry and Henry James. The psychological twists and turns in their writing were totally absorbing. I wanted to write in the style of those authors, and I felt that I needed a few psychology courses first. Dr. Charles Sumner, professor and chair of the psychology department at Howard, influenced my life for many years.

I have never had a professor more brilliant than Dr. Sumner was. His extremely difficult exams were legendary. Students moaned before attending his classes; I could hardly wait to get there. Aside from Miss Utley in high school, I had never had a mentor. I became Dr. Sumner's protégé, and I lived and breathed clinical psychology. When Dr. Sumner died, I left Howard University. I returned to Chicago and entered Roosevelt University, the great liberal private university named after Eleanor Roosevelt. Within the walls of that urban university there was a general absence of racial discord among the students. Unfortunately, the professors brought their prejudice baggage with them; as many continue to do everywhere in this nation. I received a bachelor of arts in clinical psychology. Later, after another marriage and divorce, I earned a master of arts, also in clinical psychology, at Roosevelt.

Many of my early jobs had little to do with clinical psychology. I could have been best defined then as an urban sociologist. My first position was with the Chicago Welfare Department as a vocational counselor; I was an urban renewal worker; and I also worked in the antipoverty program as a planner and community action trainer. All of my employment was change-oriented, even my administrative stint at Planned Parenthood. I felt that I was doing something good for people of color, the poor, and the oppressed; I believed that I was changing society. When I worked as a clinical psychologist, I tried to bring a new perspective to my assignments, counseling, for example, unwed, pregnant adolescents and incarcerated juvenile delinquents. When I was a psychologist at the Chicago Psychiatric Institute, I probably did more counseling than diagnosing of the court-referred clients. I really *believed* I was changing society. And I was wrong.

During my stint as a "soldier" in the war against poverty, I became involved in training and program development and evaluation. I learned to do all types of training: culturally sensitizing white police officers and middle-management U.S. Department of Labor personnel; teaching grass-roots community groups how to be leaders and effective members of advisory boards; training community workers to reach out and change people in the Hispanic barrios and African American ghettos of Chicago. I know I got through to hundreds of people, but my efforts did not change the world. It is indisputable that this nation is in worse racial and economic shape today than in the 1960s poverty program era.

Late one hot and humid Chicago summer, a former psychology professor of mine, who was now the department chair at Roosevelt, called and asked me to teach a course. At the last minute, the professor who was to teach the course had backed out, leaving the department in a bind. Despite my vigorous protestations, the chair insisted that if I could train, I could teach. He was right—I loved it. For the next three years, I taught psychology part-time at Roosevelt and also at two other colleges in the Chicago area. A master's degree was not enough to be effective, so I decided that I had to earn a Ph.D. I was working on my fourth divorce, and therefore, in view of my established life pattern, it seemed logical to get a doctoral degree.

Backing into Sociology

At that time, to my knowledge, there were only three universities in the Chicago area that had doctoral programs in clinical psychology: Northwestern, Loyola, and the University of Chicago. As a part-time graduate student, I had accumulated all but about eighteen hours toward the doctorate. Ironically, the University of Chicago, where I had originally placed out of all math as a freshman, insisted that I would have to take calculus and other advanced math courses to be in their program. The waiting lists were so long at Northwestern and Loyola that it would take almost four years to be admitted.

I mentioned my frustration to a close friend, with whom I grew up, who was a member of the University of Illinois Board of Trustees. He assured me that I could be admitted to Illinois. Unfortunately, the Chicago Circle campus did not have a program in clinical psychology and I could not attend the campus in Champaign, Illinois. Since most of my work as a clinical psychologist had involved the juvenile and criminal justice systems, I decided that studying criminology would be a legitimate move. Criminology was a part of sociology, so, with my trustee friend's assistance, I was admitted to the graduate program in sociology at Chicago Circle Campus. Three years later, Ph.D. in hand, I headed for Florida to save the South.

Seventeen White Men and Me

Somewhat naively I thought that academe was above the usual pettiness found in the "real" working world. I envisioned intellectual "rap" sessions with my colleagues, collegiality, and faculty and students happily drinking pitchers of beer together as we solved the problems of the world and the mysteries of life. I was, of course, wrong again.

Although at the time I was unaware of it, the School of Criminology at Florida State University (FSU) was under a faculty hiring freeze because of their poor racial minority hiring record. Despite the fact that my credentials were just as good as, if not more impressive than, a number of the faculty members, I was immediately viewed as "the *minority* candidate." This negative stereotype stuck with me most of the twelve years I was on the FSU faculty. There was no rationale for this stigmatization: I published more than most of the faculty and, despite some deliberately set roadblocks, I went from assistant to full professor within eleven years. I had hoped to become a full professor after ten years. The dean thought that such a move would be premature, and he advised me to wait an additional year. He reasoned that since eleven years was the average length of time that it had taken for the men before me to make full professor, I would not receive the faculty vote if I went for the promotion sooner. I reluctantly followed his advice, and I was made a full professor with the exact vita of the year before.

A brilliant Harvard law school graduate, Carolyn Watson, was hired the same semester as I was. We were the only women criminology faculty, and we became fast friends. Our sincere and deep relationship lasted until she died of cancer about seven years later. We were put far in the back of the department in the two smallest offices because, it was explained, "as the only women faculty in the School, we thought that you two would like to be together." Carolyn lasted only two years before she left in frustration. For almost a decade, there were seventeen white men and me on the FSU School of Criminology faculty. During my last year, Jane Gray, a dynamic and exciting sociologist from Ohio State, joined the faculty; we were practically joined at the hip for that wonderful year. Thus, my first two years and my last year at Florida State were marvelous primarily because I had female peers with whom to share the misery.

During the dry spell when I was the first and only person of color and the lone woman on the School of Criminology faculty, I had to appeal the denial of my tenure, make salary inequity a formal issue twice, and challenge my male colleagues for not receiving doctoral directive status. I won each of these battles by using gender, not race, as the basis of my arguments. I could have gone either way, but I reasoned that gender was the less explosive argument.

A Black Rapunzel in the Ivory Tower

The woman professor isolated in the ivory tower of academe is the modern-day Rapunzel. Whereas the Rapunzel of the fairy-tale world had the problems of her tower and her time, women in the academic ivory tower face a multitude of unique problems in this era. When Rapunzel let her hair down, she was rewarded by a loving prince climbing to be at her side. When a woman professor lets *her* hair down, there are few rewards and there are usually sanctions. She is stereotypically defined as being "typically female," which is not in keeping with her role as a professor. In my view, the many roles of professor for a woman are not the same as those of a man in the same vocation. If minority racial status, especially African American, is added to this mix, there is a *double backlash* from her white, male colleagues. Unfortunately, though less frequently, this backlash comes from her white, female colleagues as well.

In the discipline of criminology, the teaching assignments of women professors typically include "women's subjects": female courses; introductory courses in the field; and courses on children and on juvenile delinquency. Introductory courses are usually required "teaching" courses, which means that student interest cannot be taken for granted. Such courses do not auger well for popularity because the classes are larger and they emphasize graded assignments, roll taking, and other measures seen by students as negative, oppressive, or punitive. In contrast, the assigned role of "professor" means that one "does not need the institutional apparatus of grades and compulsory attendance for support" (Bernard 1964, 118). Thus, there is less potential student/professor conflict than student/teacher conflict. For these reasons, in twenty years of teaching I have taught only upper-level and graduate courses.

Committee assignments for female professors are different from those of their male counterparts. There seems to be a penchant for male administrators—and most administrators are men—to assign women to "affirmative action" and other "social welfare" committees (Florida State University 1976, 19). Other "female" assignments include orientation meetings and reception attendance. This novel approach to wooing parents and their offspring to a particular discipline is seen by male administrators as "natural" for a woman because of the social "hostess" nature of the function and also because such a role involves parents and youths.

The subtle effects of academic sexism and racism on a female professor's morale, motivation, and psychological well-being can be devastating. With the exception of my two dear former colleagues Carolyn Watson and Jane Gray, I can count on my two hands the times that I have been part of a social scene at any white colleague's home that was not department affiliated. While I am not bitter about this double jeopardy status, I do stay damned angry a lot of the time. I have learned to use that anger in a positive way; I produce. In fact, I usually out produce my white counterparts.

After fifteen years of being the only racial minority and most of the time the only female in a department, I experienced a fantastic four years when, at Indiana University, I had the pleasure of being a friend, mentor, and colleague to criminologist Charisse Coston. Similar to my Florida State experience, when Carolyn Watson and I were put in the offices in the back, Charisse and I were located in the farthest back hall of the department next door to each other. Since we were not the only women in the criminal justice department, I assume that the unverbalized message here was "as the only African American women faculty in the department, we thought that you two would like to be together." It seems that academically I have come full circle.

I think that I have also come full circle in my life. I am painting again. I plan to have my piano tuned, and I will try to relearn how to play it. I have outlined three novels, and I started writing the first one, *Popcorn and Oranges,* knowing that I will have to reread O. Henry and Henry James once more. I also doubt that anyone will ever call me "chocolate drop" or any other racist appellation again. I would raise "holy hell"; which, after all, is my destiny.

Coramae R. Mann

REFERENCES

Bernard, Jessie S. 1964. *Academic Women.* University Park: Pennsylvania State University Press.

Florida State University Task Force. 1976. "Excellence with Equity: Report of the Florida State University Task Force on the Status of Women." Unpublished report.

Sixteen

Marginality, Motherhood, and Method
Paths to a Social Science Career
and Community

Shulamit Reinharz

In this essay I focus on one of many threads in my life—becoming and being a social scientist. Because this volume deals with women's lives, I have explored how this thread is interwoven with becoming a woman, a wife, and a mother as well. As is true of many other people, I became interested in social science because of the marginality and sense of otherness I have experienced since early childhood. Although marginality has taken on a rather negative tone in social science literature, in my case I feel that the opposite is true. I experienced marginality as a resource until I reached adulthood. Only then did I feel the need to express a core professional identity. At that point, I sought a community, and fortunately, I found it.

The Holocaust Legacy and Growing Up in the United States

The most profound element of my earliest sense of self and marginality is the fact that my parents are Holocaust survivors. Their survival is still unfathomable to me. My parents were middle-class Jewish teenagers in Germany in the late 1930s, when, as everyone now knows, German society turned into a massive collective killing machine. My parents are two of the fortunate few who found a way to flee: they discovered a way to escape to Holland, where they became farmhands, with no previous experience.

Having saved the money they earned to buy tickets to sail for the United States, they had even put their belongings on a ship, scheduled to depart the next day, when Hitler invaded and my parents were literally trapped. For six years they lived underground, sometimes together, sometimes separately, escaping death daily because of sheer luck and the assistance of daring, virtuous people, many of whom were no older than they. My parents lived like Anne Frank, at times in a room behind a false wall or in a field or in a closet. For years, my father did not go outdoors in daylight. Somehow, they were not caught even though many of their friends were discovered and killed. In fact, only 10 percent survived of those who had decided to hide.

When Canadian troops liberated the Dutch population and an Allied victory was proclaimed, my parents found a rabbi and married. Soon thereafter I was born in Amsterdam. My mother's parents had been killed in a concentration camp (her father had been a judge in Germany, her mother had been a housewife); her sisters had escaped to Palestine, where one died of illness and another still lives. My father's parents had escaped to the United States via England, and his two sisters had been smuggled out as well. Almost no other relatives of my mother or father had survived. When the war was over, my parents mistakenly thought that *all* their relatives had been murdered. But the International Red Cross, which had taken on the task of locating survivors, discovered, much to my parents' amazement, that my father's parents were alive and living in Malden, Massachusetts, where my grandfather had been working as a physician for the previous five years. Upon hearing this incredible news, my parents and I left for Boston, arriving in 1947. I was about eight months old, yet the strictly law-abiding immigration officer compelled my parents to sign a statement verifying that I, as a female, was not a prostitute! This may have been my father's first experience of what he constantly showed me was the absurdity of bureaucracy.

In Malden, we were an unusual German-speaking household. I say "unusual" because, although my parents could not help speaking their native language, they did not want to hear "that language of hate coming out of their children's mouths." Nevertheless, unwittingly, they spoke German to me all the time; to this day, I can understand, but not speak, German.

During that year of recuperating from six years in hiding, and enjoying the miraculous existence of their newly formed three-generation family in Malden, my parents decided to move to Israel with their Zionist friends from Boston. The State of Israel had been established in 1948 in part as a haven for those who had gone through hell. Israel, at the time, was an extremely poor country that had just emerged from its own war of independence.

We arrived in Haifa in 1948 and moved to a shack in the middle of a wooded nature preserve near the city. To my parents, this idyllic setting might have represented an escape from the horrors of "civilization" that they had just endured. Photographs my parents took at the time show me standing next to flowers in the middle of a field or taking a bath in a metal tub outdoors. It certainly was romantic, but on the other hand, there was no running water and no electricity in our shack. Nor was there much food to be had, or transportation, or peace. In fact, the area in which we lived, the Carmel Forest, was surrounded by hostile Arab communities. Under these unusual conditions, my parents produced a new life. In June 1949, my mother rode on a donkey led by my father to the city of Haifa, where she gave birth to my sister. Because my infant sister did not thrive and my father became seriously ill, my parents decided to return to the United States to recuperate.

Back in Malden later that year, we lived with "our suitcases packed," ready to return to Israel. Although I was only three years old, my parents sent me to a Hebrew-speaking nursery school designed for people planning to immigrate to Israel. My father looked for work that would bring in more income than selling ties at Woolworth's, his first actual job after road-building in the Mount Carmel nature preserve. The Nazi regime had forced my father to leave high school before graduation, and he had not yet gone to college. Because of his Zionist connections, however, he found work as a fund-raiser for Israeli institutions. My mother's untitled job was to try to make ends meet, that is, fashion a life for our little family without much money. My father began attending college in the evenings, and he gradually earned a master's degree in literature, becoming proficient in English. Perhaps his language skills reflected the fact that in order to help pass the time in the underground, he had taught himself Russian. Somehow my mother learned "psychological testing" and earned some money doing that. They were beginning to climb back into the middle class.

One day, my father informed us that he had gotten a good job with a major Jewish organization in New York and that we would all be moving to New Jersey. I had just completed first grade in a horrible public school that practiced corporal punishment—even on first graders—so I was happy to move. When the move was complete, I found myself living in an apartment in a New Jersey suburb. Soon after that, my mother gave birth to my brother—the only one of her children born in the United States, and the only child who was delivered by physicians, who made it a miserable experience for my mother, she claimed.

My memories of elementary school include not wanting to recite "The Lord's Prayer" every morning (since it was not a Jewish prayer); discovering that we were going to sing "Hava Nagila" (a song that has nothing to do with religion) in the Christmas concert and not knowing whether I should correct the teacher's pronunciation of the Hebrew words; refusing to sign a school birthday card for President Eisenhower since I knew my parents were Democrats; developing a friendship with a black boy; and having a Jewish girl who was my classmate become my best friend although she lived in a house and I lived in an apartment. I also remember a man having parked his car at the curb of the street on which I walked to school and beckoning me for directions. When I approached the window, he exposed himself.

For show-and-tell I brought materials from Holland, and I told my classmates proudly that that was where I came from. I also remember being given a psychological test, as was every other child in my grade. One question asked "How far do you expect to go in your education?" At the extreme end was listed "Ph.D." I had no idea what a Ph.D. was, but I checked it. Somehow I must have ingested the idea that I could reach the highest goal.

In sixth grade, at the age of ten, and about three months before I was to graduate from elementary school, my family bought a house in a neighboring New Jersey suburb, a little bit further away from New York. The move was not difficult for me because the new house provided me with my first "room of my own" and my new teachers even took some interest in me. For example, one teacher asked me to write a paragraph on the spot about "anything," but did not explain the reason for this assignment. Not knowing what to write about, I went to the *World Book Encyclopedia* in the classroom, took out the volume with the essay on "Israel," and copied a paragraph. When I told my mother, she was delighted. At graduation three months later, I learned that I had won the penmanship competition on the basis of that paragraph!

On our block, all our neighbors were Catholics or Protestants, and my father used to tell me that he wondered which of them would hide us if we needed to be hidden. I never thought it strange to evaluate people in terms of their willingness to shelter us and put their lives at risk. At the time, my mother taught at a Hebrew School, and I attended a different one regularly and liked it. Although I had the distinct impression that my father never respected her job as "a real job," it was, nevertheless, income-producing employment. And thus my mother was not quite what has come to be known as the stereotypical 1950s housewife. And I, perhaps, was not the stereotypical frivolous 1950s teenager, because I had to baby-sit for my brother after school at least three times a week—my first unpaid, and in that sense stereotypical, female job.

My father was a rabbi of sorts, and he had a German-speaking congregation in New York City. Going to High Holiday services there meant a continuous reintegration of my parents' past German experience with my growing up in America. In this congregation of old survivors with very few children, my brother, sister, and I were novelties; we experienced a kind of pleasant marginality. Similarly, almost none of my grandparents' friends had children, and when we visited them in Malden on other holidays, we served as the surrogate children of the entire group. A pleasant marginality.

Since there were very few Jews in my town (and no blacks), I was a novelty there as well. I remember walking home from school with my friends explaining what Hanukkah was. They seemed fascinated. The story was edited, of course. I didn't explain that we—as do most Jews—put the Menorah in the window to make sure everyone knows who we are. I told them about the meaning and beauty of the holidays, not about their psychological significance. For me, at least, at some deep, unarticulated level, the Holocaust had not quite been eradicated from the suburbs (see Brienes 1992). Somehow, danger always lurked, even if it was only the danger that we projected. History does not stop for the refugees who move into their safe haven. It seeps into everyday life.

I also remember that after I spent the whole summer of 1958 in Israel with my mother and brother, visiting her sister, I returned to find a story in the high school newspaper, "Shula Rothschild Visits the Far East!" People seemed confused.

My name itself was rather exotic and required continuous explanation of its meaning and pronunciation. My name made me feel special, interesting, and different in a way I valued. A few tough girls in junior high hurled antisemitic insults against me when they cornered me in the bathroom, but generally I felt my life was "almost" the same as everyone else's: dances, marching bands, proms, homework, phone calls, music, football games, pajama parties, and boys, boys, boys. Still, I wondered what it would be like to be really "in," really in the center and not on the margins. I couldn't help, also, thinking about the nature of my high school culture in the light of my familiarity with Israel. There, too, of course, I was marginal. In the summers, I went to Zionist summer camps, which taught us to disdain "bourgeois values." In the fall, I would plunge right back into "bourgeois U.S.A."

High school had its fill of academic pressure, focused on grades and the SATs. My parents and I did not always have a clear understanding of high school culture, so, for example, in honor of my taking the SATs, they bought me a new dress, which I wore when I took the exam. I was in the honors track (called "enriched"), and I remember the teacher of one of our classes rearranging our seats to reflect how we scored on the SATs! My scores were very high, although not the highest, and again, I felt different, but it wasn't a bad feeling.

One of the clear, yet implicit, messages of high school was that competition is good. That is the way history was taught, as well. World War II was not taught in terms of describing the Holocaust, but rather as if it were another football game, and the Allies won. I remember wondering why the teachers always spoke about the United States as being "the best country in the world," and why they referred to the present as if it were the "best period in history," the culmination of civilization. My marginality was leading to what I thought were interesting questions.

The Experience of College

Despite my rather rigorous high school classes, I felt completely unprepared for Barnard College, the school I chose for its prestige, location, and relatively low cost. In college, for the first time I began to feel different in a negative way. In particular, I felt poorer than my peers. In high school some girls had more clothes than others, but basically we had the same middle-class standard of living. In college, I was plunged into a more diversified group of young women. Some were very wealthy; a few were quite poor. I felt like an utter stranger there.

Having parents who had not gone to college in the United States, I had no idea what college culture was all about when I arrived on campus. I don't remember receiving any orientation or undergoing other procedures to ease the transition. We did get a lot of rules, however, designed to repress our (hetero)sexuality, although this was not explained explicitly. For instance, we were told we could not enter a men's dorm, but we were not told why nor did we question the ruling openly. Many of us violated the rules covertly, of course, which I believe we experienced as demeaning.

All entering students in my class (1967) were asked to read Betty Friedan's *The Feminine Mystique* (1963) before entering school, a book I couldn't relate to at all. The reason was not so much the book itself but that I had not yet begun to think. The first book I read that gave me the sensation of thinking was Erich Fromm's *The Art of Loving* (1956), which I liked in part because a survivor wrote it. In that book, I recognized the working out of ideas, and I wanted to try my hand at it.

I was a commuter student at Barnard College. Being a commuter was another negative form of difference because I was missing out on what college was all about. I probably spent as much time in the subways as I did in the classroom. I spent even more time in the library, however, because I did not have the money to buy books. Because I took notes from books I did not own, college was somewhat like a high-school experience. I lived at home and went to school every day. That was it.

I had no idea what courses to take in college when I started, and the advising system did not help me at all when I tried to choose among literature, science, and the social sciences. Somehow, English literature wasn't "my" literature, and I didn't have the single-mindedness that I thought a science career demanded. Anthropology focused on physical materials, which did not interest me. Thus, because the distribution system required my taking a social science course or two, I decided to try sociology, and I was eager to have a good experience. In sociology I could take an unabashed look at my adopted home—the U.S.A. As luck would have it, I had an excellent teacher, Roberta Simmons. She was methodical, clear, and systematic. She gave me tools to work with, basic sociological concepts. She explained who the important sociologists were—such as Robert K. Merton across the street at Columbia—and she made me feel connected to them.

With this strong foundation under my belt, I was ready to learn more. I walked into the classroom of Mirra Komarovsky, and I was completely entranced by her European style, her engagement in research that could unlock the secrets of our society, and her mass of yellowed notes from which she lectured. I wanted to be like a combination of Roberta Simmons, who represented America, and Mirra Komarovsky, who represented Europe, unbeknownst to them. And then I met Renee Fox, who taught us about going into the field and collecting data about other countries. It was getting very exciting. Philip Zimbardo taught social psychology; Gladys Meyers taught social welfare; Susan Sontag taught Susan Sontag; Amitai Eztioni taught a kind of political science course. I was being turned on to ideas.

In my junior and senior years, I stopped commuting and moved in with an older woman who needed a bit of companionship. This was a step closer to the "inside" of the college community than commuting had been, but it was not really all the way "in." My housemate was an alumna of the class of 1907, while I would soon be an alumna of the class of 1967! She helped me understand gerontology, which was to become a lifelong interest.

In my junior year I was getting more adventurous. I began tutoring a young black junior high student whose family life was different from anything I had ever seen. That summer I got a job as manager of a small hotel. There were countless difficult situations at the hotel, all of which became my responsibility. Returning to school in the fall, I no longer felt naive, and I began to learn how important it is to say no. For example, I took a job as a waitress in a Hungarian pastry shop close to campus. When mold grew on unsold pastry, the owner asked me to scrape it off and add some more whipped cream. I quit. I then took a job as a private typist for a male faculty member from another university. The typing was to take place in his apartment. The first session nearly ended in rape. I quit. I called the Barnard Employment Bureau the next day to warn them not to send students to replace me. They called his employer, and he, in turn, began harassing me on the phone. It took me a few weeks to realize that he could harass me only if I answered and stayed on the phone. When I stopped, he stopped. I also went out with a guy who hit me when I wouldn't have sex with him. When he apologized and said he would never do that again, I told him I would never see him again. I quit. I experienced great strength in having overcome these awful, yet typical, situations. In a sense, my life was providing me with an unofficial education in women's studies, since women's studies had yet to be born.

Adopting what I believed was the role of sociologist, I took a job as a research assistant at the Bureau of Applied Social Research, a survey research organization affiliated with Columbia University. In my view, the particular research project on which I worked was conducted in ways that were similar to the management of the pastry shop. At the same time, I was studying sociological research methods at Barnard. The distance between the research model in the classroom and the reality in the research organization was glaring. I decided that, unlike in the pastry shop case, I was not going to walk away. Instead, I was going to study what was going on. I was going to build on my strengths (I had taken honors in sociology) and change the world! In practical terms, it meant that I applied to graduate school in sociology.

The Experience of Graduate School

The only application I made was to Brandeis: It was young, feisty, "alternative," just like who I thought I was. In addition, one of my Barnard professors, Alan Blum, was a friend of a Brandeis professor, Larry Rosenberg. I'm sure the phone call Blum made didn't harm my chances, although when I think back at how cocky I was during my Brandeis interview, I marvel at the risk I took. Or perhaps I already sensed that that was the preferred demeanor in the department.

In another place, I have written about the Brandeis sociology department's faculty and philosophy (see Reinharz forthcoming). In a more general sense, in graduate school, I recognized that if you have a liberal arts degree, you haven't studied that much of any one thing. I wanted to learn more psychology and history. I wanted to learn about mental health and illness—so I studied family dynamics and mental hospital environments. Sociology was in turmoil; American society was in turmoil. I learned that there was no single homogenized entity known as "American society" from which I was marginal. Rather, there were many different versions, and the mix was always changing. Sociology itself interested me: sociology as an object of study, sociology as a set of practices.

The start of my graduate education at Brandeis coincided with the start of my marriage to a historian and, perhaps unsurprisingly, to an Israeli. Israel had become a magical symbol for me. Somehow it was "the road not taken," the eternally young, moral place established to protect people. When I met a handsome Israeli teenager in reality, someone who looked just like the dreams I had been having for years, I had to marry him and live out the script. Being married to an Israeli suddenly meant, however, that I was the "insider" in the couple, and he was the relatively "marginal" one. Being married to a historian also meant that we had lots of opportunities to contrast sociological and historical perspectives. My view was that data are selective constructions; his view was that archives provide "facts."

Getting adjusted to married life was an education in and of itself. Suddenly there was the question of the division of labor in a household—who would do what for the collective unit? I rebelled utterly and somewhat successfully against a gender-based set of rules: that I should do the laundry in the local laundromat "because" I'm a woman made no sense to me.

It was 1967 and the world was changing rapidly on the outside—the Six-Day War, the war in Viet Nam, the assassinations of Robert Kennedy and Martin Luther King, the civil rights movement—but what about on the inside? The woman still does the laundry? Every Friday night my husband and I had a Sabbath dinner at my grandparents' home in Malden, even though as a sociology graduate student I was engaged in a critique of every aspect of society. I felt as if I lived multiple, contradictory lives.

The Brandeis sociology department encouraged me to write about "alternative visions" and "critical conceptions." For example, my master's thesis was entitled "Alienation, Education and Zen," and we students did yoga with our teachers and spent a lot of time together. My husband and I traveled to Europe every summer on what seemed like less than $5-a-day. We were trying to understand America from another perspective as much as we were trying to learn what Europe was about. We visited concentration camps; we argued with leftists in Berlin; we were nearly arrested by anti-Zionist border police in East Germany and nearly arrested by Communist police in Yugoslavia. Then we spent a year in Israel. My husband did archival research while I tried to help people cope with experiences such as being the target of rocket shelling. Out of this work came my first publications, coauthored with Israeli psychiatrists. The papers were decent first efforts, but were not satisfying as collaborative work.

Back in graduate school, the emphasis was less on professional training and more on personal growth and social reform. I left school before finishing my degree. Although I had a lot of experiences under my belt; my husband had his degree in hand. Off we went to Ann Arbor, Michigan, where he had gotten an excellent job. I didn't quite know where Michigan was or what I would do when I got there.

As it turned out, I found several jobs: teaching group dynamics in the social work school; teaching group dynamics in an extension course; supervising group-therapists. Then I picked up another slot—director of the undergraduate experiential education program in the psychology department. Called Project Outreach, this program espoused a pedagogic philosophy we called "experiential education," as described by Paolo Friere, whom we brought to campus to make the point. I loved directing this immense program, although at times there were intense personal conflicts among the staff that I found difficult to handle.

Being a sociologist in a psychology department, I was comfortably at home once again as a "marginal" person. Moreover, the segment of the psychology department with which I was affiliated was itself marginal in the department. This sort of marginality allowed me to criticize from the inside. I put all of this under the rubric of "sociology" and became valuable to the department because the program was large, generated lots of credit, and was much appreciated by the students.

Yearning for Motherhood

I had gotten pregnant in 1973 soon after we arrived in Ann Arbor, when I was naive enough to think that I could hold down a full-time job and be a mother as well. My husband and I traveled to Israel shortly after I became pregnant, and after being there for a month, I suffered a painful, completely unexpected miscarriage. Soon thereafter, following the outbreak of the Yom Kippur War, I became terribly ill. My experience of the war revived memories of my parents' experience during "their war." I thought we would all die, and many did, in fact, die, including the son of the obstetrician who was caring for me at the time.

We returned to Ann Arbor in the dead of winter. I had a demanding job, no Ph.D., had suffered a miscarriage, and was too ill to contemplate becoming pregnant again. My work began to be boringly repetitive, and I did not have the inner peace to resume writing my dissertation. Semester after semester, I developed a huge educational program, but aside from student satisfaction and community service, there was nothing to show for my efforts.

Lack of a Ph.D. made me marginal in a way that was anxiety-producing in a university as distinguished as the University of Michigan. Despite my success, I was increasingly dissatisfied, unhappy, and anxious. Lack of a Ph.D. paralleled lack of children: I felt empty. Whereas formerly it had been "interesting" to be different, now it was paralyzing. What was I going to do with my life? To make matters worse, I developed a chronic illness. The strange thing about it was that I appeared normal most of the time, while actually I wasn't normal at all. Such an experience is deeply alienating. This debilitating state, made worse by insensitive physicians, continuously diminished my sense of well-being. I could not write my dissertation if I didn't know who I was; and I could not figure out who I was unless my health improved and I wrote my dissertation. I remember once crying into a tape recorder and playing it back, thinking I could detect some meaning in that.

When I reached what I felt was the bottom of the pit, I acted. I took a leave from my job and—unsurprisingly—moved to Israel, letting Israel save and heal me as it had so many Jews. There I planned to confine myself to a room and write. By arranging the appropriate physical environment, having the assistance of my husband, and marshaling the force of sheer willpower, I forged ahead. My reward for finishing the first chapter was a one-week trip through the Sinai Desert with a friend.

Motherhood and a Ph.D. at Last

My reward for finishing the next couple of chapters was to allow myself to get pregnant. I returned to Ann Arbor that summer, pregnant, with a dissertation sans conclusion in hand, and with my health somewhat under control. I resumed my old job, revised the dissertation, wrote the conclusion, and defended it with a ten-week-old baby in my arms. I was not surprised that mothering came naturally to me—all it took was to look closely at our daughter and try to understand her "language." It was rather similar to being a participant observer. I did not connect being a good mother to some sort of biological essence I had as a woman. Rather, I felt that being a decent, thoughtful person enabled me to be a good mother. Those qualities could also be found in men.

My dissertation concerned the multiple conflicting strands within sociology, and it was published in 1979 as *On Becoming a Social Scientist: From Survey Research and Participant Observation to Experiential Analysis*. It addressed the question I had in mind when I entered graduate school ten years earlier, which was "How should sociology be done?" Things were coming together for me at last.

With a Ph.D. in hand, I finally had the prerequisites for being a real person in a university environment. Thus I felt entitled to change my job and become less marginal. No longer would I direct the large undergraduate psychology program; rather, I would apply to be a faculty member in a more "regular" unit. My appointment was as assistant professor of community psychology, the unit within the 150-or-so-member psychology department that was most sociological in orientation. I began to work closely with graduate students because I had real empathy for them. I began to find that rather than training in a particular field, logic was sufficient. Sociological thinking was one form of logic, and it fit well into the community psychology program. I began to consult with human service organizations, and, recognizing how important it was to publish, I wrote up whatever I was doing. I strove to publish in prestigious publication outlets, but I used whatever outlets came my way. The point was to do what was needed to meet the requirements of my position. If psychology was going to be my chosen area, though, I knew it would be wise to participate in professional organizations. So I joined the American Psychological Association and the Midwest Psychological Association, among others. I attended conferences, presented papers, and worked hard. I began to get small grants to do my work, and I even won a prize as the most promising untenured female faculty member at the University of Michigan. That certainly was a boost.

As a community psychologist, I thought it would be helpful to study another community in depth. So in 1979 and 1980 I took a leave from the university to do intensive participant observation on a kibbutz, focusing on how the community responded to the needs of its aging population. In preparation for this research, I taught a course in gerontology. Thus, when my dissertation-based sociological book appeared, I was actually living on a kibbutz with my young daughter (my husband lived in Jerusalem so he could do archival research), and I was engaged in a community psychology study. It was then that I began to receive invitations from sociologists to contribute to their anthologies. While doing the community study of the kibbutz, I realized that the methods and theory I was relying on were the methods and theory I had learned as a budding sociologist in graduate school.

Although I knew I could go back to being a "community psychologist," and I even coauthored a textbook on the subject with my colleagues (Heller, et al. 1984), I longed to be among sociologists—people who spoke my language. For example, in Ann Arbor, I was continuously "explaining" grounded theory and qualitative methods to my colleagues, just as I had explained Hanukkah to my adolescent friends. I wanted to be in an intellectual environment where I would be pushed further rather than having to explain the foundation. It was tiring to be marginal in my own profession. In fact, even as an adolescent, explaining Hanukkah to others was fun precisely because I didn't have to explain it at home. I wanted to feel that my profession was also a home, a place where I did not have to explain everything.

Becoming a Feminist Academic

Upon my return to Ann Arbor from the kibbutz in 1980, I received a shock. University of Michigan graduate students told me that my book, *On Becoming a Social Scientist*, had been discussed extensively at the annual meeting of the National Association of Women's Studies while I had been abroad. The implications of what I had written about women's ways of knowing and doing social science were important, they had said. These students and a few feminist faculty then asked me to join an informal "feminist research methodology study group." Subsequently, the women's studies program invited me to teach an introductory course. I understand, of course, that one cannot attribute a direction taken to an invitation alone. One has to be ready to accept the invitation. Nevertheless, these were propitious offers; they helped me reshape my career in a feminist direction. It is not surprising that after this enthusiastic recognition I attempted my first single-authored sociologically based, theoretically driven article in a refereed journal. I wrote and rewrote, revised and resubmitted and was ultimately successful (Reinharz 1983).

My work in women's studies raised many sociological concerns for me, the most basic of which was "What had women done thoughout history?" I posed the question after having lunch with the community psychologist Annette Rickel, who showed me the table of contents of her projected anthology on women's problems. "Did women only *have* problems?" I asked her. "Didn't they also *solve* problems?" Didn't women *do* things? What, in fact, had women *done?* I decided to try to develop a conceptual framework for the material I would collect on this issue. The result was "Women as Competent Community Builders," a piece that underpins much of my subsequent work in women's studies (Reinharz 1984).

I had another question. I was beginning to write the book based on my fieldwork in the kibbutz, and in preparing the introductory chapter explaining the history of the kibbutz movement, I embarked on a new project about the woman who developed the ideology underpinning the creation of kibbutzim. I also wrote about the current state of sociology in Israel, trying to integrate my interest in the discipline and the country (Reinharz 1989a).

I had by then fully accepted the idea that my personal experiences could have sociological significance. The "feminist group," for example, illustrated the creation of new settings that reflected people's changing needs and values. Similarly, as I wrote about issues that were important in my own life, I clarified them for myself, thereby enhancing my personal experience.

Since my life was becoming more stable, I allowed myself to get pregnant again. I also applied for an opening at Brandeis as an assistant professor of sociology, where I could finally return to being a sociologist. My husband applied for a job in his field at the same university, and, miracle of miracles, we both succeeded. Thus in fall 1982, I was a thirty-six-year-old mother of two preschoolers; I had a Ph.D. in sociology and had taught psychology for nearly ten years and women's studies for a year; and I was returning to my graduate department to teach. I also received another invitation: to be the coeditor of the journal *Qualitative Sociology* with Peter Conrad. Moreover, I was given responsibility for the field-methods training in our department. I began to attract a large number of graduate students and help them produce what I believe are very worthwhile sociological studies. I had really come into my own, and I actually had a position of authority. Peter Conrad and I evaluated manuscripts from all over the country and tried to strengthen the standing of qualitative work in sociology. After what now seems like a ten-year detour, I had the opportunity of teaching, writing, and editing sociology again.

Returning to Sociology

There are many tales to tell of my evolution as a sociologist beginning at the point of joining the Brandeis faculty and in that sense becoming a member of a department fully invested in my becoming one. Perhaps that was the first time I no longer felt intellectually marginal and instead felt like an insider. Surprisingly, many of the problems I did encounter in this new job were caused by women, not by men, which led me to develop a more sophisticated understanding of women's roles in society. When I gave my "job talk," for instance, a female junior faculty member seemed to do her best to embarrass and undermine me during the question-and-answer period. Another woman in my department later said, "One feminist is enough in each department, and I was here first."

Although I was shocked in both cases, I discovered that I had the strength to deal with them effectively and that feminism was not going to blind me to the problems that existed in some relationships among women. I learned from these experiences how damaging competition—that form of interaction so highly lauded in my high school curriculum—can be. It seemed to me that the strength of women's bonds was nothing in comparison with the forces that tear us apart. I also learned from these experiences how important aspects of my own definition of feminism are to me: "If you've got power, use it to help another woman; if you're going somewhere good, take another woman along." I want to define the women's movement as a supportive community. A supportive community, rather than a competitive hierarchy, is my objective for the women's studies program at Brandeis, which I now direct. My definition of my role as a full professor (the first woman to hold this position in my department), is to be a mentor to others who are interested in having me as a mentor.

Most of the tales I have to tell of the sociologically significant aspects of my ten years in the department (in which I traversed the mine fields of tenure and promotion), concern trusting my intellectual responses to problems. For example, when I taught introductory social psychology during my first semester and used Peter Berger's *Invitation to Sociology* (1963), I noticed for the first time the deep misogyny embedded in this work. First, I attempted to convert this observation into writing about how important this problem was. I labeled my response "feminist distrust" and showed how feminists read through the lens of distrust in order to detect and correct misogynist bias (Reinharz 1985/1988). I remember nearly shaking with rage but disguising my response with humor in an article called "Patriarchal Pontifications" (Reinharz 1986).

I also knew that this observation required action. And so I developed a course called "Women and Intellectual Work" in which I could trace the history of women's work as sociologists, thereby sidestepping misogynist sociological work. I tried to locate other feminist sociologists who were engaged in rewriting sociology from a feminist perspective, and I discovered the work of Mary Jo Deegan (1991), whom I greatly admire. My contribution to Mary Jo's reference work on female sociologists was a chapter about my teacher, Mirra Komarovsky, thereby renewing my connection with her (Reinharz 1989b, 1991).

As I continue to write this essay, I find that I have a story to tell for each publication and that the writing of each one feels almost like the birth of a child. My series of articles on miscarriage, for example, begins with the story of my having written a description of my miscarriage in 1973 that was so full of rage that friends of mine urged me to not publish it. I put the paper in a drawer and tried to go on with my life, although a part of me was always mourning. The paper itself was a kind of miscarriage: It didn't go anywhere. Ten years later, I received a request to submit an article for a journal's special issue devoted to women's concerns. Because I was so involved in mothering, teaching, and writing at the time and could not carry out additional fieldwork, I committed myself to writing a series of articles on miscarriage utilizing textual materials (Reinharz 1988a, 1988b, 1993a, 1993b).

In the mid-1980s I wanted to write a book about the issues I had been thinking about since first being asked to join the "feminist research methodology group" at Michigan. That ten-person group and subsequent similar ones I joined when moving to Boston have been extremely important to me. They represent a kind of "alternative university" in which members present their work to one another, provide useful critiques from a feminist perspective, and then help each other find avenues for publication. All the members of the first Boston-based group have gone on to earn full professorship or the equivalent in part, I believe, because of the support we gave one another. Our discussions concerning what a feminist research method might be led to my desire to write an integrating work that would reexamine the literature I had read and answer some questions. With *Feminist Methods in Social Research*, I feel I have laid the questions to rest, at least for myself (Reinharz 1992).

Since January 1991, I have been director of women's studies at Brandeis in addition to my full-time position in the sociology department. I am amazed at how much time and energy I have wanted to pour into my new role. Clearly it has become my new baby. In two short years we have transformed the program into one that engages ten times as many faculty as before and has added many new components in addition to an upsurge in student interest. Most notable are a thirty-member National Board for Women's Studies at Brandeis University, a Visiting and Resident Scholars program, a graduate degree–granting program, an internship program in the prevention of violence against women and children, a Working Papers series, a video series, an endowment drive, and a monthly meeting of all members of the community. The principle reason I enjoy directing the women's studies program is the opportunity it offers to implement what I have learned in community psychology, sociology, and feminist scholarship. Since women's studies is my new baby, I want to help it thrive. Women's studies also seems to represent "positive marginality."

Concluding Thoughts

It is comforting to recognize, as I write this, that opportunity and effort (tempered by difficulty and pain) have characterized my life so far. For this reason, I consider it my duty to help create opportunities for others and to continue to try to transform my discipline and my life. Like many other feminist sociologists, I feel very fortunate to have found my voice. Many of us are poised to take extraordinary intellectual leaps and to work for the improvement of our discipline, our universities, and our communities. We can live with our marginality as long as there is some place where we are "at home." The tension between being marginal and having a community characterizes feminists' lives, but the future seems more promising than ever. I think we have something good to pass on to the next generation.

Shulamit Reinharz

REFERENCES

Breines, Wini. 1992. *Young, White, and Miserable: Growing Up Female in the Fifties.* Boston: Beacon.

Deegan, Mary Jo, ed. 1991. *Women in Sociology: A Bio-Bibliographic Sourcebook.* Westport, Conn.: Greenwood Press.

Heller, Kenneth, Richard Price, Shulamit Reinharz, Stephanie Riger, and Abraham Wandersman. 1984. *Psychology and Community Change.* Chicago: Dorsey Books.

Reinharz, Shulamit. 1979. *On Becoming a Social Scientist: From Survey Research to Participant Observation to Experiential Analysis.* San Francisco: Jossey-Bass. Rev. ed., New Brunswick, N.J.: Transaction Books, 1984.

———. 1983. "Consulting to the Alternative Work Setting: A Suggested Strategy for Community Psychology." *Journal of Community Psychology.* 11:199–212.

———. 1984. "Women as Competent Community Builders: The Other Side of the Coin." Pp. 19–43 in *Social and Psychological Problems of Women: Prevention and Crisis Intervention,* edited by Annette Rickel, Meg Gerrard, and Ira Iscoe. New York: Macmillan.

———. 1985/1988. "Feminist Distrust: Problems of Context and Content in Sociological Work." Pp. 153–72 in *The Self in Social Inquiry*, edited by David Berg and Ken Smith. Newbury Park, Calif.: Sage.

———. 1986. "Patriarchal Pontifications." *Transaction/SOCIETY* 23 (6): 23–39.

———. 1988a. "Controlling Women's Lives: A Cross-Cultural Interpretation of Miscarriage Accounts." Pp. 2–37 in *Research in the Sociology of Health Care*, edited by Dorothy Wertz. Greenwich, Conn.: JAI Press.

———. 1988b. "What's Missing in Miscarriage?" *Journal of Community Psychology* 16 (1): 84–103.

———. 1989a. "Sociologists Working in Israel." *Footnotes* 18, no. 4 (April): 3–4.

———. 1989b. "Finding Her Sociological Voice: The Work of Mirra Komarovsky." *Sociological Inquiry* 59 (4): 374–95.

———. 1991. "Mirra Komarovsky." Pp. 239–48 in *Women in Sociology: A Bio-Bibliographic Sourcebook*, edited by Mary Jo Deegan. Westport, Conn.: Greenwood Press.

———, with the assistance of Lynn Davidman. 1992. *Feminist Methods in Social Research*. New York: Oxford University Press.

———. 1993a. "Empty Explanations for Empty Wombs: An Illustration of a Secondary Analysis of Qualitative Data." Pp. 157–78 in *Qualitative Voices in Educational Research*, edited by Michael Schratz. London: Falmer Press.

———. 1993b. "Miscarriage." Pp. 260–62 in *Encyclopedia of Childbearing: Critical Perspectives*, edited by Barbara Katz Rothman. New York: Oryx Press.

———. Forthcoming. "The Chicago School of Sociology and the Founding of the Graduate Program in Sociology at Brandeis University: A Case Study in Cultural Diffusion." In *A Second Chicago School? The Development of Midcentury Sociology at the University of Chicago*, edited by Gary Alan Fine. Chicago: University of Chicago Press.

Seventeen

Kaddish and Renewal

Gaye Tuchman

I have been given the rare chance to explicate my own text. As an ethnographer, I know that every time I describe a phenomenon I select some details and omit others: Selection is a purposive activity designed to tell a sociological story. I did not write this essay to do sociology. I wrote the first part to come to grips with my feelings. I wrote the second because my mother asked me to. I present them here because both bits of prose help to explain who I am.

Whenever I teach the sociology of gender to undergraduates, I ask them to interview their mother and her mother to learn about the impact of our changing society on women's lives. They always ask for guidance. Unfortunately, I have never had a comparable essay about my family. One grandmother died before I was born; the other when I was six; and I have never interviewed my mother—just talked to her, almost daily since the birth of my son, daily since my father died. (We speak after supper; my sister and mother speak every morning.)

So, after asking my students to listen for the sociology—the story of assimilation, the story of patriarchy, and the story of how your family looks different to you as you get older—I read them the first part of this essay. It's melancholy and nostalgic. I'm not even sure whether all the myths I learned in childhood are true. But it expresses who, most of the time, I feel myself to be: the accomplishment of the Sugarmans, of my unusual father, and of my mother who very much wanted me to achieve a life of my own.

1977

My family, more accurately my mother's family, is dying. When I was a child, there were spurts of gladness at a new life, a *Bar Mitzvah*, a wedding. Life replenished death. Today I learn about death. The telephone calls me to the grave site of my mother's father's first cousin. The funeral corteges have grown progressively smaller. No one phones to say that my grandfather's first cousin's granddaughter has had a child. I don't know that distant cousin, now living in Florida or California or even here in New York. She was reared in suburban Long Island or Westchester and I, in New Jersey.

My friends tell me that my sprawling Jewish family is unusual. We own two large cemetery plots, one in Long Island where my great-grandparents lie and where my parents will be buried, and one in New Jersey where space is allotted for me and for the grandchildren of cousins my age who are married and giving birth. We have a scholarship fund to assist each year an excellent prospective college freshman. It is carefully administered by trustees representing each branch of the family; each is bound to withdraw from the deliberations when a high school senior with too close a specified degree of affinity enters the competition. Last October, the Sugarman Family Circle held a dinner dance to celebrate the fiftieth year of its incorporation. About 125 of my cousins and quasi-cousins attended—perhaps one-third of the people whom I have been taught to call my family.

This degree of organized activity is a sloughing off of family bonds. Twenty-five years ago, before my generation left the New York area to go to college, many never to return, the dinner dance was an annual event, as was the yearly Hanukkah party and the June picnic. My great-uncles laughed; cousins and in-laws did the fox-trot with fervor. Older women danced together, holding each other's elbows in a loose embrace.

The family gathered once a month at the Hotel McAlpin, now defunct, to meet on such questions as where to buy a second cemetery plot for the children of my generation. Men played pinochle and chewed their cigars. Women gossiped and pinched the cheeks of children. We children ran through the hotel's hallways and flew paper airplanes. Today the Family Circle meets every few months in someone's home; fewer than thirty assemble. I don't go, although I religiously attend professional meetings.

When I met some of my cousins for the first time in twenty years at the Fiftieth Anniversary Celebration, we reminisced about my Great-aunt Stella, who weighed well over 350 pounds and had the fiercest pinch. We remembered thinking, as children, that her grip on our cheeks was so strong that she could lift us up and throw us across the room. We shared the experience of once having encountered numerous relatives whose names we could not remember but who could recite what we had looked like as infants and name our degree of affinity.

Some of us once-children did not recall one another. We weren't quite sure how we were related. The dinner dance committee should have handed out family trees at the doorway, someone suggested. Another cousin remembered that the family tree hasn't been updated in ten or fifteen years—since Stella died. My organized family has assimilated and modernized.

When still on the Lower East Side of Manhattan, many Jewish families had founded cousin's clubs. The Sugarman family seemed different because it had been organized well before its official incorporation in 1927. Julius Zacharanu, my great-grandfather's youngest brother, came to the United States as a teenager in 1888. I don't know why he was selected to lead to migration or how he came to buy a tobacco farm in Connecticut. As others did, he sent for his brothers and sister, their children and spouses. But not all at once. They came to work the farm and to learn English. A master of the new language and the mores of the new land, the immigrant would depart for the Lower East Side to be replaced by the next brother or nephew. I used to think the Sugarmans brought every Jew from Kodiesht, the small Rumanian village of their birth. My New Jersey–born Uncle Meyer tells me they brought only close relatives—through first-cousins. But all passed through the farm on the way to the Lower East Side, to enter New York as English-speaking Yankees. As old men, they reckoned their ages according to the country where they had been born or *Bar Mitzvahed* and by the sequence of *B'nai Mitzvah*. Their calendar was firmly rooted in their religion, their family, and the pattern of migration.

The Sugarmans settled on a Rumanian block on the Lower East Side. They married their neighbors' children. My uncle and aunt relate the story of how my grandmother came to marry my grandfather. She and her sister had wanted to marry brothers, but their mother was convinced that the arrangement was unlucky. Great-grandmother Nagler discussed the problem with her neighbor, Gussie Sugarman, for whom I am named. "Don't worry," Gussie supposedly said, "My Isreal will marry your Becky." Those were the days, my father recalls (extending his generalization through the 1930s), when one decried intermarriage if a *Litvak* (a Lithuanian Jew) married a *Galitziyaner* (a Galcian Jew).

The family was extensive and absorbing. It absorbed in at least two ways. Every in-law became a member of the family. Our organization was not a mere cousin's club. (We never used the word "club," a slight word naming friends who played bridge or gin or poker.) Ours was a Family Circle, ever enlarging its perimeter. When I visit the cemetery today, I spot the graves of people I knew in my childhood: the brother-in-law and sister of a great-uncle's wife; my grandfather's first-cousin's wife's sisters, brothers, nieces, and nephews. Only now do I know there was no tie of blood. At the Fiftieth

Anniversary Dinner Dance, the president of the Family Circle—the brother of another great-uncle's wife—gave life to that pattern of expansion. He asked descendants of the three brothers and sister of my great-grandfather's generation to rise, when he called out the name of their forbearer: Jeal, Mordechai, Julius, Esther. Then he added that those who had entered the family as he did, through the marriage of a brother, sister, uncle, or aunt to a Sugarman, should also rise when the name of the forbearer with whom they were associated rang out. I felt pride when the largest group to stand was my branch, the descendants of Mordechai.

The family had incorporated after the bonds to the common Rumanian past had already begun to weaken. The plaque by the entrance to the Sugarman enclave in Mount Hebron Cemetery, Queens, announces the fifty-three original members and three junior ones. (In 1927, the junior members were older than thirteen, unmarried, and younger than twenty-one. That is, they were bar mitvahed but not old enough to vote.) The graves of my great-grandfather's generation date to that period: the oldest stone announces in English and Hebrew the death of my great-grandmother, 1864–1921, reinterred to be with her family. (I can't read the inscription chiseled on the other old stone, that of Great-great-uncle Jeal; only his name appears in English.) Shortly before 1927, the family began to scatter to different parts of the New York metropolitan area. My grandfather, one of his brothers, his two sisters, and a first cousin settled near Passiac, New Jersey. Others went to Long Island, Westchester, Upper Manhattan, or the Bronx. Having the Family Circle meant they would all assemble once a month at a central location, the hotel on Manhattan's Herald Square.

Through the 1950s, the Sugarmans continued to be absorbed in one another. They transferred the close living arrangement of working-class ethnic groups to the suburban section of the mini-industrial town where I was reared. I can still map the pattern of residences and visits. During World War II, while my father soldiered and my mother and I lived with her parents, six homes of relatives stood nearby. After my grandmother's death in 1949, my mother, her sister, and her father reproduced immigrant closeness by living in two-family houses. My grandfather lived downstairs; my aunt and her family, upstairs. We lived next door. After my grandfather remarried, he moved to another house less than a mile away, and we moved to his former residence. Such arrangements are relatively rare among the middle class. And my grandfather had been successful; my mother still delights in recalling that he owned a car throughout the 1920s and 1930s and that her mother bought her a $100 cloth coat when she was of marriageable age.

Sometimes I think that the family began to die when the old men died. I remember the old men much more vividly than I do the women of my grandfather's generation. The family was quietly, but actively, patriarchal. I smile at the thought of two of my grandfather's first cousins, brothers whom I could tell apart only because when they drank *sliwowitz* (plum liquor) or rye, Ike's nose got redder than Abe's. I recall another man in that generation who chased all the ladies at the annual dinner dance. Perhaps he pinched them. They giggled. He was naughty.

I also remember whispered stories about arrangements that no one likes to talk about and that would never happen now. A son who worked with his father embezzled some money from the firm. ("A terrible thing," everyone agreed, "a *shande*" [mortification].) The family chipped in to handle the problem. Before my birth, a cousin of my mother's generation was sent to California and told never to return when he refused to be swayed from his announced intention to marry a non-Jew. Before the couple was married, the family gathered money to set him up in business. Then they said *kaddish* (mourner's prayer). Now, half of my first cousins are married to non-Jews. When the first of those marriages took place in the mid-1960s, all "children" under the age of forty who were members of my branch actively told their parents not to intervene. Matters that in the 1930s evoked passion across the entire *mishpuche* (extended family) were declared "none of our business" in the 1960s.

Perhaps I think that the family began to die when the old men began to die because my grandfather was the oldest of his brothers, sisters, in-laws, and assorted first cousins to reach the age of seventy and "pass on," as we politely say. At the time, it seemed a harbinger of what was to come, much as the recent death of his youngest sister-in-law at age sixty-eight brought a new kind of grief. My oldest uncle is sixty-three. Only three women and two men over seventy are left. The cemetery, neatly arranged by date of birth and family branch, is filling in.

The family began to die long before my grandfather's terminal illness. It died a little when the second large cemetery plot was purchased in New Jersey. The life passed out of the monthly meetings where the men had filled ten years of talk with endless debate about the best location. The family had begun to die with the continued and accelerated education and prosperity of the men and their movement to the suburbs. In the second generation, two men had become professionals. George, the son of Great-great-uncle Julius, owner of the tobacco farm, went to Yale and became a dentist. Bernie, my grandfather's youngest brother, became a pharmacist in the 1920s. Others in that generation were economically comfortable, some in cigars and later in textiles.

The wealthiest of Jeal's sons became the family patriarch, endowing the scholarship fund to keep us all together through the years, donating a dormitory to a Yeshiva in B'nai B'rak. But even with wealth, that generation had maintained traditional patterns. The patriarch's brothers drove to Passaic from New York almost every Sunday to gossip and to joke in Yiddish and to share schnapps (a drink, often rye). Assorted cousins would visit. Visits were not required; they came to be called *mitzvot* when the patriarch aged and grew ill.

Family visits were still the rule in my youth, but they had a different quality than the closeness my mother recounts. When she speaks of her youth and adolescence, I hear the presence of moral injunctions: first and second cousins of approximately the same age must both like and love one another. One must make allowances for family. In my generation, those commandments disappeared.

Several of my first and second cousins attended Thomas Jefferson Junior High School and Passaic High School when I did. Our classmates took our measure by criteria foreign to the family: Does she clutch her books to her bosom or hold them under her arm? Does he wear a buttoned-down shirt? We applied those same modes of judgment to our out-of-town cousins. In school, we learned that it was wrong for teenagers to go to Family Circle meetings and so to maintain our childhood. Participation in family functions came to seem shameful, a sign of lack of involvement with friends. One by one, those in my age-group disappeared from the monthly gatherings. Although a parent might approvingly announce the presence of an adolescent cousin at the last meeting, his attendance seemed an indication of social retardation, not of healthy attachment to family as my mother claimed. His parents were old-fashioned; he wasn't hip. My younger sister and I successfully begged out soon after our upstairs neighbor, a first cousin six weeks younger than I, convinced his parents that he no longer had to attend. I was in high school then. I had stayed with the family longer than most.

My parents say I was brought up to have family-feeling. I think I stayed so long because I was immature. I prefer to think that the pertinent factor was that my father, a second-generation American from a poor orthodox family, had been embraced by the Sugarmans. He had not been graduated from high school. The parents of my multitudinous cousins were third-generation; many had attended college.

My mother dropped out of teacher's college when she married my father in 1937. Her brother is a lawyer. Her male first cousins are doctors, engineers, and schoolteachers. Most of the women did not go to college. My mother's sister took a job after high school and married as soon as she could. Some of her cousins, but not all, left the area to get educated. They returned. All of my New Jersey cousins left for their education. Many went on for advanced degrees and moved wherever their work took them. For some, their profession was an excuse to flee the too-constricting bosom of the family, as though Great-aunt Stella's love-pinch had become its painful symbol.

Our separate paths took another toll. The weddings of those my age have passed, as have many of the *Bar* and *Bas Mitzvahs* of their children. Except for my mother's nieces and nephews, I see some of my cousins only at the cemetery. I never see others. We few who watch the graves fill in are the constant mourners of the past. We, the faithful, mainly convene for the funerals of members of our branch and the unveiling of their tombstones. I can no longer recite the names of age mates from other family branches.

At these brief encounters, I remember how much I loved my cousins' parents. Sometimes we speak of our mutual past. Someone always says we must get together on happier occasions. We never do, for we don't know one another any more. If we were to chat across a dinner table some evening, we might discover each other as people. We might learn of our antithetical tastes, our opposing politics, our conflicting urban and suburban life-styles. We might learn that we love our memories of one another but not our current selves. We might learn that the bonds of our family started to strain when groups scattered through the New York area well before our births, when the second family plot was purchased and there were to be no more ritualized debates, when virtually everybody became upper middle-class and there was little need to quietly assist one another, when friends taught us that old-fashioned family-feeling was a sign of social awkwardness—when we became American.

The feeling of belonging to a mammoth entity called family will not be passed on to the fifth generation of Sugarmans in the United States, the generation after mine. But I have Jewish friends, whose families were more recent immigrants to America, who are taken aback by my ability to reel off distant ties. One of them said recently, "You mean, the guy who sat across from you at the Fiftieth Anniversary Party wasn't a relative." "Of course he is," I answered. "It took two minutes to figure out that our grandfathers were first cousins." I added a thought unspoken at the celebration: "My grandfather financially supported his." From the days of the *B'nai Mitzvahs* in Rumania and the passage through the Connecticut tobacco farm, our family lasted longer than most.

1989

We are here today to dedicate the gravestones of Meyer Sugarman and Jack Tuchman, men we knew and loved. Treasured husbands, fathers, brothers, grandfathers, uncles, and friends, both of these men lived meaningful, even blessed lives. We and they are surrounded by the graves of people we knew and loved: parents, grandparents, great-grandparents, uncles, aunts, cousins. They reminded us of the continuity of life and of love—that we have sprung from their roots and that others will follow us—to laugh as they laughed, to love as they loved us, and to try to do good in the world.

My uncle was a Sugarman; the tombstone of his mother, Rebecca Nagler Sugarman, wife of Isreal, is just over there. It tells us that Meyer bore the name of his grandfather, Maier Nagler. My father married into this immense family. They treasured his virtues and understood his foibles. He was one of the first men of his generation to be elected president of the Sugarman Family Circle.

On first blush, my uncle and my father seemed very different people. They had very different life-styles. My father loved to travel. My uncle loved to read maps. Their educations were very different. Their jobs were very different. My father loved to amuse children. In his prime, he was a world-champion tickler. My uncle loved children with a fond seriousness. My father loved to tell jokes. My uncle loved to listen to them. But both men loved to talk to one another. Sometimes they would monopolize the conversation at holiday meals, talking about what was happening in Passaic and exchanging their understandings of people and situations. They respected one another. They were brothers-in-law and friends for over fifty years. Fifty years is a very long time, and in all that time, Jack Tuchman and Meyer Sugarman never exchanged a harsh word.

Perhaps my uncle and my father got on so very well because at heart they shared basic values, Jewish values. Each man was an avid reader, always in the middle of at least one book and delighted to share what he had learned. Each man was so proud of his children and grandchildren that their friends were frequently regaled with tales of our accomplishments.

Most important, each man understood that one purpose of life is to help other people. Sometimes my uncle forgot to charge clients for his services. To him, money was not as important as ideas. I think every *schnorer* (beggar) in the greater metropolitan area knew that if he went to the Jefferson Bake Shop, my father would give him a contribution. He once even sent *chai* ($18 dollars) to a television evangelist whom he felt encouraged virtue and love of God. After he retired, he took a blind man swimming every week and helped the man keep in his lane.

Both Meyer Sugarman and Jack Tuchman understood the basic teaching of the *Pirkay Avot:* It is our task to lead an ethical life; a life that honors people is marked by joy in others' accomplishments and by service to the community. Meyer's deeds are marked in the history of New Jersey. He was one of the leading estate lawyers in New Jersey, a lawyer's lawyer, a town prosecutor, and counsel to the ethics committee of the New Jersey Supreme Court, a high honor indeed. Jack's service to the community is marked on the walls of his *shul* (synagogue), the Ahavas Israel, on the walls of the Beth Israel Hospital made cheerier by the many pictures he donated, and in the marriages he assisted by buying a *chupa* (wedding canopy) for residents of the displaced persons camp where he served immediately after World War II. We are also their accomplishments, for they reared and taught us.

All of us feel great sadness that Meyer Sugarman and Jack Tuchman died. We miss them greatly. But we also dedicate their gravestones with appreciation of the beauty of their lives and our hope that we, our children, and our children's children can do as they did—live with joy and live an honorable and an ethical life.

1992

My mammoth extended family taught me what, as a sociologist, I do best: watch, listen, and try to make sense of the social interactions around me. Since my early life was geared so much toward adults, among my peers I feel myself to be ever socially awkward, someone who never quite fit in, an observer of my own participation, a participant observer.

My father taught me to write. He certainly never thought that either my sister or I would write for a living. First, he taught us indirectly: He gave us the gift of telling stories, preferably funny ones delivered to enchanted groups. He entertained so well at family meals that I sometimes think that the very worst sin we could have possibly committed was to have been inarticulate.

He taught me more directly about writing when I was in fifth grade and attended private school. I want to back into how he did that. When I was nine, my piano teacher had convinced my parents to send me to the local private school: I hated it. There were few Jews. There were lots of rich kids. I made social gaffes that still make me cringe. Invited to Emily's house, I mentioned that we drank our morning orange juice out of the Howdy Doody glasses that grape jelly came in. There was a crushing silence. Invited to the wealthiest home in town, I came in the back door and saw a white woman loading a washing machine, so I said "Hello, Mrs. Jones." And it was the maid. I had never heard of a white maid, though I had seen the corner in front of the A&P near my father's bakery, where black women waited for a day job as a "cleaning lady."

One day in fifth grade, the teacher told us to write an essay. I panicked. I didn't know what an essay was. My father wrote the first sentence of a story and told me to finish the rest. (I smiled when in graduate school I read *The Golden Notebook,* where Lessing and her lover exchange first sentences and again when I saw the same practice in de Beauvoir's *Mandarins.* Other people had also been blocked. And since I would like this essay to be more truthful than not, I should admit that I still can't begin an article or book without a good first sentence.) My father explained that an essay is a story using facts. Then he told me to use the simplest words I could. Good writing, he said echoing a Hemingway he had not yet read, is writing anyone can read. Now, when I write, I talk at my computer, pretending I'm addressing a culturally diverse, Queens College class who need me to use the plainest words I can. Or sometimes I pretend I'm explaining my ideas to my parents, avaricious and sophisticated readers who won't put up with multisyllabic airs.

This parental gift of gabbing on paper has been essential to my career as a sociologist. Supposedly, we sociologists of the academy get paid to teach, but ultimately we get tenured and promoted for our writing. Because research and writing can be so very difficult, one could also say we get paid for our *sitzfleish,* our ability to sit and keep at it. When I am interested in something, I can sit forever. That ability is also a gift from my father. He bribed me to learn. In ninth grade, he payed me twenty-five dollars for each A+, a considerable amount of money in those days. He set me obscure research questions; some were Masonic secrets and some easily discovered by reading the Sunday magazine of the *New York Times.* He paid me for correct answers. He clearly pushed me in ways that I now think misguided and try not to do to my child. But at the same time, when I bragged about my own child's precocity shortly before my father died, he reminded me, "I always told you. Never try to be the smartest one. There's always someone smarter. Just keep at it."

Both the parental push to achieve and parental advice "to keep at it" help to explain why I am a professor. My parents certainly hadn't planned for me to become a professor, although inadvertently they helped me to discover that secret desire. When I was in (public) junior high school, my mother went back to complete her college degree. In the mid-1950s, I had not realized how daring her action was: She was a pioneer. My mother took me to some of her classes, including an astronomy fieldtrip and a class on the history of Western religions. The informality of the classroom and the lecture were fascinating—so engrossing that as soon as my mother had taken the final exam and no longer needed to monopolize her books, I did the reading for the course on religion. From then on I harbored an unarticulated wish to be a college professor. Unarticulated, because I was ashamed to tell: Women weren't college professors.

I don't know what my father wanted me to be. I never asked him, and he never told me. When I was seven or so and going through my "a" period—I would be an anthropologist, archeologist, or astronomer—he never said my ambitions were silly. He wanted me to be popular, something I just didn't know how to pull off. He wanted me to be a good Jew. He demanded respect. When he uttered "respect," that word resonated with a fulsome, angry, patriarchal, class-based tone.

I always thought my mother wanted me to be a schoolteacher. Perhaps I was fourteen or so when my mother told me that school teaching was a good job for a woman, because you could be there when the kids get home. Several weeks ago, my mother said she had always hoped I would be a lawyer. I would have been a lousy lawyer; I hate the perpetual confrontation that seems endemic to practicing most kinds of law. My uncle, the estate lawyer, must have felt that way too. His specialty is not noted for courtroom disputes.

My secret wish to be a professor didn't surface until February of my last semester of college. I had not yet applied for a job, and I knew that becoming a "gal Friday" in New York was an appalling thought. The field of law flitted through my mind and flitted out again. Then, women needed higher grades and better law boards than men to get admitted to any decent law school and I was a mere B+ student who hated confrontation. A friend thought I should apply to Harvard Business School, but business school just didn't seem right either. And school teaching was out.

I had gone to Brandeis University, a Jewish school. My parents had encouraged me to apply to Brandeis. Like many middle-class people from immigrant backgrounds, we had not heard of many top private colleges out-of-state. My parents knew about the Seven Sisters and *Time* magazine had recently done a story about Brandeis. I applied to some of the Seven Sisters and got into two, felt scared, heard my parents' unspoken advice, and went where there were sure to be lots of Jews. I took one course from a woman—the required freshman course in great books of Western civilization—and saw one other woman professor.

Those were years of bewilderment. Both the professors and the other students were sophisticated. My freshman roommate had read the *Iliad* in high school; I had never heard of it. I clearly enunciated "goythee," when I came upon the name Goethe. I read the work of Herbert Marcuse, a Brandeis professor and campus hero, with a dictionary. Others read his work without one. The first semester of my freshman year I received a C+—in introductory sociology. I decided that sociology was just common sense. After several years of watching the people around me, I realized that different things are common sense to different groups.

The Brandeis professors and students were politically outspoken; I had been taught not to be. The anti-Semitism of World War II had had a profound impact on my family. My father had worked in a camp for displaced persons, where his first language—Yiddish—helped him to assuage the pain of inmates who both mourned the past and yearned to build new lives. Some of my father's relatives had died in the concentration camps; others had survived. My father had experienced deep anti-Semitism in the army. My mother still tells me of the anti-Semitism of her childhood—other children had called her "dirty Jew"; my father had the same experience in Brooklyn. The lessons my parents derived from the Rosenberg trial concerned anti-Semitism, not anticommunism. The judge, the lawyers, the defendants were all Jews: The Gentiles had used Jews to prosecute Jews. Together with the hearings of the House Unamerican Activities Committee, the Rosenberg trial meant, "Watch your step. Don't sign anything. Never discuss politics outside your home."

At Brandeis, students spoke freely of politics, although almost all of them were also Jewish. My roommate brought me to a demonstration at the local Woolworth's to protest the refusal of the chain to serve at its lunch counters people who were then called Negroes. Another student brought me to a SANE (Committee for a Sane Nuclear Policy) march—from Brandeis to the Watertown arsenal, where we met protestors who had walked from Harvard and M.I.T. Sociology professors participated in those demonstrations, too. When anthropologist Kathleen Gough did not receive tenure, supposedly because she had spoken publicly against American foreign policy, the campus was in an uproar about this infringement on freedom of speech. Brandeis was a strange liberal world where you were supposed to say what you thought—no matter what the consequences. In that world, students giggled about the hand-lettered sign abutting the muddy path from the dormitories to the library: It said "Ho Chi Minh Trail." That sign introduced me to what was to be the major protest of my graduate school years: antiwar activity. It affirmed that it was okay—even morally necessary—to disagree with American foreign policy.

In my junior year, I took sociology again. A course on the sociology of literature seemed relevant because I was majoring in English and American literature. I noticed that there were some really interesting questions implicit in this course and two other sociology courses I took later that year. My male professors, especially Lewis Coser, Maurice Stein, and Kurt Wolff took the time to talk to me. They didn't treat my questions as naive, though they were. They took me seriously. Something extraordinary happened: I found out that education is not about grades. I learned that my fascination with social arrangements—my years of trying to make sense of my family and of trying to understand my peers—could be an intellectual enterprise. I had found my chance to be me. But I was slow to grasp it.

Many of my friends applied to graduate school when we were seniors. These women didn't seem to think that their plans were unseemly. After a day of crying because I seriously felt I was condemning myself to a sterile, familyless life, I, too, applied. I mailed my applications too late to get financial aid from any of the "really good" sociology departments; the Brandeis sociology department had yet to accept one of its own undergraduates as a graduate student. So I went off to a mediocre state institution that gave me full support. I hated it. Not only was I surrounded by non-Jews, a scary experience for someone who had been as insulated as I, but most of the male professors—all but one were male—were what I would now call pretentious pigs.

The same professor taught both research methods and statistics. In those precomputer days, we hand-selected national samples and used a calculator to derive chi squares and partial correlations. With a fellow student who had taken a terminal master's degree from Brandeis, I worked on these truly boring tasks with fervor. I started a never-finished master's thesis on a topic that I knew was mainstream, and therefore, acceptable, but I never finished. I wanted out. After a year of being in cultural exile, I transferred to Brandeis. Subsequently, the methods and statistics professor took aside the man with whom I had done the work for his classes and asked him something like, "You know that really good work you did. You did it all, didn't you?" I fume in retrospect. I don't think that any of the other women in that department—there were only three of us—ever finished a doctoral thesis.

Brandeis was very different. There were no women on the sociology faculty, although the men hired Rosabeth Moss Kantor after we students demanded what was then termed a "role model." But half of my cohort were women. I was awed by my fellow students. Several of them, including Barrie Thorne, held Woodrow Wilson Fellowships. They loved ideas and avidly debated Marx, Durkheim, Weber, Simmel, Freud, and Schutz. They were politically serious. Nancy Stoller had helped to found the organization that was to become SNCC (Student Non-Violent Coordinating Committee) and went South to organize, as did two of the men. Before it was fashionable, the women founded consciousness-raising groups and joined Bread and Roses. I felt too awkward to participate in a consciousness-raising group, but I joined them at demonstrations. Mostly I participated in a vision that we at Brandeis were a link to the ethnographic tradition of the Chicago School, that we had broken from American functionalism in a creative way that let us do our research knowing that the study of sociology was the study of social life and social lives.

Everett Hughes taught that life informed sociology. With Barrie Thorne and Janet Billson, I took a reading course from Hughes and learned to listen to his sometimes rambling stories as tales about the sociology of the everyday world. Hughes told stories of his youth. The Ku Klux Klan burned a cross on his front lawn of his childhood home after his father, a minster, had preached racial equality. The boys with whom he had grown up had wanted to become blacksmiths because it was an occupation they could observe. Serving with the Union in the Civil War, a great-uncle encountered a West Virginia nephew fighting for the South and ordered him to go home. Hughes spoke about when Robert Park introduced him to Langston Hughes, whose family had also come from West Virginia; they called each other "cousin," because in previous generations their families had probably been intimately involved with one another. Hughes' way of teaching—telling stories—forced me to see that my own family was the stuff and substance of sociology, that sociology concerned the relevance of the past to the present, and that sociology should stress the need for change.

My dissertation was about news—how reporters, editors, writers, and cameramen made news. (Again in the news organizations I studied, I was surrounded my men.) I called it "News, the Newsman's Reality." (On my curriculum vitae I now list it as "News, the Newsman's [sic] Reality.") I completed it in 1969. sometime in the late 1970s, I realized that I had studied news not only because of its relevance to the conduct of the Vietnam War, but also because, as Robert Park had written, news was a form of gossip. I had grown up surrounded by talk about the people in my town and by family-gossip—although, unlike newsworkers, we were not supposed to repeat those stories. As I had done my research, I had realized that participant observation of the newsrooms reminded me of family rules: Don't repeat tales from one person to the next. Be careful as you negotiate your path within the extended family. What I had thought was a politically motivated dissertation was intensely personal.

My first organizing activity as a feminist was also intensely personal. From Brandeis, I had found myself a job at the State University of New York, Stony Brook, then an up-and-coming sociology department. My male colleagues told me that I had the (to me odious) distinction of being the only full-time woman in a major graduate department. They had rifled through the *Guide to Graduate Departments* published by the American Sociological Association to prove it. (They didn't mention that with a Ph.D., I earned $10,000 and that they had offered $11,500 to a man who had yet to complete his dissertation.) Twenty-six years old, the token woman invited to be a mascot at the boys' poker games, I felt very lonely. After my first year on the faculty, I participated in the meetings of the American Sociological Association and helped found Sociologists for Women in Society (SWS). At the 1971 convention and at the SWS organizing meeting held at Yale earlier that year, I experienced intense relief. I was doing something politically meaningful in the sphere in which I felt most at home: work. I was organizing on my own behalf and that of other women. And I was surrounded by other women who were sociologists and who, at their jobs, felt the same isolation I was experiencing. I felt they were family.

Since the birth of my child, before my father's death but after the deaths of six friends and relatives in two years, I have not attended many professional meetings. My son has made it quite clear that he does not want me to travel without him, and bringing a child along is a major expense. In ways that I could not understand when, before his birth, we in SWS fought for child care at professional meetings, a child changes all aspects of your world. My child renewed my life; he has taught me more than how to play Nintendo. When he was three, he explained that flowers are like people; they come in many hues. When five, he asked why New York City built such ugly houses for poor people and why people threw poison (empty crack vials) on the playground. He has wondered why there are so many poor people in New York and seem to be so few where we now live in Connecticut. When he admired the way the paint drips down a huge canvas by Miro, he looked in ways I can no longer see. When we last visited New York, he asked to be taken to see the Rembrandts at the Metropolitan Museum and so reminded both me and my sister, an art critic, of our childhood family outings to New York's many art museums. We both still harbor a wish to roller-skate down the ramp of the Guggenheim. More cautious than we, too familiar with aspects of cities we never saw as children, he fears it might be hard to stop.

The world of sociology has also changed since I received my doctorate in 1969. I have had many colleagues who are women and feminists. Soon I will again attend professional meetings. When I finally leave the classroom and the word processor to participate more fully in the changed world of sociology, there will be a different kind of reminder of what has passed and what has come. There is still much work to do, especially for the undergraduates finding their identity during the post–Reagan-Bush years and the women graduate students who have returned to school from working-class homes. They have had the audacity to dare to be. But still some do not know that a woman need not cry because she really wants to be a professor.

Gaye Tuchman

Eighteen

Becoming an Active Feminist Academic
Gender, Class, Race, and Intelligence

Pamela Ann Roby

I am a feminist sociology professor who has worked, with others, toward social change for over two decades. I envision a world free of sexism, classism, racism, and all other forms of oppression. I seek a society in which *all* children receive the attention and care they need along with full access to many areas of knowledge so that they can realize their full human potential. I believe it is possible for our world to be organized in such a way that everyone has clean air and water, good health care, decent housing, nutritious food, adequate rest, and satisfying work that contributes to their own and others' well-being.

While this larger vision of full human liberation is always with me, I have concentrated on issues of gender, class, and race. My work as a sociologist has involved developing new courses and major university undergraduate and graduate programs; teaching lower division, upper division, and graduate classes; drafting federal legislation; writing articles, proposals, and books; presenting professional papers and public speaking; networking; leading workshops; creating new organizations; and reshaping the organizational structures and processes of existing ones to make them more compatible with human needs (Roby 1990a, 1990b). In these efforts, I have worked not only with colleagues and students but with union activists, members of the U.S. Congress, grass-roots community groups, and others.

Gender, class, and race shaped who I am today. In addition, early emotional neglect and abuse, which were complicated by silence and denial, resulted in my functioning as a child at a level labeled "low IQ." In working to attain social change and conserve positive gains, I have struggled with feelings emanating from this past. At the same time, my rich variety of activities as an academic and an activist have rewarded me with new friendships; the joy of creative, cooperative work; and a sense of taking charge. They have motivated me to continually expand my perspectives, knowledge, and skills. And they have given me the occasional satisfaction of achieving goals that are important in their own right as well as steps toward larger goals.

Class in a Midwestern Suburb

In general, mixed-class backgrounds are little discussed and less understood. However, like multiracial backgrounds, mixed-class upbringings shape what we think we can do, how we perceive the world, and how the world perceives and acts toward us. Perhaps one of the reasons issues of class are so confused in the United States is that many of us have mixed-class backgrounds, and there is little discussion or understanding of the meaning and implications of these multiple heritages.

I grew up the third generation of my family to live in Shorewood, which in the 1940s and 1950s was an all-white, upper middle-class Wisconsin suburb, the first suburb north of Milwaukee on Lake Michigan. My father's family had moved to Shorewood from the South Side of Milwaukee in 1919, when he was in sixth grade. Dad's father, a kindly doctor, was not a good businessman, so, although his family lived comfortably, they were not as well to do as most of Shorewood's other professionals and executives. Dad dropped out of college during the depression of the 1930s. Although he and my mother settled in Shorewood, they were clearly downwardly mobile.

Until I was in sixth grade, I lived in a two-bedroom, very sooty, white-frame "Milwaukee bungalow." I considered the house "our home" and hadn't much noticed who owned it until we were evicted. After fourteen years of Dad's faithfully paying rent, he was late one month when his father was seriously ill, and the landlord grabbed the opportunity to evict us because he wanted the house for his soon-to-be-married daughter.

Although the eviction and our moving to Grandma's house on the other side of the village were the major events in my life for a year or so, I discussed them with no one. I didn't tell anyone in my school, larger family, or church about how the sheriff arrived unannounced at our door or about my mother's deep upset as soon as he left. At twelve, I had already internalized middle-class patterns of silence about that which was deemed shameful. Most other children at school—and certainly the ones my parents suggested I play with—were from families who owned large houses. Each child had her own room and often a playroom as well. My brother and I shared a single room. My home—the house we had until we were evicted—was also different because it was dirty. It wasn't dirty on the inside. Mother carefully dusted, vacuumed, and cleaned at least once a week. But it was one of the last homes to have a coal furnace, and it had not been painted for eighteen years. Its white exterior, covered with many layers of gray soot, was a public statement of difference and marginality.

My home was not the only thing that distanced me from the majority of more well-to-do children at school. I was the only child of nearly one hundred in my grade who wore hand-me-down clothes. All my clothes except my once-a-year Sunday School Easter dress (which, like the clean inside of our home, was not visible at school) were hand-me-downs from my cousins in Michigan and Texas.

I liked my home. I liked my clothes. I especially liked the skirts I got, wrapped up in a big brown box, from my cousin in Texas. I still remember favorites: the cotton skirt with famous paintings printed on it, the yellow-flowered flounced skirt, and the blue plaid one. Nothing was the matter with these clothes. They were clean. They were not torn. And they fit. I even liked the designs and the fact that they came from my older cousins whom I liked and admired, if for no other reason than they were older. But these lovely skirts and all the other clothes I wore were out-of-date, and that mattered to others. My bicycle was also obviously old and "used." Everyone else had brand new Schwinn bicycles. One couldn't tell what make mine was because it had been repainted so many times. So, although my bicycle rode just fine, something important about it was missing in my peers' eyes. Not that anyone in this upper middle-class community would be so crude as to tell me that *my* bike was substandard. But as I listened to everyone boast about the particular features that made *their* bikes special, I felt awkward and out of place.

On one hand, I belonged in Shorewood where my family had lived for over thirty years. On the other hand, there were these continual reminders that we fell short of community standards and were therefore in important ways outsiders. I lacked a language and a framework with which to understand my position and that of my family within the class structure of my school and community. Nevertheless, without the word "class" ever being mentioned at school or at home, I was learning a great deal about class and classism. Not until years later did I learn that there were other people—people outside of Shorewood, outside my family—who were also evicted from their homes and wore hand-me-down clothes.

Women, Work, and Family: Active Foremothers

Like all children, I was shaped by my gender as well as my class. While a young girl, I learned that my foremothers had paid dearly when they abandoned careers for family. Not only did they lose work they enjoyed, they lost control of their lives as well. I began to feel that a professional life would give me more freedom to be myself, more control and less unhappiness.

My mother's mother, Nanny, a warm, friendly woman who was fond of me, had taught public school mathematics after leaving the family farm in Michigan. As a child, I sensed that it was unusual for a woman to teach a "man's subject," and I was proud that Nanny had taught mathematics. She left teaching when she married my grandfather. I noted that she treasured the copper kettle that she had used to make tea in her classroom and spoke fondly of her times there. I felt that it was too bad she had stopped teaching. Her kettle now sits on my living room table.

My Grandma Roby was raised by an independently wealthy mother and aunt, and she developed her own goals. By her late teens, she had founded the Beaufort, South Carolina, Public Library with other young women friends. Both her mother and aunt opposed Grandma's decision to go to medical school, saying it was improper for a young lady. Grandma waited until she came of age to control a trust fund. Then she traveled west to Chicago and entered the Hahnemann Medical College. All twenty-one of her professors were men, but seven of her forty-seven classmates were women. Grandma, then Winifred Reed, graduated from medical school in 1902 second in her class.

Despite her success in medical school, Grandma never practiced medicine. Two years into her studies, she began seeing Harlow Roby, a student in the class ahead of hers. After a year and a half of courtship, they married and moved to Milwaukee, where Grandpa started his practice, and Grandma had four children. Her children and the fact that doctors were on call around the clock kept Grandma from practicing medicine.

According to numerous comments by her children, Grandma always regretted leaving medicine. By the time I lived with her during junior high, her regret was common family knowledge. I concluded that it was important to not allow "falling in love" to interrupt one's professional life and passions.

My mother's experience also reinforced my desire to be an independent woman. Mom taught kindergarten for one year before and several years after marrying Dad in the midst of the Depression. They waited for four years before Dad felt that he was earning enough to afford having children. Before having children, Mom decided she would devote herself fully to motherhood and a few volunteer activities, and I remember her work with my Girl Scout troop and the Protestant Home for the elderly. But her work changed when we were evicted from our home and needed money.

While a full-time mother and housewife, Mom always had neck aches, headaches, and shoulder aches. Once Mom returned to teaching kindergarten, most of her pains disappeared. A year later, our family physician noted that her relief was a perfect example of the beneficial effect that work could have on a woman's health. His observation made a lasting impression on me.

While the women of my family gave me mixed messages about the importance of family over work, I responded to their observable unhappiness by deciding that work of one's own was most important. For a time, my father approved of my studies. He had always said that he expected *his* children to complete college without pausing, and he was pleased when I went on for my master's degree. However, when he learned I was pursuing a Ph.D., he expressed concern. One afternoon, two and a half years into my graduate studies, he telephoned me. During what was an exceptionally long talk for us, he told me of his worries. He feared that I would end up unhappy like the women working around him at the telephone company. I was shaken. What seemed to me like a chance to continue living a full, useful, and interesting life was to him a path to loneliness.

Developing a Passion for Research and Writing

Like many academics, much of my work centers on research and writing. Two Shorewood High teachers gave me tastes of what were to become my passions. One was Mr. Elmer Jacobson, my high school biology teacher. I remember realizing in his class how much I liked learning through doing research. My second outstanding teacher, Dr. Zelma Oole, taught creative writing. She began her classes by telling us that she did not intend to teach grammar. Rather, she simply wanted us to write. During her classes, we all wrote whatever we chose, and met with Dr. Oole one at a time, for about fifteen minutes each. During these sessions, she read over our manuscripts, asked us to tell her more about what we wanted to say in particular passages, and pointed out parts that she especially liked. I absolutely loved writing! I started waking up at 3:00 or 4:00 in the morning to write most days of the week. I wrote and wrote: poems, short stories, essays. Twice a year, under Dr. Oole's editorship, we published a student creative writing newspaper, *The Gleam*. I was proud to have several manuscripts appear in the paper.

Growing up as a "poor relative" in a well-to-do family sensitized me early on to social inequities that were to become the heart of my sociological research. When my family drove through one of Milwaukee's African-American ghettoes and Father would say "roll up your windows, lock your doors, this is a bad part of town," I would stare out the window. I saw homes and people who were as much poorer in relation to me as I was in relation to my classmates and cousins. I wanted to know who they were and what they felt and thought. I wondered why some people ended up rich and others poor. Barred from interaction with these human beings, I felt imprisoned and deprived.

My Congregational church youth group expanded my vision and profoundly shaped the choices I was to make. At our church camp, missionaries told stories and showed slides about conditions in third world nations. Our church's ministers participated actively in early civil rights organizing. Their actions reinforced my questions about inequities between rich and poor, black and white. They took us on visits to inner-city storefront churches and recreational centers, had inner-city black ministers visit our group, and helped arrange an integrated all-city Protestant youth choir that was several hundred strong. I deeply admired the ministers and their work. But over Sunday dinners, Father and I argued about their social activism, civil rights, and other issues. Father's anger about the ministers' involvement in civil rights grew until he organized a group of fellow church members who eventually asked the head minister, Dr. McNair, to leave. Dr. McNair moved to Tougaloo and became a professor of theology. Mother commented that she couldn't "imagine a white person wanting to live with all blacks." I knew that Dr. McNair saw people differently, and I suspected that he would find the students and faculty at Tougaloo more congenial than the white church members who had fired him. The gulf between my parents and myself hurt. I kept arguing with them, but they did not respond. I did not realize until years later that their beliefs were grounded in their early hurts that my angry arguing did not address.

The Social Construction of Reality: The Denial of Intelligence

Along with learning about class, gender, and race, I was also struggling with the effects of early emotional neglect and physical/emotional abuse. My parents' first child was a much desired son who died at eighteen months. The doctor told them the way to get over their grief was to have another child. The result was my birth. At that time, my mother was capable of basic physical care. Otherwise, she was silent, distant, and angry. Father, when present, provided respite but colluded with Mother's distance by telling me to keep secret any affection between us. Swamped with feelings, and sensing it was not safe to speak, I didn't start talking until I was three.

In kindergarten I continued to be extremely quiet and spoke in a garbled, hesitant manner. Teachers planned to hold me back from first grade until I became intrigued with a class weaving project and showed enough promise to be promoted. Although I "passed" kindergarten, in first grade, second grade, third grade, fourth grade, I was in the lowest group of everything—reading, math, everything. Authorities termed me "low IQ," and teachers solemnly told my parents they shouldn't expect me to complete high school.

My days were filled with awkward, embarrassing moments. Being at the bottom of the class and having to leave it once a week for speech therapy marked me as different. For example, in fourth grade, my teacher had the students in the top three math groups buy spiral notebooks for their math problems. Those of us in the bottom group were to continue using workbooks. Though humiliated by my status in all subjects, I felt I could do something about this. Using change saved over weeks from my small allowance, I bought a spiral notebook. Walking home that afternoon, clinging to my purchase, I felt as if I was almost the same as the other children. The next morning my teacher looked down at me from the front of the class and said so that all could hear, "Ohhh, Paammm, *you* don't *need* to have a spiral notebook." I was painfully embarrassed and felt too ashamed to talk with anyone about her comment.

Although my speech was never declared "all right," at the end of fourth grade, my speech therapist decided that I no longer needed therapy enough to warrant continuing. In any case, it had been pretty minimal: I practiced various phrases over and over, and memorized and recited poetry. As far as I know, only once did anyone connect my speech and learning problems with emotional distress. My fifth grade teacher arranged an evening appointment with my parents and myself and recommended that we get family counseling because she thought it would help my school performance. Father replied that our family had never needed help and never would.

During these early years of school when not smarting from embarrassment, I mostly felt like an amoeba enmeshed in fog, continually moved by the flow of things first in one direction and then another. I was unconnected at school, hiding at home. Then, when we were vacationing in northern Wisconsin, our family visited a farm with a litter of thirteen puppies. We chose a friendly black and white one, whom we named Cherry, and took her home. I trusted and felt closer to Cherry than to any person I knew. We walked, ran, and played together. When I returned from school, Cherry wagged her whole body with delight and jumped up and down. After calming down from licking me, she would cuddle close.

Cherry was a great solace. When I was sad, we'd sit together in a big old overstuffed rose-colored chair. I'd talk and talk and slowly pet her. She'd lick my cheek and steadily gaze at me with her big brown eyes. Tears would roll down my cheeks, and I'd hold her more tightly. Sometimes I'd cry and cry.

As Cherry listened to me time after time, the fog in my head and my feeling of formlessness began to lift. After we moved to Grandma Roby's, Grandma became someone else who was glad to see me. She listened to me sing hymns and peck out tunes on her piano. In contrast to my parents' disappointment in me, she presented an alternative reality. But as my family's stay with her lengthened, my parents became more and more frustrated with Grandma and often shouted angrily at her late into the evening. Now in seventh grade, I wanted to stand up for Grandma, but I knew no more how to stop my parents' shouting at her than I did their shouting at me. Instead, I concentrated on my studies in an effort to shut out the loud angry voices. Lo and behold, at the end of the first semester of seventh grade, I received a report card with an "A" in metalwork and "B"'s in a couple of academic subjects.

Suddenly I was no longer "low IQ"! Grandma, Dad, and others began to praise my achievements. My mother, however, believed praise led to a "swelled head," and if she acknowledged my change, she did not say so. I began to find reading, writing research papers, and other forms of study a refuge. Some subjects interested me in their own right. But studying was also a form of personal liberation, liberation from the low IQ label and realities of being at the bottom of the class. While studying for exams was tedious, reading and writing were not. Although I was never in a popular group, I flourished academically. Rather than being unable to complete high school as my grade school teachers had predicted, I was selected for the National Honor Society and wore its pin as I walked down the aisle to receive my high school diploma. I began to feel that I could take charge of my life.

Becoming a Sociologist: From Psychology to Social Change

When I left Milwaukee for Denver University (DU), I knew I wanted to work with people. During my first years at DU, I planned to double major in psychology and education. I chose psychology because my high school dean of women suggested that I would be a good school counselor. I chose education because, after my first year at Denver, Dad reminded me that he and Mom were paying for most of my schooling and said that he wanted me to get an elementary school teaching certificate "in case anything happened to my husband." I complied with his suggestion and completed a teaching credential, but I continued to follow my own interests.

In the latter part of my sophomore year I took a psychology class that included an internship at Fort Logan, the state's mental health center outside Denver. After working with a few patients, I concluded that they were basically no different from my friends and me except that they seemed more distressed by various pressures and/or less willing to bend to the wishes of others around them. I remember one woman in particular, Carolyn. She composed music. Fortunately each cottage had a piano, an unusual amenity for mental institutions. Each time Carolyn returned to Fort Logan, she composed several pieces. After copyrighting her work and getting "well" over a half year or so, she would be released to her family of four children and a husband. Once home, Carolyn would last about a year, at which point she would again streak nude down the main street of Denver. Police would return her to Fort Logan. To me it was clear that Carolyn was much more interested in composing music than in being a housewife and mother with little or no assistance.

It was not Carolyn's inner psychological processes that caught me, but her being trapped at home and unable to compose the music that she loved. Her story resonated with my memories of my foremothers' lives and alerted me to a larger social issue. Not long after meeting Carolyn, I decided that I wanted to help shape society to meet the needs of individuals rather than to try to fit individuals to society. At this point I changed my primary major from psychology to sociology.

In my sociology classes I began to wonder about my own life as a woman student on a campus defined by men. Conditioned to silence in the face of authority, I, like most of my classmates, respectfully listened to my professors without questions. Yet when a particularly kindly white male professor lectured on minorities, I asked him after class, "Aren't women a minority too?" He was surprised by my question and said "No, after all, women are 51 percent of the population." Unable to articulate my sense that his answer was woefully inadequate, my mind shut off and I went no further.

Then, a few weeks later, at the 1962 Associated Women Students' National Meeting, I was introduced to the women's movement by Betty

Friedan, whose book *The Feminine Mystique* had yet to be published. For the first time, I heard someone publicly address educated suburban women's pain and anger about their limited roles. I still remember the goose bumps on my arms as I heard her speak to several thousand of us active women students who had gathered at the University of Oklahoma. Surrounded by these thousands of women, I suddenly felt in my bones that collectively we women could change the world that had so limited and bound us.

Throughout my years at DU, I was active in and an officer of many campus organizations. Probably because the university lacked a sociology graduate program and graduate student role models, I did not consider pursuing a Ph.D. in sociology while I was an undergraduate. Rather, I applied to graduate programs in administration in higher education because I wanted to continue working on university campuses.

At Syracuse University the following fall, I found an elective course, S. M. (Mike) Miller's "Poverty and Social Inequality," most exciting. Not only was it sociology, but it focused on poverty and inequality, which had remained my key interests since childhood. At the end of the term, Mike suggested that I submit my research paper for publication, and he asked me to work with him as a research assistant. Over the next months, I learned much from Mike and other research assistants, and I attended my first American Sociological Association meetings.

I also learned much from social activism. I joined several sociology faculty members and a dozen graduate students in the Congress on Racial Equality (CORE)–led picketing of Niagara Mohawk, the city's electric power company, which employed two token African Americans in a work force of sixteen hundred that served consumers who were 10 percent black. I was inspired by sociology professors' active involvement in civil rights, by George Wylie's resignation as a Syracuse chemistry professor to work full-time with CORE, and by Rev. Martin Luther King, Jr., who spoke eloquently about civil rights at a university dinner.

The civil rights movement pushed the United States to recognize the realities of poverty. Soon after I began working with Mike Miller in 1965, the Ford Foundation awarded him a large research grant to evaluate the War on Poverty. Mike invited me to work as a research assistant on the project at New York University (NYU), where he was moving. I eagerly accepted, and I also enrolled in NYU's Ph.D. program in sociology. At NYU, Mike and I coauthored *The Future of Inequality* and several articles (Miller and Roby 1968, 1969a, 1969b, 1970a, 1970b, 1970c, 1970d, 1971a, 1971b; 1972; Roby 1968, 1969a, 1969b; cf. 1974). I loved this work, which consisted largely of secondary analysis and writing, but also included interviewing, archival research, and participation in relevant conferences. In addition, Mike and I helped found, and volunteered at, the New Community Center, which focused on empowering and assisting the poorest of the poor in New York's Lower East Side, a twenty-minute walk from NYU.

When not working on these projects, I participated in a women's consciousness-raising group with seven others, and in civil rights and peace demonstrations with tens of thousands. In different ways, each of these helped me think about and shaped my perspectives on power and social change. These experiences, coupled with the inspiration of Mike Miller and later senior women sociologists including Alice Rossi, Jessie Bernard, Pat Sexton, and Mirra Komarovsky, gave me a sense of what was possible as well as desirable.

New Research and Activism

I have always felt excited about my research and writing because I have always designed my research to probe issues that I have been involved with as an activist. As a result of my concerns with gender, class, and race, I examined the development and revision of New York State prostitution laws for my Ph.D. dissertation. I reported my dissertation findings to several thousand members of the National Organization for Women (NOW) at its 1972 meeting, on Barbara Walters's daytime show, "Not For Women Only," and in the *Nation* as well as in two professional journals, *Social Problems* and *Criminology*. The NOW convention voted to include my and others' recommendation that states decriminalize prostitution in its legislative agenda for local NOW chapters.

This same concern about the ways women's lives were shaped by gender expectations led me to look more closely at the lives of the women around me and to my editing *Child Care—Who Cares? Foreign and Domestic Infant and Early Childhood Development Policies* (1973b). The book, which the Ford Foundation supported, examines issues affecting day-care programs in eight high-income industrialized nations. In doing research for the volume, I learned much about the eight nations' social histories and how much stronger many of their policies affecting women were than ours in the United States. Child-care advocates in many U.S. cities and states have used the volume as they have sought to expand and improve child-care legislation.

Teaching and Amending the Vocational Education Act

My first teaching position was at George Washington University (GW), followed by two years at Brandeis, where I joined the sociology and social welfare faculties, both of which had strong doctoral programs. Two years later, in 1973, I accepted a tenured position at the University of California, Santa Cruz (UCSC), where I have remained for the past twenty years with the exception of times as a Mellon fellow at Wellesley College and as a visiting scholar at the University of Washington.

During my years at GW and Brandeis, I met women union leaders through my child-care research. They introduced me to organizations of union women. I was especially inspired by the founding meeting of the Coalition of Labor Union Women (CLUW), which was held in Chicago in March 1974. I learned more about working women's concerns by teaching "Women and Work" at UCSC and doing initial research for my book, *Women in the Workplace* (1981). These influences led to my organizing a national working conference on research on women in working-class jobs and the National Commission on Working Women with the late Barbara (Bobbie) Wertheimer, then director of Cornell's Trade Union Women's Institute, and Joyce Kornbluh, director of University of Michigan's Trade Union Women's program.

During the same year, David Goslin, with whom I had worked at Russell Sage and who was now executive director of the Assembly of Behavioral and Social Sciences of the National Academy of Sciences (NAS), invited me to join the NAS Committee on Vocational Education Research and Development which, after considerable struggle, much work, and organizing, resulted in S.2603, "A Bill to Amend the Vocational Education Act of 1968 to Assure Equal Educational Opportunities in Vocational Education for Individuals of Both Sexes" (Mondale 1975; cf. Roby 1975b, 1976, 1972a, 1973a, 1975a). Over the following weeks, S.2603 was amended and incorporated into a larger bill that was passed and signed into law as the "1976 Education Amendments" (P.L. 94-482, 90 stat. 2239).

Making Room for Women in Sociology

During these years, dozens, and then hundreds, of us who were feminist sociologists learned to organize within sociology. I have written elsewhere about our creating Sociologists for Women in Society (SWS) and our work within the American Sociological Association (ASA) (Roby 1992).

Two examples of the numerous changes that were created in American sociology during these years are the representation of women among the ASA's annual meeting participants and on the ASA's council. Between 1948 and 1968, women consistently comprised less than 10 percent of the ASA's annual meeting participants. Similarly, the ASA council had no women members in the years from 1962 to 1966, one woman member from 1967 to 1969, and no women members in 1970. The women's caucus first met at the 1969 ASA meeting, the ASA committee on the status of women in sociology was founded in 1970, and SWS, which included most of the women who had participated in the women's caucus, was founded in 1971. Following the founding of these groups, women's participation in the ASA's annual programs more than tripled, to over 30 percent between 1980 and the present. Starting in 1971, the proportion of the ASA council that was comprised of women increased unevenly but steadily (I served on the council from 1975 to 1978 and as president of SWS from 1978 to 1980). Today, over half the council is comprised of women. Progress in the representation of women of color on the ASA council has been much slower than that of white women. Elected as ASA vice-president in 1991, Doris Wilkinson was the first woman of color ever to sit on the council. Evelyn Nakano Glenn was the second woman of color to join ASA's highest decision-making body. She was elected to a three-year term as a council member the following year. The representation of women of color in the ASA continues to be a SWS concern.

With knowledge gained through our efforts to degender the American, British, Canadian, and other national professional sociological associations, several of us began organizing a research committee on women in the International Sociological Association (ISA) at the 1970 World Congress of Sociology held in Varna, Bulgaria. At the Varna meetings, like all previous congresses, women's issues were discussed only in the research committee on the family, if at all. No one knew much about the protocol for organizing a new research committee, but a handful of us invited others to a meeting in Elise Boulding's hotel room. At the appointed time, about twenty of us from many nations crowded into Elise's room. We agreed to circulate a petition to form an ISA research committee on the study of women in society.

After obtaining over a hundred signatures and submitting our petition to the ISA's executive office, we became concerned that the ISA was not giving our petition proper attention. We knew that four years would elapse before the next congress. Therefore, a number of us formed an unannounced welcoming committee at the entrance to a dinner for ISA executive officers. We each told as many officers as we could about our desire to have a research committee on women in society. I do not know whether the ISA was in fact processing our request more slowly than others', but our action brought attention to women's issues!

Those of us who became a coordinating committee organized "Research Committee 32 on Women in Society" primarily by mail and telephone between the 1970 and 1974 congresses. Elise Boulding took major responsibility for the committee, and she was its first chair. In 1974, we met as an officially recognized committee and had paper sessions at the World Congress of Sociology in Uppsala, Sweden. Starting that year, RC 32 on Women in Society has had one of the largest and best attended programs of the congress! In 1976, RC 32 elected me as its representative to the ISA's research council. Two years later, the research council elected the late Magdalena Sokolowska of Poland and me to the ISA's executive committee. We were the first women to be part of this body, which had been comprised solely of men for the ISA's first twenty-five years. For the past ten years, women have comprised about a third of the ISA's executive committee and have increasingly participated in the congress's programs but have yet to be appropriately represented in the congress's most visible plenary sessions.

And Did It Matter?

This progress within professional sociological associations and the profession as a whole means that thousands of us have spoken who would not have done so if the ways of the past had continued. Our speaking means not only that colleagues have heard our research findings but that we have been able to learn from others' responses to our work. In the process, we have further developed our skills and increased our confidence in our thinking, work, speaking ability, and leadership. Our process of breaking through barriers that silence us is still incomplete, and sometimes success generates attack rather than appreciation. But we have learned and are learning the meaning of liberation and the value of fighting for it.

Second, to many colleagues in my generation—women historians, anthropologists, psychologists, radical political economists, as well as sociologists—this organizing means that we have our fields of scholarship—women's studies, gender studies, feminist studies—within our disciplines as well as forums in which to discuss and develop critical perspectives on our disciplines. Without organizing, challenging, and confronting, we would have continued to have been bystanders, and our fields of study would not have existed. Along with men of color and white men allies who have worked for and attained change, we also know through our experience that organizing is inextricably linked to the attainment of truth in the social sciences and to the attainment of understanding and justice in our larger society.

Third, our organizing means that feminists of other nations are not subjects but sisters in a common struggle. It means that we know some of these women personally. We know that our differences must be recognized, respected, and reflected in our collective goals. Such recognition not only makes possible but enhances our efforts and enriches our individual lives.

Fourth, many of us have gained know-how and confidence by using a wide range of leadership skills within the special environments provided by feminist professional organizations and committees.

Fifth, we as a feminist cohort know from our experience, from our cores, that change is possible and that by joining collectively with others we *can* make a difference.

Finally, I know that I do not stand alone in saying that my life has been much enriched by my participation in all this organizing and feminist activity. My life has been enriched by the sisterhood and love that are part of organizing. I don't want to romanticize the sisterhood. It included lively conflicts, but, for hundreds and probably thousands of us, this sisterhood has been a very real, powerful, wonderful force in our work and lives.

Gender, Class, and Race

From 1988 to 1991, while doing research on how gender and race affect trade union stewards' leadership in working-class job sites, I directed the UCSC doctoral program in sociology and chaired the campus wide graduate council. I accepted these positions despite yearning to have more time to write, because I wanted more diversified graduate programs for myself and others. Although not all shared my concerns and there were never enough resources allotted to meet the needs we were attempting to address, I was never alone in seeking greater racial and gender diversity. Many faculty *wanted* to diversify our graduate programs, and race and gender were part of our affirmative action agendas. Class issues, however, remain relatively invisible.

In all three divisions—the natural sciences, the humanities, and the social sciences—although gender issues persist, we have made much more progress in increasing the proportion of Ph.D.s awarded to women than we have to working-class students and U.S. students of color. In the sociology graduate program, which has always had an approximately even representation of women and men students, we have had some success over the last few years in racially diversifying the student body. However, although the program, like the university and most institutions of higher education, keeps no records about students' class backgrounds, I can see from my own observations that graduate students from working-class and poor backgrounds, regardless of race, have been the least likely to complete more than a year or two of the program. While directing the program, I learned that I personally, and we collectively, have much to learn about ridding our institutions of class bias so that students who are raised working-class and poor, particularly students of color, can successfully complete graduate school and contribute to our society as sociologists. Financial support, which we could offer while I was graduate director, is a necessary but far from sufficient condition for us to realize this goal. Over the past two decades, those of us who worked actively in SWS and the ASA learned that degendering our profession meant making changes at many levels: emotional, social, interpersonal, and organizational. I think that at least this much will be required for us to diversify sociology and our institutions of higher education in terms of class and race.

Re-evaluation Counseling: Recovering Occluded Intelligence

Throughout my early years of involvement in liberation movements, I was repeatedly struck by how these movements faltered because of interpersonal dynamics between movement members. I puzzled over why people who held important social goals in common so often became intensely angry with one another. And why, with or without this intense anger, did people often "burn out" and leave movement activity after months or years? It seemed to me that some understanding, some process, something was missing.

While asking these questions, I struggled with my own issues. Although I was successful in graduate school and in my early years of teaching and research, I often felt inadequate, out of place, isolated and/or overwhelmed—much like I did when I was young. Nothing I was learning in sociology addressed these feelings. I visited a friend's therapist once, but I felt that the effort I would spend in raising money to pay for therapy would outweigh any benefit. Most public speaking and formal presentations still brought up my childhood feelings of terror and remained a struggle for me. A university psychiatrist prescribed tranquilizers to help me through a graduate seminar presentation. He gave them to me after I saw him for five minutes at the health clinic, much as physicians dispensed cold medicine. A number of other students I knew had already been using tranquilizers for years, so I didn't question taking them. These pills numbed my old fears and other feelings sufficiently for me to get through graduate school and to remain a committed activist.

I was searching for answers to these movement and personal issues when I first heard of Re-evaluation Counseling. "RC" is a system of "co-counseling" that teaches people ways of listening to one another so they can figure out problems and release distress that is getting in the way of their functioning as well as they would like. In this way, co-counseling addresses the dilemma noted by several scholars that generally many more people are trying to speak and be heard than are listening, especially listening without interruption (West and Zimmerman 1983; Derber 1979).

When I moved to Brandeis in 1971, I found that hundreds of students were learning RC theory and the fundamentals of co-counseling in sociology classes. Most of the students who spoke enthusiastically about RC were also actively involved in one or more of the early 1970s liberation movements. A few months after I arrived, Diane Balser, a sociology graduate student who later became a good friend and director of the Massachusetts Women's Statewide Legislative Network, suggested that some RC techniques and theory might be helpful in my teaching. Soon after, an outstanding undergraduate made the same comment. I admired both women, and the following summer, I decided to try a RC class to see what it could offer. RC turned out to provide some of the most crucial skills and understandings of my personal and professional life.

RC theory assumes that everyone who is not seriously brain damaged is "born with tremendous intellectual potential," the ability to love and work cooperatively with others, and joy, but that these qualities have been inhibited and submerged in adults by the cumulative effect of distressing experiences throughout our lives. It assumes further that "any young person would recover from such distress spontaneously" by raging, talking, crying, trembling, laughing, and other forms of emotional release. When adequate emotional discharge can take place, the person's thinking, feelings, and behavior are freed from rigid patterns left by the hurt (see Jackins 1983; Scheff 1979; Weissglass 1990). In co-counseling sessions we divide whatever time we have, whether it be thirty minutes or two hours. Then we essentially take turns listening with full, respectful attention (as the counselor) and being listened to (as the client).

I use my own co-counseling sessions to discharge the distresses that I used to numb out with tranquilizers; to celebrate and really let myself feel accomplishments; and to talk and think through particularly challenging portions of my writing and issues at work as well as major life decisions. For example, I wrote much of this chapter with ease, but I had trouble writing a couple of sections, particularly the one about having been considered "low IQ" in grade school. So, in a co-counseling session, I told Julie Olsen Edwards, a friend and colleague, about the feelings that part brought up. After talking about it, I cried and cried. The next day I woke up with the section practically written in mind. I quickly wrote it out. But then I thought, "No, I can't say that!" In my next counseling session, I laughed a lot about how embarrassing it was to have been considered "low IQ." At least twice my laughter turned to tears as I reaffirmed my commitment to write as truthfully as possible because I think that our lack of knowledge about what life is really like for one another is part of what holds oppression in place. My co-counselors did not give me advice. Rather, they allowed this process to happen by listening with full, interested attention and relaxed body postures that communicated that they expected that I could and would figure out exactly what I wanted to say and say it.

But individual healing is not enough. Freeing our own intelligence and that of others from distress also requires transforming oppressive institutional and societal structures and ideologies that support them. Starting in 1973, when several women organized the first RC Women's Liberation Workshop, held outside of Santa Barbara, California, many different groups of co-counselors have networked, published journals, and organized liberation workshops throughout the world. Three years after participating in the first women's workshop, I organized the first of a continuing series of RC weekend-long workshops for college and university faculty.

"RC Colleague" workshops generally include both women and men faculty from many disciplines, types of institutions, and backgrounds. In the faculty groups, we share information about teaching and other aspects of our work, deepen our understanding of the specific oppressions and internalized oppressions under which we have lived, and learn how to better support one another as allies. The purpose of the work is to "think and respect thinking, to allow no invalidation of any scholar or teacher including ourselves, to refuse to be isolated from our colleagues or to act as agents of oppression, and to use our full knowledge and power for the creation of a just world." RC theory and practice in combination with human goodness and intelligence and humane social movements and organizations are my greatest hope for our realizing the vision of human liberation I described at the beginning of this chapter.

Tomorrow

I feel fortunate to be a woman and an active feminist sociologist at this time in history. As women, feminists, and sociologists, we have an unprecedented understanding of society and ourselves in terms of not only gender but class, race, and many other identities. I look forward to our continuing to create a society in which all people, including ourselves, can learn, play, work, and grow free of all forms of oppression, a society in which all are nurtured in a healthy environment and with the caring that is our birthright.

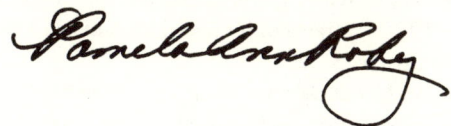

Acknowledgments: I am especially grateful to my friend and co-counselor, Julie Olsen Edwards, for helping me think through and more clearly communicate these issues and for her editing. I thank Ann Goetting, Lynet Uttal, and Doris Wilkinson for encouraging me to write this essay and for their advice. For their many suggestions, not all of which I have heeded, I thank Frank Barrett, Diane Beeson, Bob Connell, Virginia Draper, Kathleen Fong, Guadalupe Friaz, Amanda Konradi, S. M. Miller, Howard Robboy, Dale Roche, Lillian Roybal Rose, Diane Schaffer, Tilly Shaw, Laurie Talcott, Candace West, and Jane Zones. I also thank Judy Burton and Wenonah Williams, for their help with this manuscript, and Angela Ginorio, Herbert Costner, Judith Howard, and others of the Northwest Center for Research on Women and the department of sociology, University of Washington, for the colleagueship and research support they gave me as a visiting scholar.

REFERENCES

Derber, Charles. 1979. *The Pursuit of Attention: Power and Individualism in Everyday Life.* New York: Oxford University Press.

Jackins, Harvey. 1983. "The Art of Listening." Pp. 173–90 in his *The Reclaiming of Power.* Seattle, Wash.: Rational Island Publishers.

Miller, S. M., and Pamela Roby. 1968. "The War on Poverty Reconsidered." Pp. 68–82 in *Poverty: Views from the Left,* edited by Jeramy Larner and Irving Howe. New York: Morrill Press.

———. 1969a. "Education and Redistribution: The Limits of a Strategy." Pp. 45–55 in *Racial Crisis in American Education,* edited by Robert L. Greene. Chicago, Ill.: Follett.

———. 1969b. "Poverty: Changing Social Stratification." Pp. 64–84 in *Understanding Poverty: Perspectives from the Social Sciences*, edited by Daniel P. Moynihan. New York: Basic Books.

———. 1970a. "Social Mobility, Equality, and Education." *Social Policy* 1(1): 38–40.

———. 1970b. "Urban Change and Schools of Education." Pp. 166–74 in *The World Year Book of Education*, edited by Joseph A. Lauwerys and David Scanlon. New York: Harcourt, Brace, and World.

———. 1970c. *The Future of Inequality*. New York: Basic Books.

———. 1970d. "Creaming the Poor." *Transaction* 7(8): 38–45.

———. 1971a. "Social Problems of the Future." Pp. 673–96 in *Handbook of Social Problems*, edited by Erwin O. Smigel. New York: Rand McNally.

———. 1971b. "Strategies for Social Mobility: A Policy Framework." *The American Sociologist* 6:18–22.

———. 1972. "Educational Strategies for the Disadvantaged." Pp. 47–69 in *Opening Opportunities for Disadvantaged Learners*, edited by A. Harry Passow. New York: Teachers College Press.

Mondale, Walter. 1975. "S. 2603." *Congressional Record*, 94th Cong., 1st sess., 1975. Vol. 121, pp. 34668–70.

Roby, Pamela Ann. 1968. "Educational Aides in Inner City Schools." *Integrated Education* 6(6): 47–56.

———. 1969a. "Politics and Criminal Law: Revision of the New York State Penal Law on Prostitution." *Social Problems* 17: 83–109.

———. 1969b. "Inequality: A Trend Analysis." *Annals of the American Academy of Political and Social Science* 385:110–17.

———. 1972a. "Women and American Higher Education." *Annals of the American Academy of Political and Social Science* 404:118–39.

———. 1972b. "Politics and Prostitution." *Criminology: An Interdisciplinary Journal* 9:425–48.

———. 1972c. "The Politics of Prostitution." *Nation* 214:463–66.

———. 1973a. "Institutional Barriers to Women Students in Higher Education." Pp. 37–56 in *Academic Women on the Move*, edited by Alice K. Rossi and Anne Calderwood. New York: Russell Sage.

———, ed. 1973b. *Child Care—Who Cares? Foreign and Domestic Infant and Early Childhood Development Policies*. New York: Basic Books.

———, ed. 1974. *The Poverty Establishment*. Englewood Cliffs, N.J.: Prentice-Hall.

———. 1975a. "Sociology and Women in Working-Class Jobs." Pp. 203–39 in *Another Voice: Feminist Perspectives on Social Life and Social Science*, edited by Marcia Millman and Rosabeth Moss Kanter. Garden City, N.Y.: Anchor/Doubleday.

———. 1975b. "Vocational Education and Women." Pp. 102–14 in *Sex Discrimination and Sex Stereotyping in Vocational Education*. Hearings before the Subcommittee on Elementary, Secondary, and Vocational Education of the Committee on Education and Labor, House of Representatives, 94th Congress, 1st Session. Washington, D.C.: U.S. Government Printing Office.

———. 1975c. "Shared Parenting: Perspectives from Other Nations." *School Review* 83:415–31.

———. 1976. "Toward Full Equality: More Job Education for Women." *School Review* 84:181–211.

———. 1981. *Women in the Workplace.* Cambridge, Mass: Schenkman.

———. 1987. "Union Stewards and Women's Employment Conditions." Pp. 139–55 in *Ingredients for a Women's Employment Policy,* edited by Chris Bose and Glenna Spitz. Albany: State University of New York Press.

———. 1990a. "Sociology of Leadership: A Course Plan and Reading List." Pp. 88–95 in *Leadership Education 1990: A Sourcebook,* edited by Miriam B. Clark and Frank H. Freeman. Greensboro, N.C.: Center for Creative Leadership.

———. 1990b. "Feminist Research: A Graduate Seminar Plan and Reading List." Pp. 188–96 in *The Sociology of Sex and Gender,* edited by Virginia Powell. Washington, D.C.: American Sociological Association.

———. 1992. "Women and the ASA: Degendering Organizational Structures and Processes." *The American Sociologist* 23:18–47.

Roby, Pamela, and Lynet Uttal. 1988. "Trade Union Stewards: Coping with Union, Work, and Family Responsibilities," Pp. 215–48 in *Women and Work,* vol. 3, edited by Barbara A. Gutek, Laurie Larwood, and Ann H. Stromberg. Beverly Hills, Calif.: Sage.

Scheff, Thomas J. 1979. *Catharsis in Healing, Ritual, and Drama.* Berkeley: University of California Press.

Weissglass, Julian. 1990."Constructivist Listening for Empowerment and Change." *Educational Forum* 54:351–70.

West, Candace, and Don Zimmerman. 1983. "Small Insults: A Study of Interruptions in Cross-Sex Conversations between Unacquainted Persons." Pp. 103–18 in *Language, Gender, and Society,* edited by Barrie Thorne, Cheris Kramarae, and Nancy Henley. Rowley, Mass.: Newbury House.

Conclusion

"Editing" Women, Memoir, and the Sociological "I"

Sarah Fenstermaker

There's more to the self than Mead's, the 'I'. —Anonymous

The only time I have seen my coeditor I was suffering from an occupational crisis of growing proportions. I had recently finished three years as founding chair of the campus women's studies program at UC Santa Barbara, and I had just assumed the post of associate dean of the graduate division. By then I had become addicted to the exhilaration of cross-disciplinary institution building, and a work life with relatively little time for scholarly contemplation. Yet, I was beginning to feel out of touch with my identity as a sociologist, and I longed for a new project to shepherd from start to finish. I don't think I could have been more ambivalent about where I was headed than at the social gathering where I met Ann Goetting.

I can't easily reconstruct the basis for my agreement to collaborate with Ann on this volume about senior women sociologists. It was certainly not a rational assessment of each other; we were complete strangers. Perhaps it was the hour, or the drink, but nevertheless I impulsively agreed. In that moment, it seemed just the project to resolve my ambivalence about my own work life and this loosening connection to sociology. Besides, I knew I was happiest when collaborating with others.

Not any edited collection would have sufficed. Facing mid-life and mid-career myself, I needed to see past that to longer lives lived productively in the profession, and to be reminded of the invigorating intellectual vision that sociology can bring. And not just any group of sociologists would have appealed to me. Elsewhere (Fenstermaker 1993) I have described the roots of my attraction to sociology, to feminism, and the intimate connection of my growth in each during graduate school in the 1970s. I have spent my adult life as a feminist sociologist listening for the voices of women and what I can craft sociologically from them.

We began with the concept of "analytic reflections" to describe to ourselves and to prospective authors what we hoped would result. It seemed a term specific enough to guide a first draft, yet vague enough to accommodate many styles and approaches. In his book *The French Worker: Autobiographies from the Early Industrial Era* (1933, 27), Mark Traugott lists the common narrative strategies found in autobiography, for "like any managed form of self-presentation, they inevitably privilege certain bits of information and lead to the concealment of others." In each story collected here we see a specific set of themes, chosen for a variety of purposes and within specific conventions. Indeed, the organizing section headings that Ann and I selected after the fact point to the choices authors made to convert a life lived into a life communicated: stories of missed and seized opportunity, isolation, adversity, adventure, intellectual growth, despair, and redemption.

In this context, I thought long and hard about the book as a feminist undertaking. I know that when I was encouraging prospective authors to submit chapters, a number asked me, I thought a bit warily, if this book would be "feminist." I told them that if they were asking whether the *editors* were feminist, I was, but that I wasn't sure what Ann would say. If they were asking whether all the *contributors* must be feminists, the answer was no. On its face, of course, the publishing and thus legitimation of women's reflections on the past suggests, if not a feminist, at least a woman-*centered* project. However, simply assembling women was not enough. Over the years, I have become convinced that good feminist scholarship must represent not only a valuable product but also a *way of working* where each decision values, and makes valuable, women's experience, where, if one is seeking the representation of women's voices through memoir, those voices are not ignored in the process. Not only did this belief influence virtually every interaction I had with Ann, authors, and publishers, it also made a great deal of difference when we decided on the editor's place within the volume.

Early on, we thought we would contribute autobiographical chapters ourselves. It seemed to violate the spirit of the volume to keep our distance from our own authors—as if we were somehow outside the process of the construction of these lives as tellable stories. But when the number and quality of the chapters kept growing, we gave up that idea for the notion of periodic, essay-like integuments placed between themes in an effort to tie them together. Eventually, we saw that they would be an overbearing presence, very like an introductory sociology text, where one is told what things mean at every opportunity. We had to assume that the readers of this volume were capable of making all the sense we did of the pieces—and their own as well. We abandoned our earlier ideas as unnecessary intrusions, and happily confined ourselves to an introduction, a conclusion, and some nominal organizing headings.

A number of related but quite specific questions shadowed the editing process throughout as well as the development of a clear direction for the volume. They remain unresolved, but I can now invite readers to ponder them with me: What is unique, and uniquely shared, in sociologists', and *women* sociologists', autobiography? What ultimately constitutes common and different in the context of women's autobiography? And finally, what promises do these memoirs hold for the future?

Editing Women's Lives

> *Why were the questions about social structure and personality, the power of the group, the inevitability of social hierarchy, and the lure of the sociological imagination so compelling?*
> —Suzanne Keller

> *I walked over to sociology—it was nearby.* —Beth B. Hess

The *theoretical* underpinning of the volume, reflected in its title, was one that sociologists had been wrestling with for some time. In broadest strokes, it spoke to the problematic connections between biography and history, individual agency and social structure, individual choice, constraint, and institutional change. Philip Abrams (1982, 227), who calls for an abandonment of these categorical dualities and for a "sociology of process" writes, "Society must be understood as a process constructed historically by individuals who are constructed historically by society." The implications of such a statement guided our crafting of this collection. Understanding what Ann calls "fictions of the self" requires attention not only to the history that makes them, and the history they make, but also to the unique process from which both are outcomes—a process which is *itself* a product of individual action and social structuring. Our assemblage of senior women sociologists' autobiographical offerings seemed a way for readers to complicate those old, unshakable dualities. Moreover, a forum for the women of sociology seemed long overdue, for in previous autobiographical collections they had often been relegated to the equivalent of a "women's section" (for example, Berger 1990).

The *editing* of the volume, however, and the stories themselves, made those old problematics real and reaffirmed the need for a "sociology of process" to supplant our conventional notions of individual actions as against an independent social system. Nowhere can the fluid relation between the development of an autonomous individual—dependent on the social group and the legacy of history, yet independently altering both—be better illustrated than in autobiography. Thus, the practical process of "editing" women kept me far closer to the original theoretical interest than I had first imagined.

The editorial choice to let the contributions "speak for themselves" is not a trivial one, for it raises the question of whether there is a women's sociological perspective (or "voice") whose most important dimensions are discernible without analysis. Foremost in these tellings is the theme of sociology and women's place within it. This is no surprise, of course; we did, after all, solicit *women* to tell of their lives in *sociology*. But we must ask, do we hear distinctive voices here? A single story told eighteen different ways? Eighteen very different stories told in much the same way? Is it the *lives* of women sociologists that seem to share a common thread revealed here? After all, and despite their age differences, as women they each confront a single, albeit changing, profession. Or, is it the way those lives are *told*, through the lens of a single discipline, to which each woman was socialized and from which each draws a distinctive way of seeing? In fact, it is the stories themselves that constitute the best evidence for the complex relation between the two, reducing the traditional question of which came first, the individual sociologist or sociology itself, to so many chickens and eggs.

I once conceived of this concluding chapter as a kind of sociological stroll through our authors' lives, where I would encapsulate the shared and unshared dimensions of the stories told. But the more closely I read the stories and the more I took them on their own complicated terms, the more I realized that such an approach loses almost everything in its own construction: This many reported childhood experiences that sensitized them to injustice; this many had fathers (or mothers) who encouraged aspiration; this many confronted the terrors of tokenism; this many discovered the joys of teaching in a profession that seldom rewarded it. And so on. If there are distinctive voices to be found within these memoirs, they are fragile ones, and they are not easily subjected to conventional sociological framings without great loss.

Perhaps like you, I found myself in my colleagues assembled here. I recognized my own development, my own bitter and bittersweet trials with childhood, graduate school, tenure, and the isolation of the woman scholar. And even though I was only twenty-six when I began my first job as an assistant professor, now as a middle-aged single mother, I can appreciate the stories of those who gallantly juggled academic career and family. Throughout, I felt a clear connection as I heard the voices of those who speak my disciplinary language, observe what I might observe about places I have never been, and who share what feels to be a natural fascination with social life and its inventions.

At the same time—and the simultaneity is important to note—I felt *unconnected* to some of these experiences and points of view. These stories do, after all, stretch across the globe and over a half-century of experience. They cross boundaries of class, race, nation, ideology, and religion. Differences are everywhere, even among the lives that I still think of as "like me" or "like me enough."

The editing of a volume limited to elder women sociologists has taken me far beyond my initial regret and sense of loss when I realized that an assemblage of predominantly white middle-class women would be the result of our call for submissions. By drawing from older women sociologists, we inherited the result of racist and class-bound institutional practices that excluded virtually all but a small number of privileged white women. We had stacked the deck against achieving race and class diversity, with the predictable outcome, and I worried a great deal about what readers would then value in the experiences that were represented.

The worry has led to a novel encounter with questions I have been struggling with as a feminist and a sociologist for more than a decade: What does it mean to share historical and social location? What does it mean to share age, race, and class categorical memberships? And what is the sociological import of the many differences left over? If we speak through our own stories, what differences must we gloss or leave out, to win a reader (and ourselves?) over to the familiar? What is "common" and "different" when lives are the text?

As Ann points out in her introductory chapter, autobiography finds itself anew in each reader's life, where "confirmations are comforting; without them one feels isolated and marginal." That experience of connecting with another woman's experience is what much of feminist activism, scholarship, and the historical reclamation of women is about. Yet in the last decade, as more voices were heard, and more lives resurrected, we questioned the practice of ignoring those experiences that were not easily nestled into existing, easily recognizable histories. Many feminists now see that the sentimental glow of connection and likeness must coexist with the *un*connection of difference, or women's lives will once again be erased. But the glow is a seductive one, for we are motivated to define away disconcerting difference and invent another layer of abstraction to accommodate and reconfirm essential likeness. But what of the life that illustrates the veracity of what we do *not* hold true? What of the life we have judged eccentric or tainted or squandered? And what of the life whose experiences are so removed from one's own that connection seems unfathomable?

When Suzanne Keller tells her story of her flight from Nazi occupation, I am moved by her story, but I must use all my imagination to picture it.

> And what extremes of human behavior to integrate: on one hand, the horror of the crematoria, on the other, the generosity of countless strangers.

Similarly, when Coramae Mann describes the contrasts of Minnesota and Chicago, I must simply take her word for it.

> In Minnesota, my friends were of all colors and there was no discernible racial segregation of any kind. When I returned to Chicago for vacations, I again experienced the mindless racial prejudice and ghetto life with only faces of color and segregated beaches and other "public" facilities. . . . The "chocolate drop" of Ohio became the "nigger" of Chicago.

And when Martha Gimenez remembers a girlhood Argentina, where "coup d'etats and rumors of military uprisings were ordinary events," there is intellectual appreciation, but not necessarily connection.

In reading these stories, difference is of the greatest value when it sparks more than the comforting ring of the familiar. If, in an act of faith—for me a feminist act—I can understand and appreciate the women's story that is *not* mine, the story that does *not* provide the easy exhilaration of recognition, the story of women I do not respect, or even *like* very much, then I have gone beyond the narrow confines of my own experience and its limiting connections.

Ultimately, it is the individual reader who becomes the most important reference point to decide the meaning of common and different. Each of us brings our selves to these accounts, our own normative notions of what a life *should* include, how lives *ought* to unfold, and what is sociologically significant about what the sociological "I" experiences and reports. Once again, it is not a survey of same and different that is in order, but an act of faith—an appreciation for the complexity of "common" and "different" in the context of so many years, so much history, and such rich individual experience.

The two broad themes that spoke to me across these stories were the ones that originally motivated the volume and that address the experiences of the women of sociology, many of them (though by no means all), distinctly sociological and distinctly feminist: An early sense of, and appreciation for, the social margin and the outsider, and a lifetime of struggle as an academic woman. One cannot argue that the themes themselves are unique to these memoirs. Life inevitably demands that each of us locate herself or himself in some relation to a socially constructed inside and outside. And certainly one story of *every* life is its encounter with adversity. Yet through the stories told here, one can get a feel for the way in which these individual women *as social observers* interacted with, and changed, and were likewise changed, by the lives they constructed. The themes of marginality and professional survival are those that exemplified the process—as a process—for me. Such broad strokes, however, are still best suited to a chapter that should be read only *after* the individual memoirs themselves, particularly since I unabashedly ignore the very different historical contexts in which professional lives unfold. There are many, many other experiences that shaped the lives of these individuals and their profession more generally, and many more insights to be drawn from them than are found in this chapter.

Living Outside

> *I did okay [in calculus], until one day, at the blackboard, the professor flipped an eight on its side and started talking about "infinity." Now there was a concept worth grappling with! I was captivated. No one else seemed to be. . . . Meanwhile, I thought about infinity and lost my way.* —Diane Rothbard Margolis

It has been noted elsewhere (Willie 1988), that it is characteristic of sociologists to think of themselves as marginal, as outside some mainstream, however fluid its boundaries. This is certainly borne out in these accounts. References to feelings of marginality are mentioned often, experienced as states of personality discovered in childhood, but prompted by many different conditions. Helen Hacker, for example, says that "I am attracted to unpopular causes and outsiders; people on the margin. I have always been out of sync."

As only one of the authors whose sense of otherness results from war, Britta Fischer remembers the pride in the legacy of her grandparents who had sheltered Jews.

> [The stories] nourished our sense of decency. We were different and proud of it. . . . I learned to empathize with other outsiders in other times and places. . . . I would try to imagine what Anne Frank must have felt when she rode in a freight car to the concentration camp.

Shulamit Reinharz, who credits an early sense of otherness for her interest in social science, recalls the profound impact of the war on her family.

> For me, at least, at some deep, unarticulated level, the Holocaust had not quite been eradicated from the suburbs. Somehow, danger always lurked, even if it was only the danger we projected. History does not stop for the refugees who move into their safe haven. It seeps into everyday life.

Whatever its source, the marginality cited conveys the image of being exiled, a refugee in one's own life.

For Elaine Hall, an exile of sorts resulted from her choice to abandon femininity to avoid the debilitating oppression of "the marriage road," as she calls it.

> Looking at my mother through the lens of my own dreams, I saw only the limitations, the pain, and the loneliness of her life. . . . The dilemma for me was not whether to be a feminine or an unfeminine woman; rather, it was whether to be a woman or some unwomanly entity defined as the opposite of that "feminine thing." Rejecting my model of a feminine woman, I chose to be an Unwomanly Person.

Certainly, these authors return to "outsider" status frequently to account for their interest in social life and social inequity. Pamela Roby writes that "growing up as a 'poor relative' in a well-to-do family sensitized me early on to social inequities that were to become the heart of my sociological research." Gaye Tuchman observes:

> My mammoth extended family taught me what, as a sociologist, I do best: watch, listen, and try to make sense of the social interactions around me. Since my early life was geared so much toward adults, among my peers I feel myself to be ever socially awkward, someone who never quite fit in, an observer of my own participation, a participant observer.

I think of myself similarly affected by an "otherness," which was forged in very early childhood by illness and by the strong sense of the unspoken and unacknowledged in my family. It left me with both a fascination and a facility for unveiling the hidden realities in social life, skills obviously shared by our authors. One observation that struck a chord of recognition in me was from Suzanne Keller. She writes about the Nazi occupation of Vienna, a generation and a world removed from the secret discoveries of my own childhood.

> This then was the real truth: the old verities, namely, the flag, adults in control, a sense of order, were just provisional after all. It was obvious even to a child that these depended on invisible social forces to sustain—or destroy— them.

This notion of the unseen truth, but one knowable with the right combination of skills, is a compelling one. It renders the social world as mysterious and exciting to the sociologist as the natural world is to the biologist, or the chemist. This collection of stories suggests that it is from the margin that one comes to such an experience.

Living Inside

> *Whatever gave me the audacity to think I could make a place for myself as a woman in sociology, I'll never know.*
> —Lynda Lytle Holmstrom

This was never intended to be a book of sociological success stories; we did not fill it with the handful of sociological stars whose stories have been told and retold. Yet, each author bears the mark, and the burdens, of academic *survival*—the string of successes and failures that combine to make any professional life. There are eighteen stories of college, graduate school, and academic life in a culture that severely limits most women's chances for meaningful work and supportive surroundings. The stories are by no means alike, but each reflects a struggle for intellectual place, recognition, and opportunity—as all women's lives do. Survival is success.

Feeling the outsider certainly suits one for the ideologies of American sociology. However conservative the academic profession as a whole, sociology fancies itself standing apart, and thus able to make conventional social practices and the workings of social institutions a scholarly problematic. Very often, it tolerates and even seeks out those who as Suzanne Keller says, are "more fox than hedgehog, to follow a more serendipitous rather than single-minded course." Yet Lynda Lytle Holmstrom comments on the choice of Brandeis over Harvard.

> Both institutions looked as if they would judge me by my marital status rather than by my accomplishments—the same thing that happened to Mother a

> generation earlier at the bank. . . . Who knows? I might have gone [to Harvard] and been mired in Parsons's "pattern variables" for years!

Men (and a very few women) trained women sociologists over the last fifty years. For example, these stories would not be told the way they are without the mentoring of Paul Lazersfeld and Everett Hughes. This has something to do with the unintended preponderance of accounts from Columbia, Brandeis, and Chicago, yet in this volume, these two can stand for all those men who trained women for the last fifty years. Years ago, Paul Lazersfeld was reported to have explained to his student, a now well-known feminist sociologist, that there was "always room" for the exceptional woman. So there has been. For feminist academics, who have spent much of their lives transforming the discipline and its canon, this is a curious legacy, for so many of our intellectual fortunes rested on the powerful male— whether father, husband, or sociologist/mentor—who made us "exceptions," and made a kind of room. As Hannah Wartenberg remembers:

> At Columbia, however, my peers expressed the hope that now I would return to doing "real sociology." . . . Only Paul Lazarsfeld was not opposed to such research. When he asked to see my thesis, and I replied deprecatingly, "Oh, it's just about women going back to work," he commented, smiling, "I like autobiographical theses."

One of my favorite images is Herbert Blumer to Jane Prather: having been denied graduate admission because she was married, Jane was seeking Blumer's intercession. Said Blumer, "Married?" That's no reason!"

I am a Hughes student once removed, so I found the Hughes testimonials in these accounts quite moving. Lynda Lytle Holmstrom has written about the Hughes legacy elsewhere (1984), and writes in her account here that "Everett both saw the conceptual importance of studying women's careers and was helpful to women students and colleagues." Gaye Tuchman notes that "Hughes's way of teaching—telling stories—forced me to see that my own family was the stuff and substance of sociology, that sociology concerned the relevance of the past to the present, that sociology should stress the need for change."

Reading these accounts, I found it easy to get lost in a warm revisitation of my own graduate school days at Northwestern, where I was mentored by, among other men, Howard Becker and John Kitsuse. But Datha Brack's comment reminded me that these are, after all, primarily stories of isolation and tokenism—isolation from the congenial, from an affirmed sense of intellectual direction, or a rightful place in the academy: "In all the years I studied at Columbia, I'd never had a woman professor or been assigned a text written by a female scholar." Diane Margolis remembers a typical exchange during her "reentry" to graduate school.

> "Why are you getting a Ph.D?" some man would challenge at a dinner party, insisting that I was frivolously wasting my husband's money and a place in graduate school that a young man should fill.

Once there, it was often no better. Judy Long writes of her stay on the faculty at Chicago.

> The history of women faculty at the University of Chicago is a ghostly one, haunted by the absence of women scholars who have been "disappeared." . . . For all I know, feminism persists at the University of Chicago in the same distinctive form: each one teaches one and then expires.

And Gaye Tuchman writes of Stony Brook that, at "twenty-six years old, the token woman invited to be the mascot at the boys' poker games, I felt very lonely." As Suzanne Keller recalls the place for the "exceptional woman":

> Being the token woman in a man's world could be a plus if that token woman managed to combine a conventional "feminine" style with unconventional feminine performance. . . . I knew instinctively that to succeed in the "men's house," I had to act the woman at some points and the man at others. . . . But keep in mind the special social conditions that made this the case: The women were a tiny minority, who excelled in, but did not challenge the system.

Coramae Mann remembers of her time at Florida State University:

> We [she and a colleague, Carolyn Watson] were put far in the back of the department in the two smallest offices because, it was explained, "as the women faculty in the School, we thought you two would like to be together."
> . . . Thus, my first two years and my last year at FSU were marvelous primarily because I had female peers with whom to share the misery.

It is, of course, not just gender than produces the experience of the token. Helen Hacker describes her interview for an ABD post at Randolph-Macon College, where, "never having had one, they were looking for a 'nice Jew' to be on their faculty." Similarly, Janet Lever says, "I remember being shocked by the recruitment letter from a noted scholar at a major university saying his department already had a woman so they were seeking a 'black negro.' " Nor were men the only impediment to success. Shulamit Reinharz recalls that "another woman faculty member in my department later said, 'one feminist is enough in each department, and I was here first.' " And for many of us, the inequities of graduate school, however glaring they seem to us now, were simply accepted. Elaine Hall remembers the not-so-turbulent sixties.

> We never had a woman sociologist as a role model; we never saw a woman as the professor, the researcher, and the scholar we were studying to become. ... For all our demands for personal relevance, we neither grasped nor collectively challenged the exclusion of women and gender from our curriculum.

For these "exceptional" women, out of this exclusion came real change and community. Notable is the number who prevailed over committees and faculty colleagues to study the experiences of women as fit subject matter for sociology. I remember it as quite difficult enough to struggle with a *willing* dissertation committee to "allow" me to study household labor. All the more remarkable is to read of the work of Beth Hess (with her mentor Matilda White Riley), Hannah Wartenberg, Helena Lopata, and Judy Long, who each began work on women well before we could imagine the explosion of scholarship that would come later. Judy Long writes:

> The journals devoted to feminist scholarship came into existence only after I had been writing and publishing on women for almost two decades.... I have no doubt that if I had been "smarter" and concentrated on the rules rather than the questions, I would be more "successful" today. Maybe I would also be burned out, disillusioned, and even meaner than I am.

And Helena Lopata, recalling her work on widows, notes that "the concept of support systems has been so deeply integrated into sociology that my name is no longer identified with it."

The changes they helped to make in the discipline, particularly in the areas of curriculum and feminist scholarship, are remembered by them as the most satisfying. And the building of a community of women scholars, exemplified by the development of Sociologists for Women in Society (SWS), is mentioned frequently. Hannah Wartenberg speaks of being "saved" by SWS. Beth Hess concludes about it, "The company of feminist sociologists remains my most congenial environment, and SWS has given me much more than I can ever give back." And Helen Hacker speaks of feminism as the "beacon that I follow even as its trajectory changes."

It is here where I am most aware of the reflexive quality of these women in their connection to each other and to the profession in which they work. Quite apart from their own sense of themselves as political actors, as scholars, and as teachers, they were part of the development of the feminist critique of social life—at its core a *sociological* critique—that changed their own lives. And, they daily determined the future of a profession where the study of women could be counted as scholarship, and where the company of women was given value.

Untold Stories

> *Instead, I concentrated on my studies in an effort to shut out the loud angry voices.* —Pamela Ann Roby

There is richness in these stories, but there is also the unspoken, stories not told but which make their ghostly presences felt nonetheless: stories of childhood abuse, betrayal, and infidelity. The emotional roller coaster rides that involve children, spouses, lovers, and parents. Struggles with health and disability. Sex and sexualities. Marriages, present and past. Those stories. To one extent or another, such is the case with every autobiography and every human account. Only sometimes are we wise enough to fill in the blanks, as we try to imagine what is absent. The rest is lost, even as its presence is felt.

And there are sociological observations that could be made, but are not, and that, too, is notable. For example, there is much made here of direct experience with discrimination and inequality, but little is made of how privilege is manifest in one's own biography, and the way in which it shaped each life. Perhaps it is no surprise that those born outside the United States seem most cognizant of the privileges at work in their adopted cultures. For example, Britta Fischer recalls her college days at Barnard.

> The irony of Barnard students going on freedom rides while our school carefully limited black students to four, or 1 percent, of each entering class of four hundred was not lost on me.

Martha Gimenez observes:

> Having grown up in a society where class divisions and identities prevail and where domestic servants were taken for granted in most middle-class households, I could not help being critical of theories about women in general.

For most, class, race, and/or heterosexual privileges helped soften the blows of gender discrimination and provided some of the opportunities that determined the life courses represented here. The fascinating question that remains unanswered is how for each life privilege operates, in counterpoint to inequality, to shape women's lives and their ultimate reflections on them.

Conclusion

> *Today there is little mobility, but lots of movement.* —Judy Long

I would not be so foolish as to predict in any detail what sociology, and a sociology for women, will become in the next fifty years. The changes in store for higher education in general are hard to imagine. But, if not a "feminized" sociology, we can expect that many more women will find their way into sociology and the professoriate, and many more will find their way into every level of academic institution. We can hope that the stories of women will be those of collegiality and community rather than isolation. Yet, for academic women of color, who must still negotiate the rocky shoals of white men, white women, and men of color, we must hope that all women come to appreciate *both* their shared interests and their empowering differences. If there can be a common vision among us, this is the way to achieve it.

Finally, as I think of my own daughter, now ten, I can better imagine the future—the stories from *her* cohort, and those beyond. Rather than memories of perceived marginality and isolation, perhaps they will be ones of entitlement—to education, to satisfying work, and to relationships untainted by inequity. What sort of sociologists, and sociology, will result, I can only imagine. But I can't wait to read the stories.

REFERENCES

Abrams, Philip. 1982. *Historical Sociology*. Ithaca, N.Y.: Cornell University Press.
Berger, Bennett. 1990. *Authors of Their Own Lives: Intellectual Autobiographies by Twenty American Sociologists*. Berkeley: University of California Press.
Fenstermaker, Sarah. 1993. "Telling Tales Out of School: Three Stories of a Feminist Sociologist." Paper presented at "Gender Life Histories and Human Agency: 'The

Missing Feminist Revolution in Sociology' Revisited," a conference held at Berkeley, California, February.
Holmstrom, Lynda Lytle. 1984. "Everett Cherrington Hughes: A Tribute to a Pioneer in the Study of Work and Occupations." *Work and Occupations* 2(4):471–81.
Merton, Robert K. 1988. "Some Thoughts on the Concept of Sociological Autobiography." Pp. 17–21 in *Sociological Lives: Social Change and the Life Course*, vol. 2, edited by Matilda White Riley. Beverley Hills, Calif.: Sage.
Riley, Matilda White. 1988. "Notes on the Influence of Sociological Lives." Pp. 23–40 in *Sociological Lives: Social Change and the Life Course*, vol. 2. Beverley Hills, Calif.: Sage.
Traugott, Mark, ed. 1993. *The French Worker: Autobiographies from the Early Industrial Era*. Berkeley and Los Angeles: University of California Press.
Willie, Charles Vert. 1988. "Commentary on *Sociological Lives*." Pp. 163–77 in *Sociological Lives: Social Change and the Life Course*, vol. 2, edited by Matilda White Riley. Beverly Hills, Calif.: Sage.

About the Editors and Contributors

Datha Clapper Brack taught sociology at Fairleigh Dickinson University in Rutherford, New Jersey, and at Bergen County Community College in Paramus, New Jersey, specializing in women's studies. She wrote and reviewed books for *New Directions for Women*. She is currently retired and lives in Ithaca, New York, with her husband.

Sarah Fenstermaker is a professor of sociology and women's studies and the associate dean in the graduate division at the University of California, Santa Barbara. She has published widely in the areas of gender, work, and domestic violence and is perhaps best known for her book *The Gender Factory: The Allocation of Work in American Households* (Plenum, 1985). Her current work focuses on the theoretical articulation of race, class, and gender in women's work.

Britta Fischer is an associate professor of sociology at Emmanuel College in Boston. She received her B.A. from Barnard College and her Ph.D. from Washington University. She has published several articles in the areas of technology and the professions, and she is currently engaged in historical research on Brazilian culture.

Martha E. Gimenez is an associate professor of sociology at the University of Colorado at Boulder. She has written numerous articles and book chapters in the areas of the political economy of population, Marxist theory, and feminist theory. She is coeditor, with Jane Collins, of *Work without Wages: Comparative Studies of Domestic Labor and Self-Employment* (SUNY Press, 1990).

Ann Goetting is a professor of sociology at Western Kentucky University. Her publications in scholarly journals span a wide range of topics within the areas of family and criminology. She is author of *Homicide in Families and Other Special Populations* (Springer, 1995).

Helen Mayer Hacker is emerita professor, Adelphi University. She currently teaches one course at the New School for Social Research. She continues to review books and papers and to serve on committees for professional journals and organizations. Occasionally, she conducts some original research, most recently on attitudes toward "outing." Her interests now center on feminist methodology, women and religion, and sexuality.

Elaine J. Hall is an assistant professor of sociology at Kent State University. She teaches courses in inequality, race and ethnicity, and feminist research. In addition to conducting research on waitressing, she publishes on sociology's conceptualization of race, class, and gender ("Visual Image of American Society," *Gender and Society,* 1990) and the construction of adoption and abortion as pregnancy resolution options ("The Social Construction of Abortion and Adoption in Marriage and Family Textbooks," *Family Relations,* 1994).

Beth B. Hess is a professor of sociology at County College of Morris in Randolph, New Jersey. Her publications include: four editions of *Growing Old in America,* with Elizabeth W. Markson (Transaction); five editions of *Sociology,* with Peter J. Stein and Elizabeth W. Markson (Macmillan; Allyn and Bacon); *Analyzing Gender,* with Myra Marx Ferree (Sage); and two editions of *Controversy and Coalition: The New Feminist Movement,* with Myra Marx Ferree (Twayne).

Lynda Lytle Holmstrom is a professor of sociology at Boston College. Her publications include: *The Two-Career Family* (Schenkman, 1972); *The Victim of Rape: Institutional Reactions,* with Ann Wolbert Burgess (Wiley, 1978); and *Mixed Blessings: Intensive Care for Newborns,* with Jeanne Harley Guillemin (Oxford, 1986). Her current research, with David A. Karp and Paul S. Gray, is on family dynamics during the college application process.

Suzanne Keller, professor of sociology, is the first woman granted tenure at Princeton University (in 1968). Her books include: *Beyond the Ruling Class* (Transaction, 1991); *The Urban Neighborhood* (Random House, 1968); *Sociology,* with Craig Calhoun and D. Light (6th ed., McGraw Hill, 1994); *The Social and Career Lines of Three Generations of the American Business Elite* (Arno Press, 1980); and *Building for Women* (Lexington Books, 1980). She is currently completing a book on the genesis of community.

Janet Lever is an associate professor of sociology at California State University, Los Angeles. She is also a consultant-in-residence at RAND in Santa Monica, California, where she researches and writes on sex and health-policy issues. She and Pepper Schwartz coauthor *Glamour* magazine's monthly "Sex and Health" column.

Judy Long is a professor of sociology at Syracuse University. Her publications include: *The Second X: Sex Roles and Social Roles* (Elsevier,

1979); *Sexual Scripts: The Social Construction of Female Sexuality*, with Pepper Schwartz (Dryden, 1977); and numerous articles in professional journals. Her new book, *Telling Women's Lives: Subject/Narrator/Reader/Text*, is forthcoming.

Helena Znaniecka Lopata is a professor of sociology at Loyola University, Chicago. She was born in Poland, and she obtained her Ph.D. from the University of Chicago. Her fields of specialization are symbolic interaction, social roles, social roles of women, and occupations and professions. Her latest books are: *Circles and Settings: Roles Changes of American Women* (SUNY Press, 1994) and *Polish Americans* (Transaction, 1994).

Coramae Richey Mann is a professor of criminal justice at Indiana University, Bloomington. Her research has been directed toward those oppressed by the juvenile and criminal justice system: youth, women, and racial/ethnic minorities. She is the author of three books: *Female Crime and Delinquency* (University of Alabama Press, 1994); *Unequal Justice: A Question of Color* (Indiana University Press, 1993); and *Women Murderers: Deadliest of the Species?* (forthcoming).

Diane Rothbard Margolis is a professor of sociology at the University of Connecticut, Stamford. She is the author of *The Managers: Corporate Life in America* (William Morrow, 1979). Currently, she is completing work on an analysis of contemporary conceptualizations of the self.

Jane E. Prather is a professor of sociology at California State University, Northridge. Her research focuses on the decoding and advertising of psychotropic drugs targeted for women and on analyzing teenage girls' magazines for implicit messages about the significance of education, employment, and body image.

Shulamit Reinharz is a professor of sociology and the director of women's studies at Brandeis University. Her books include: *On Becoming a Social Scientist* (Jossey-Bass, 1979; Transaction, 1984); *Psychology and Community Change*, with others (Dorsey, 1984); *Qualitative Gerontology*, with Graham Rowles (Springer, 1987); and *Feminist Methods in Social Research* (Oxford, 1992). One of her major interests is the history of women's sociological work.

Pamela Ann Roby is a professor of sociology and women's studies at the University of California, Santa Cruz. She is a founder and former president of Sociologists for Women in Society. Her publications include:

The Future of Inequality, with S. M. Miller (Basic, 1970); *Child Care—Who Cares? Foreign and Domestic Infant and Early Childhood Development Policies* (Basic Books, 1973); *The Poverty Establishment* (Prentice-Hall, 1974); and *Women in the Workplace* (Schenkman, 1981).

Gaye Tuchman is a professor of sociology at the University of Connecticut, Storrs. She was one of the eighteen founders of Sociologists for Women in Society. Among her books are *Making News: A Study in the Construction of Reality* (translated into Spanish and Japanese, sections in Italian and Hungarian; Free Press, 1978) and *Edging Women Out: Victorian Novelists, Publishers, and Social Change,* with Nina Fortin (Yale, 1989).

Hannah Schiller Wartenberg is an adjunct associate professor at the University of Miami in Coral Gables, Florida. Her areas of interest are mass communication and gender roles. Her most recent research concerns Cuban Jewish women in Miami.